PINK FLOYD

THEIR MORTΔL REMΔINS

PINK FLOYD

THEIR MORTAL REMAINS

V&A Publishing

THE CONTENTS

008 Foreword: Becoming Pink Floyd
—AUBREY POWELL

The Band

014 'Lift Off': Syd Barrett, Pink Floyd and the London Underground
—JOE BOYD

036 What Have We Done to England? Pink Floyd and the Lure of the Pastoral
—ROB YOUNG

056 A Long-Term Prospect
—JON SAVAGE

080 'Painters, Pipers, Prisoners': The Musical Legacy of Pink Floyd
—HOWARD GOODALL

112 Great Gigs in the Sky: Pink Floyd and the Architecture of Rock
—VICTORIA BROACKES AND ANNA LANDRETH STRONG

The Albums
—MARK BLAKE

148 The Piper at the Gates of Dawn
162 A Saucerful of Secrets
172 Soundtrack from the film *More*
176 Ummagumma
182 Atom Heart Mother
192 Meddle
204 Obscured by Clouds
214 The Dark Side of the Moon
228 Wish You Were Here
238 Animals
248 The Wall
272 The Final Cut
278 A Momentary Lapse of Reason
292 The Division Bell
302 The Endless River

308 Storm Thorgerson, Photo Designer
—AUBREY POWELL

312 The Notes
313 The Picture Credits
314 The Acknowledgements
316 The Collaborators
317 The Index

FOREWORD
BECOMING PINK FLOYD

Pink Floyd have always been an enigma. Offstage, from the very beginning, they seemed to shy away from publicity. Onstage, they played wild sonic soundscapes, but were often hidden behind a multicoloured, experimental light show. They performed in church halls, dingy basements and at the capital's hippest club, UFO, where the cognoscenti of the '60s underground scene considered them London's premier psychedelic group.

As individuals, Pink Floyd were invisible. It was always about the event, and of course the music: a unique mix of John Cage meets Karlheinz Stockhausen meets Bo Diddley.

Those visiting UFO for the first time in spring 1967 probably found the experience hard to fathom. But the attraction of being a part of something 'new', something 'avant-garde', was unique and infectious.

Pink Floyd offered a fresh alternative to the chart toppers of the time; they were more thoughtful, more 'serious'. However, it's hard to survive on reputation alone. Slowly, by degrees, Pink Floyd found themselves making their way into the mainstream world of pop culture, by employing managers, signing record contracts, touring and developing songs that were more approachable, but still wildly unpredictable.

Before long, Pink Floyd had a couple of hit records and became mildly famous. However, hallucinogenic drugs began to take their toll on guitarist and songwriter Syd Barrett. Syd wasn't cut out for the do's and don'ts of the pop game and he became empty, unfulfilled and shattered. Unable or unwilling to play, he was dropped from the band and his friend David Gilmour, a talented guitarist, stepped up to replace him.

I was there at the time, assisting for Pink Floyd's lighting crew and later sharing a flat with the capricious Syd. It was a time of fear, anguish and uncertainty. With their frontman and main songwriter gone, Pink Floyd could have fallen apart. But the band, yet to realize their full potential, were ambitious and with a fresh line-up took off in a new direction.

By chance, David Gilmour took me and our mutual friend, Storm Thorgerson, with him on this journey. Hipgnosis was Storm's and my fledgling design company. The Hipgnosis name was suggested unwittingly by Syd Barrett, and Storm, Roger Waters and Syd had been friends at school. When the opportunity to design a cover for Pink Floyd's second album, *A Saucerful of Secrets*, came along, Storm raised his hand. A few years later, *The Dark Side of the Moon* became our most acclaimed artwork.

Hipgnosis' creative path followed Pink Floyd's for a decade, until *The Wall* in 1979. It began again for Storm after Roger Waters left the band in the mid-'80s. Storm carried on lending his creative talents to Pink Floyd until his death in 2013, when the baton was passed back to me. It has been an extraordinary ride.

In the years that followed their debut album, 1967's *The Piper at the Gates of Dawn*, until the gigantic *Wall* tour of 1980 and '81, Pink Floyd became even more distant from their audience and critics as their shows became bigger and their albums sold in the millions. Pink Floyd insist it was never deliberate, but there are very few photographs and no film footage of them performing live between 1972 and '89, and one would be hard pressed to say it was by coincidence.

For the launch of *The Dark Side of the Moon* in 1973 at London's Planetarium, they sent cardboard cut-outs. Only one member of the band showed up. A tour poster from the time shows them turning their backs to the camera. Before a concert during their 1977 *Animals* US tour the band walked out among the crowd. No one recognized them.

Pink Floyd became known as the 'thinking person's band'; a label they neither embraced nor commented on. They preferred to be known for the quality of their music and theatrical staging. Albums such as *The Dark Side of the Moon*, *Wish You Were Here* and *The Wall* were cerebral, musical masterpieces that dwelt on subjects including emotional detachment, wealth, childhood, war, loss, separation and madness. It was hardly your average pop fare.

Roger Waters' traumatic departure from the band in 1985 created another vacuum. However, David Gilmour and Nick Mason, along with Richard Wright, went on to produce two more classic Pink Floyd albums: *A Momentary Lapse of Reason* in 1987 and 1994's *The Division Bell*, both followed by huge world tours. But still they kept their distance.

References to past problems were, and are, frequently made by band and commentators alike. This tends to add further intrigue to one of the most successful rock bands of the last 50 years. And the rumour mill continues to buzz, especially following the band's memorable reunion for Live 8 in 2005. A working connection between the band members still survives, however tenuous.

After five decades, the veil is finally lifted in this book and the exhibition it accompanies, *The Pink Floyd Exhibition: Their Mortal Remains*. Both reveal, for the first time, Pink Floyd's extraordinary personal archive of notes, lyrics, letters, diary entries, photographs, artwork, films, equipment and more. These artefacts offer a unique glimpse into the band's private and professional lives.

It's a treasure trove hidden for decades in lockups, storage facilities, old studios, at the back of dusty shelves and in long-unopened tour cases. In a warehouse, old, perished plastic pigs flown years ago at Pink Floyd concerts were found abandoned, never to be re-inflated. Yet among the detritus was an inflatable TV set and fridge, relics from the 1977 *Animals* tour – and still in perfect shape. This was a typical day in a two-year journey of discovery. In some rare instances, we did find material that had been archived carefully. It was a joy to discover that Nick Mason's hoard of memorabilia, including photographs and posters, had been thoroughly catalogued.

All this dredging and sifting has unearthed many unseen, worthwhile objects, and makes for a fascinating back-story to the exhibition. For the first time, an audience can peek into the world that was, and is, Pink Floyd: their instruments, bespoke album designs, reproductions of their stage shows with all the accompanying films, inflatables and lighting effects, not to mention the extraordinary music and the back-room creative talent that helped them along the way.

The V&A welcomed the proposal for a Pink Floyd retrospective with open arms. The Museum team, including curators Victoria Broackes, Anna Landreth Strong and Geoffrey Marsh, have been generous with their experience and creative input, as has Kathryn Johnson in the creation of this book. The exhibition includes some wonderful pieces from the V&A's extensive Theatre and Performance Collections.

My own team of co-curator Paula Webb Stainton and archivist Tracey Kraft have been unsurpassed. Meanwhile, none of this would have been possible without the architectural genius of Ray Winkler and his associates at Stufish, Peter Curzon from StormStudios and the Real Studios team. The belief and backing of Michael Cohl, and the tenacity of Paul Loasby, have been invaluable, not to mention the complete co-operation of Pink Floyd: namely Roger Waters, David Gilmour, Nick Mason and the estates of Richard Wright and Syd Barrett.

Hopefully, through the book and accompanying exhibition, you will get to know this most enigmatic of bands a little better.

—Aubrey Powell
Creative Director and Curator, *The Pink Floyd Exhibition: Their Mortal Remains*

THE BAND

'LIFT OFF'
SYD BARRETT, PINK FLOYD AND THE LONDON UNDERGROUND

Joe Boyd

When David Bowie visited David Gilmour backstage before his 2006 Albert Hall concert, he agreed to sing a song so long as it was 'Arnold Layne'. 'Why "Arnold Layne"?', asked a journalist afterwards. Because, said Bowie, Syd Barrett's vocal on that record changed his life; it taught him to sing in his own voice, his own accent, just as he talked, not trying to sound American, or black, or cool, just to be himself.

Pink Floyd mythologized Syd as their founder and guiding spirit, but it's not so often recognized how dramatically he, Roger Waters, Richard Wright and Nick Mason altered Britain's (and hence the world's) musical landscape. As close as I was to their explosion – producing their first single and presenting them at UFO throughout those magical months of 1967 – and as much as I revelled in their startling originality, I could never have predicted their enduring impact.

△

1 · PAGES 6–7 · Pink Floyd, Belsize Park, London, 1970. Photograph by Storm Thorgerson / Aubrey Powell at Hipgnosis

2 · PAGES 10–11 · Aubrey 'Po' Powell with Roger Waters and David Gilmour, backstage on the British Winter tour, Birmingham, 1974. Photograph by Jill Furmanovsky

3 · PAGE 14 · Syd Barrett, Hampstead, London, June 1967. Photograph by Andrew Whittuck

4 · OPPOSITE · 'Summer Sadness for John Hopkins', *International Times*, no.14.5, 9 June 1967. Designed by Hapshash and the Coloured Coat (Michael English and Nigel Waymouth). V&A: E.1748–1991

In June 1965 Allen Ginsberg headlined the International Poetry Incarnation at the Albert Hall. The following spring, word reached London (via antennae at the counter-culture bookshop, Indica Books) of Ken Kesey's Acid Tests in San Francisco and New York's Lower East Side musical heroes, The Fugs. Months-old copies of the New York *Village Voice* carried reviews of underground films by Jack Smith and Jonas Mekas, while Situationist happenings shocked Paris and the stoned and bearded Provos emerged as a political force on the Amsterdam city council.

London had its creative eccentrics, but its primary function in this murmuring revolution seemed to be as a transit hub. Extraordinary characters stopped over on their way from Paris to Ireland, New York to Morocco, or San Francisco to Delhi. The central drama of *Don't Look Back* is Bob Dylan's 1965 visit to London. The city, after all, had The Beatles and The Rolling Stones and miniskirts and King's Road, all well-established and profitable 'overground' phenomena. By the summer of 1966, new drugs-and-politics-fuelled energy was bursting forth all over the world but there was no sign that London's revolution would be anything special: so far, the excitement was largely imported.

Then, in early autumn, came stirrings in W11. All accounts of London's 'psychedelic underground' begin with the Powis Square benefits for an idealistic attempt to bring the Revolution to Notting Hill Gate known as the London Free School. The lights, the music, the atmosphere, the freaks, the drugs, Pink Floyd onstage, the dancing … suddenly, there was a focus, a regular event to talk about, to look forward to, to compare with other events. The ripples of joy that spread through W11 in their wake were palpable. We had *lift-off*!

The joy lasted just under a year. There are many analyses of the rise and fall of Freak London during those 11 months and some have much to recommend them. Around the time of The Rolling Stones' drugs bust trial in June 1967, for example, John 'Hoppy' Hopkins, editor of *International Times*, co-proprietor of the UFO club and all-round inspirational figure, was jailed for eight months, plunging most of us (to say nothing of Hoppy himself) into a gloom that took a long time to lift. Weekend hippies now outnumbered the original Freaks at concerts and demonstrations. But those 11 months also marked the arc of Syd Barrett's trajectory across the London sky. His retreat into silence coincided with the evaporation of our joy.

Is that too pat? Too sentimental? Let's look more closely at the music that inspired that magical year. The sort of extended improvisations for which the Syd-era Pink Floyd are famous can be – and often are – quite tedious; think of Dantalian's Chariot, the Graham Bond Organisation, the less-interesting bits of The Crazy World of Arthur Brown, Colosseum and even Soft Machine when Robert Wyatt and Kevin Ayers weren't singing. But if the guitarist at the heart of it is a genuine original and if the jumping-off point is a jaunty, slightly demented but hook-filled and very English melody, those trippy excursions into the abstract become something else entirely.

The Band—Joe Boyd

5 · ABOVE LEFT · 'Nite Tripper', the first UFO club poster, December 1966. Designed by Michael English. V&A: E.1695–1991

6 · ABOVE RIGHT · UFO club poster, January 1967. Designed by Michael English. V&A: E.1696–1991

7 · OPPOSITE TOP · UFO club poster, February 1967. Designed by Michael English. V&A: E.1697–1991

8 · OPPOSITE BOTTOM · *International Times* UFO poster no.2, January 1967. Designed by Michael English. V&A: E.121–2002

*All movement is accomplished in six stages
And the seventh brings return*
—'Chapter 24', 1967

Where did that tune come from? It has little to do with The Beatles and nothing to do with The Stones or Dylan, the blues, or anything else then afoot in pop music. It was so surprising it made a roomful of stoned kids look up and grin, first at the stage, then at each other.

Light shows were central to what happened to the band in 1966. In the colourful gloom the four members of Pink Floyd looked so serious, so self-effacing, as they stared down at their instruments while inky blobs of colour bubbled and covered the stage; you could barely make out any individual features. There is nothing remarkable about hiding like that unless the audience is trying to pierce the murky darkness where Syd's sparkling eyes always shone. Self-effacement is only interesting when the singer is that beautiful.

That year was supposed to have marked the birth of a counter-culture in which the usual ambitions of capitalism were forsworn, but the scene was full of hustlers, schemers and dreamers. I know – I was one of them. Desires and competitive urgencies surged among us all, even amid the tripped-out and loving currents that energized everyone on stage, backstage and in the crowds. Syd might have been the most ambitious of us all but he never showed it; his aimless

18 The Band—Joe Boyd

9 · ABOVE · Publicity shoot with Pink Floyd, Hampstead, London, June 1967. Photograph by Andrew Whittuck / colour treatment by Peter Curzon. Pink Floyd Archive

unconcern was the hurricane's eye around which the storm blew. The brilliance of his songs, casually tossed into our midst, gave us the confidence to create what we did, certain that our soundtrack was not a local whim, but world-class.

Without Syd, we might have been just a colony of the American Cultural Revolution. With him, a new world of unabashedly English music was born, owing almost nothing to the blues that had inspired the British pop revolution, from skiffle right up to the spring of 1967.

△

'The Sixties' have been credited as fount of many revolutions: sexual, chemical, spiritual, political and musical. The musical revolution has many subsections, but one rarely examined is the capture of the high ground by the middle class.

Before 1965, pop music was like boxing or football or crime, an escalator out of poverty. Little Richard, Elvis, Bill Haley, Ray Charles, The Ronettes, Billy Fury, The Beatles ... Rock 'n' roll's first decade was dominated by working-class kids and pioneering producers who created hits by tapping into those singers' authenticity.

Bob Dylan, a middle-class boy from Minnesota, far from the cradle of American musical authenticity, has described in *Chronicles* his outsider's fascination with the roots of American music. He drank in the old 78 records reproduced on the Harry Smith *Anthology* as well as the mid-'50s Southern rock 'n' roll that was fast being muscled aside by crafted, corporate pop. As Dylan began making his name in coffee houses, big money was regaining the hold on youth culture that had been shaken loose by buccaneering independent record labels such as Atlantic and Sun. Working-class singers – Elvis being the most blatant example – didn't much mind whether the A&R man wanted them to sing R&B with a sparse, tight band or croon a ballad swamped by strings, so long as it was a hit.

But Dylan was on a journey that balanced ambition with a spiritual quest. His pilgrimage led him from the coffee houses of Greenwich Village to concert halls and eventually the stage of the 1965 Newport Folk Festival. There he transformed popular music by strapping on an electric guitar and singing his defiantly obscure lyrics in front of a band blending South Side Chicago blues musicians with white kids who had studied blues like students taking a university degree. The group blasted out Dylan's vision of a modern sound that leapfrogged both the Brill-Building 'walls of sound' and the polite acoustic harmonies of coffee-house folk, connecting directly to the black and white music of old, southern, rural America.

The avalanche set loose that night opened the door for such bourgeois offspring as Jerry Garcia, Grace Slick, Neil Young, David Crosby, Jim Morrison, Paul Simon and Harvard boys Kris Kristofferson and Gram Parsons, while instigating transformative shifts by Brian Wilson and Carole King – just the start of an endless list. Being essentially rootless, they were free to pick and plunder from any tradition that struck their fancy.

These Americans were guided and inspired by the very British phenomenon of art-school blues bands, the fruits of a fleeting moment of post-war, government-abetted social fluidity in which bright working-class and lower-middle-class kids could make an intellectual as well as economic escape from their backgrounds. In their leisure time, they played precious copies of American blues and R&B records until they were worn out.

If cross-cultural mimicry succeeds, it is usually through failure. In attempting to copy their American heroes, British blues aficionados – from John Lennon to Keith Richards to Van Morrison to Eric Burdon to Rod Stewart to Eric Clapton – created something completely new and very commercial. But time never stands still; by 1966, the initiative was tilting West and it was time once again for the British to pay heed to America, or at least to Bob Dylan.

△

When some friends from Regent Street Polytechnic (now London's University of Westminster) and Camberwell School of Arts decided to form a band, it had to be a blues band. But this was not a group of grant-reliant art students escaping poor-ish backgrounds; Syd, Roger, Nick and 'Rick' (as Richard Wright was then known) were from comfortable, if somewhat unconventional, families. All but Nick and Rick, moreover, had grown up in Cambridge, where they had been exposed in early youth to adventurous minds, intellectual ferment, stimulating teachers and Bohemian circles.

10 · OPPOSITE TOP · Roger Waters and Nick Mason rehearsing with Sigma 6 in the student common room at Regent Street Polytechnic, London, 1964. Left to right: Clive Metcalfe, Sheilagh Noble, Keith Noble, Roger Waters, Nick Mason and Vernon Thompson

11 · OPPOSITE BOTTOM · David Gilmour and members of Joker's Wild, October 1965. Left to right: 'Sunshine' Geoff Whittaker, David Gilmour, Johnny Gordon, Clive Welham and Tony Sainty. Pink Floyd Archive

12 · LEFT · *Untitled* or *Abstract in Blue* by Syd Barrett, 1965. Given to Libby Gausden for Christmas 1965 together with a large blue glass bauble. Collection of Libby Gausden Chisman

Among them, only Syd, the last to join in 1964, was an art student. For most art-school rockers, the connection between their music and their studies was oblique at best. Not for Syd. In his excellent biography, *A Very Irregular Head* (2010), Rob Chapman shows Syd's pop career as a continuation of the drawings, paintings and other creations that had dazzled his teachers and fellow-students. To Syd, making pop music was a kind of performance art.

Like many budding British guitarists, Syd worshipped Bo Diddley. But he was equally excited about the paintings of Jim Dine, Chaim Soutine and Robert Rauschenberg, the writings and illustrations of Edward Lear, the absurdist humour of Hilaire Belloc and Peter Cook as well as William Burroughs' and Brion Gysin's cut-ups. And then he encountered the acronyms that would provide his most profound influences, AMM and LSD. Long before Lennon and McCartney bragged about dabbling in psychedelics, Syd and some Cambridge friends had opened their minds with the pure, Swiss hallucinogen. Boundaries between what Bo Diddley was after with his boogie'd-up Latin clave rhythm and the sort of juxtapositions Gysin and Rauschenberg were chasing dissolved in the flick of an acid tab. Now Syd was ready. When he saw AMM guitarist Keith Rowe applying lessons learned in art school to the guitar, it made complete sense to him.

Rowe was confronting the same issues as Syd and other British guitarists, but starting from a different point. He was a jazzer, a follower of American masters Jim Hall and Wes Montgomery, playing West Coast cool at night while studying the abstractions of Jackson Pollock at art school by day. Rowe decided to tear down the walls between his two artistic personalities; soon afterwards, Syd followed.

'Lift Off': Syd Barrett, Pink Floyd and the London Underground

13 · RIGHT · AMM rehearsing at Langtry Road, London, 1968. Photograph by Frazer Pearce

14 · OPPOSITE · The Tea Set, later to become Pink Floyd, 39 Stanhope Gardens, London, 1965. Left to right: Bob Klose, Syd Barrett, Roger Waters, Nick Mason and Richard Wright. Pink Floyd Archive

Rowe and AMM rejected all notions of 'entertainment'. They committed to moment-by-moment inspiration, which might mean turning on a short-wave radio, spinning the dial and letting it join in the improv, or running a cigarette lighter up and down the guitar or piano strings. Observing Rowe convinced Syd that there was more to playing guitar than technique. For a start, he experimented with laying the guitar across his lap where it stopped being a phallic extension and became an object he could control in any number of different ways.

In abandoning virtuosity (a goal of most British guitarists from Eric Clapton to Jeff Beck to Albert Lee to Richard Thompson to Jimmy Page), Syd was moving British pop further along a road it had already travelled. I've always believed that British groups' lack of instrumental fluency gave them an advantage. The archetypal American band was full of great 'pickers' fluent in country-rock, blues, R&B, folk or maybe a bit of jazz. Every town in the US has bars with live music until long past British pub-closing times, with work aplenty for the dedicated muso. After-hours sessions, dressing-room jams, home get-togethers and casual pick-up gigs, are all largely American phenomena. Mastery, I'm convinced, can flatten out originality.

British groups were formed to get girls, glory and money (usually in that order) and generally consisted of boys who could, at the start, barely play their instruments. All they needed was to learn the chords to songs created by the band's strongest personality. Far from being a problem, this 'handicap' resulted in music that had the instrumentation and some of the texture of American rock 'n' roll and R&B but was startlingly original. They couldn't play the clichés well enough to fall back on them.

Led by their first lead guitarist, deft jazz buff Bob Klose, The Tea Set (as Pink Floyd were initially known) made desultory attempts to cover some Elmore James and Jimmy Reed numbers. But when Klose failed his mid-term exams,

24   The Band—Joe Boyd

his parents made him quit the group to concentrate on his degree; such were the middle-class anxieties that thrust Syd Barrett to the forefront of the not-much-longer-to-be-called Tea Set.

I used to have a hash-burn-studded copy of the Philips gatefold blues reissue dedicated to the 1930s recordings of Blind Boy Fuller, an itinerant Carolina blues man who was once so popular that Big Bill Broonzy recorded a song in which he threatened to come to Charlotte and take away all Fuller's women. Paul Oliver, a British blues expert whom most musicians viewed with awed respect, contributed a lengthy set of sleeve notes in which, setting Fuller into context, he mentioned other wandering singers from the same area. We don't know whether Syd ever listened to the record – certainly nothing in his playing reveals Fuller's influence – but buried in Oliver's notes are the names Pink Anderson and Floyd Council, which Syd appropriated, Rauschenberg-like, as the group's magical talisman. Nothing could be further from Dylan's reverence for the Harry Smith anthology.

Two further developments in the evolution of Pink Floyd arrived soon after the name-change. One was the discovery of how much they enjoyed playing in front of a moving collage of coloured lights. Mike Leonard, a friend who taught at Hornsey College of Art, invited them to rehearse in his campus studio where he was experimenting with abstract projections on a wall; they loved jamming as the lights played on and around them. This meshed perfectly with their other new discovery, the Binson Echorec, a primitive tape-reverb unit that had been used in a most prosaic manner on early records by The Shadows. At gigs, they began extending their versions of 'Dust My Broom', hiding their personalities

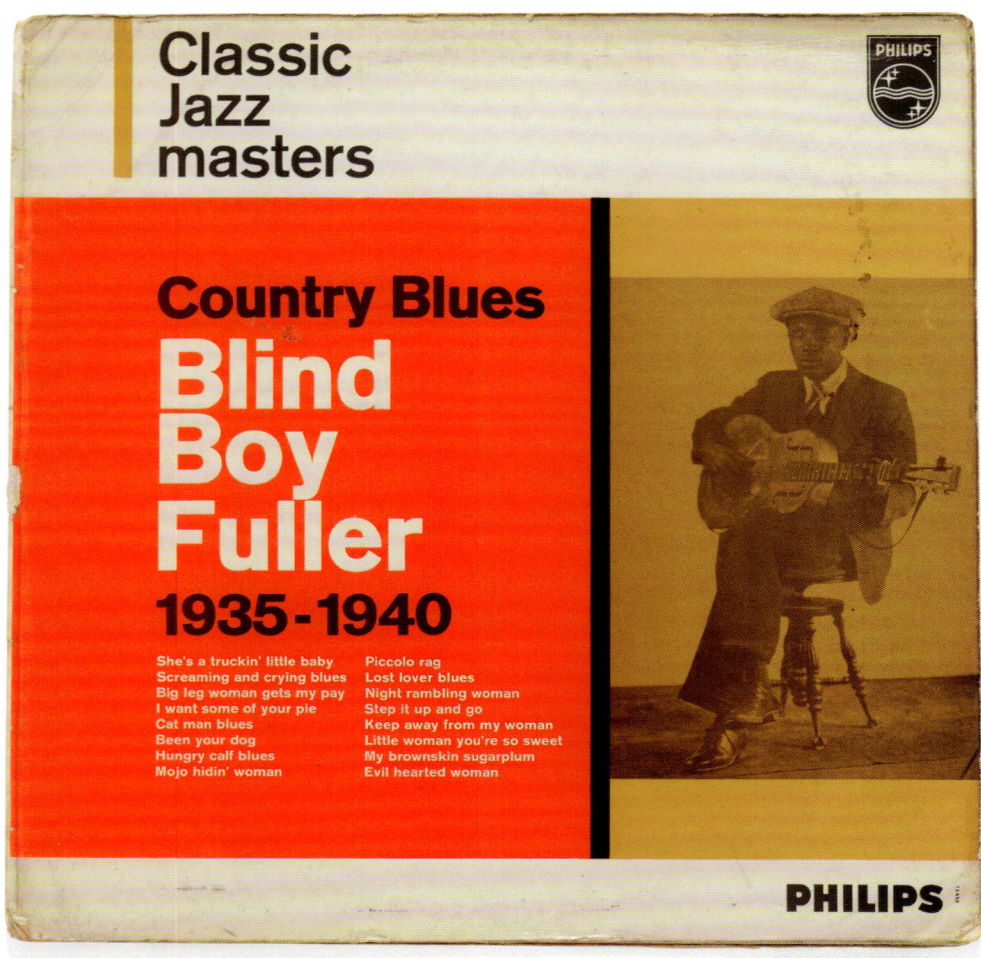

15 · ABOVE · Blind Boy Fuller, *Country Blues 1935–1940*, Philips, UK, 1962

16 · RIGHT · 'Butterfly' vinyl record showing the band's change of name from The Tea Set to Pink Floyd, January/February 1965. Pink Floyd Archive

26 The Band—Joe Boyd

in the bubbling lights and drowning the individual notes of their solos in reverb as the Echorec filled the room, creating dense atmospheres of sound. Gigs morphed into a kind of performance art that retained enough of the surface template of 'pop group' for them to get paid.

Then Syd started writing songs. Syd's drawings and paintings were very English, harking back to that peculiarly Edwardian genre of blissfully childish nonsense: E.H. Shepard's drawings for *Winnie-the-Pooh* and *The Wind in the Willows*, Edward Lear's 'The Owl and the Pussycat' and John Tenniel's illustrations for *Alice's Adventures in Wonderland*. His teachers and fellow students adored them, viewing him as the artistic star of both his Cambridge grammar and Camberwell School of Arts. In his biography, Chapman reports a quality that would mark Syd's life and career: praise seemed to hold little interest for him. He drew or painted and moved on, uninterested in exhibitions, reviews or grades, carelessly handing out finished works to friends. When he began composing, echoes from the same sources infused his lyrics: deceptively childish, truly innocent, in love with the English countryside and anchored in a world of fanciful tales, anthropomorphic creatures and wonder. His experiences with LSD seemed to connect him even more closely to this very English, very nostalgic, slightly fey world.

Syd's jaunty lyrics and cheerful melodies made the instrumental adventures that followed inspiring, uplifting, trippy in the best sense of the word. Lengthy instrumental jams can often instigate head-nodding scowls; but when the Floyd played 'Set the Controls for the Heart of the Sun' at the UFO club, I remember the faces in the audience wreathed in smiles. I once wrote of Syd's songs as green, fertile planets, welcoming visions appearing out of the void at the end of a long journey into outer space. The dour seriousness of much instrumental pop was almost entirely absent from Pink Floyd's music, both before and after Syd's departure. Roger Waters, Rick Wright, Nick Mason and David Gilmour learned his lessons well.

17 · **ABOVE LEFT** · Pinkney 'Pink' Anderson, undated. Photograph by Kip Lornell. Blues Archive, Special Collections, The University of Mississippi Libraries

18 · **ABOVE RIGHT** · Floyd Council, undated. Photograph by Kip Lornell. Sheldon Harris Collection, Blues Archive, Special Collections, The University of Mississippi Libraries

△

19 · OPPOSITE · Letter from Syd Barrett to Jenny Spires, late 1965. Collection of Jenny Spires

Writings about the London psychedelic underground movement of 1965 to 1967 talk about Pink Floyd providing the soundtrack for an irresistibly triumphant spread of fashion, aesthetics, ideology, liberation and enlightenment. Rear-view-mirror perspectives can endow such historic shifts with an air of inevitability. But the London underground needed all the help it could get.

Fortunately, in John 'Hoppy' Hopkins, Syd found a kind of doppelgänger, a man equally imbued with an inspiring, joyful sort of genius, an extrovert to balance Syd's contained nature. Hoppy called the first meeting of the London Free School, organized Pink Floyd's first benefit concert, created (with Barry Miles) *International Times*, invited Pink Floyd to play at its launch party and joined me in establishing UFO, the club that launched the band into the West End and stardom. The wheels started to come off the underground in June 1967 when vindictive authorities threw Hoppy in prison, around the same time Syd started losing interest in being a pop star.

Hindsight is not required to see those magical times as reliant on Syd's music and Hoppy's inspiring leadership. Both were charismatic stars, Pied Pipers with opposite personalities – one an apolitical artist, the other passionately committed to social and political change – but each essential to what was accomplished in those months. The underground proclaimed itself anti-matter to hierarchies, but without Hoppy and Syd it would have remained a minor historical footnote.

London's underground was a sexy place. Hoppy adored women and rarely limited himself to one girlfriend. For his part, Syd's image may have been androgynous but he was most emphatically heterosexual. His songs are full of lust, longing and passion; beautiful desired girls populate his compositions. Syd's fans didn't scream or faint or crowd the front of the stage for him, the scene was far too cool for that sort of behaviour, but the girls all knew he was there. He added a dimension of sex appeal that was notably absent from most other 'underground' outfits.

Syd's beauty and intelligence had always made him a focus of attention, but now he was centre-stage and, in his own understated way, dominant. When, as producer, I went into the studio with the band in January '67 to record 'Arnold Layne', I talked mostly to Roger, with Nick and Rick chipping in their opinions. Syd sat and listened, but when an important decision had to be made, all eyes turned to him.

We had chosen our song a few weeks earlier. Like so many of Syd's compositions it was deceptively simple; after his father died and his older sisters left home, Syd's mother began renting rooms to girls from Homerton Ladies' College across the road. In those pre-tumble-dryer days, frilly underthings would be hung in the backyard and lodgers would occasionally complain about a missing pair of knickers. Then there was a local court case about a man convicted of stealing underwear. So 'Arnold Layne' is really a kind of folk song in the antiquated sense, a report on local goings-on with a moral attached. But it also touched a nice '60s nerve, the sexual revolutionary sneering at the sad life of a repressed, hypocritical older generation: *'Oh Arnold Layne, it's not the same, it takes two to know...'*

The Band—Joe Boyd

Dear Girl, here is the letter I wrote last week for you about you. It breaks me up to think how pretty you are — your body, your face, your voice — everything pretty. I tried to make the letter pretty — it is quite pretty isn't it? I dont like the black bit on the right though. That was a mistake. The bit with the arrow.

avegroovehipsterbabydollswitchedontwistravegroovehipsterbabydo

Write and tell me about Stevenage if you feel like it little one.

When I got back to London tonight, the others had painted the van with a white stripe which looks good with our name on it.

You cant see the name because it is too small. You cant see me because I'm in the back.

20 · ABOVE · Nick Mason loading kit into the band's Bedford van, Rock Road, Cambridge, October 1965. Pink Floyd Archive

21 · OPPOSITE · 'Arnold Layne', EMI Columbia, UK, released 10 March 1967. Collection of Warren Dosanjh

Our objective was to compress the atmosphere of a UFO gig into three minutes and we made a reasonably good fist of it, with Wright's swelling organ solo triggered by a 'psychedelic' drum effect. Sound Techniques' engineer John Wood loved the song and came up with effects to augment the sound. Whether or not it worked aesthetically, it was certainly commercial enough. Within weeks, the group had been signed to EMI (who had no interest in trusting Pink Floyd's recording future to an independent producer such as me), the record was in the charts and the queues outside UFO stretched around the block. The band were soon booked on tours and in clubs where kids expecting to hear short catchy pop songs like 'Arnold' were bewildered by the spacey excursions. Bottles and other objects were sometimes thrown at the stage; class conflict in a Mecca Ballroom.

To Roger, Rick and Nick this was all very exciting. The interviews, 'Top of the Pops' lip-synching, the hostile audiences, were all part of this fantastic, life-altering new territory. I, too, was excited by the eruption of the underground into the mainstream; it gave me a chance to get over my chagrin at being excluded from a Pink Floyd future.

The revelation in the spring of '67 that Beatles had taken LSD was but one manifestation of the cultural war that began raging on the streets of British cities. Neither side reckoned with the power of the other. The police began busting drug-holders in the UFO queue on Tottenham Court Road while the

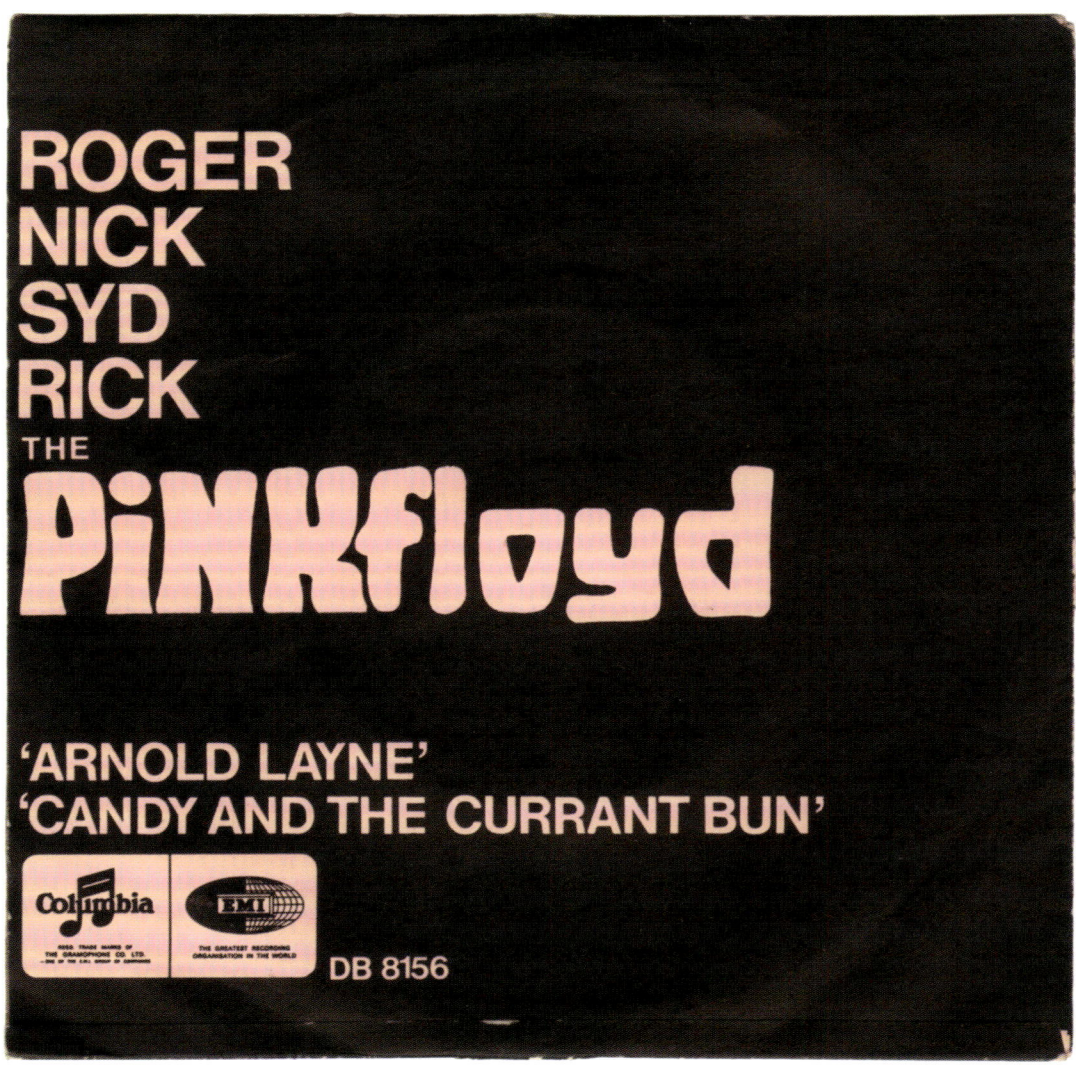

tabloid press splashed their front pages with lurid 'sex-drugs-teenagers' stories. Hoppy, the exposed leader of our ragtag army, was busted and sent to prison. UFO was evicted from its comfortable Irish dance-hall home to the bigger and costlier Roundhouse in Chalk Farm; without Hoppy's wise counsel, I vainly tried to compete with the professional promoters who were booking our bands and copying our light shows. By October, UFO was no more.

Rob Chapman makes a well-argued case that Syd, far from being the 'acid-casualty' of received mythology, was rebelling against the strictures of the pop industry, the demand for 'follow-up' singles, the endless interviews and the uncomprehending audiences. UFO crowds had spoiled Syd; they adored everything he offered them, be it abstract 10-minute guitar noise excursions or a haunting song from the I Ching. The destructive cocktail of drugs he seems to have consumed during the Summer of Love may have been more a symptom than a cause of his retreat.

But for all its outrage and vindictiveness, the Establishment couldn't hold back the tide. A tripping John Lennon delivered his Papal benediction on the underground by turning up at 'The 14-Hour Technicolour Dream' to watch the Floyd bring up the sun, Orpheus-like, over Alexandra Palace. By the end of June, the tripped-out sounds of *Sgt. Pepper's Lonely Hearts Club Band* were everywhere. The Rolling Stones bust, a campaign by the *News of the World* and the drug

'Lift Off': Syd Barrett, Pink Floyd and the London Underground   31 squad to humiliate the long-haired degenerates, ended by holding the authorities up to ridicule – with even the staid op-ed pages of The Times piling in. The reverberations of that summer altered society in ways that to this day cause reactionaries to splutter satisfyingly with bitterness and resentment.

But London's Year of Syd, which lasted from September 1966 to August 1967, ended with Hoppy in Wormwood Scrubs, the quality of drugs and the ideals they embodied in tatters, the original core of UFO freaks disillusioned and our hero standing onstage, hands at his sides, while the group placed David Gilmour on stand-by.

△

In July 2006, the weekend after Syd died, I was driving near Cambridge on the M11 on my way to give a talk about the Sixties at that monument to middle-class music, the Latitude Festival. Suddenly, his voice was on the radio: *Last Word* on Radio 4. They played an excerpt from the May 1967 interview with Hans Keller, who can barely contain his disgust that these musical vandals are being allowed to perform in the Queen Elizabeth Hall – imagine! 'why has it all got to be sooo terribly loud?!' After a short response from Roger, Syd takes over. Like the clever grammar-school boy he was, he explained rock 'n' roll volume levels as if talking to a child: 'we play in large halls where volume is necessary and when people dance, they like volume.' Keller seems stunned. 'Well, that's interesting', he admits.

I pulled over to the side of the road to listen. The only occasions in almost 40 years that I had heard Syd's voice were those snippets of painful studio chat on the two solo albums released in the years following his departure from Pink Floyd. I put each album away after one listen and they never darkened my turntable again. But yes, now *that* voice was the Syd I knew; I'd almost forgotten. It was back where it belonged, on that audio life-blood of the English middle-class intelligentsia, Radio 4. The sound of it struck me to my heart.

A few months later, after being asked to help mount a tribute concert to Syd at the Barbican, I could no longer avoid listening to those albums. What good songs! Matching them with the singers – Chrissie Hynde, Captain Sensible, Damon Albarn, Mike Heron, Kevin Ayers, Nick Laird-Clowes from The Dream Academy, Martha Wainwright and Kate McGarrigle – was wonderfully enjoyable work. I still mourned the long-lost reel-to-reel demo of five songs Syd gave me in January 1967, songs that didn't work for the group and that he thought I might have some use for. I vividly recall one in particular called 'Boon Tune'; it resurfaced five years later on *Madcap Laughs* as 'Here I Go', with Syd's voice a shadow of what it had once been.

Those albums are still hard to listen to. They ache for a band to support Syd's hesitant singing, but stand forever in testimony to the damage done by whatever happened to him that summer of 1967. Perhaps a non-fiction scientist of the future will combine a remote analogue signal reader with an infra-red scanner and a perfected GPS device and locate that tape in some rubbish dump or dusty attic. A future generation will hear the beautiful sound of Syd and guitar and five great songs sung with the joy and confidence of innocent youth.

Syd's post-Floyd life falls somewhere between Brian Wilson and Nick Drake. He was clearly both too fragile and too uncompromising to lead a band on tour after world-conquering tour, but no one contemplated leaving him back at base to write songs and create a very English, avant-garde masterpiece in the manner of *Pet Sounds*. And, if he did grow as reclusive as Nick Drake, at least he had his time in the spotlight, the adoration of girls, the knowledge that audiences loved him.

Syd's music shares with Drake's an uncompromising Englishness; it is, no doubt, that stubborn, well-bred confidence that has made them both so resonant. Syd's influence was felt immediately, of course, in the sound of the group that carried on without him. Assessing the level of continuity is tricky; I always felt they sounded very much the same band, just different. Chapman sees a wider gap and quotes Syd to make his point. Early Pink Floyd was all freedom and adventure; the Roger Waters and David Gilmour Floyds were more about structure. As Syd once said, his old mates 'thought as architecture students'. Which, of course, they were. They took some of Syd's chord progressions and the sound textures they'd explored with him and set them in organized, concrete shapes, a triumph, perhaps, of form over freedom, but what a triumph!

Pink Floyd never turned away from Syd, helping to produce his solo albums, writing songs in his honour, making sure he got his royalties and telling everyone what a key figure he was. I'll leave it to musicologists to parse out the

22 · **ABOVE** · Pink Floyd onstage at 'Love-in Festival', Alexandra Palace, London, 29 July 1967. Photograph by Michael Putland

23 · OPPOSITE · Syd Barrett practising yoga at his home, Wetherby Mansions, Earl's Court, London, 1970. Photograph by Aubrey Powell

level of influence or continuity. What is clear is that Syd's songs gave birth to a genuinely English phenomenon that was completely out of step with the blues-based, America-centric music that had come to dominate Western popular culture – and which still does. Almost every hit record that has emerged from London, New York, San Francisco or Los Angeles can trace its DNA back to the sword-and-gunpoint diaspora of African slavery. Except Pink Floyd, the whitest, most European, most intellectual of them all. Did they hold the door open for Kraftwerk and Abba? No doubt.

1967 marked the apex of pop music's Age of Exploration. The startling originality of The Doors, Frank Zappa, Love, The Velvet Underground, Cream, Jimi Hendrix and The Who spiralled down, slowly in some cases, overnight in others. The Beatles eventually went from 'A Day in the Life' to 'Maxwell's Silver Hammer', Dylan from 'Like a Rolling Stone' to 'Lay Lady Lay'. Singer-songwriters in the James Taylor/Joni Mitchell vein would dominate the next wave of innovation. But England kept coming up with eccentric one-offs: David Bowie, Roxy Music, Marc Bolan, Kate Bush, Jarvis Cocker and Damon Albarn (whose father worked at UFO). Perhaps you can't hear Syd in them the way you hear Muddy Waters or Robert Johnson in The Rolling Stones or Eric Clapton, but they are all forcefully English in a fashion hard to imagine listening to pre-1967, pre-Syd British pop. You can certainly hear him in Robyn Hitchcock, who 'grew up with my nose pressed against the glass of the sixties'.[1] The miracle of Syd was that it came out so perfectly formed and then it went, all done by the time he was 25. He didn't dilute his talent, he squeezed the tube dry.

△

My favourite Syd Barrett song, 'Bike', could also serve as his epitaph.

> *You're the kind of girl who fits in with my world*
> *I'll give you anything, everything*
> *if you want things.*

'*If you want things.*' That was Syd's problem, he didn't really want anything badly enough to fit himself into the way things were going. The rest of us paid lip service to craving freedom from society's constraints but Syd, like Hoppy, actually lived it. We – the new Pink Floyd, me, Barry Miles, most of the other groups that played at UFO – all of us had some sort of conventional future ahead of us, just a bit more off-centre and idealistic than the rest.

In 1967 we thought we were at the beginning of something really big. We didn't realize we were nearing the end. Everything we created in those years of optimistic freedom wound up on a corporate website. Maybe Syd saw it coming, like the small animal that runs out of the forest two days before the earthquake.

> *I know a room of musical tunes*
> *Some rhyme, some ching*
>
> *Take a couple if you wish, they're on the dish.*

The Band—Joe Boyd

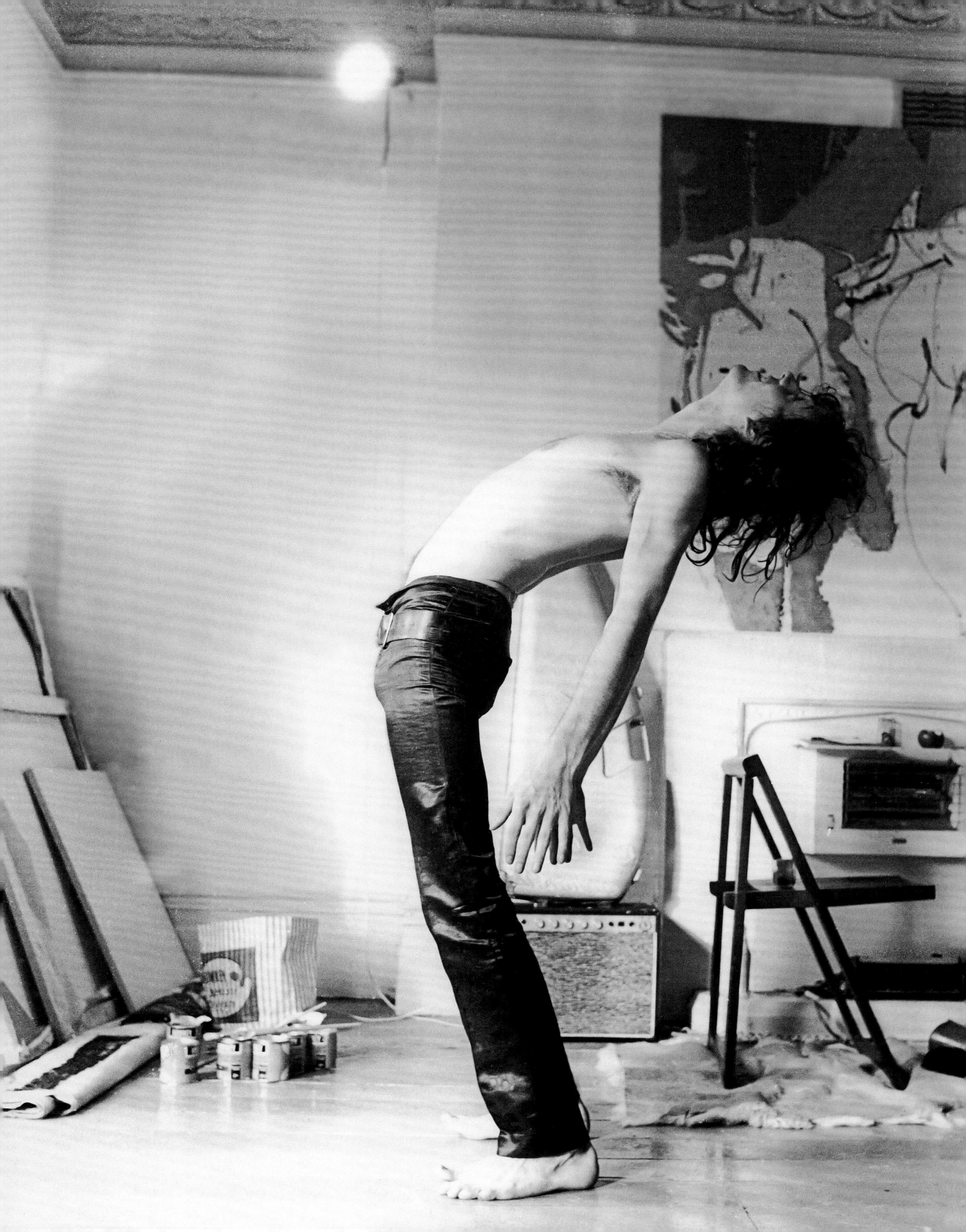

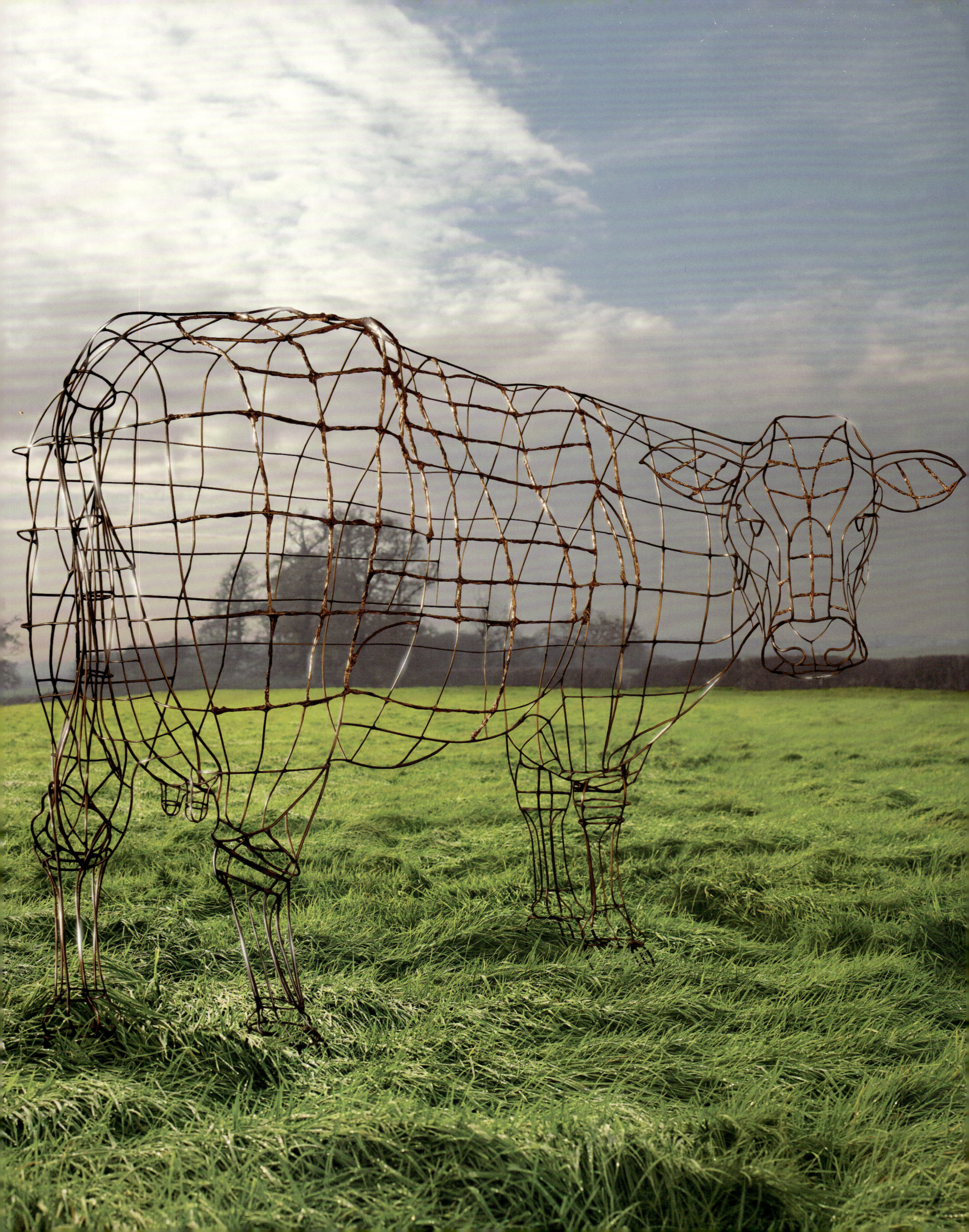

WHAT HAVE WE DONE TO ENGLAND? PINK FLOYD AND THE LURE OF THE PASTORAL

Rob Young

… would I were
In Grantchester, in Grantchester! –
Some, it may be, can get in touch
With Nature there, or Earth, or such.
And clever modern men have seen
A Faun a-peeping through the green,
And felt the Classics were not dead,
To glimpse a Naiad's reedy head,
Or hear the Goat-foot piping low …
  —Rupert Brooke, 'The Old Vicarage, Grantchester', 1912

24 · PAGE 36 · 'Wire Cow', created and photographed for the 40th anniversary edition of *Atom Heart Mother*, 2010. Designed by Storm Thorgerson and Peter Curzon, as a visual pun on the question 'Why a cow?', provoked by the original album artwork.

25 · BELOW · Roger Waters with actors Kevin McKeon and Christine Hargreaves on the film set of *Pink Floyd – The Wall*, 1982

Yesterday Waters, 59, now a millionaire, said: 'I spent many, many happy hours fishing for roach with a bamboo rod and a piece of bread in that bit of the River Cam. I have powerful memories of the warmth of summer mud oozing up between my toes. That time turned out to be creatively important for me – my work is coloured to a certain extent by the sound of natural history.'
—'Rock star whose lyrics defined a landscape enlisted to help save meadows', *Guardian*, 30 June 2003[1]

A sleepy English suburban garden, 1944. The silent pram stands near the birdbath, the birdsong approaches its late afternoon crescendo, a mother dozes in the sunlight.

The scene recurs in *Pink Floyd – The Wall*, Alan Parker's 1982 film based on autobiographical recollections by Pink Floyd founding member Roger Waters. The film, which was a consolidation of the narrative on the album *The Wall* (1979) and the group's 1979–81 touring show, is loaded with heavy rhetorical imagery, but this scene is where the bombardment pauses for a few brief instants, a dreamlike, fantastical moment of domestic harmony. The peace is a fleeting lacuna between aerial bombing raids. For the baby in the perambulator, a period of blissful ignorance that he has just lost a parent: his father killed while fighting in Italy.

38   The Band—Rob Young

In this garden, secretly, stealthily, the law of the jungle holds sway. A predatory black-and-white cat stalks a white dove. Later, 1950s schoolchildren shoot each other with pretend pistols and tommy guns in the playground. The grotesque cartoons of Gerald Scarfe animate a gigantic metropolis of tower blocks and smoke-belching factories trampling across empty countryside. Eventually it is the Wall itself – psychological, metaphorical, actual – that bulldozes its way through the meadows. One of the film's earliest shots shows the silhouette of a tiny boy running across a rugby field. The distant, H-shaped goalposts could be the first right-angled strokes of a sketch for the edifice of brick and cement that will come to eat up the entire screen, and consume the consciousness of its damaged protagonist.

The Wall project (kept alive through later stage iterations by Roger Waters, right up to the tour of 2010–13, which also featured Scarfe's animations) may seem like an unlikely place to begin thinking about Pink Floyd's connections with the English visionary and pastoral tradition. But as the product of the same group – or at least, the same franchise – that composed 'See Emily Play', 'Grantchester Meadows' and *The Piper at the Gates of Dawn*, it must be considered as part of the same portfolio. The lifespan of most groups associated with the golden age of British psychedelia in the late 1960s was short. Due to financial troubles, personal crises, musical divisions, drug or alcohol damage, the majority were cut down in their youth. Pink Floyd had their share of difficulties too, but the unit survived long enough to outlive its adolescence, grow old with the century, and gain a veteran's perspective upon their earlier depictions of innocent pleasures. And as we'll see, even in the psychedelic-pastoral heyday, those pleasures were always tempered with darker apparitions lurking in the woods.

26 · ABOVE · Animation of 'The Teacher' processing children through a mincer, projected onstage during Pink Floyd's tour of *The Wall*, Earl's Court, London, 16 June 1981. Designed by Gerald Scarfe. Photograph by Peter Still

What Have We Done to England? Pink Floyd and the Lure of the Pastoral

27 · OPPOSITE · Shell Guide to Cambridgeshire, 1964. Designed by John Northcote Nash. Issued by Shell Mex and BP Ltd. V&A: E.1506–1963

Pink Floyd was founded at the source of some of the ripest imagery of the English idyll. An hour's train ride north of London, the medieval university town of Cambridge can be a disorientating place, in which innovative intellectual activity takes place amid architecture and traditions of behaviour unchanged for decades, even centuries. There are places of extreme stillness, not just the ancient courtyards of the university. Along the slow-winding River Cam, fringed by verdant fields, tearooms and hamlets, England's poetic memories are preserved and entombed. Rupert Brooke lived in the Old Vicarage there in the years before the First World War. 'I lead a lovely and dim and rustic life there, and have divine food,' he wrote to a correspondent during a trip to Germany in 1912. On the same trip he penned 'The Old Vicarage, Grantchester', a poem more often alluded to than actually read. It's a mostly tongue-in-cheek memorandum of Cambridgeshire place names and the types of folk who dwell there. However, its most evocative lines have become idiomatic of an airbrushed and romanticized image of archetypal Englishness – rooted, at least, in aristocratic leisure, and celebrated in the films of Merchant-Ivory and the TV series 'Downton Abbey' – tea served on a sun-drenched lawn where one afternoon is much like another.

I like to imagine it's Rupert Brooke lounging by the Cam in David Gilmour's song 'Fat Old Sun' (on *Atom Heart Mother*, 1970), which paints a Samuel Palmer-like panorama of a blissful English summer evening with its '*Distant bells, new mown grass smells so sweet/ by the river holding hands…*'. Or that it's Brooke's footsteps we can hear in the closing seconds of Pink Floyd's 'Grantchester Meadows', included on their 1969 LP *Ummagumma*. One of the band's most celebrated pieces, it's an acoustic pastoral reverie, sung in a reverberant chamber to the accompaniment of a double-tracked guitar and a tape loop of a chittering skylark. Humming honeybees, honking geese and running water fade in and out, counterpointing Roger Waters' solemn, chanted evocation of the glorious stretch of field by the River Cam: a Georgian poet puffing collyweed. Its rusticity is made stranger, though, by the dead, dry air around the field recordings: that aviary is on a very short tape loop. And as the lyrics later reveal, this is only a meadow of the mind, recalled in the chill of an urban winter: '*Basking in the sunshine of a bygone afternoon/ Bringing sounds of yesterday into this city room.*' The dream is rudely thwacked awake with a fly-swatter.

△

The English pastoral is not without its complications. To the city dweller a bucolic existence in the countryside can appear both desirable and threatening, a feeling amplified by the timelessly strange sleeve of *Atom Heart Mother*. The Friesian cow, name of Lulubelle III, haphazardly photographed by Storm Thorgerson near a motorway just north of London, gazes balefully while proffering her rump end towards the LP purchaser with ill-concealed contempt. '*Hanging on in quiet desperation is the English way*', Pink Floyd sing on 'Time', from *The Dark Side of the Moon* (1973) – a desultory song about enervation, creative stagnation and time slipping away with promise unfulfilled. It is, perhaps, the true soundtrack to those miserable Edwardian terrace teas, plagued by wasps and impending thunderclouds. The lyrical tone recalls both the small-town isolationism and despondency of the poet Philip Larkin, as well as George Orwell's comment, at the conclusion of *Homage to Catalonia* (1938), about the 'deep, deep sleep of England'. Both Larkin, who to some extent walled

The Band—Rob Young

Painted by John Nash

Shell guide to CAMBRIDGESHIRE

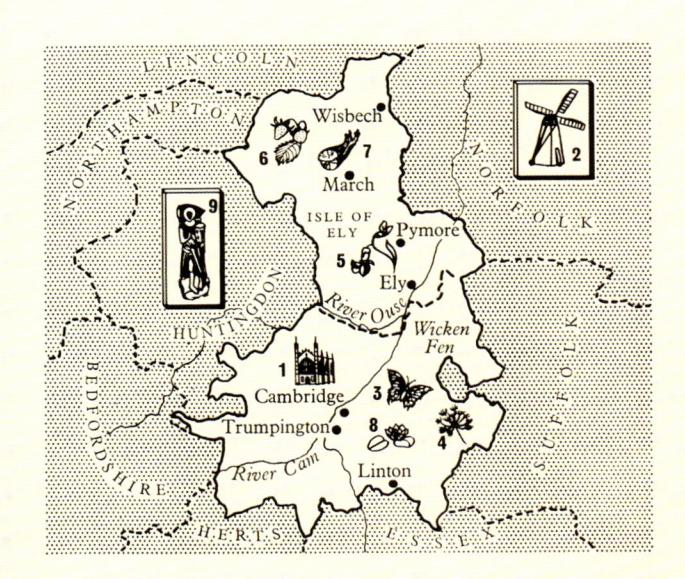

A county which contains Ely Cathedral, King's College Chapel (1) and the city of Cambridge, the Fens, and Swallowtail butterflies, must be numbered among the most remarkable of all counties in Britain; and if huge skies and a flat or else flattish landscape are not everybody's taste, here you feel you are seeing all of the sky and all the world's surface at a glance. Dykes and the pumps of windmill (2) and beam engine have turned the Fens into the richest land. A plaque on the 1830 engine-house at Pymore says:

> *These fens have oft times been by water drowned.*
> *Science a remedy in water found.*
> *The power of steam, she said, shall be employed:*
> *The destroyer by itself shall be destroyed.*

The 680 acres of Wicken Fen, a nature reserve maintained as much as possible in its original state, are the home of the Swallowtails (3), whose food plant, "Carrot" to the Fenman, is the tall Milk Parsley (4), which exudes a white sap. The Marsh Pea (5) is another rare plant of Fenland, and of Wicken. In the foreground are not only the Fenland farmer's strawberries (6), but one of the ancient bog oaks (7) of a dry pre-historic era which he has to remove from his black earth. Reeds, punts and water-lilies (8) on a long dyke or lode, and pollard willows complete the picture—together with undergraduates, and the famous brass (9) of Sir Roger de Trumpington, set in Trumpington Church in 1289, the second oldest brass in England.

YOU CAN BE SURE OF **SHELL** *The Key to the Countryside*

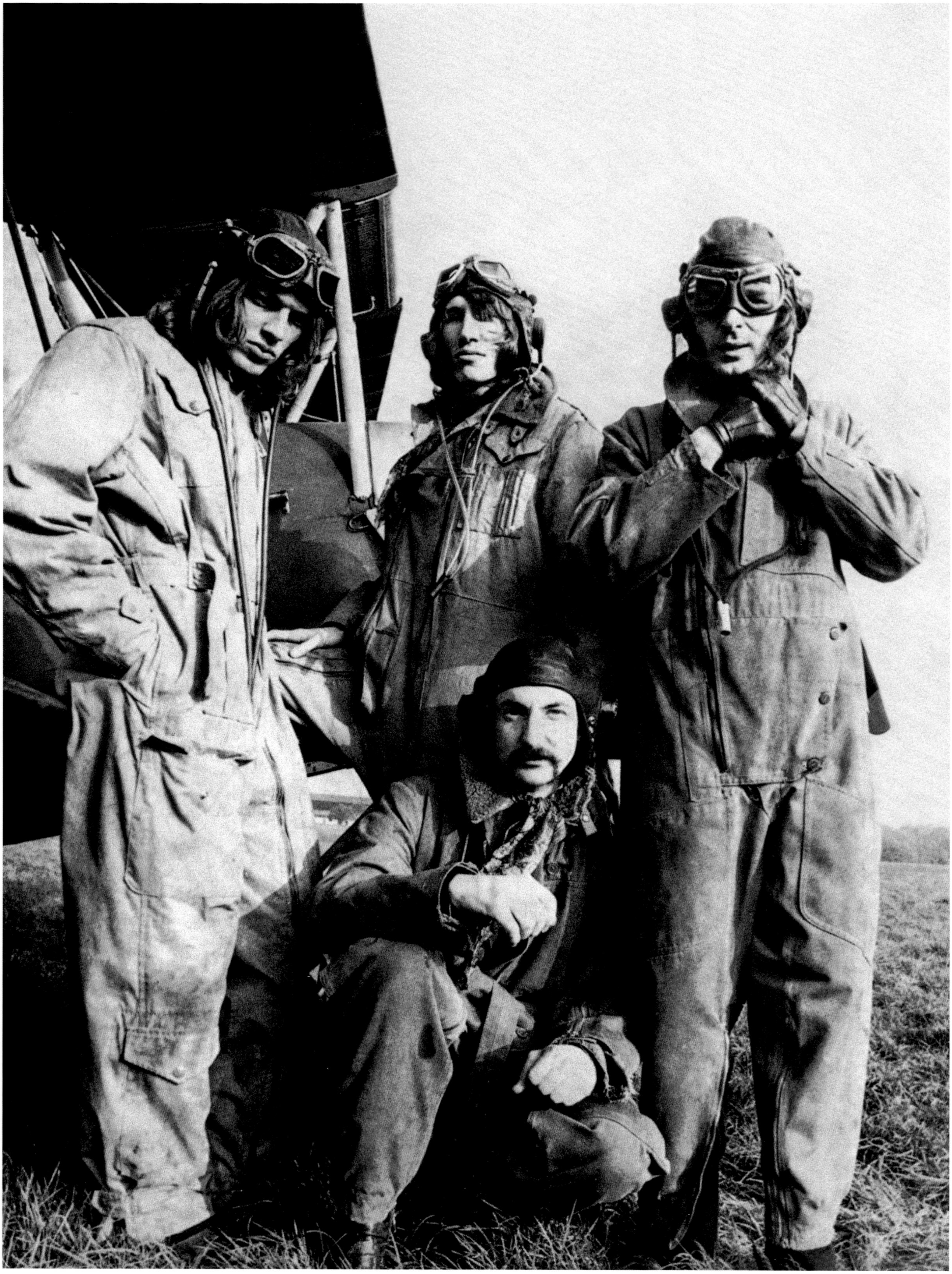

himself up in his home town of Hull and kept himself aloof from mainstream public life, and Orwell, who concerned himself with the impoverishment of civil life under the political conditions of the twentieth century, and whose *Animal Farm* (1945), surely influenced Pink Floyd's bleakly satirical socio-political concept album *Animals* of 1977, appear as guiding spirits behind the band's oeuvre. His sentence about the somnolent nation concludes with the words, 'I sometimes fear that we shall never wake till we are jerked out of it by the roar of bombs.' Orwell's paradox of domestic peace being purchased by the noise of conflict is picked up and echoed throughout the work of Pink Floyd.

The 'fortress built by Nature', the 'Precious stone set in a silver sea': Shakespeare's famous phrases, spoken by John of Gaunt in *Richard II*, circumscribe the experience of British identity. Preserved from external harm by serendipitous geography, the British Isles defended its sea-lined borders while harbouring slow-changing rural environments. When the artillery in Flanders was heard rumbling on the southern coast of England in the First World War (an aural phenomenon commemorated in the 1914 poem 'Channel Firing' by Thomas Hardy), when the Channel Islands were occupied by Nazi forces in the Second World War, and when bombs started raining on the nation's major cities, Britain's island paradise was threatened more tangibly than it had been for a millennium. The parental generation of Pink Floyd and their peers lived and fought through it. Pink Floyd were supposed to enjoy the fruits of peace, but of course it was not so simple.

England may be this 'other Eden', but in reality every acre of British land is marked by history: there are few expanses of untamed wilderness. It's all owned by someone. The British birthright is actually a land of lost content, a land that is perpetually beyond reach, out of bounds, unaffordable. There it stands, shining plain, but – John of Gaunt again – 'leased out ... like to a tenement or pelting farm'.

Just as Rupert Brooke sat in a gloomy Berlin café in 1912, dreaming of the church clock standing at ten to three and wondering if there was still honey for tea, so Pink Floyd's early music often recollects the English countryside in tranquillity. Nostalgia, as the saying goes, ain't what it used to be. *La nostalgie anglaise* has taken countless forms over the decades – a longing for a perceived golden age; a deeply embedded folk memory of a time before agrarian simplicity was eroded by enclosure, industrial revolution and urbanization. Here, it is suggested, is where the rot set in. The animated sequences in *Pink Floyd – The Wall* are highly compacted expressions of precisely this outrage at the destruction of heritage.

The English utopia is located in the realm of nature, the village, the empty field, the stone circle. It has the whiff of the pagan, of the folk, of eternity about it. The high Edwardian moment, in the twilight Indian summer of imperial history leading up to the First World War, is potent in the English imaginary: the last time patriarchal class nuclei held their molecules together, a final basking in the polarized pink sunset of the Victorian Empire before the digging of the trenches. The English utopia is not only located in physical and temporal space but also in the arts: literature, poetry, painting, music. From the *Pilgrim's Progress* of John Bunyan (and Ralph Vaughan Williams' opera of the same name) to the enlightened Albion of William Blake and Peter Ackroyd; from the poetic and

28 · OPPOSITE · Promotional photograph for Pink Floyd's single 'Point Me at the Sky', featuring the band in flying suits beside a De Havilland DH.82A Tiger Moth aeroplane, Biggin Hill, Kent, 1968. Photograph by Storm Thorgerson / Aubrey Powell at Hipgnosis

painted landscapes of William Wordsworth, Paul Nash and Geoffrey Hill to the Arthurian visions of Alfred Lord Tennyson and John Cowper Powys, and the Nordic phantasy demesne of J.R.R. Tolkien.

The English utopia also has a political dimension, where dreams and visions of an ideal society (or 'The Celestial City') are destabilized by corruption, economics and the permanent division entrenched in Britain's creaking democratic system. One of the great utopian prophets of English culture, William Morris, combined the roles of fantasy author, organic artist and political agitator with aplomb in the late Victorian age, influencing a whole new generation in the process. Morris embodied the inherent contradiction in the British psyche: within the soul of the most fervent progressive idealist spins the germ of a conservative. Such revolutionaries often seek to revolve back to the beginning, before things got out of control. On the contrary, conservatism in Britain has in practice, in the lifetime of Pink Floyd, meant the destruction of old certainties and ways of life, in the interests of streamlining and efficiency. Nostalgia is relabelled a thought crime. This is the divided state the band has grown up in, and the conflict between the two states, at some level, has fuelled the motor behind Pink Floyd's artistic evolution over the course of more than 50 years.

Morris' work of speculative fiction, *News from Nowhere* (1890), travels forward in time to picture an England turned upside down. This communitarian world without money, wage slavery or even a functioning government is accessed by a time traveller who takes a trip on the River Thames and rows into an alternative reality. The England imagined in such vividness can never exist, but something like it may always be present in the visionary consciousness. Not all of Pink Floyd's music remained on this path beyond the band's formative years, but it continued to inform their output in a more covert fashion. Representations of Britishness, patriotic symbols and locations, references to national character and the defence of the realm, have always had a place in Pink Floyd's work. They are present in the many instances of ambient sounds from nature that preface certain tracks, acting as an underlay of memory. Memories of the Battle of Britain never seem far away either. In 1968 the group dressed in RAF pilots' overalls, leather flying helmets and goggles and posed with a Tiger Moth biplane to promote the 'Point Me at the Sky' single in press shots and on film. More overtly and exaggeratedly, they orchestrated a Spitfire flypast at Knebworth Festival in 1975, and a replica fighter plane occasionally crashed on to the stage during their early 1970s live shows. Gerald Scarfe's Nazi bomber mutating into a giant metallic eagle is one of the most haunting visions in *The Wall* film.

△

'The Pink Floyd' emerged in the mid-1960s, but the narrative of the group is complicated by its changing line-up over the decades. It has kept the same name but on a variety of projects, different personalities have led the way. The Pink Floyd of *The Division Bell* (1994) is not the same as the Pink Floyd of *The Piper at the Gates of Dawn* (1967), nor of *The Final Cut* (1983). Knowing the disharmony and fluctuating alliances within the group itself, as well as the comings and goings of personnel over time, these albums and their associated tours are best considered as individual, discrete artistic projects, steered and authored by one individual member or another, but using the group as a resource to complete the work.

An individual at the age of 16 will hold a different world view from the one he or she holds at 35. The group's adolescence can be mapped to the years when Syd Barrett was the lead singer, guitarist and principal songwriter. Pink Floyd's Barrett period (1965–8) is all about escapism, but this was true of the entire British psychedelic movement. If there's one word that sums up the spirit of the English Summer of Love, it would have to be 'carnivalesque'. It was appropriate enough, because it harked back to a spontaneous underground of street culture in Britain dating back to the dawn of the industrial age. Broadside ballads, the roadside songs of street hawkers and sweeps, fairgrounds, circuses, open-air markets, musical halls proffering 'amusements' of a predominantly comical and light-musical character, pavement theatre, the songs and stories of nomadic pedlars and Gypsies. At the same time, the Festival of Britain in 1951, when many pop stars were on the cusp of their teens, and the science-fiction books, comics and movies of the 1950s onwards, injected tantalizing glimpses of imaginary technological futures, both utopian and horrific, into the cultural bloodstream. Additionally, the visual arts exploded paradigms, from action paintings and auto-destructive art to pop art's vital reclamation of consumerism. This potent fusion of modernist and nostalgic unsanctioned culture formed the distant forerunner of post-war pop. With the wireless dial locked to John Peel's buccaneering Radio London show 'The Perfumed Garden', adherents of this new cult

29 · **ABOVE** · *News from Nowhere*, William Morris, Kelmscott Press, 1892. V&A, National Art Library

What Have We Done to England? Pink Floyd and the Lure of the Pastoral

GAMES FOR MAY
THE PINK FLOYD

On Friday, 12th May, 1967 at 7:45 p.m. in the Queen Elizabeth Hall, South Bank, S.E.1, Christopher Hunt and Blackhill Enterprises present GAMES FOR MAY — space-age relaxation for the climax of Spring — Electronic compositions, colour and image projections, girls, and THE PINK FLOYD. Tickets: 21/-, 15/-, 10/- from the box office, Royal Festival Hall, S.E.1 (WAT 3191) and agents.

QUEEN ELIZABETH HALL/MAY 12

QUEEN ELIZABETH HALL GENERAL MANAGER JOHN DENISON CBE

reached deep into the dressing-up chest of history, wrapped themselves in the floral prints of William Morris and waited for the future to engulf them.

The attempt to reclaim a lost childhood was an inevitable response from the urban generation born in the mid- to late 1940s, who had made their playgrounds in the rubble-strewn aftermath of the Second World War. Britain's blues boom of the early to mid-'60s was an attachment fantasy to an America that appeared to be a land of plenty in comparison. The challenge became to redraw rock and psychedelia in a British vernacular. Not so much a distorted Americana, more a warped Victoriana: pastoral myths for the smoke-bound consumer, hallucinatory trips to the country and a rebirth in the secret gardens of childhood. Not for nothing did Michael Horovitz title his 1969 anthology of underground and counter-cultural poetry *Children of Albion*, with William Blake's painting *Glad Day* emblazoned on the front cover. And lest we forget, the working title for The Beatles' 1968 *White Album* was 'A Doll's House'.

Pink Floyd were in the thick of it. Photographs of the band celebrating, moments after signing their contract with EMI Records outside the company's London headquarters, show them high-kicking, clad in dandy silk shirts. The group's 'Games for May', a live performance at London's Queen Elizabeth Hall in May 1967, gave vent to the contradictory aspects of pagan festivity and cosmic communion. It was billed as 'space-age relaxation for the climax of spring'; blasting through one of the first quadraphonic amplification systems, which EMI engineers installed to circulate sound around the hall, Pink Floyd improvised their work-in-progress album, *The Piper at the Gates of Dawn*, as a rock equivalent of Igor Stravinsky's *Rite of Spring*. Attendees entering the foyer were serenaded with canned birdsong, and front-row ticket holders were showered with bubbles and daffodils tossed by someone in an admiral's costume. July found The Beatles premiering the flower-power anthem 'All You Need is Love', with its music-hall brass fanfare introduction, taking the spectacle to a global level with their international TV broadcast of the song. Meanwhile, Donovan removed all traces of his Woody Guthrie-influenced past and reinvented himself as pot-headed Pied Piper come to spirit off the children of Albion to a hidden land of perpetual fried picnics. A promotional film made for a medley of songs from that year's *A Gift from a Flower to a Garden* shows Donovan in florid wizard's robes holding court on the lawn of a Cornish cottage that's been transformed into a clotted-cream Camelot.

Like Donovan, Syd Barrett was fond of whimsy and the childlike, the 'fey'. Their inspiration was the kind of child's garden of verse that recalled Victorian nurseries or the youthful protagonists of E. Nesbit stories, a fantastical and nonsensical songbook including Lewis Carroll's 'Jabberwocky' and 'The Walrus and the Carpenter', Edward Lear's 'The Owl and the Pussycat', W.B. Yeats' 'The Song of Wandering Aengus', even the deathless 'Twinkle Twinkle Little Star'. Donovan's own composition, 'In an Old-Fashioned Picture Book', was a sentimental tapestry of seafront nostalgia, as yellowed photos of a little girl called Patience found in an old album stir up '*Faint sounds of a distant brass band, who rides the donkey today?/ Will our visions of tomorrow mingle with those of yesterday?*'

△

30 · OPPOSITE · Handbill advertising 'Games for May' by Pink Floyd, Queen Elizabeth Hall, London, 12 May 1967. Designed by Barry Zaid. Pink Floyd Archive

31 · OPPOSITE · 'It isn't manners for us to begin, you know', said the Rose, Peter Blake, 1970. Screenprint inspired by *Alice's Adventures in Wonderland* by Lewis Carroll. V&A: CIRC.122–1976

Post-war British modernism blurred the canvas of the English pastoral. Urbanization and the creep of the suburbs into formerly rural zones or 'edgelands' filled the atmosphere with ghosts from the lost countryside. The disquieting marriage of twentieth-century progress and the pagan uncanny is a feature of a mass of British literature, film and television. In Pink Floyd's case, its 1960s music was made strange by the mixture of childlike imagery, effects pedals and synthesizers, and hallucinogenic drugs. The scope of their debut album *The Piper at the Gates of Dawn* is prodigious enough to contain not only juvenilia like 'Matilda Mother', 'The Gnome' and 'Bike', but also the proto-space rock of 'Astronomy Domine', 'Pow R. Toc H.' and 'Interstellar Overdrive'. 'Flaming' mentions '*lazing in the foggy dew, sitting on a unicorn*', as well as fanciful references to buttercups and '*sleeping on a dandelion*', all punctuated with primitive sound effects: tinkling bells, wind-up clocks and rattles and the call of a cuckoo. 'The Scarecrow' is an uncanny projection of Barrett's own mental condition on to a spooky feature of the agricultural landscape. 'Chapter 24' is a re-reading of the fu hexagram of the I Ching, but its references to the solstice and the seasons fit naturally with a British rural setting. As Barrett's biographer Rob Chapman points out, the song 'contains a palpable folk influence and cadences and inflections which could only have been drawn from the English hymn tradition'.[2]

Several of Barrett's songs are shaped as fairy tales populated with a Brothers Grimm cast of kings, princesses and gnomes. 'Matilda Mother' begins '*There was a king who ruled the land/ His majesty was in command...*' Barrett had grown up reading Kenneth Grahame, Lewis Carroll, Hilaire Belloc and Kate Greenaway's self-illustrated books of fables, alphabets and games, monuments to Edwardian childhood innocence. His songs, from the earliest writings to his post-Floyd solo work, are a kaleidoscopic parade of gingerbread men, mice called Gerald, terrapins and octopi, flowers, candy, currant buns and ice cream, dream dragons and unicorns. At the same time, in the early 1960s Barrett, an art student, was hit by the rush of abstract expressionism, trash and pop art and kinetic sculpture. Fuelled by the same contrasting impulses, Pink Floyd's music of this period is strangely pushed and pulled between nostalgia for the secret gardens of the child's imagination, and the space-age futurism of interstellar overdrive. Binning the operating manual for spaceship Earth, they set the controls for an accelerated oblivion. But that sunburst could equally crossfade into the endless summer memories of childhood. As Barry Miles put it:

> Syd's lyrics connected directly to shared British memories of fairytales, of Hobbits, of going down the rabbit hole, Rupert Bear being called home for tea by his mother standing at the gate; unflappable Professor Quatermass seemingly unperturbed that one of his astronauts has been somehow absorbed by the other in a cheap soundstage made from a garden shed; square-jawed Dan Dare confronting the aliens each week in the *Eagle*; Flash Gordon bumping around a cheap interplanetary set in a rocket ship that burned like a damp firework in search of aliens with angel wings; Syd and Rick's bleeps and squeals like the scary BBC Radiophonic Workshop soundtrack to the 'Red Planet' radio serial; the boy at school with a scared mouse in his pocket; Uncle Mac and BBC 'Children's Hour'; Christopher Robin; the excitement at first hearing rock 'n' roll washing in on waves of static from Luxembourg; it was all there.[3]

The Band—Rob Young

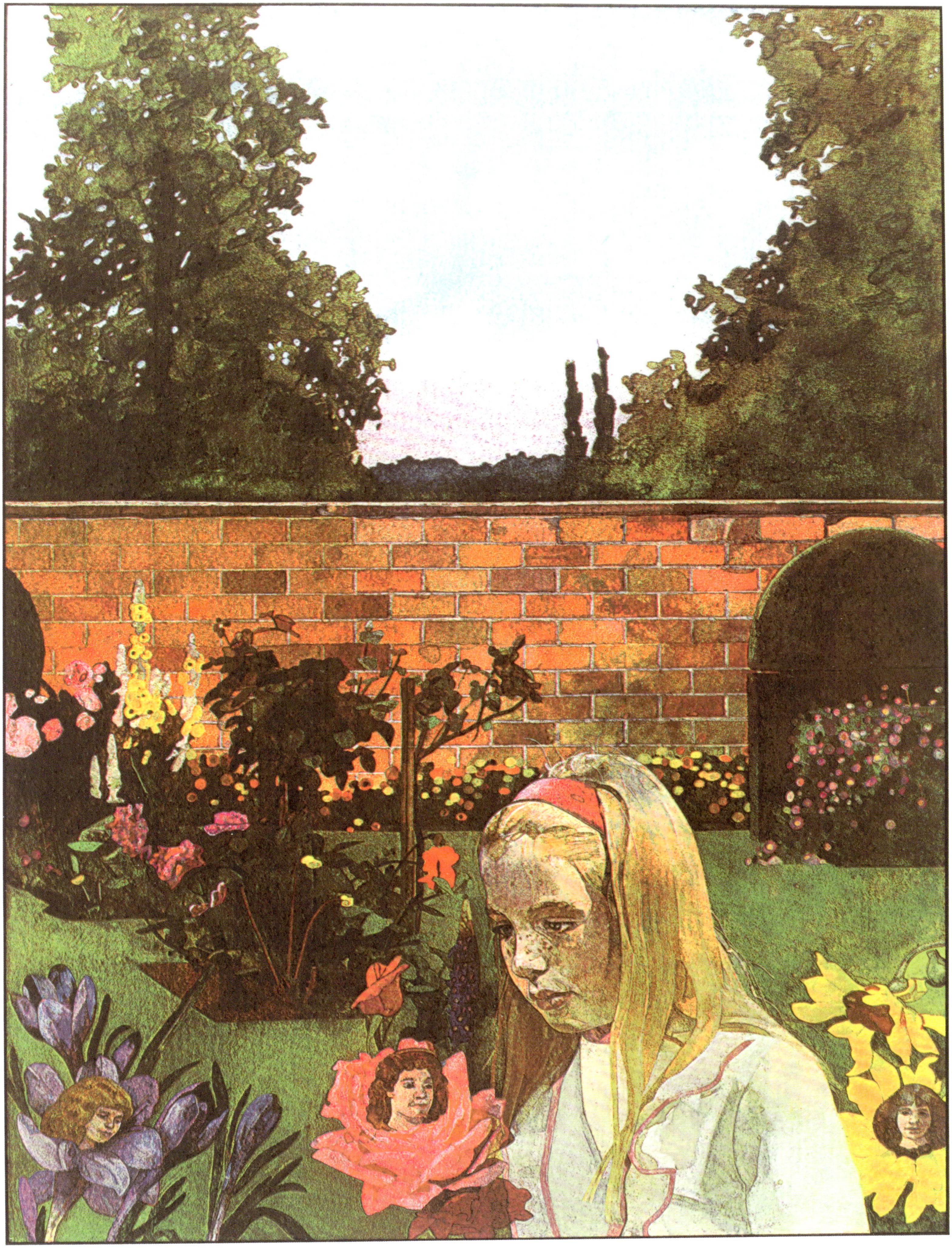

ALBION

NUMBER 1
2s.

The Piper at the Gates of Dawn lifted its title directly from chapter seven of Kenneth Grahame's classic children's novel *The Wind in the Willows*. In the chapter, Ratty and Mole take a boat out on the River Thames one evening, and as they row further out a haze seems to descend and they reach an island where the nature demigod Pan materializes. The episode, hallucinatory and misted in reverie, is an anomaly within the rest of the book. Grahame himself led, or at least promoted, the semi-indolent life of an idler:

> The Loafer may decently make some concession to popular taste by strolling down to the river and getting out his boat. With one paddle out he will drift down the stream: just brushing the flowering rush and the meadow-sweet and taking in as peculiar gifts the varied sweets of even. The loosestrife is his, and the arrow-head: his the distant moan of the weir; his are the glories, amber and scarlet and silver, of the sunset-haunted surface ... he is at peace with himself and with the whole world.

The passage comes from a book of whimsical essays entitled *Pagan Papers* (1893), not entirely as arcane as the title suggests, but a collective paean to the innocent delight in losing oneself in the countryside – at least for an afternoon or two. Pink Floyd often pined for, but rarely found, that repose. They eventually consummately rejected it out of hand: the lazy province of sheep.

It didn't take long before a discomfort began to infuse Pink Floyd's music. An uneasy combination of indolence, cynicism and righteous anger are present as far back as their second album, *A Saucerful of Secrets* (1968). It's no coincidence that none of the songs, save the final 'Jugband Blues', were composed by Barrett. In 'Remember a Day', lines about playing in sunlit apple trees are immediately followed by '*Hide from your little brother's gun*', an ominous foreshadowing of war in the midst of childhood games. The album's flagship blowout, 'Set the Controls for the Heart of the Sun', a shorter version of a piece the group improvised for lengthy periods in concert, is often described as one of Pink Floyd's most space-rock efforts. In fact, the lyrics make no mention of anything to do with rocket ships or technology; instead we find leaves trembling in anticipation, swallows resting under the eaves and love as '*the shadow that ripens the wine*'. In the twinned spirits of William Blake and Omar Khayyám, the heart of the sun is the destination of an impending voyage of gnostic enlightenment. The sci-fi elements are more prominent in 'Let There Be More Light', with its tableau of a '*mighty ship/ Descending on a point of flame*' making contact with the human race. The location of this extra-terrestrial encounter – Mildenhall, in Cambridgeshire – swings the scenario into a specifically English context and is swiftly followed up with the observation that '*the road revealed to him/ The living soul of Hereward the Wake*', in reference to the eleventh-century Anglo-Saxon outlaw who defended East Anglia against foreign invaders.

△

If Pink Floyd had split up permanently after the departure of Syd Barrett in 1968 they would now be remembered as the most inventive part of the great constellation of English psychedelia, celebrating innocence through a narcotic haze of fantastical electronic enhancements and infernal sound machines, and connecting the nursery rhyme with the pastoral with the age of space travel.

32 · OPPOSITE · Cover for *Albion* magazine, no.1, 1968. Designed by Michael English. V&A: S.45–1978

By hanging in there, they exposed their innocence to bitter experience. The fall from grace began to emerge in lyrics produced by the various band members even as early as the 1972 soundtrack to Barbet Schroeder's movie *La Vallée*, on the LP *Obscured by Clouds*. 'Childhood's End' imagines leaving the comfort and safety of the river bank for the '*sea/ of long past thoughts and memories./ Childhood's end, your fantasies/ merge with harsh realities*'. 'Free Four' describes how '*Life is a short, warm moment/ And death is a long cold rest … / So all aboard for the American tour/ And maybe you'll make it to the top … / You are the angel of death/ And I am the dead man's son/ And he was buried like a mole in a fox hole…*'

This Beckettian sense of cradle-to-grave futility creeps into many Pink Floyd songs. The reference to the mole harks back to the innocent riverside pastimes of *The Wind in the Willows*, before the savagery of the fox hunt takes over. Pink Floyd officially left the psychedelic caucus race and joined the music industry rat race in the 1970s, as evidenced by tracks such as 'The Great Gig in the Sky' and 'Money' on *The Dark Side of the Moon* and 'Welcome to the Machine' and 'Have a Cigar' on *Wish You Were Here*. After spending their formative years messing about on the river, they were now being sold down it.

But in a new era, when punk figurehead Johnny Rotten was sloganizing hate for Pink Floyd and the overbearing pomposity of progressive rock, they were forced to move onwards from the cataloguing of rock stars' luxury problems. *Animals* (1977) was a bleak, occasionally witty fable relating to the state of British politics and social mores, with little ambiguity. 'Sheep' once again opened with a rural field recording before describing the unquestioning obedience of the middle classes, being factory-farmed into submission. The same image of mass processing of individuals would of course soon be employed in 'Another Brick in the Wall', but one might argue that *Animals* found Pink Floyd at their most allegorically Orwellian, and where they truly effected a hundred-and-eighty-degree reverse on the 'medicated goo' of their early years, with a wholesale reaction against the persistence of nostalgia.

The only remembering now to be done, as the 1970s became the '80s, was the type of remembrance ritually offered to veterans of war. *The Final Cut* (1983) followed *The Wall* in drawing on the experiences of Roger Waters' father, Eric Fletcher Waters, killed in an apparently bungled mission at Anzio in 1944, leaving the singer fatherless almost since birth. The album's provisional title was 'A Requiem for the Post-War Dream', and its austere sleeve displays a dark jacket emblazoned with a Remembrance Day poppy and British medal ribbons from the Second World War. When the album came out, the decorations of the previous year's war were still being handed out, as Britain had just aggressively defended the tiny marine outpost of the Falkland Islands in the South Atlantic – a conflict that surely lies behind the exasperated title, 'Get Your Filthy Hands Off My Desert'. *The Final Cut* opens with snippets of radio news bulletins, announcing the planned construction of nuclear shelters in the East-Anglian towns of Peterborough and Cambridge. The threat of thermonuclear destruction has reached even as far as the banks of the Cam itself. '*Oh Maggie,*' sings Waters, '*what have we done/ To England?*'

△

33 · ABOVE · John Lydon, aka Johnny Rotten, wearing his infamous 'I hate Pink Floyd' T-shirt, 1976. Photograph by Ray Stevenson

What Have We Done to England? Pink Floyd and the Lure of the Pastoral

Though fragmented due to personal differences and shifting allegiances during the 1980s and '90s, Pink Floyd's field of operations moved inexorably back to the river. Specifically, aboard *Astoria*, the houseboat built in 1911, which David Gilmour purchased in 1986 and converted into a recording studio. Permanently moored at Hampton on the River Thames, the boat is situated a frog's leap away from the setting of William Morris' *News from Nowhere*. At the beginning of the first album to be recorded there, *A Momentary Lapse of Reason* (1987), we hear the sound of plashing oars – 'signs of life' along the mystic river. Mole and Ratty have returned to seek out the great god Pan one last time. The group's late output has continued to hark back to its origins, even though irrevocably tainted by experience. The bells of Grantchester peal out again and honey-bees return to their bumbling on 'High Hopes', the song with lyrics by Polly Samson and David Gilmour that closes *The Division Bell* (1994). The bell clangs rhythmically throughout the track, evoking simultaneously peaceful, glowing memories – '*the grass was greener/ the light was brighter*' – and the Division Bell itself, traditionally rung in the UK Parliament to announce an imminent vote. These summoned Fenland bells mark the azimuth where radiant possibility and unrealized dreams begin their slow, lifetime slide into entropy and responsible adulthood. Syd Barrett even hovers inside this vision, wraithlike, in the lines '*The endless river/ forever and ever*', which gesture three decades backwards to '*Float on a river forever and ever*', in Pink Floyd's second single 'See Emily Play', written by Barrett. Storm Thorgerson's cover artwork for *The Division Bell* likewise returns to the Fens: two monumental metal heads, sculpted in profile, face off in a stubbly English field. We know it's Cambridgeshire because in the space between their mouths can be seen Ely Cathedral, nicknamed 'the ship of the Fens'. These giant Janus faces resemble riveted aircraft parts fallen to Earth, with roundels for eyes. They have rotated from their customary outward confrontation with the past and the future, to gaze inward, their two halves forming a phantom third set of features. All the tensions expressed in Pink Floyd over the years between the public/private, past/future and nostalgia/progress, are evoked once more in this iconic image.

In Pink Floyd's music, the pastoral has been perpetually unstable, rarely enjoyed for its own sake but always threatening, or under threat. It is one of many tangential elements in a corpus that has ranged wide in its search for thematic content, but there is clear continuity over a 50-year stretch. The river has borne them away on their long journey, opened up many tributaries and side streams, and eventually carried them back to some kind of resolution. The last, and most likely final Pink Floyd emission was, indeed, a collection of instrumentals culled from sessions on the *Astoria* houseboat, and entitled *The Endless River*. The Thames runs softly, but its undercurrents are complex and unpredictable.

34 · ABOVE · Pink Floyd's circular screen showing the river view from David Gilmour's studio onboard the *Astoria*, from the tour of *The Division Bell*, 1994. Photograph by Denis O'Regan

What Have We Done to England? Pink Floyd and the Lure of the Pastoral

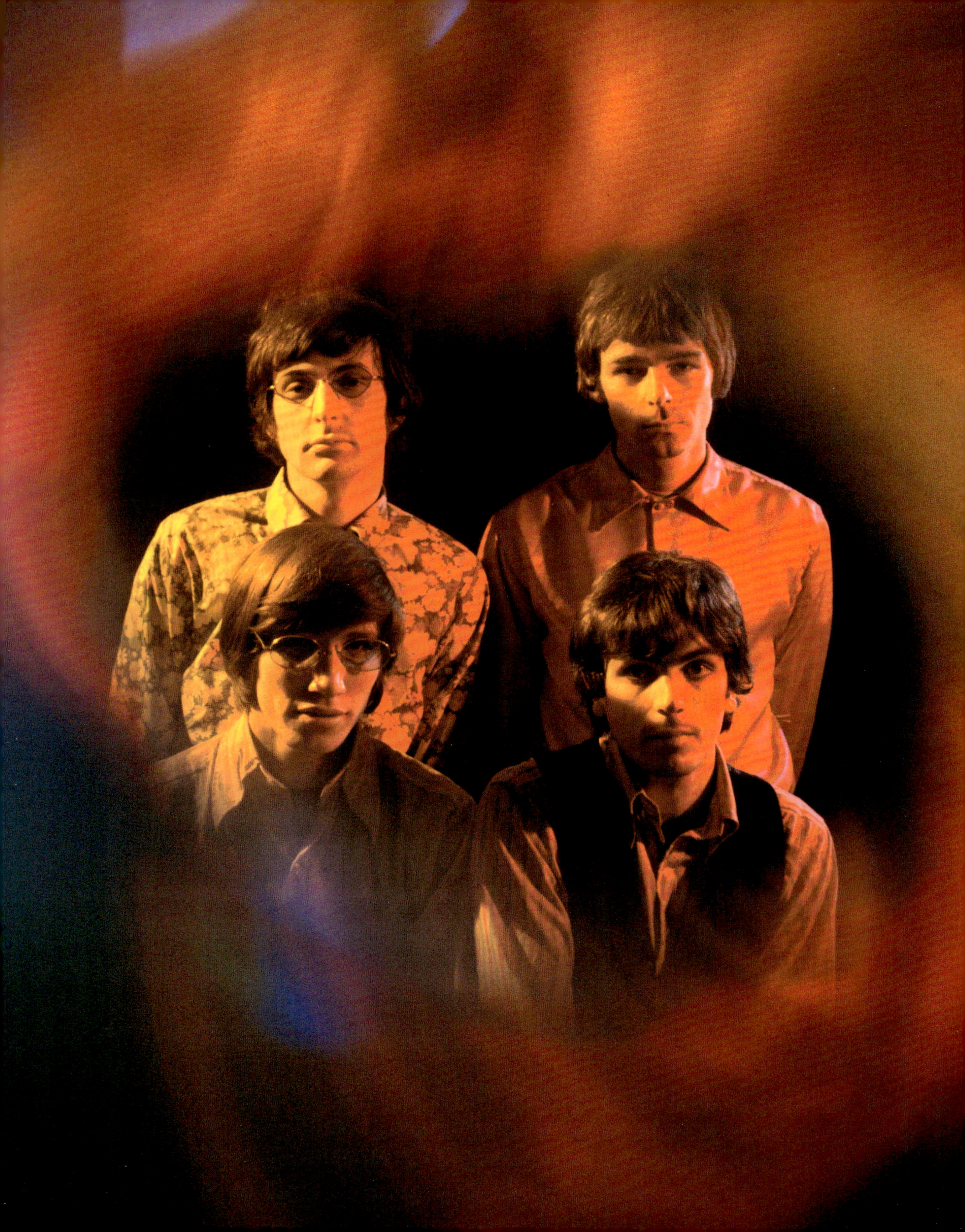

A LONG-TERM PROSPECT

Jon Savage

Pink Floyd will be a name to watch in the New Year
—'Rave-Elations: The Ones to Watch', *Rave*, December 1966

We've had bad publicity, bad records and atrocious lyrics like The Smoke's 'My Friend Jack' and the Pink Floyd's 'Arnold Layne'. I'm sick of these songs. I refuse to play any of them.
—Bob Farmer, 'Simon Dee Digs the Amazing March of SQUARES!', *Disc and Music Echo*, 8 April 1967

By spring 1967 the British pop scene was in a state of flux. The apparently holistic unanimity of the 1963 to '66 pop chart – mod Britain, swinging London – had passed along with the withdrawal of The Beatles, the gradual disappearance of the pirate radio stations and the cancellation of the influential weekly TV show 'Ready Steady Go!' Nobody quite knew what was taking its place: was it straightforward teen pop, reactionary light entertainment or the new sounds of the underground? Was it all of these or nothing?

35 · **PAGE 56** · Pink Floyd, 1967. Photograph by Marc Sharratt

36 · **OPPOSITE** · Invitation to the press launch of 'Arnold Layne' at EMI Records, 20 Manchester Square, London, 3 March 1967. Collection of Warren Dosanjh

Beginning in 1963, The Beatles had presided over an explosion of youth music and youth consciousness. In the full flowering of pop modernism, everything – art, commerce, the teenage news – had been concentrated in the pop single, with the charts as one gigantic mixer churning up beat, British R&B, soul, Motown, the start of psychedelia and the inevitable 'mums and dads' records that harked back to campfire singalongs or light operetta. The competition was intense, and the discipline even more so: everything had to be communicated in two or three minutes.

Four years later, money and time had done their work. The centre could not hold, especially when the amount of money and attention directed at youth culture prompted thoughts of social change, another kind of consciousness and generational politics. 1966 was the last year when singles outsold albums in the UK, with The Beatles' *Sgt. Pepper's Lonely Hearts Club Band* acting as the hinge between these two periods. As the progressive pop stars – as they were then called – moved towards rock and the long-playing record, a vacuum was created.

On 25 March 1967 – the week that Pink Floyd received their first write-up in *Disc and Music Echo* ('Meet the Pinky Kinkies') – the Top 10 was dominated by Light Entertainment. Engelbert Humperdinck was at Number 1 with 'Release Me', the record that famously kept 'Penny Lane' / 'Strawberry Fields Forever' off the top spot, followed by two different versions of 'This is My Song' and dreadful records by Vince Hill, The Seekers and Sandie Shaw (Britain's Eurovision entry). Clearly there had to be a world beyond this.

As far as the general public were concerned, Pink Floyd began as a pop group. 'The single was king', says their then co-manager Peter Jenner about this early phase.[1] That was the agenda, and whatever improvisations they had played for the underground cognoscenti had to be synthesized and redacted into a three-minute, catchy, hook-laden tune. Released on 10 March, 'Arnold Layne' was played to hell on the remaining pirate radio stations and made the Top 30 late that month, eventually rising to Number 20 despite the controversy surrounding a Radio London ban.

It was one of several singles to attract adverse attention early that year, as the progressive insistence in breaking the boundaries of taste came up against those whom it sought to provoke. Records by The Rolling Stones (sex) as well as by EMI groups The Game and The Smoke (drugs) had been censored or critically lashed. With its explicit storyline about transvestism, 'Arnold Layne' was asking for trouble in that climate, even though it seemed an entirely unsensational treatment and an entirely natural topic for a song.

'We can't think what Radio London are so perturbed about', Roger Waters explained, 'it's a song about a clothes fetishist who's obviously kinked. A very simple, straightforward song about one sort of human predicament.'[2] This idea, to explore the outer limits of then accepted behaviour, was hardly novel: 'Arnold Layne' fitted right in with The Who's run of Top 5 hits between 1966 and '67, psychological songs that examined hints of incest ('Substitute'), transvestism ('I'm a Boy'), mental impairment ('Happy Jack') and masturbation ('Pictures of Lily').

The Band—Jon Savage

This is it!

THE NEXT PROJECTED SOUND OF '67

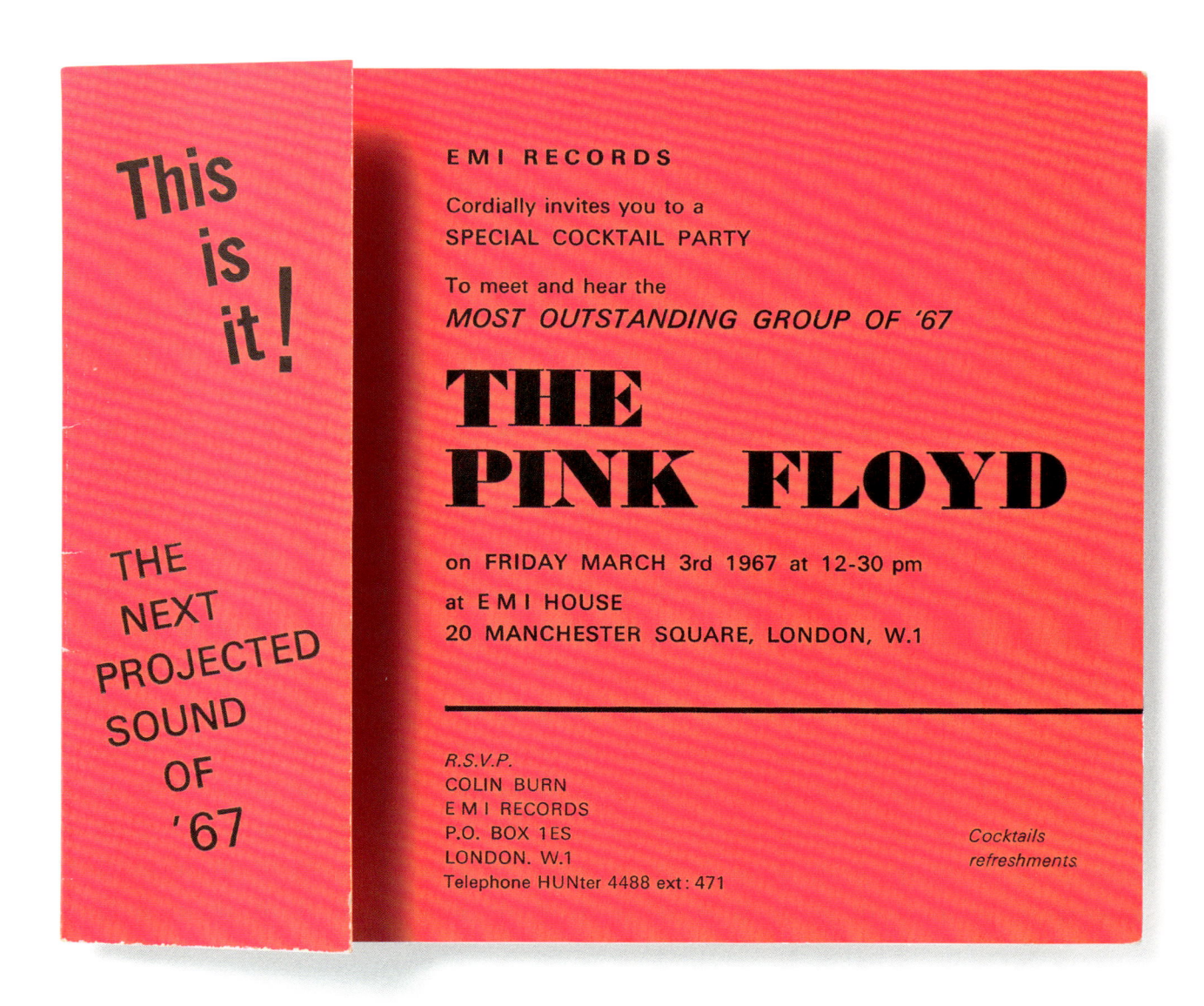

EMI RECORDS

Cordially invites you to a SPECIAL COCKTAIL PARTY

To meet and hear the MOST OUTSTANDING GROUP OF '67

THE PINK FLOYD

on FRIDAY MARCH 3rd 1967 at 12-30 pm

at E M I HOUSE
20 MANCHESTER SQUARE, LONDON, W.1

R.S.V.P.
COLIN BURN
E M I RECORDS
P.O. BOX 1ES
LONDON. W.1
Telephone HUNter 4488 ext: 471

Cocktails refreshments

Signed to EMI through its prime label Columbia, Pink Floyd were assured a high profile from the off: their first single was advertised as 'The Next Projected Sound of 1967' and the *Disc and Music Echo* profile called them 'four very advanced young men of pop'. With their long hair, flowing clothes, penny round shirts, ethnic waistcoats and square sunglasses, they appeared as harbingers of a new era where synaesthesia ruled in the form of 'projectors, spot lamps and liquid slides' – pop not as entertainment but environment.

With 'Arnold Layne' hovering around the Top 30 for several weeks, *Disc* allowed Pink Floyd a follow-up feature in early April. Clearly the uncredited writer was unconvinced: 'are they just a brief bubble on the pop scene or have they the ability to last?'[3] The four were interviewed separately. Roger Waters described himself as 'aggressive' and gave the writer a hard time. Nick Mason was the most approachable. Richard Wright was 'easy-going and exceedingly absent-minded'.

Syd Barrett was 'the best looking of a rather ordinary bunch'. He commented on the 'apparent swing to the squares' then plaguing British pop: 'Teenagers in Britain are great. Possibly, they are not buying the bulk of records, but they come to life as audiences. Just because Humperdinck, closely followed by the Ken Dodds [sic], is doing so well is not indicative of apathy on the part of teenagers.' As he concluded: 'Freedom is what I'm after. That's why I like working in this group. There's such freedom artistically.'

37 · OPPOSITE · *Disc and Music Echo*, 22 July 1967. Cover photograph of Pink Floyd by Colin Prime

Late in the next month, the June issue of *Rave* hit the stands. 'Britain's Most Influential Young Magazine' was hedging its bets, with features on latest teen sensations The Monkees and Dave Dee, Dozy, Beaky Mick and Tich, with a fetching picture of Cat Stevens on the cover. Right inside the back cover was a spread on Pink Floyd, illustrated by a colour picture of the group in their early 1967 psychedelic finery, their light show projected onto their loose shirts and scarves.

Maureen O'Grady called them 'one of our most futuristic groups', and her interview caught a group torn between their underground origins and the demands of the marketplace: 'at the UFO club in London, the people there are so blasé that they are bored to death with "Arnold Layne" because it's become a pop song', Roger Waters observed, while Nick Mason admitted that 'we really didn't want "Arnold Layne" to become our first single ... we tried to stop it being released, but we couldn't. Still, it doesn't matter now.'[4]

With a news-stand date of late May, the *Rave* interview was presumably conducted sometime earlier that month, while 'Arnold Layne' was still in the charts and the group were preparing for their big multimedia extravaganza, 'Games for May', at the Queen Elizabeth Hall. Two days later, on 14 May, Syd Barrett and Roger Waters were interviewed by Hans Keller on BBC's 'The Look of the Week': a clip that still exists. In a few days they were in EMI Studios recording their next single.

'See Emily Play' was the song that broke everything wide open. It was a big hit, reaching Number 6 and staying in the charts for nearly three months. A month after its release, the group's status was recognized by a *Disc and Music Echo* front cover, the picture taken from their April shoot with Colin Prime in Camberwell's Ruskin Park. It was a light-hearted session, contrary to later interpretations, with Syd Barrett obviously the leader in gesture and appearance – the most attuned of the four to psychedelic fashions.

This was Pink Floyd's pop zenith. The colour cover trailed a half-page feature and a quarter-page ad for their forthcoming LP *The Piper at the Gates of Dawn*. They were trailed, again, as trailblazers: 'part and parcel of London's new underground movement'. Their co-manager Peter Jenner described their music as 'an environment', and spoke of the band's collective desire to create their own situations rather than play in established clubs: 'we'd like to have a large marquee and travel the country. "The Freak Out Comes to Town", it could be called.'[5]

Nobody reading this article on publication would have known it, but the tensions between pop and underground, between the demands of the music industry and what Syd Barrett needed – 'he believes in total freedom', reported *Disc* – were on the point of curtailing this first, hit-making phase. During the next year and a half, Pink Floyd would release three further 45s, none of which would be successful. Forced to dive deep into their own resources, they began to concentrate on albums, sympathetically staged shows and film collaborations.

Albeit unintentionally, Pink Floyd marked the change between singles and albums, between pop and the new rock. The band's inability and/or refusal to sustain the hit-making momentum, was the embodiment of the fact that the time-honoured sixties pop dynamic – a single every three months, a constant

DISC
and MUSIC ECHO 9d
JULY 22, 1967   USA 20c

LENNON 'war' film secrets: exclusive
SCOTT McKENZIE speaks to DISC!

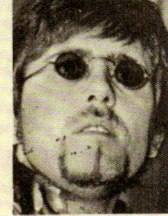

HOLLIES tour shock —page 16

PINK FLOYD HIT 8: ALBUM ALL SET

PINK FLOYD, up to No 8 in the chart this week with "See Emily Play," fly to the States in September to promote the disc which is released there at the end of this month.

Their follow-up single, for September release, will be either "Old Woman With A Casket" or "Millionaire," both Syd Barrett songs.

Pink Floyd's first album, "Piper At The Gates Of Dawn," is released next Friday (July 28) and includes a 10-minute track entitled "Interstellar Overdrive."

The group go to Germany on August 1 for two days of TV appearances and are also set for a four-day visit to Denmark from September 9. Tonight (Thursday) they start a three-day Scottish tour at Elgin.

● FREAKING - OUT WITH THE FLOYD: SEE PAGE 7.

stream of dates and package tours – was no longer applicable for the new breed of musicians, who saw their work not as a simple commercial process, but as a form of art and a kind of exploration. Pink Floyd had willingly entered this arena, but circumstances forced them to change their terms of engagement.

1968 would be the transition year. Nobody knew whether it would work, but the group had no choice but to plough on. While seeming perverse to some observers – 'during the past year, there have been so many paths for the Pink Floyd and not all of them have been easy and sometimes it seems as though they have taken the wrong one', John Peel wrote that year[6] – the choices that they made set them up for another decade and a half. Survival takes great courage: it's harder to go up and come back down than it is to ascend in the first place.

1967

> But remote in other haunts than these the rural Pan is hiding, and piping the low, sweet strain that reaches only the ears of a chosen few. And now that the year wearily turns and stretches herself before the perfect waking, the god emboldened begins to blow a clearer note.
> —Kenneth Grahame, 'The Rural Pan. An April Essay',
> *Pagan Papers*, 1893

Two film sequences bookend Pink Floyd in 1967. The first was shot by Peter Whitehead on 11 and 12 January 1967. Whitehead had known Syd Barrett in Cambridge and, after seeing the band play at UFO, decided to use them in his forthcoming documentary film *Tonite Let's All Make Love in London*. Beginning with stop-frame light movement, a Swinging London montage and live footage shot the next day at UFO, Whitehead's sequence shows the group improvising two long numbers, 'Interstellar Overdrive' and 'Nick's Boogie'.

It's an invaluable document of a new kind of sensibility within pop: intuitive and experimental. Syd Barrett is at the centre, hunched over his guitar, swaying in time to the rhythm, spinning out reverberated filigrees through his Binson Echorec. He is slightly bearded but still fresh faced. Much of his improvisation is pure texture, scrapings and pluckings, sudden runs of high liquid notes that play off Richard Wright's organ. At one point during 'Nick's Boogie' he applies his cigarette lighter to the guitar in an echo of AMM's Keith Rowe.

The second was filmed in the last month of the year for the Central Office of Information, to be distributed in North America in a series called 'London Line'. The clip begins with a close-up of Syd Barrett, with his pop-star perm and kohl-rimmed eyes. As he sings the melancholy waltz of 'Jugband Blues' he stares into the camera, frozen in stasis. During the free-form instrumental break, the lights flicker in the studio, framing the four-man group in shadow. They are together, but apart.

Few groups were more attuned to film than Pink Floyd: they played bathed in moving light, and it was a short step from light show to movie camera. It's fitting that their hyper-speed trajectory of 1967 was captured, not just by these extraordinary films but by outlets as diverse as 'American Bandstand', 'Top of

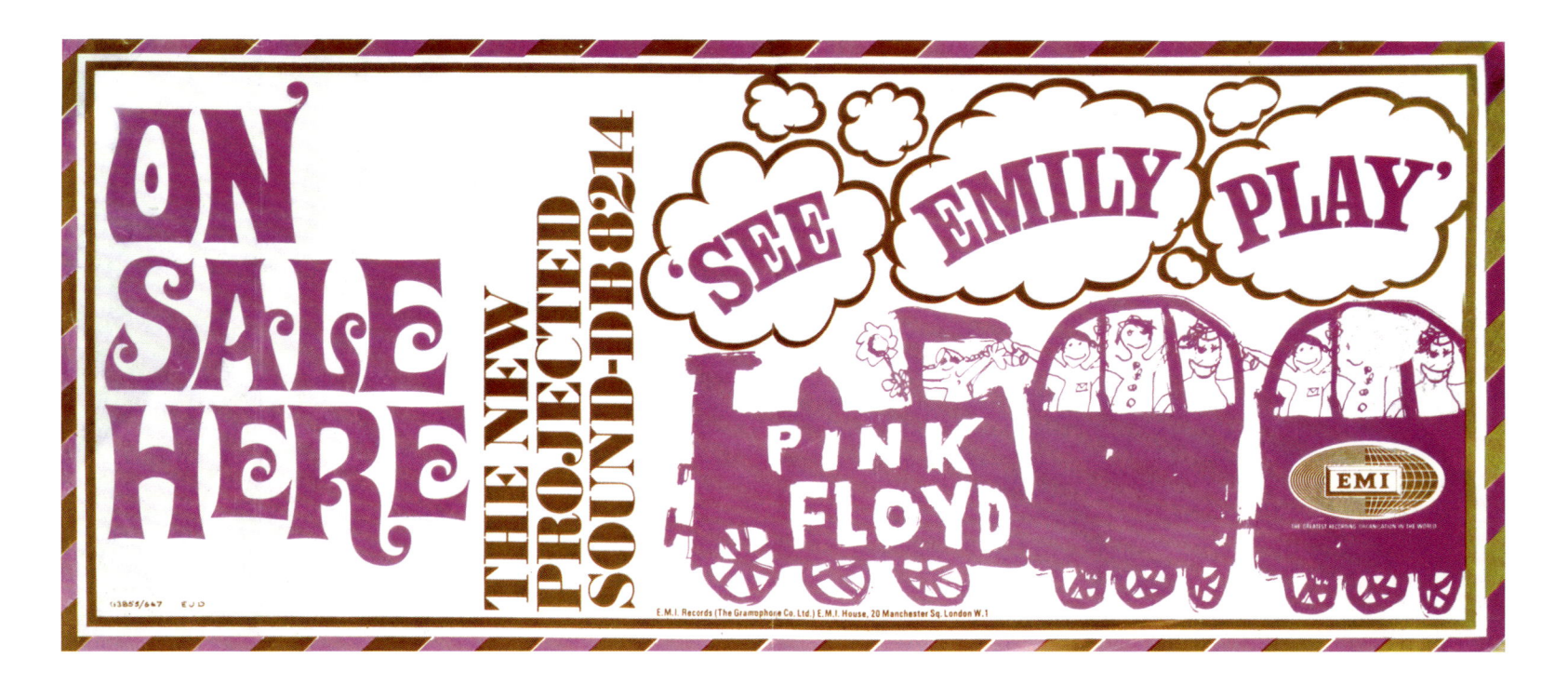

38 · **ABOVE** · Promotional poster for 'See Emily Play', June 1967. Illustration by Syd Barrett. Pink Floyd Archive

the Pops' and Pathé News. Just as in The Beatles' newsclips and promo videos, these films capture a group, and in particular an individual, at the cutting edge of musical and social change.

As Peter Jenner recognizes:

> it was such a strange world to be working in, the pop business, the speed of the success was just what happened in the pop business. The Beatles had a record out and the next thing, people were going mad, and they were all over America. The pop business does foreshorten these things. You have a hit, and you're a hit act. The hit takes three weeks to become a hit, maybe a month, but it's an incredibly short period of time. It became normal, it's just what happens. An incredible acceleration, in hindsight.[7]

Pink Floyd had begun as a student pastime and had quickly developed into an artistic experiment, a harbinger of a new kind of music-making and its alternative society. With 'Arnold Layne' and even more intensely with 'See Emily Play', the group were pitched into the heart of the pop world: press, TV, promo, endless one-nighters around the country, and the expectation of a follow-up single that was expected to be a hit. Suddenly, they were in the grid, and Syd Barrett, in particular, hated it.

'The whole era of the (Syd) Floyd was about a year,' Jenner says; 'it started in the autumn of '66, and by the autumn of '67, they were blowing up. Disintegrating. Syd was going crazy.'[8] As often happens with charismatic frontmen who vacate the stage, hindsight is applied to every action, yet it was not a given that Barrett would react the way that he did. Indeed, given the evidence of the last session that Barrett performed with the group, BBC's 'Top Gear' on 20 December 1967, he was still capable of good coherent work.

1967 was a year of extraordinary achievement for Pink Floyd that slowly subsided into a confusing ebb and flow. The evidence is there not only in the films,

A Long-Term Prospect

39 · ABOVE · Publicity shoot for EMI Records, 20 Manchester Square, London, 3 March 1967. Photograph by Dezo Hoffman. Pink Floyd Archive

but also in the actual records, which oscillate between profound outer-space exploration, childhood wonder and convoluted disturbance if not actual terror. This is the group's mythic period, with Syd Barrett as the archetypal, self-destructive Romantic boy wonder, but the focus granted to this one year only makes their subsequent renaissance all the more extraordinary.

With its swirling organ and soaring instrumental break, 'Arnold Layne' was immediately arresting. Barrett's vocal was unusual in its frank Englishness: there is no attempt to sound American and, as on 'Lucy Leave', he drags out the syllables – '*Layne*', '*strange*' – in a manner that makes the sudden interjections – '*he hates it*', '*why can't you see*' – all the more surprising. Beneath the controversial topic, a very British kind of perviness, this is a cautionary tale with a definite sting: '*takes two to know – why can't you see?*'

Oscillating between the third person and direct address yet concise and melodic, 'Arnold Layne' was a successful introduction – ushering in a distinctive new voice. Pink Floyd gave their experimental aspect a slightly freer rein on the B-side, 'Candy and a Currant Bun', even though the lyrics had been altered from the overt drug reference of 'Let's Roll Another One'. Beginning in a haze of fuzz, the song explodes in the middle break that merges organ and viciously riffing guitar, before resolving into repeated bursts of babbling Binson echoes.

It's clear that EMI signed Pink Floyd as a long-term prospect. Even before 'Arnold Layne' was established as a success, the group were in Abbey Road recording songs for their first LP. This was to be a mixture of both song and improvisation – with one of the first tasks being to capture their forte number, 'Interstellar Overdrive'. At the same time, the group were out on the road, far from UFO and the Roundhouse, doing one-nighters in Malvern, Ross-on-Wye, Portsmouth, Nottingham – rowing clubs, railway clubs, floral halls.

Their reception was mixed. Late 1966 had seen the beginning of subcultural split between the nascent hippies – which included the sharp end of British pop – and the hardening mods, determined to stay within their amphetamined version of Black American soul music. Clearly long improvisations and songs about gnomes, transvestites and the I Ching weren't going to play well with that crowd. 'Some places up North flip over us,' Richard Wright told *Rave*, 'while others are cold for no apparent reason.'[9]

When the group played the California Ballroom, Dunstable, on 12 February, the audience reacted by throwing beer mugs. As Roger Waters told *Zigzag* magazine a few years later, that 'was the one where they were pouring pints of beer on us from the balcony, that was most unpleasant and very very dangerous too'.[10] At the Feathers pub in Ealing a couple of months later, Waters was hit by an (old) penny, 'which made a bloody great cut in the middle of my forehead. I bled quite a lot … I was glowering in a real rage'.[11]

'We play what we like and what we play is new,' Roger Waters told *Record Mirror*'s Peter Jones:

> I suppose you could describe us as the house orchestra of this new movement, because we're the only people doing what the fans want to hear.

> We're really part of the whole present pop movement. We're not, repeat NOT, an anti-music group. In fact, we're very much in favour of a lot of things, including freedom and creativity and doing what you want to do, but of course tempered by social conscience. We're not really anarchists.[12]

As the apparent leaders of a new movement, Pink Floyd began to attract mainstream attention. On 14 May, they played a brief snatch of 'Astronomy Domine' on the BBC's 'The Look of the Week'. With this live transmission happening two days after the 'Games for May' event, the campaign for the mid-June release of 'See Emily Play' was up and running. The single was promoted with a child's drawing and was well reviewed: 'Excitement as expected', wrote Peter Jones in *Record Mirror*; 'this is the group's best so far and it builds well enough to be a substantial hit. The instrumental phases later on are way-out, clever and certainly different. Very well done, gents.'[13]

'See Emily Play' begins like a rocket: the guitar and the organ propel the song forward at warp speed, before snaking into the first verse. The lyric taps into English archetypes – '*Float on a river forever and ever*' evokes John Everett Millais' painting of Ophelia – while pressing the psychedelic trigger with words like 'dreams', 'mind', 'games'. The setting is pastoral, the mood apparently ecstatic. The middle eight is brief, another rocket launch with a 'Tomorrow Never Knows'-style Goons piano.

Now considered a Summer of Love classic, 'See Emily Play' has a strange undertow that went unnoticed at the time: '*Soon after dark, Emily cries*', '*you'll lose your mind and play*'. This ambiguity – between heaven and hell – was common to early psychedelic songs, before the beatific gloss of the Love Generation took over. Only the perceptive critic Penny Valentine caught the paradox: even though not a fan, she found it 'another one of those songs which appear childishly innocent on the surface but actually carry messages of doomy evilness'.[14]

'See Emily Play' launched Pink Floyd into full-blown pop stardom. On 6 July the group made the first of three appearances on 'Top of the Pops'. The footage, which resurfaced only recently, is dominated by an out-of-focus swirling effect but shows a coiffed and smart Syd Barrett miming without any obvious reticence. Wearing a multicoloured '*gown that touches the ground*', he is every inch the psychedelic pop star – with only a hint of glassiness around the eyes.

The pressure – to be there, to do that, to be that kind of person – was increasing. Nick Mason, Roger Waters and Richard Wright adapted easily enough: after all, as Mason told *Zigzag* later, 'we were a rock 'n' roll band'.[15] With his insistence on 'total freedom', Syd Barrett found that being a pop star was a responsibility, if not an actual trap, such as he had never before encountered in his life. The group's schedule for July included several TV appearances, interviews and concerts in Birmingham, Northwick, Redcar, the Isle of Man and a short tour of Scotland.

On 27 July, Pink Floyd made their third appearance on 'Top of the Pops'. This time, Barrett was less than enthusiastic. The next day, he walked out of BBC's 'Saturday Club' show. In the chart of that week, published on 29 July, 'See Emily Play' reached its highest position, Number 6, but that night, Pink Floyd played a double header – with an evening show in East Dereham in Norfolk (where the

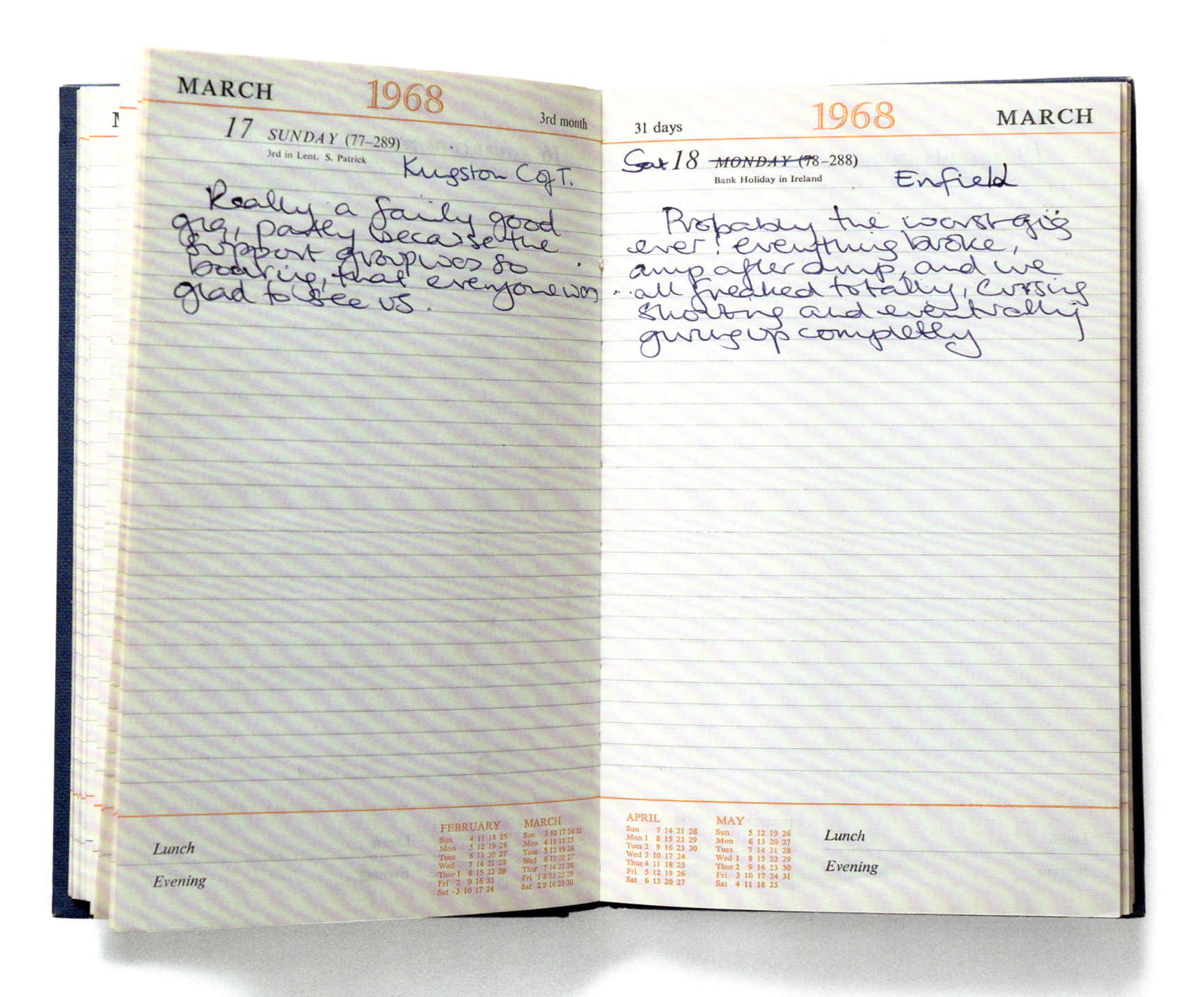

40 · ABOVE · Diary entries by Nick Mason referring to Pink Floyd gigs at Kingston Technical College and Enfield College of Technology in March 1967, written in a 1968 diary. Pink Floyd Archive

A Long-Term Prospect 67

punters threw glasses) followed by an early morning appearance at the 'Love-in Festival' at Alexandra Palace that was 'notably uninspired' by one account.[16]

The zenith had been reached: in the short term, the only way was down. Not that anyone outside the group's inner circle knew it at the time. Although there were reports of cancelled dates, the pop press was full of news about the Pink Floyd's forthcoming US trip, their next single ('either "Old Woman with a Casket" or "Millionaire", both Syd Barrett songs', reported *Disc*)[17] and the release of their debut LP *The Piper at the Gates of Dawn* – which, as *Record Mirror* observed, had 'plenty of mind-blowing sound'.[18]

For a moment, Pink Floyd had it all: pop success, artistic credibility and subcultural status. They were innovative yet successful, experimental yet disciplined. It was all focused and poured into 11 songs that, ordered into a sequence with a title taken from Kenneth Grahame's 1908 novel *The Wind in the Willows* – a masterwork of Elysian nature mysticism from that seeming 'golden age' before the First World War – built up to a definitive statement of English mysticism: the wonder of Albion.

The Piper at the Gates of Dawn is, on one level, rooted in place. It is a very Cambridge album, blissfully pastoral yet with psychic undercurrents, cocooned yet with ever-present traps for the unwary. It's split between instrumental improvisations – 'Interstellar Overdrive', Roger Waters' 'Pow R. Toc H.' – and short, structured songs.

Only The Beatles' album *Revolver* and The Kinks' *Face to Face*, both released in 1966, had achieved this level of musical variety and empathy, and neither had the perceptual touches of *The Piper at the Gates of Dawn*, which is suffused with clicks, percussive vocal tics (most notable on 'Pow R. Toc H.') and sounds that are just out of the reach of immediate comprehension. The album balances artistic experiment and commercial discipline with very few signs of strain or compromise.

Barrett's refusal to be bound by the dictates of the music industry was part of a dogged yet mercurial personality. His innate bounciness masked fears that could not help but be expressed in the songs that he wrote: his burst of inspiration took him deep, not just into the collective consciousness but into his own psyche. In 'Candy and a Currant Bun' he had half-mockingly warned (in an echo of Johnny Kidd and the Pirates' 'Please Don't Touch'): '*Oooh, don't touch me child/ Please you know you drive me wild/ Please you know I'm feeling frail.*'

But what is real and what is a joke? There are hints strewn beneath the euphoric surface of *The Piper at the Gates of Dawn*, just as there had been in 'See Emily Play'. The line in 'Flaming' – '*Screaming through the starlit sky*' – and the passivity in 'Scarecrow': '*The black and green scarecrow is sadder than me/ But now he's resigned to his fate/ 'Cause life's not unkind – he doesn't mind.*' He is up the clouds and with the stars – the locus of dreams and religious visions – but will he ever come down?

This first version of Pink Floyd relied on the delicate balance of Syd Barrett's psyche: the very quality that made their music so distinctive, his unusual metres

41 · ABOVE · Rehearsal for 'See Emily Play' on the set of the BBC's 'Top of the Pops', Lime Grove Studios, Shepherd's Bush, London, July 1967. Pink Floyd Archive

A Long-Term Prospect

A HEMS PRESENTATION · SUNDAY AT THE SAVILLE

OCT 1 by arrangement with the Brian Morrison Agency
THE PINK FLOYD
TOMORROW featuring KEITH WEST
THE INCREDIBLE STRING BAND
THE FAIRPORT CONVENTION

OCT 8 THE JIMI HENDRIX EXPERIENCE · THE CRAZY WORLD OF ARTHUR BROWN · THE CRYIN' SHAMES

SAVILLE THEATRE

BOOK NOW
STEM 4011

SHAFTESBURY AVENUE

and lightning mood switches, began to unravel on one of the last songs to be recorded for the album. On the one hand, 'Bike' is a gentle love song, but there is a quaver in Barrett's voice, and the sense that he is straining to keep in time. It ends with a burst of *musique concrète* – bells, clocks, violin, gongs etc. – that resolve into reversed laughter, looped and accelerated, like the calls of insistent birds.

Two days after the album's release, Pink Floyd were back in Abbey Road recording new material: there was little rest from what Waters would later call 'the machine'. Although five weeks of dates were cancelled after Barrett's climactic refusal at the 'Saturday Club' session at the end of July, there was the demand for a single to follow up 'See Emily Play'. The group was approaching a crisis, and the two songs they recorded reflected this state, pointing as they did towards an end and a beginning.

Written during July and mooted as the group's third single, 'Scream Thy Last Scream' lasts for nearly five minutes and is a terrifying portrait of disintegration. In the wildly clanging lyrics – '*blam beam your pointers point your pointers*', '*flittin' and hittin' and hittin' quack quack*' – and the accelerating middle break with its R&B bass line and sarcastic Barrett interjection, '*oh sock it to 'em*', it captures the madness of the 'Old Woman with a Casket' all too accurately. Fading on ambient sound and children's cries, it is at once coherent and deeply disordered.

In contrast, 'Set the Controls for the Heart of the Sun' is ordered, logical, calm. Roger Waters' first great song, it begins in texture – a simple bass riff, echoed xylophone runs, low organ notes – before Waters' whispered vocal enters. The lyric switches between an appreciation of the new dawn and existential questions: '*Witness the man who raves at the wall/ Making the shape of his questions to Heaven/ Whether the sun will fall in the evening/ Will he remember the lesson of giving?*' Seagull noises enhance the ambient mood, as the melody circles in a loop.

This one song illuminated a way forward for the group, but in the short term, things had gone badly wrong. Photographs from a brief September tour of Sweden and Denmark show Barrett still coiffed and smartly dressed, yet with a haunting, wide-eyed stare. A live recording in Stockholm on 10 September opens with a riff-heavy instrumental called 'Reaction in G' – a response to the group's unpleasant touring experiences in the UK. The buried vocal sound throughout only exacerbates the flickering, ragged improvisational feel.

This freedom was, of course, what Barrett wanted, while his management and his bandmates still wanted hit singles at that point: this would later change. This stand-off deepened during the autumn, as the psychedelic subculture that Pink Floyd had spearheaded began to lose its bloom. Barrett was still expected to come up with the commercial goods and, in mid-October, Pink Floyd made a second attempt at a third single in a session that resulted in three finished songs, 'Remember a Day', 'Jugband Blues' and 'Vegetable Man'. What came across was regret and frustration.

On the beautiful 'Remember a Day', Richard Wright uncannily channels the lost childhood so well evoked by Barrett: the song's psychedelic production renders the lyric – '*Remember a day before today/ A day when you were young*' –

42 · OPPOSITE · Saville Theatre poster for NEMS Enterprises concerts. Designed by Hapshash and the Coloured Coat (Michael English and Nigel Waymouth). V&A: E.1735–1991

A Long-Term Prospect

a reflection on the loss of personal and cultural innocence. The three-part 'Jugband Blues' is a direct comment on Barrett's alienation from the group he once fronted and indeed from himself: *'I'm wondering who could be writing this song.'* It ends with a profound question that is at heart of psychedelia: *'and what exactly is a dream.'*

If 'Jugband Blues' shows Barrett's awareness of his position, 'Vegetable Man' takes us right into the maelstrom. Set to a lurching, crunching rhythm, the lyrics are crammed into the riff without concern for rhythm or rhyme. They were composed under extreme pressure: as Peter Jenner remembers, '"Vegetable Man" was written in my presence, in my sitting room, we had to go out to the studio, and it was, "we need a new single, Syd". He wrote the lyrics there and then. It's just a description of him.'[19]

What comes over with clarity is both Barrett's ability to see himself in an unflattering light – *'in my paisley shirt I look a jerk'* – and his acute commentary on the conflict between external appearance and inner self image. After reciting his hippy finery he observes: *'It's what I wear, it's what you see/ It must be me, it's what I am/ Vegetable man.'* In the nature of all his multi-part songs from this period, he suddenly switches to a direct address: *'I've been looking all over the place for a place for me/ But it ain't anywhere, it just ain't anywhere.'*

Barrett was clearly still in possession of his musical abilities at this point, although the patience of his bandmates was sorely tested. His songs were still remarkable, albeit disturbing: as Peter Jenner observes, 'I actually think that "Vegetable Man", "Scream Thy Last Scream" and "Jugband Blues" should be compulsory listening for anyone in psychiatric training. To me they're like those Van Gogh paintings with the swirls, the crows, the corn field. You can see the mental state much better than some old fart talking at you for hours on end.'[20]

Pink Floyd finally nailed their third single, the upbeat although decidedly odd 'Apples and Oranges' – another slice of Syd life delivered almost without mediation on 45 – before travelling to America for their first US tour. Apples and oranges, chalk and cheese: no clip illustrates the gulf between Barrett and the group better than their 7 November appearance on 'American Bandstand'. Looking at once childlike, wide-eyed and 'not here', Barrett stares at the camera, refusing to mime, while Roger Waters tries to pull the whole thing together.

'Syd turned into a very strange person,' Waters told *Zigzag* in 1973. 'We were definitely reaching a stage where all of us were getting depressed just because it was a terrible mistake to go on trying to do it. He had become completely incapable of working in the group.'[21] And yet Barrett's rebellion seems to have been selective: while television appearance and live shows did not go well, the group's two 'Top Gear' sessions from that autumn are both excellent, with no sign of dishevelment or conflict.

'Apples and Oranges' flopped, and Pink Floyd were sent out on one of the last great package tours, a three-week long affair that featured The Jimi Hendrix Experience, The Move, The Nice, Amen Corner and Eire Apparent. Expected to compress their hour-long sets into 17 minutes or so, Barrett found the whole experience intolerable and was only present in body and not in mind. A group

43 · ABOVE · 'Apples and Oranges', Columbia, Netherlands, 1967. Cover photograph by Andrew Whittuck. Aubrey Powell Collection

A Long-Term Prospect

44 · OPPOSITE · Publicity shoot for Blackhill Enterprises, Bayswater, London, January 1968. Photograph by Peter Jenner

photo of all the acts from the tour shows him looking at the camera in what is obviously considerable distress.

Around Christmas time, the three other members of Pink Floyd approached their Cambridge friend David Gilmour to join as an extra guitarist – the idea being that Barrett could continue in a Brian Wilson-style role, as a writer but not a concert player. (This is what the lead Beach Boy had arranged in early 1965 after finding touring intolerable.) But the break had been made. In the December film for 'Jugband Blues', Barrett looks at the camera without affect. He keeps the same posture throughout, but as the song ends on the final, unanswerable question, he turns away without expression – out of the film, out of the group.

1968

> *Isn't it strange*
> *How little we change*
> *Isn't it sad we're insane*
> *Playing the games that we know and in tears*
> *The games we've been playing for thousands and thousands and ...*
> —Roger Waters for Pink Floyd, 'Point Me at the Sky', December 1968

It begins with a fast, looped bass figure – at once technological and trance-like. Around 75 seconds in, a cymbal crash segues into a slower, circular riff that announces the verse. The chorus is marked by a surge of instrumentation: Pink Floyd's upwards trajectory is continued, but at a more deliberate pace. The scenario is grave: the arrival of a spaceship from outer space, containing a superior being who heralds all the ambiguities and dilemmas familiar from 1950s science-fiction films such as *The Day the Earth Stood Still*. It ends in a rousing, spiralling guitar solo.

As the opening track on Pink Floyd's second album, 'Let There Be More Light' is both a continuation and a development. It is still firmly rooted in psychedelia – with its multi-part structure, outer-space theme and echo of 1967s naivety, '*for there, revealed in glowing robes/ was Lucy in the Sky*', but the mood is more serious, measured, indeed disciplined. The earlier intuitive explorations are replaced by carefully erected musical structures – aural architecture – and a less intense musical palette: not so many highs, but not the lows either.

Order emerges out of the previous two years of improvisation. The Binson effects are almost gone, replaced by an echo of those looping effects in the repetitive riffs and circular melodies. There is less thought of the singles market: with its allusive, complex lyrics and five-minute length – 'Let There Be More Light' points forward to the group's concentration on albums, the format that allowed them the space and the fidelity to establish, with carefully accreted musical motifs, a mood and a theme over 40 or so minutes.

Pink Floyd were in it for the long haul, and *A Saucerful of Secrets* is a statement of intent. Although it contains several tracks recorded with Syd Barrett – 'Remember a Day', 'Jugband Blues' and 'Set the Controls for the Heart of the Sun' – it has an entirely different feel to *The Piper at the Gates of Dawn*. The 12-minute

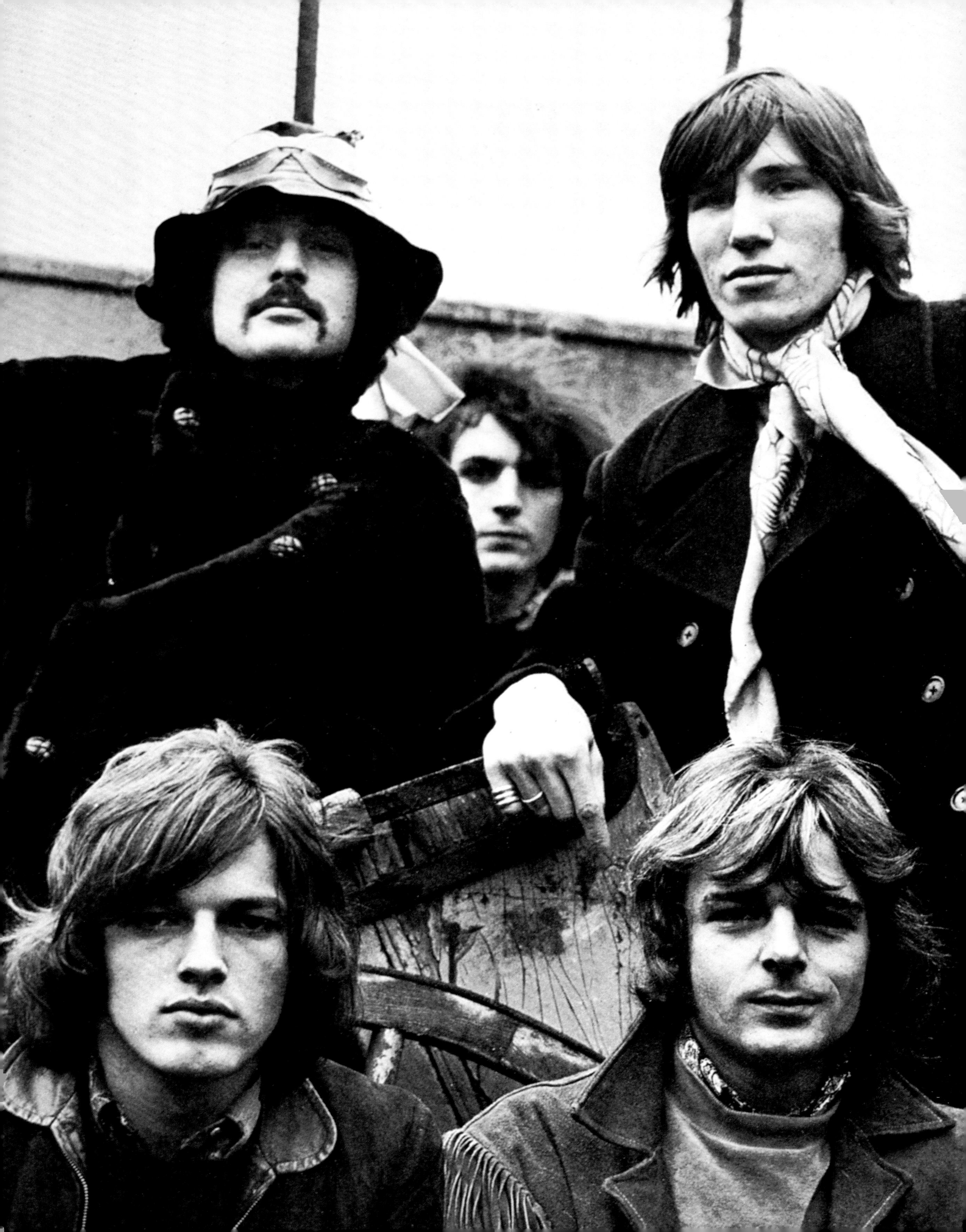

45 · OPPOSITE · 'No More Singles from Pink Floyd', *Record Mirror*, 3 January 1970. Pink Floyd Archive

46 · FOLLOWING SPREAD · 1969 scrapbook belonging to Nick Mason, containing Roy Shipston's article 'Are Spacemen Floyd on the Way Back to Earth?', published in *Disc and Music Echo*, 22 November 1969. Photograph by Aubrey Powell at Hipgnosis. Pink Floyd Archive

title track points to the neo-classical grandiosity that would mark much of Pink Floyd's future work, while 'Corporal Clegg' heralds the arrival of an important theme: Second World War damage and its impact on the post-war generation.

With David Gilmour, there is more care, more musicality. At a time when the group was falling apart in the face of Syd Barrett's wild experimentalism, he offered security, dexterity and professionalism. In talent and temperament, he was well-suited for the situation facing Pink Floyd in early 1968, which was survival. The fact was starkly revealed by the fate of their first post-Syd Barrett 45, 'It Would Be So Nice', described by Roger Waters as 'complete trash'.[22]

Nobody liked it, neither the public nor the group: 'it was awful that record, wasn't it,' Nick Mason told *Zigzag*, 'at that period we had no direction'.[23]

Syd Barrett's departure was announced in March, and with him in April went Peter Jenner and Andrew King: in their place, Pink Floyd were managed by agent Bryan Morrison and Steve O'Rourke. With an allusive cover by the designers Hipgnosis (their Cambridge friends Storm Thorgerson and Aubrey 'Po' Powell) that blended astrological and science-fiction symbols as well as an image from Marvel Comics' *Dr Strange*, *A Saucerful of Secrets* was released at the end of June. Despite mixed reviews, it reached the album Top 10.

The new structures were falling into place. On the day of the album's release, the group played the first major free concert at the Cockpit in Hyde Park. 'I have never heard them play better', John Peel wrote at the time; 'there was no anger or violence in what they did.'[24]

Shortly afterwards, they left for their second tour of the United States. During the summer and autumn, they played underground venues like Mother's in Birmingham and Middle Earth in Covent Garden, as well as the burgeoning student-union circuit.

Just before the end of the year, Pink Floyd released their fifth stand-alone single – a two-sided classic. On the flip was an early, nearly six-minute draft of 'Careful with that Axe, Eugene', a flowing but ominous instrumental that would become a centrepiece of their live set. On the A-side was 'Point Me at the Sky', a complex creation with a slow spacey verse (sung by Dave Gilmour) segueing into a surging chorus with a heavy, crunching riff. After a slow choral bridge widens everything out, the afterburner goes on and the song ends with an anthemic fade-out, somewhat in the style of The Beatles' 'Hey Jude'.

With its complex structure, soaring interludes and philosophical lyrics about flight, escape and future possibilities, this was a compressed masterwork worthy of 1967 – a late psychedelic flash. However, despite a promo film featuring the group in a vintage Tiger Moth, 'Point Me at the Sky' completely failed to chart. Pink Floyd had outgrown the format: henceforth they would concentrate on longer tracks and conceptual albums. They would release no further singles in the UK for 11 years, by which time their music had become harsher to fit the times.

The Band—Jon Savage

record mirror

21st CENTURY PEOPLE—an A to Z guide to the people who made the '60s swing
CROSBY, STILLS, NASH, YOUNG—their views.

THE BEATLES' DECADE-by John Lennon
DONOVAN talks to Keith Altham about, drugs, meditation and his music

Week ending January 3rd, 1970 — A Billboard Publication — Price 1/- Every Friday

No more singles from Pink Floyd

IT WAS 1967 when film director Michaelangelo Antonioni went in search of America. It was dreamtime in San Francisco's Haight Ashbury; the new American Revolution. Hippies, rock music, student revolt, black power...

Antonioni's search ended in California's Death Valley, 1969. The result was "Zabriske Point", due to be shown in England next month. Specially commissioned to write and play the music for the film were the Pink Floyd.

It is the second film-score they have written.

Said Dave Gilmore, the Floyd's guitarist: "We did the music to a film called 'More' a few months ago. It's due out here sometime — it's a big film in the States and France at the moment.

"It's about drugs, and sex and stuff.

"Since then we've been asked to do a couple of film scores—including Antonioni's "Zabriske Point". The album of the music should be out shortly.

"We like to do film scores because it's an overall concept—not just a string of songs.

"But the film I'd like to have produced the music for was "2001, A Space Odyssey". We could have done it and done it very well. But as it was, of couse, it worked out very well. We'd heard about

Basic problem

the film before it came to London, so when it came I knew what it would be like.

"The music's tremendous. But the film companies have this basic problem. Either they use an orchestra and research all the music carefully or they commission people like us to write the music.

I suppose we come quite high on people's lists for writing film music these days".

The Pink Floyd have expanded from their pop origins. Their last album, "Umma Gumma" reached the top ten of the best selling album charts while they've given up singles all together.

Difficult

"We've found it difficult to produce singles. We've needed to think that they have to be perfect. So we've decided to concentrate on LP's. In the studio there are so many things you can do. One person in a studio can do things that would require ten people on stage to do. "Umma Gumma" was a bit difficult though, because it was partly recorded live at a session we did in Manchester. We did two takes and the second best of the two at the time came off better on record. The better of the two didn't come off on record.

Future plans for the Pink Floyd include a visit to the States in February or March. Their previous visit last year was for one day—to guest during a Science Fiction Festival. The next day they had to be in Manchester.

WIN AN L.P.

A major feature begins this week on the centre pages of Record Mirror. It is called 21st Century Pop People. And it is OUR guide to the people who have changed, or are changing the face of the pop scene. Now YOU can join in. Choose a letter and invent an imaginary character who MIGHT have contributed to the pop scene during the 60's. Like Mr. L. S. Dee for instance. Then let your imagination run riot for about 100 words — describing him or her. Send it to Record Mirror (Comp.) 7, Carnaby Street, London, W.1. Funniest entries get an L.P. — and we'll print them!

Pink Floyd: (back) Roger Waters, Dave Gilmour, (front) Rick Wright,

Are spacemen Floyd on the way back to earth?

By Roy Shipston

OK YOU can come out now! Pink Floyd only want to communicate — not frighten or destroy people with an overdose of decibels as they appeared to be trying to do in the early days of the psychedelic thing.

I first saw them about four years ago, before they made those two hit singles—the very mention of which makes them visibly sick these days.

Then, their music seemed limited to playing in one key, lyrics were practically non-existent, and I was convinced that the beautifully coloured bacteria shapes on the back-cloth were there only to draw attention from the row they were making.

They don't need light-shows now. Their music has matured to become acutely interesting and exciting. But what are their aims and ambitions? What is the point of the Pink Floyd?

"We just want to get on and get through to people with the things we do. We want to get through to every person in the country, to every person in the world even. It's just communication, that's what it's all about," says guitarist Dave Gilmour.

"I suppose we all want to improve the world, make it a better place to live in, like everyone else. There is a great revolution taking place at the moment which seems to have emerged from the pop movement, the Underground scene. The same thing is happening in all the Arts.

"We all have very strong views, differing views, but we try to keep it out of our music. Some of it comes through in our writing, obviously, but we are mainly concerned with just communicating with people through our song.

"I don't think it's wrong if someone well known uses his position to get over his beliefs, or influence people. Why shouldn't he? It could be wrong if it is a bad belief.

"We're just not very good at writing that sort of song.

"We never really set out specifically to protest about violence or anything. We don't want to come across with some incredible message."

How does he define their music?

"There's not really much to explain. I don't know why it works out like it does. There's no special thing that we deliberately work at. We are just trying to move ahead, to get things done—for enjoyment and soul.

"We find that people dig what we are doing, and the way we work is to do things that we like at the time, rather than things they will like us to do. It's always been that way and it seems to work.

"Of course you have to do some numbers that they know, but they're ones that we still enjoy doing."

Why is so much of Pink Floyd's music space-orientated? "We don't deliberately try and make everything come out like that. It just works out that things happen that way. We all read science fiction and groove to '2001,' it's all very good. But some of our things happen completely accidentally."

It is difficult to imagine what sort of music Floyd will create in, say, a year's time. Their style has not changed much since the beginning. It has evolved significantly, but a style can only be exploited so far. If perfection is ever reached, the Pink Floyd, in their field, are probably as near to it as possible. So how will they progress?

"I don't know how it's going to go. It's tended to get a little less 'spacey' lately. It's just a matter of doing new things, new pieces of music, and seeing what happens.

"You can have an idea, then when the whole group gets together it will change completely. How a song is originally and how it eventually turns out may be two different things.

"The group has changed a lot since the early days, and come a long way. The worst period was after the two hit singles. We went right down then because people expected us to do them and we wouldn't.

"Now we are as busy as we want to be. We do two or three gigs a week, and that keeps us going. But I never seem to have any cash—it's such an expensive business. We are also a bit slow, especially on recording. It takes us months to get out an LP.

"We get in the studio for a couple of days then someone else, like the Beatles, wants to record and we get shoved out. So a couple of weeks later we go back and we've forgotten the mood. It takes a lot of time getting back into the thing.

"What we really need is a block session to get something done in one go. We have great fun in the studios mucking about. But I don't think I could go on recording without doing appearances. It's great to do a live gig, but we can do so much more recording. I don't see why we should limit ourselves on record to what we do on stage.

"There are a lot of things we haven't really touched on yet. Television, for instance, which is good publicity. We have been approached about doing programmes but nothing's ever come of it. I thought we had some nice ideas for a TV show—they'd probably still be OK. But TV generally is so boring.

"I suppose everybody's ego would be satisfied by a lot of fame, but it seems that if you have a record in the charts you are rejected by the so-called Underground movement. Hit parades do spell death for our sort of group, but if we did a single I'd be quite happy if it got into the charts.

"Our main thing is to improve, and we are trying all the time. We are striving to improve our amplification, on stage and in the studios, we want to clean-up the sound equipment.

"But I don't foresee any drastic changes. We've used a choir and brass section and we tend to play any strange instruments that happen to be lying around. We don't feel limited.

"One of our hang-ups is that people who haven't seen us come along believing that we're going to be good before we start. And we're not always quite what they expected.

"Myself, I don't think we'll ever get through to the masses . . ."

Mason.

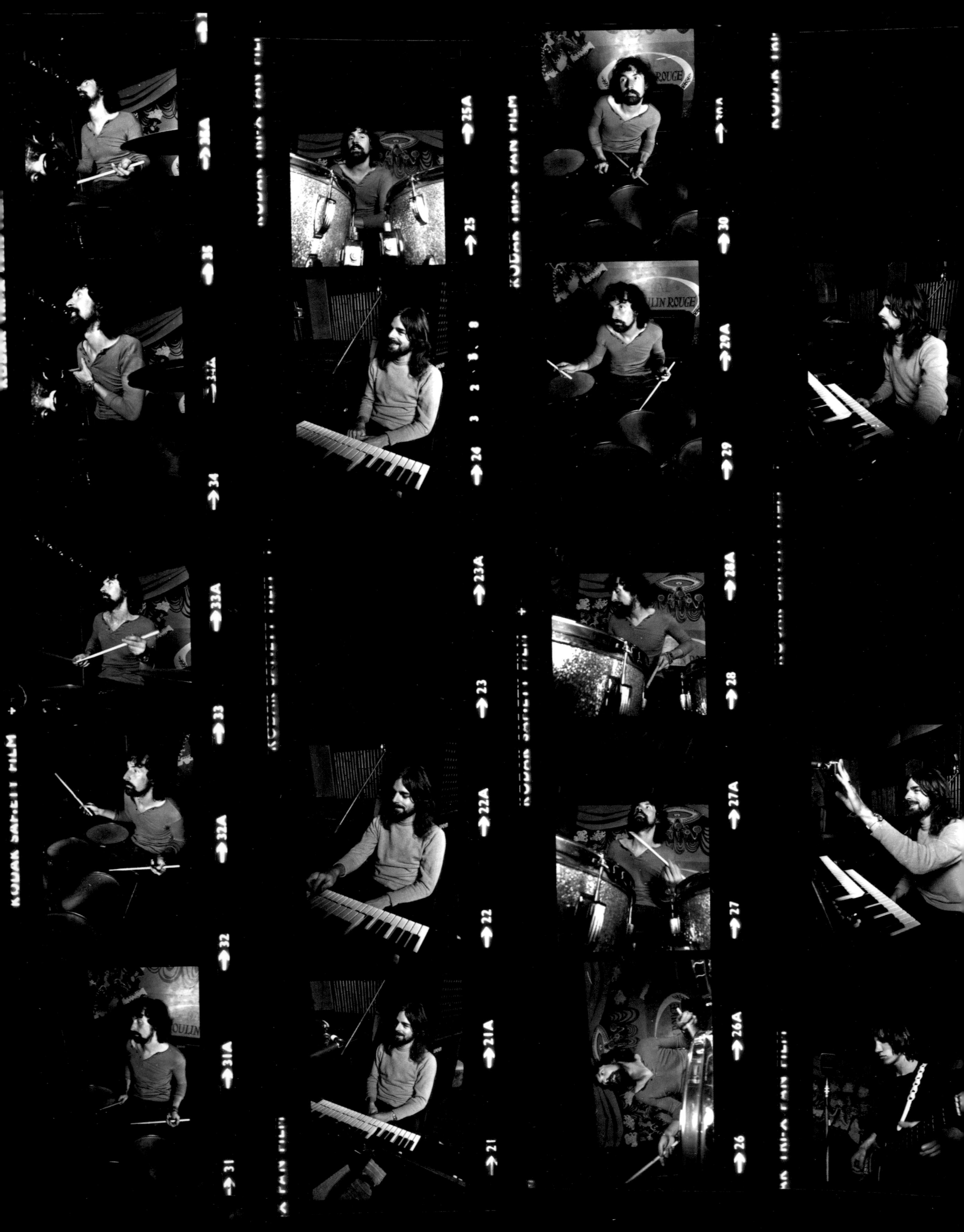

'PAINTERS, PIPERS, PRISONERS' THE MUSICAL LEGACY OF PINK FLOYD

Howard Goodall

Even the greatest of all musicians in history shine brightly for a while, blazing a trail others follow, then gently recede from the foreground, consolidating their expertise and influence. Almost every composer in Europe wanted to sound like Beethoven, Wagner and Debussy for a decade or so, before other voices became more fashionable, or more innovative. In popular music, the same could be said for Elvis Presley between 1957 and 1961, for The Beatles between 1964 and 1970, and for Stevie Wonder between 1973 and 1979, even though the secondary impact of these artists continued for many decades thereafter. Between the releases of *Meddle* in 1971 and *The Wall* in 1979, Pink Floyd also enjoyed a status among music-lovers and musicians alike that caused them to shape the musical world around them. How they did so is the subject of this chapter.

47 · PAGE 80 · Contact sheet from Pink Floyd rehearsal, Moulin Rouge Bar, Ainsdale, Southport, May 1971. Pink Floyd Archive

48 · OPPOSITE · Recording session for *Obscured by Clouds*, Strawberry Studios, Château d'Hérouville, France, 1972. Photograph by JD Mahn

The musical universe we inhabit in the twenty-first century is fundamentally different from that of the late 1960s and early '70s, when Pink Floyd was emerging as a distinct, collective musical voice. It is easy to forget that what was once their field of experimentation is now our commonplace. What was once their haphazard exploration of the combining of sound and imagery is now the accepted starting point for millions of new recordings and many thousands of new artists. Their embrace of showmanship, their exploitation of the 'coolest' passing fad (in their case, psychedelia), their plundering of any and all technological innovations available to them in the recording studio, particularly but not exclusively those developed by George Martin and the engineering team at Abbey Road Studios in the 1960s and '70s, their search for longer forms, to break free from the straitjacket of the three-minute single, their need to wrap an album's content into an overarching 'meaning', to find alternatives to the then standardized formulae of lyric architecture, their self-consciously public sharing of their private journey towards acceptance, success and disenchantment, all of these aspects of their early progress are now the bread and butter of a huge, worldwide, still-evolving music industry. For Pink Floyd, on the other hand, these possibilities were new and often disorientating. Which is not to say that they were alone in these discoveries. Indeed, even with the benefit of hindsight, their dramatic pulling away from a pack of similarly arty, similarly curious, similarly male, similarly musically self-taught, similarly British bands of that era, all seeking a vinyl-flavoured sundae of fame and fortune, still seems unexpected.

Changes in – and conflicts among – personnel, so often destructive in the upward curve of many a band's story, had in Pink Floyd's case the opposite effect: it galvanized their creativity. Except for brief periods, particularly in the unfolding process that led to the successful completion of *The Dark Side of the Moon*, Pink Floyd appears to the outsider to have been in almost permanent internal turmoil. That turmoil gave rise, without doubt, to some of the most universally adored, intelligently conceived popular music of the past half century, carving out a musical identity that for all its myriad references to the particular post-war British upbringing of its writers, managed to be at the same time spectacularly non-parochial in its appeal. They weren't simply 'in the right place at the right time', their fortune was much more complicated, burdensome and painfully human than that, and the resulting music far richer for it.

Named after two of Syd Barrett's favourite blues artists, Pink Anderson and Floyd Council, in 1965, the band formed in a period of rapid proliferation of British groups hoping to emulate the unprecedented success of, among others, The Beatles, The Rolling Stones, The Animals and The Who in the USA (the blues and early rock 'n' roll of which had been a major impetus for the success of the Beatlemania-led pop explosion in the UK in first place). Stylistically speaking, Pink Floyd's quirky first chart singles, 'Arnold Layne' and 'See Emily Play', for all the bike-shed titillation of their subject-matter, a cross-dressing underwear thief in the case of the former and the hint of an under-age, aristocratic schoolgirl's drug-induced 'losing her mind' in the latter, can be seen as fairly mainstream for the year in which they were released, 1967, the zenith of the psychedelic, flower-power craze. They may have stepped a little further towards prompting genuine alarm in the minds of more conservative listeners ('Arnold Layne' was banned, briefly, by the BBC and by pirate station Radio London) but the two singles can clearly be seen alongside The Kinks' perky lampooning of London's mod fashion scene, 'Dedicated Follower of Fashion' (1966), their homoerotic 'David Watts' (1967), The Rolling Stones' innuendo-laced 'Lady Jane' (1966), and – in the broader context of novelty character songs intended to provoke amusement or consternation – The Who's 'Boris the Spider' (1966) and 'Pictures of Lily' (1967), David Bowie's 'Maid of Bond Street' and 'The Laughing Gnome' (1967 – released a few months before Pink Floyd's own album track, 'The Gnome'), and Manfred Mann's 'Semi-Detached Suburban Mr James' (1966). Holland Park student Emily Young, known to her friends as 'the Psychedelic Schoolgirl', the supposed subject of 'See Emily Play', was one of a clutch of young women during London's hippy heyday celebrated in dreamy hit song, a list which included models Linda Keith (Keith Richards' 'Ruby Tuesday') and Jenny Boyd (Donovan's 'Jennifer Juniper').

What musical edge Pink Floyd's early singles exude emanates from two key ingredients: the band's habit of creating their songs from long, meandering, improvised sets performed live onstage (mostly at London's UFO club in Tottenham Court Road at this time) and the wayward, charismatic leadership of frontman Syd Barrett, whose influence is equally pervasive on the debut album that followed, *The Piper at the Gates of Dawn* (released August 1967).

The artistic fruits of *The Piper at the Gates of Dawn* demonstrated one possible future for the band. Had Syd Barrett – talented, mercurial, engaging, handsome, amusing, inventive though he reportedly was – continued as the leading creative force driving Pink Floyd, their future would have been radically different.

49 · ABOVE · Nick Mason playing his Ludwig hand-painted 'Wave' double bass drum kit on tour with Pink Floyd, USA, 1975. Photograph by Storm Thorgerson

The band may have continued on a path of exuberant adventure and idiosyncratic mirth – a course that might, incidentally, have given its members more enjoyment, peace of mind and a lifetime of less overall stress – but it is unlikely they would have attained their spectacular worldwide success and approval. There were many other Syd Barretts plying their art-school trade as semi-pro musicians at that time, the easy cool of mucking about with a few mates in a band in Swinging London being something of a gold-rush industry in the mid- to late '60s, and comparing the Barrett-led *Piper at the Gates of Dawn* to the other albums released that same year of 1967 is instructive. Consider just this handful – *Sgt. Pepper's Lonely Hearts Club Band*, *The Velvet Underground and Nico*, *The Doors*, *Are You Experienced* (The Jimi Hendrix Experience), *Songs of Leonard Cohen* and *Disraeli Gears* (Cream), while The Beach Boys' Brian Wilson, fresh from the revolutionary *Pet Sounds* and the single 'Good Vibrations', was busy developing and then abandoning 'Smile' (a version of which was released in the form of the album *Smiley Smile* in September '67). The musical maturity of this list is staggering, making the Pink Floyd of *The Piper at the Gates of Dawn* sound like a youthful, playful group, still not settled in their musical skin.

Notwithstanding the dizzying hullabaloo of the expansive space-rock anthems 'Interstellar Overdrive' and 'Astronomy Domine', there is little evidence of the band's impeccable later grasp of the long-form song, no hint of their subsequent mastery of musical architecture, and no sign yet of their uncanny ability to blend instrumental and sung passages together to weave out of them both a deeper meaning from the given song's governing idea. 'Interstellar Overdrive' may have been electrifying as a live experience in a club, but its nine minutes 41 seconds on the album feel somewhat exhausting after the first 50 energetic seconds, in which the gripping main riff is established. That is not to say that, for example, the iconic *The Velvet Underground and Nico*, probably the closest creative cousin to *The Piper at the Gates of Dawn* on the list, does not have its moments of self-indulgence and musical incoherence, most of 'European Son's frantic, ridiculous seven minutes 47 seconds, for a start. While Lou Reed, though, was attempting, chillingly, to recreate in song the building hysteria and unstoppable acceleration of a heroin trip in the extraordinarily manic, seven-minute 'Heroin', Barrett's Pink Floyd offered the waggish '*I've got a bike, you can ride it if you like/ It's got a basket, a bell that rings and/ Things to make it look good...*', or '*The black and green scarecrow as everyone knows/ Stood with a bird on his hat and straw everywhere.*'

There was definitely an audience for this kind of whimsy. The album went gold in the UK, where Pink Floyd had a passionate, substantial following even at this early stage, and subsequent rock journalism has accorded it retrospective status as a landmark of the psychedelic rock era, but what there was not, in 1967, was a future for it. Psychedelic rock and English pop-whimsy yielded to other fashions very quickly, and personal crisis was to force on Pink Floyd unforeseen creative avenues.

The departure from the band of Syd Barrett in March 1968 was to have two far-reaching outcomes. The short-term change of personnel re-shuffled the musical pack, bringing about changes in direction which were immediately apparent in the album of that year, *A Saucerful of Secrets* (though Barrett contributed to three tracks on the album). The responsibilities accorded to the remaining band members and the newly introduced David Gilmour prompted a transformation of the sound, lyrics and general musical discipline that was to result, after some period of further trial and error, in forging a distinct, unmistakable character to the structure of Pink Floyd songs and the albums into which they were shaped. Whether they were conscious of the effort at the time remains uncertain, but the period also seems to have brought about new priorities in which the individual members' playing improved markedly (for example, the solidity and intensity of Nick Mason's powerful, looped drum-groove in the 'Syncopated Pandemonium' section of the otherwise mainly rudderless title track has no equivalent on the previous album, and acts as a marker for many further drum-pattern-driven tracks thereafter). The second, equally significant fallout, manifest in the emotional toll Barrett's mental illness and absence had on his former bandmates, was to find exquisite, heartbreaking expression in two subsequent albums, *The Dark Side of the Moon* and *Wish You Were Here.*

A Saucerful of Secrets' defining track is the moody, modal, free-jazz-influenced 'Set the Controls for the Heart of the Sun'. With dreamlike lyrics by Roger Waters quoting medieval Chinese poets Li Shangyin and Li He, it may have been composed by Waters, and its trademark hypnotically repeated riff is played by him on bass. But the collaborative contributions of other band members to the richness of its texture, particularly Richard Wright on organ, vibraphone and celesta and Nick Mason giving a masterclass on tom-toms, give the song the overall impression of a group effort, a group, moreover, seeking for and beginning to discover a form of musical coherence. Over its five-and-a-half minutes' span, the song unfolds and develops. Though it includes what may be improvised passages from all players, architecture and form are clearly becoming a concern for a group for whom live performance was an essential playground where new material could be tested and honed (for most other bands of the period, and especially in the decades since, the purpose of live touring was to promote and sell existing recorded material). It is worth noting that another of the album's tracks, 'Corporal Clegg', establishes one of the recurrent themes of Roger Waters' writing in the ensuing dozen years – his coming to terms with, or not, the death of his father in the Second World War and that of his grandfather in the First World War. The former acted as the starting point of *The Wall*'s narrative in 1979, while the latter was still troubling him enough to provide emotional inspiration to the harrowingly delicate 'The Ballad of Bill Hubbard' on Waters' underrated solo album of 1992, *Amused to Death*.

Two albums followed in 1969, *Soundtrack from the film More* in June, and *Ummagumma* in November. The first of two soundtrack projects that were to prove useful, if slightly rushed, as supplementary studio sessions between larger-scale album commitments, *More* contains the seeds of an important hybrid Pink Floyd were to cultivate – the atmospheric pastoral ballad with acoustic guitar and gentle, double-tracked vocals embedded in a slowly evolving 'pad' of (here) organ, with judicious application of mood-setting sound effects, as trialled on the ethereal 'Cirrus Minor'. It cannot have been known even by band members at the time how central to the eventual soundscape of Pink Floyd this kind of song would become. The smooth, sustained wash of keyboard sound (the 'pad' of keyboard-geek parlance) that Richard Wright developed, initially on Farfisa and Hammond electronic organs but later on synthesizers, was not only to become ubiquitous on Pink Floyd records but more or less everywhere else too. By the late 1970s and the increased commercial availability of 'polyphonic' synthesizers (which could play chords, not single notes, the limitation of all early synthesizers using individual, voltage-controlled oscillators to create their waveforms), the 'pad' had become so familiar a default that its pre-set sounds were labelled as such, and still are to this day.

A similarly atmospheric pastoral ballad complete with chirruping birds, 'Grantchester Meadows', was a highlight of the subsequent major album release, *Ummagumma*, reminiscent in its vocal harmonies and close-miked six-string guitar of the enormously successful (and influential) Simon and Garfunkel albums *Sounds of Silence* (released January 1966), *Parsley, Sage, Rosemary and Thyme* (released October 1966) and *Bookends* (released April 1968). Much of *Ummagumma* was devoted, by prior decision, to what might be described as a laboratory of exploration for each member of the group in turn. Thus, new electronic keyboards and techniques were put through their paces by Richard Wright in the extended 'Sysyphus' section, David Gilmour, reluctant at first, tried various instrumental ideas out in 'The Narrow Way', Nick Mason did the same for drums in the three-movement 'The Grand Vizier's Garden Party' and Roger Waters eschewed conventional musical content altogether in his offering to the altar of experiment, 'Several Species of Small Furry Animals Gathered Together in a Cave and Grooving with a Pict'. Pretentious though these extended 'noodlings' may seem to us now, there is much in this material that would inform the aural landscapes of later recordings and, as we shall see with the long-form experiments of *Atom Heart Mother*, sometimes finding oneself in a blind alley helps one forge a route to a destination ahead with greater, more focused determination than before. Not many artists these days, if any, are allowed the luxury of actually publishing and selling their unvarnished work-in-progress, or what amounts to rehearsal audio, to an accepting public. In the late 1960s audiences were far more forgiving of, and interested in, experiment for its own sake, and the fans' forbearance was to be rewarded a hundredfold in due course.

One thing that shines through the Pink Floyd story is that the classic, three-minute-format pop song did not, and never has, suited the temperaments, musical proclivities and instrumental ambitions of its members – after the departure of Syd Barrett. It is therefore no surprise that before spectacular commercial success allowed them never to have to undertake the necessary evil of time-consuming, spirit-sapping creative negotiations with film directors or producers who might have ideas of their own, they should have been attracted to the challenge of recording film soundtracks. Here, they could take the small nucleus of an instrumental idea and improvise with it without the distraction of needing to find a vocal line or text, committing it directly to tape (it is notable how often Pink Floyd 'songs' began life as instrumental atmospheres and chord progressions, until, eventually, a vocal line and lyric were added, even where the source was not one of their film soundtracks). While orthodox film scoring called for just that – *scoring* work, on to paper, orchestrating it then recording it to picture in as synchronized manner as the technology of the time allowed – Pink Floyd's forays into the field, *The Committee* (1968), *More* (1969) and *Zabriskie Point* (1970), were essentially extended instrumental 'responses' to the themes of the films concerned, not synchronized frame by frame, rather scene by scene

50 · **ABOVE** · Richard Wright performing with Pink Floyd at the Lanchester Polytechnic Arts Festival, Locarno Ballroom, Coventry, 3 February 1972. John Halsall Archive

51 · **FOLLOWING SPREAD** · John Alldis conducting the orchestra during recording sessions for the 'Atom Heart Mother' suite, EMI Studios, Abbey Road, London, 1970. Photograph by Richard Stanley

'Painters, Pipers, Prisoners': The Musical Legacy of Pink Floyd

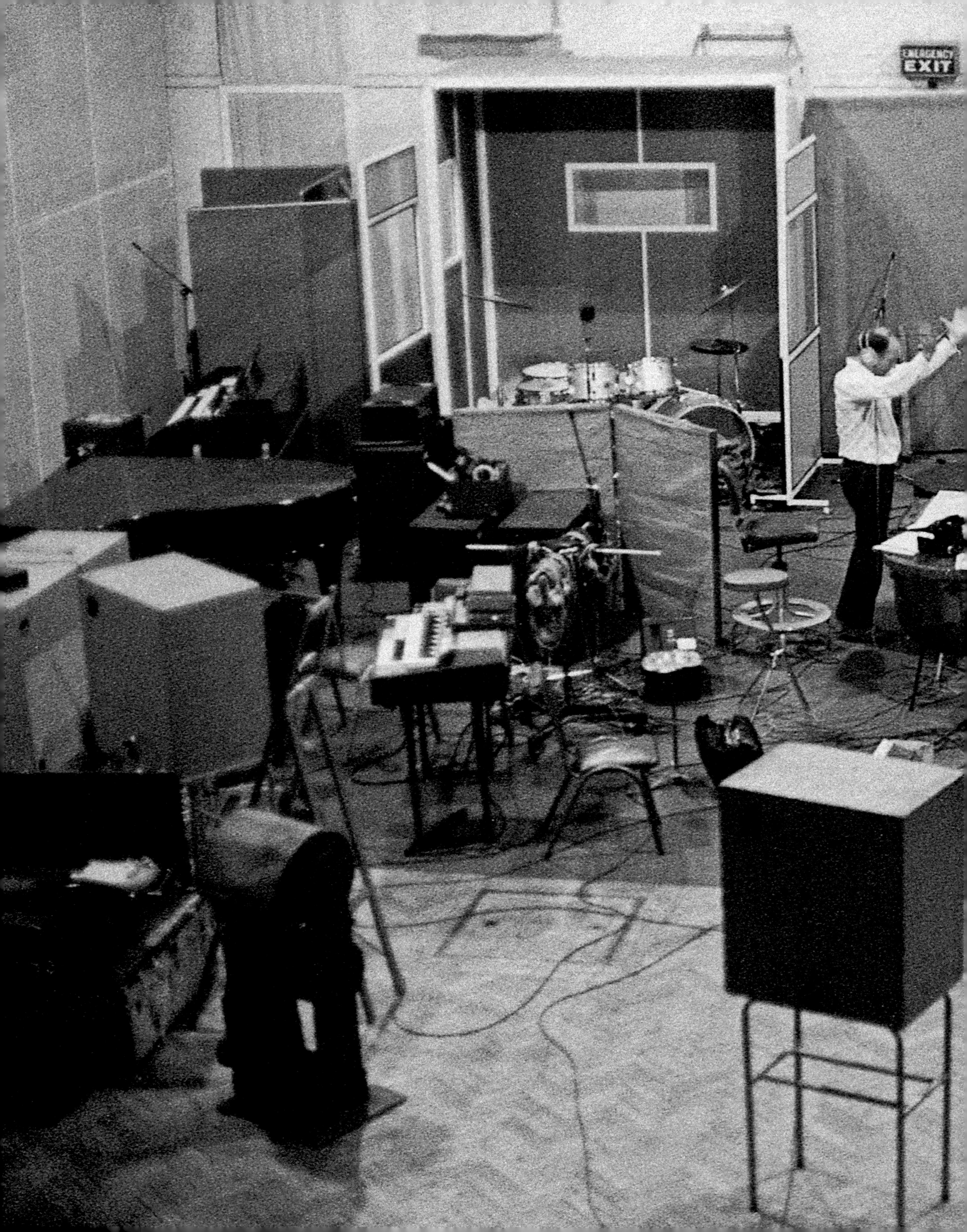
EXIT

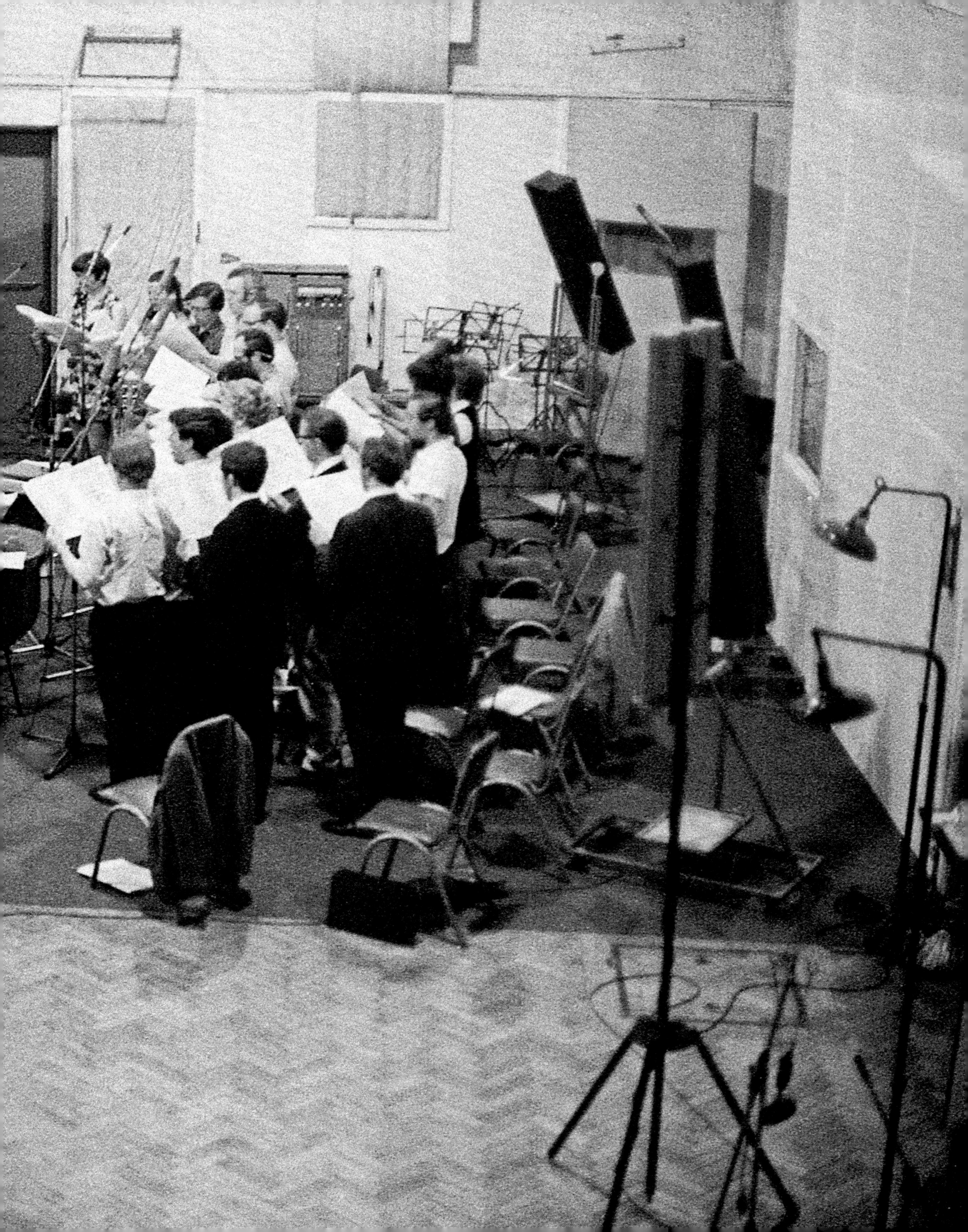

(in more than one case they were not even responding to the final cut). Clearly, the experience of collaborating with Michelangelo Antonioni on his film *Zabriskie Point* was somewhat unsatisfactory for both parties, and a melancholic passage composed for the film's violent final sequence, not added to the eventual released cut, was recycled by the band three years later, with voice and lyric, to become the song 'Us and Them' on *The Dark Side of the Moon*. What Antonioni had wanted all along was a more disturbing track for the footage and he had had in mind Pink Floyd's deranged 1968 B-side, 'Careful with that Axe, Eugene', an item that had first emerged as part of the soundtrack, as it happens, to Peter Sykes' and Max Steuer's film *The Committee*.

It was perhaps inevitable that musicians as curious, and as admirably unshackled by the possibility of failure or critical disapproval as Roger Waters, David Gilmour, Richard Wright and Nick Mason would at some point in their development, looking for solutions to longer-form musical architecture that would support a continuous 25-minute side of a vinyl album, attempt some kind of semi-symphonic expedition into the classical realm. Such an enterprise formed the first side of their October 1970 album *Atom Heart Mother*, incidentally their first Number 1 album in the UK charts.

They weren't the first pioneers in what seemed like a possible *rapprochement* between classical and progressive rock after the shock to the system that *Sgt. Pepper's Lonely Hearts Club Band* had caused, thanks to its widespread integration of classical instruments into a mainstream pop album. Classically trained rock keyboardist Keith Emerson, with his then band The Nice, released an album in 1967 called *The Thoughts of Emerlist Davjack* that first exposed his ambition to bring classical (and jazz) themes and forms into the rock arena. This was followed in November 1968 with *Ars Longa Vita Brevis,* which along with passages of Miles Davis-influenced bebop improvisation, included various self-standing items based on classical sources (for example, Sibelius' *Karelia Suite*) but also an extended 19-minute suite divided up into six contiguous classical-style movements. *Ars Longa Vita Brevis* made semi-prominent use of an orchestra. In October 1969 Emerson and The Nice (and now a full-sized symphony orchestra) went one stage further, recording live at a concert hall their new *Five Bridges Suite*, celebrating the city of Newcastle upon Tyne, released as an album nine months later. Divided into five movements, 'Fantasia', 'Second Bridge', 'Chorale', 'High Level Fugue' and 'Finale', with stylistic nods to and pastiches of – among much else – Gershwin's *Rhapsody in Blue*, Tchaikovsky's *Serenade for Strings*, jazz artists Bill Evans and Dave Brubeck, and an Austrian composer-pianist who particularly inspired Keith Emerson, Friedrich Gulda.

It is inconceivable that Pink Floyd were not familiar with *Ars Longa Vita Brevis* and *Five Bridges* (apart from anything else, they had shared the stage with The Nice at festivals more than once during this period), the latter reaching Number 2 in the UK album chart. In any case, the 24-minute 'Atom Heart Mother' suite, which takes up the whole first side of the album that bears its name, marked a departure for Pink Floyd, one that was in part prompted by a creative impasse on the extended track after it had been honed by the band through studio improvisation over many months. The idea to have the suite expanded to incorporate a classical orchestra and choir came from Roger Waters, who had been working with Scottish experimental composer and orchestrator

Ron Geesin earlier that year (1970) on the soundtrack for a documentary film directed by Roy Battersby, *The Body*. On that project, Geesin and Waters had constructed a sound collage from recorded samples of noises from the human body (breathing, laughing, whispering, slapping, grunting, farting etc.), sometimes termed 'biomusic'. These sounds were interwoven with folk ballad-style song segments from Waters (one of which is a gentle, environmentally themed plaint called 'Breathe'), some treated ('prepared') piano figures and modernistic string quartet interjections crafted by Geesin. Track titles for the 'Body' project were clearly intended to amuse, 'Lick Your Parents', 'Bridge Passage for Three Plastic Teeth', 'Piddle in Perspex', 'March Past of the Embryos' and 'More Than Seven Dwarfs in Penis-Land' set the slightly smirkish, at-the-end-of-a-long-session tone. The final, more traditionally structured song of the collection, 'Give Birth to a Smile', involving the other members of the band as guests, also features female gospel singers, a choral idea that would return triumphantly in 'The Great Gig in the Sky'.

Buoyed by the fruits of the collaboration with Geesin, Waters set him the task of finding orchestral-choral interludes to give extra weight and shape to the band's existing skeleton of the 'Atom Heart Mother' suite, which until well after the recording process was simply called 'The Amazing Pudding', perhaps acknowledging that what had gradually derived from hours of improvisation was in danger of appearing formless. This danger was never fully averted. The given titles of individual movements in the suite ('Father's Shout', 'Breast Milky', 'Mother Fore', 'Funky Dung', 'Mind Your Throats Please', 'Remergence') also

52 · ABOVE · Composer Ron Geesin with musical score for 'Atom Heart Mother', EMI Studios, Abbey Road, London, June 1970. Photograph by Richard Stanley

53 · ABOVE · Recording session for *Obscured by Clouds*, Strawberry Studios, Château d'Hérouville, France, 1972. Photograph by JD Mahn

suggest that no-one was taking the endeavour too seriously. Sound effects of trains, motor vehicles, cavalry at war, explosions and so on were added as were avant-garde tape effects and sound-sample collages. The idiom of Geesin's contributions, though modern in the sense of their being composed in 1970, was, by contemporary classical music standards a fairly tame melange of dissonance and pseudo-majestic. Since the overall structure had been laid down on tape in long, uninterrupted takes of bass and drums (owing to limitations placed by the eight-track console at Abbey Road Studios, brand new admittedly, yet struggling under the demands of the collective Pink Floyd imagination), the symphonic breadth that might have been available from marshalling classical forces was restricted to outbursts between the core band instruments' featured moments.

Often, the solo guitar, Hammond organ, bass and drums passages hint at the sound of The Beatles' recent *Abbey Road* project (another example of the trend for melding an entire record side into one whole, led chiefly by one member of the band). Overall, the 'Atom Heart Mother' suite surely proved that if the long-form, 25-minute format was going to be the band's medium of choice thereafter, the semi-symphonic, classical route was not one that was going to serve them well. Since Pink Floyd never returned to this type of collaboration again, with the exception of Michael Kamen's skilled but subordinate arrangements for *The Wall* and *The Final Cut*, one would have to conclude they recognized this too. The album was indisputably commercially successful, they took a leaf out of Keith Emerson's book and performed the suite live with various choirs and orchestras subsequently and all in all gave considerable delight to multitudes, not least school kids studying music like me at the time, hoping that it signalled the hoped-for end of the tedious classical/pop apartheid. With the benefit of hindsight, however, it did not; and was not creatively especially fecund in itself, even if it did lead Pink Floyd out of the pseudo-classical cul-de-sac (into which others, notably a berobed Rick Wakeman, plunged exuberantly) to a different way of building longer forms. This they found and made their own, without being beholden to classical templates, with which, on the basis of the 'Atom Heart Mother' suite, they were in any case ill at ease. Other clues, on side two of *Atom Heart Mother*, were being laid as to the direction of travel. Roger Waters' 'If', with its simple two-chord pendulum, its keening David Gilmour solo guitar and its fearfully vulnerable lyric, '*If I go insane, please don't put your wires in my brain…*', opened the door to a more personal vision of the band's musical outlook, one that was, at least for a passing window of congruity, to be both liberating and rewarding, even if it was to mean confronting anxiety, uncertainty and distress head on.

Meddle, released in November 1971, indicated that lessons had been learnt from the mixed blessings of the previous year's projects, with a far greater degree of formal discipline in its tracks and in the harnessing of special effects and new technology. Ideas were less liable to run on until exhausted, momentum was maintained in the longer, developmental songs like its dynamic Dr Who-ish opener 'One of these Days', and even the monumental 23-minute 'Echoes' wasted far less of its span haplessly transitioning between ideas, as had been the habit on previous sprawling epics. The album is characterized by a sense of cohesion, and perhaps a stabilizing of the balance of creative input between the four members, whose other influences include the sky-gazing beauty, vocal transcendence, hints of Indian mysticism and doubled acoustic and 12-string guitar fluency of George Harrison's 1970 triple album *All Things Must Pass* and John Lennon's towering *Across the Universe* (composed 1968, released 1970) – the shadow of which hangs particularly strongly over 'Echoes', both musically and lyrically. Compare Lennon's

> *Images of broken light which dance before me like a million eyes,*
> *They call me on and on across the universe*
> *Sounds of laughter, shades of earth are ringing*
> *Through my open ears inciting and inviting me …*

with Waters'

> *Cloudless every day you fall upon my waking eyes*
> *Inviting and inciting me to rise*
> *And through the window in the wall*
> *Come streaming in on sunlight wings*
> *A million bright ambassadors of morning …*

The golden rule of composition is not that you shouldn't borrow ideas or influences from elsewhere but that when you do, they should be the best available. Tick. The weight of 'Echoes's quintessentially Pink Floydian character is so great that accusations of picking up tips from Lennon or Harrison are, anyway, misplaced. 'Echoes' is in its own right an outstanding, musically mature piece of collaborative work by all members of Pink Floyd. By way of balance, it is also worth acknowledging *en passant* that one of the most distinctive riffs in

54 · OPPOSITE · Promotional flyer for Pink Floyd concert, Tokyo-To Taiikukan, Tokyo, Japan, 6–7 March 1972. Pink Floyd Archive

'Echoes', a downwards-then-upwards-driving chromatic major third phrase, was to re-surface, doubtlessly unintentionally, as the most recognizable motif of Andrew Lloyd Webber's *The Phantom of the Opera* score.

Experimental techniques, particularly those relating to what might be possible by pushing electric instruments and their associated effects beyond what was in the user manual, feed into the song's mood and atmosphere and are never simply placed for their novelty alone. The 'pinging' at the opening of 'Echoes', which at first hearing might be thought to be a recording of a submarine echo-locator, is in fact created by sending the amplified signal of a single piano note to the (rotating-fan) Leslie cabinet of the Hammond organ. Throughout, musical solutions were found from the players themselves and each unfolding section presents sound worlds that were entirely new: what sounds like wailing, moaning voices at the end of the song was achieved by setting up running tape machines at a delay to each other at opposite ends of the studio, the ghostly organ chords climbing and falling as they recorded and fed back to each other. 'Echoes's form is dictated not by any half-appropriated classical designs but feels, even now, nearly half a century later, organic, fresh, innovative in its own terms: rock music, rock instruments, rock techniques, rock rhythms and patterns, rock potency and impetus.

What *Meddle* demonstrates, above all, is that the band were gradually falling out of love with – in Gilmour's own words – 'the psychedelic noodling' that had characterized much of their earlier recordings. What they were unveiling was a knack for combining experimentation with a seductive accessibility, an amalgamation that was to propel their reputation around the world in a quite astonishing manner in the ensuing half-dozen years. Listeners to *Meddle* who were most excited by the cutting-edge fearlessness of 'Echoes' may not have been the same listeners whose favourite song was the sensuously languid, chimerical 'A Pillow of Winds', a song inspired by the band playing mahjong together in the south of France, but the coming together of those two aural universes was about as potent a recipe for universal acclaim as the popular music of the 1970s could offer. The distance travelled from the take-it-or-leave-it, rag-week japes of *The Piper at the Gates of Dawn*, just four years earlier, was already immense.

It is hard to imagine now a well-known band touring a new album's material for over a year before releasing it as a recording. This relative luxury (in that it allowed songs to evolve and improve gradually, with maximum input from all band members, before committing to a final version) is inconceivable today for two reasons. The audience expectation in buying their expensive tickets long in advance is to see and hear something they already know and adore and to minimize their 'risk' at the outlay accordingly, and the quality of what would be bootleg-able by recording or filming even on a mobile phone, and find itself on the internet almost immediately, is too threatening to the livelihood of the artists (and record companies) involved. They would, to some extent, lose control over the creative process too, with multiple versions of the same songs existing long before their definitive master. In 1972, though, bootleg copies of anything were of an appalling quality and their distribution was haphazard and thin across the overall record-buying market. So Pink Floyd were able to trial what became *The Dark Side of the Moon* more or less all over the world, chipping away at it like a sculpture. The hastily written and recorded *Obscured by Clouds*, on the other

Universal Orient Promotions presents

吹けよ風、呼べよ嵐
ピンク・フロイド

'72 3月6日(月),7日(火) pm6:30
東京都体育館

S・¥2,800 A・¥2,500 B・¥2,100 C・¥1,600

★都内各プレイガイドにて好評発売中!!
★お問い合せ (585)3045 ユニバーサル

主催●フジテレビ
　　　ユニバーサル
後援●東芝音楽工業
協賛●平凡パンチ
　　　アン・アン

Pink Floyd

hand, another film soundtrack project, this time for director Barbet Schroeder's *La Vallée,* was dispatched in under two weeks of total studio time, most of which was spent in Strawberry Studios at Château d'Hérouville near Paris, with sessions sandwiched between dates of a Japanese tour in early spring 1972.

It may have been a necessarily swift process, but it is some measure of the creative stride that the band's writers had got into by this point, midway through the development of *The Dark Side of the Moon* and just three months after the release of *Meddle,* that *Obscured by Clouds* (released on 2 June 1972) is as assured a collection of songs and instrumental tracks as it is. Perhaps the most surprising aspect of the album is the almost-orthodox pop songs nestled in among the more filmic instrumental items, such as the George Harrison-like 'Wot's ... Uh the Deal?', the West Coast-suffused 'Stay' and the sprightly 'Free Four' (the latter two were paired up for a 7-inch single in the USA a month after the album release). It's hard to imagine how these might have been conceived to fit with the film's plot-line, which follows the wife of the French Consul in Melbourne joining a group of explorers who travel into the depths of the Papua New Guinea rainforest and encounter the most isolated tribe on Earth, the Mapuga (who are heard singing in the album's final track, 'Absolutely Curtains'). 'Free Four', for example, is another step in Roger Waters' increasingly troubled attempts through song to make sense of his father's death: '*You are the angel of death/ And I am the dead man's son/ And he was buried like a mole in a fox hole/ And everyone is still on the run.*' The juxtaposing of catchier, lyrical song material and more atmospheric, explorative instrumental sections was an instinct that was to serve the group well in their next release, nearly nine months later.

The public birth of *The Dark Side of the Moon* on 23 March 1973 can be ranked alongside 1 June 1967 (*Sgt. Pepper's Lonely Hearts Club Band)* and 14 January 1977 (David Bowie's *Low*) as a great landmark in the roll call of achievements of British musicians in the twentieth century. This is of course partly because of its staggering commercial success and cultural impact but also because of the quality of its artistic endeavour. It is important not to lose sight of the brilliance and beauty of the album's music and the exquisite form into which it was shaped when marvelling at the sheer scale of its commercial triumph across the globe.

There is some debate as to what the first 'concept' album is, with The Beach Boys' *Pet Sounds*, The Mothers of Invention's *Freak Out,* The Kinks' *Face to Face* and The Beatles' *Sgt. Pepper's Lonely Hearts Club Band* all the subject of claims to the title. What is certainly the case is that after the enormous impact of *Sgt. Pepper* a floodgate was opened and by the early 1970s it was harder to find bands *not* releasing concept albums than ones that were. Pink Floyd's *The Dark Side of the Moon* came in the backwash of such conceptual gems as King Crimson's *In the Court of the Crimson King* and *In the Wake of Poseidon*, Yes' *Fragile* and *Close to the Edge*, Jethro Tull's *Aqualung*, Genesis' *Nursery Cryme* and *Foxtrot,* and Wishbone Ash's *Argus* (the opening track of which, 'Time Was', was the closest in musical style to *The Dark Side of the Moon* of them all). What all these have in common, though, and what separates *The Dark Side of the Moon* from them, is that they surf on the fashion of that moment, a penchant for ancient myth, runic legend or quasi-Arthurian hocus-pocus (the name, as it happens, of a huge progressive rock hit of 1971 by the Dutch group, Focus). 'Game of Thrones' would have sat very comfortably with the trend, though it is hard to

55 · **ABOVE** · Backing singers Venetta Fields (left) and Carlena Williams performing with Pink Floyd, 1974. Photograph by Jill Furmanovsky

see it making a comeback post-*This is Spinal Tap*. It's easy (very) to mock at this distance but pageant, Celtic solemnity and an intense familiarity with the works of J.R.R. Tolkein were an irresistible brew for so many progressive rock bands in the early 1970s and it did at least make a textual change from the two decades of boy-meets-girl platitudes that had preceded the craze.

The Dark Side of the Moon, on the other hand, knits its component parts together with a very different thread of meaning and intention. Its concerns are frank, personal and contemporary and at times intentionally disturbing – neurosis, madness, depression and the consequences and responses to insanity ('*hanging on in quiet desperation is the English way*'). In fact, in early group discussions about the binding ideas of the album, the pressures of modern life were the guiding anxieties – the corrupting effect of, and greed for, money, the steamroller of time, travel and expectation, and so on. But as the project slowly developed, Roger Waters steered it 'into a meditation on madness', in Nick Mason's words. Underpinning the melancholic power of much of the album's material was, for all members of the band, an inescapable sense of guilt at what had happened to their friend Syd Barrett, how they might perhaps have handled his mental illness and his departure from the group better, how they had 'moved on' while he had declined into a shadow of his former self, retreating from the world, from them and from music. These were strong currents in which to swim and the musical results are astonishingly assured and emotionally truthful, and – in the context of the music scene of 1973 – exhilaratingly unexpected.

56 · OPPOSITE · Saxophonist Dick Parry performing with Pink Floyd on their British Winter tour, 1974. Photograph by Storm Thorgerson

It is a paradox of *The Dark Side of the Moon* that while its subject-matter was essentially dark and melancholic, its music is throughout uplifting, warm, accessible and, at times, joyous. Music has long been able to combine the release of redemption and acceptance with the acknowledgement of suffering, African-American spirituals being potent examples. At some point in the recording process the possibility of involving the Italian-based American mezzo-soprano Cathy Berberian, the go-to singer of choice of the '60s classical avant-garde, in what might be a wordless, rhapsodic solo was discussed. The eventual introduction, however, of Clare Torry, Doris Troy and other singers with gospel, soul, blues and country in their bones injected a non-English, non-white, non-male, non-parochial grit into the album, particularly Torry's magnificent, heart-rending improvisation in 'The Great Gig in the Sky', and the album was transformed by their contribution as a result. David Gilmour has referred to the influence of the wordless, improvised singing (treating the voice as one would a guitar solo, in effect) by legendary soul singer Clydie King on electronica pioneers Beaver and Krause's 1971 album *Gandharva*, in a song called 'Walkin'. The jazz- and blues-inflected tenor saxophone solos of Dick Parry on 'Us and Them' and 'Money' reinforce the sense that the band were reaching out of their own backgrounds to a wider, less sheltered musical experience. 'Money', for all that it has a sophisticated time-signature (7/8 – almost unheard of in a century of popular music), a jazz-funk electric piano counter-riff and an inventive tape-loop of cash registers, is, stripped down to its basics, a 12-bar (minor-variant) blues. Even Richard Wright's gradual moving away from his favoured Italian Farfisa electronic organs to the Hammond RT-3 for *The Dark Side of the Moon* sessions signals a subtle gravitation towards gospel (Hammonds being overwhelmingly the organ of choice in gospel churches, and consequently in most recorded black music of the 1960s and '70s). Musical Americana pervades the album, despite the geographical specificity of the English- and Irish-accented spoken inserts and that of many of Waters' lyrics (*'For the want of the price of tea and a slice/ The old man died'*).

While many of the studio effects and techniques on *The Dark Side of the Moon* were by and large a continuation of previous recording tricks – taped sounds of the human body, sound samples spliced and re-ordered, spoken word interjections, synthesizer pads and deep bass pedals – the re-focusing of the atmospheres they helped evoke towards the experience of ordinariness, towards fundamental human emotions, inadequacies and insecurities, shed new light on their function across virtually all songs. Rather than attempting to convey a science fiction, psychedelic or future imagined state, these unusual, innovative, experimental sounds were integrated into songs concerned with the reality of being a human being, here and now. From its opening sound collage of effects, voices and the desperate, sorrowful howling that marks the climactic transition from 'Speak to Me' into 'Breathe (In the Air)', to its final heartbeat ritornello and bleak, receding spoken epigraph, *'there is no dark side of the moon, really, as a matter of fact it's all dark...'*, *The Dark Side of the Moon* fulfils its authors' aspiration to confront the listener with a realization of the need, above all, for empathy. In this respect alone, *The Dark Side of the Moon* is a departure from all previous Pink Floyd albums and from most of the other 'progressive rock' albums that were popular in the early 1970s. The mighty egos of men who strode the world's stadiums like colossi usually identified with superheroes, swashbucklers and gods. Pink Floyd instead chose here to identify with the lost, the confused, the yelled-at, the disenfranchised.

The Band—Howard Goodall

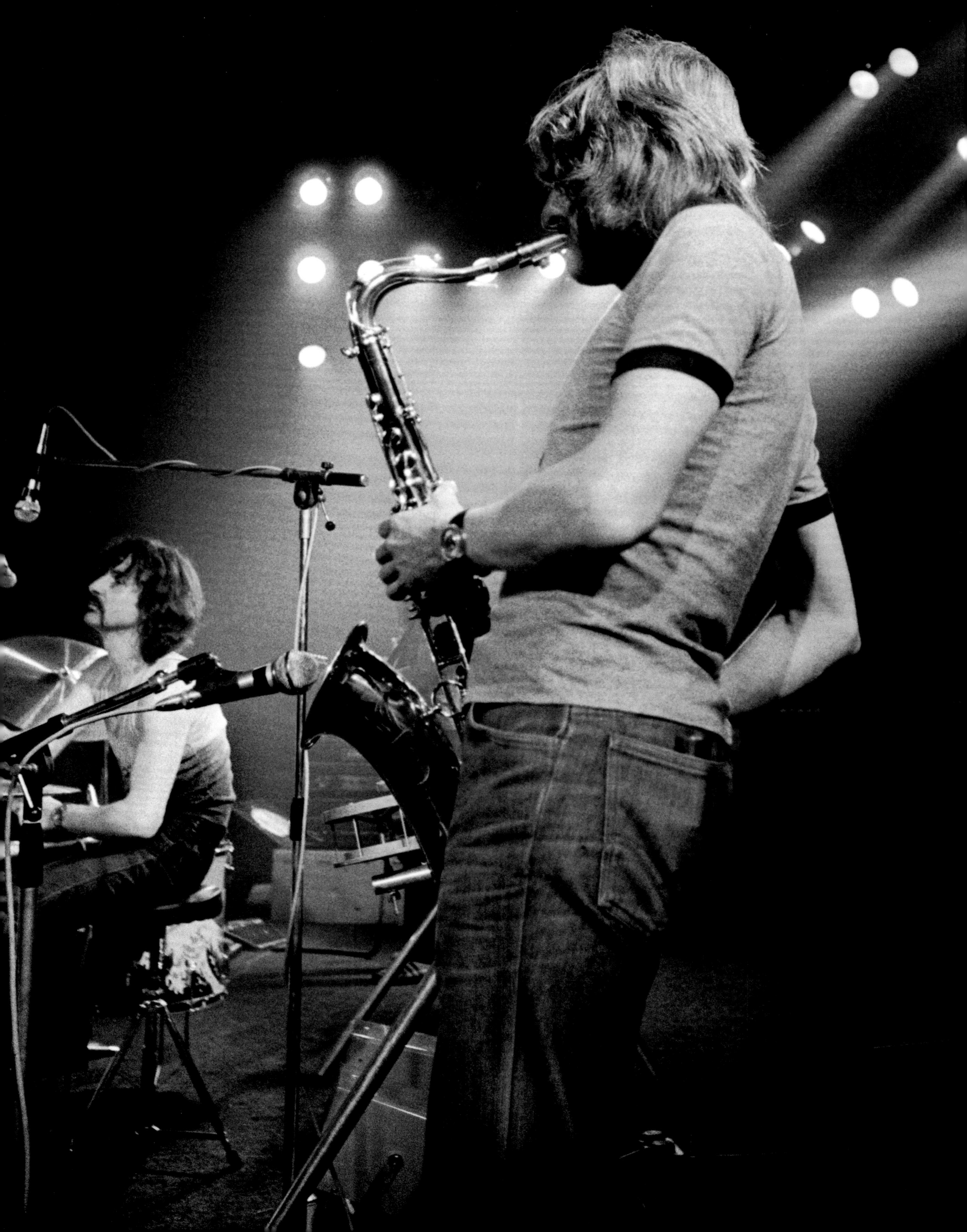

57 · ABOVE · Stage set for Pink Floyd's British Winter tour, 1974. Photograph by Jill Furmanovsky

58 · FOLLOWING SPREAD · Pink Floyd backstage on their British Winter tour, 1974. Photograph by Storm Thorgerson

Musical characteristics of this album and the one that followed it, *Wish You Were Here*, whether intuitive or studied, vastly increased the band's ability to land emotional punches where and when it mattered. An example of this is their particularly effective control of the way that harmony can be used to increase or relieve tension. What 'Breathe', 'The Great Gig in the Sky' and 'Any Colour You Like' all have in common (with 'Shine On You Crazy Diamond' from *Wish You Were Here* and 'Echoes' from *Meddle*) is a long 'verse' (or, in the terminology of classical form, 'first subject') in which two chords oscillate back and forth. In the case of 'Breathe' they are E minor 7th to A, in 'Any Colour You Like' they are D minor 7th to G, in 'Echoes' they are F sharp minor to C sharp minor, and so on. The bulk of the section of 'The Great Gig in the Sky' where Clare Torry improvises is underpinned by the oscillation G minor 7th to C9.

The effect of moving back and forth between just two chords is to create a sense of forward movement, even ones where there is an inherent pull towards the second. In 'Breathe's sequence, E minor 7th *wants* to resolve to A, but A itself in an ideal world *wants* to resolve to D, a yearning that is deliberately thwarted by a return to E minor 7th, thus re-setting the see-saw once again. These laws of orbital gravity that operate in chordal relationships are as old as the first variants of the Western tuning system, 'Equal Temperament', that theoretically allowed all keys to interlock, a system that emerged in a near-enough-is-good-enough fashion in the late seventeenth to early eighteenth centuries.

The Band—Howard Goodall

There are two dangers, though, in letting the harmony of a piece of music pivot backwards and forwards between just two chords. One is the possibility of stasis or boredom: this has to be counteracted by keeping the moving parts, as it were, constantly in a state of development and evolution. This means solo parts embedded in the texture, whether instrumental or vocal, must not stay still, repeating the same motifs over the unchanging chord pattern. Thus, in 'Breathe', Roger Waters' bass line does not simply reiterate the root notes E to A, E to A in a machine-like way, it moves between the two through various mini-melodic steps, each pattern slightly different, and David Gilmour's slide guitar phrases, while obeying the underlying logic of the Em7 to A ping-pong, in fact *voice* these chords differently over the course of the verse (voicing is the technique of moving the individual notes of the given chord to different positions in its structure – a guitar can play the chord Em7 in about 20 different ways depending on which strings play which note in its range).

Moreover, the slide guitar's ability to sustain and drift between its chord changes (much more so than a conventional guitar) allows Gilmour the additional perk of using suspensions (notes that don't belong to the underlying chord but hang over it, suspended, until they fall down on to the note position they were intended for). Suspensions were J.S. Bach's cleverest, most delicious gift to European harmony (he didn't invent them, he just did them so well everyone wanted to emulate his skill), since they deliberately frustrate the expectation of where the note should fall but in so doing contrive a supplementary chord, a more sophisticated one, as a by-product of the suspension. Thus, the fifth time the Em7 to A pattern is heard, at 35 seconds into 'Breathe', Gilmour suspends an F sharp over the Em7 chord (suspended 'above' the E where it is 'supposed' to be), creating a new, thicker chord, known to (and beloved of) jazz musicians: E minor 9th. After the Em7 to A see-saw has been played no fewer than 8 times, over a minute into the song, we are finally allowed the longed-for reward of the move away from A, not to where A *wants* us to go, D, but to the unexpected new home of C. This sudden interruption of our moment of release is, like a suspension, a way of prolonging the pleasure, moving us forward using the harmony, so our ears cannot get bored. Pink Floyd became absolutely brilliant at drawing out harmonic progressions in this way, filling what were in effect relatively simple, economic chord choices with event, surprise, mood and inner activity.

The unforgettable David Gilmour four-note lead guitar motif that begins 'Shine On You Crazy Diamond', B flat up a 5th to F, down a 7th to G, back up a 6th to E, is in essence a two-chord see-saw, G minor 7th to C, a pattern that fluctuates, apart from one brief excursion to F, for 30 seconds until the glorious release of the unexpected, E flat at 4'51" into the song. The interruption of E flat after Gm7 to C, incidentally, is an identical relationship of chords as the C after Em7 to A is in 'Breathe'. The difference in the later song is that by the time Gilmour's famous four-note motif begins, the song has already been up and running for nearly four minutes (longer than the total duration of an average pop single), sustaining the single chord G minor for its first 2'22" simply with ornamental solo lines on keyboard and guitar. How successfully the band manage expectation and release can be judged by the fact that 'Shine On You Crazy Diamond's first chord change, from G minor to D minor, is a full 2'22" into the song, and it is a fabulously satisfying moment when it does eventually arrive. Mastery of long-form was being achieved by ingenious management of the hidden gravity available in basic chord progressions.

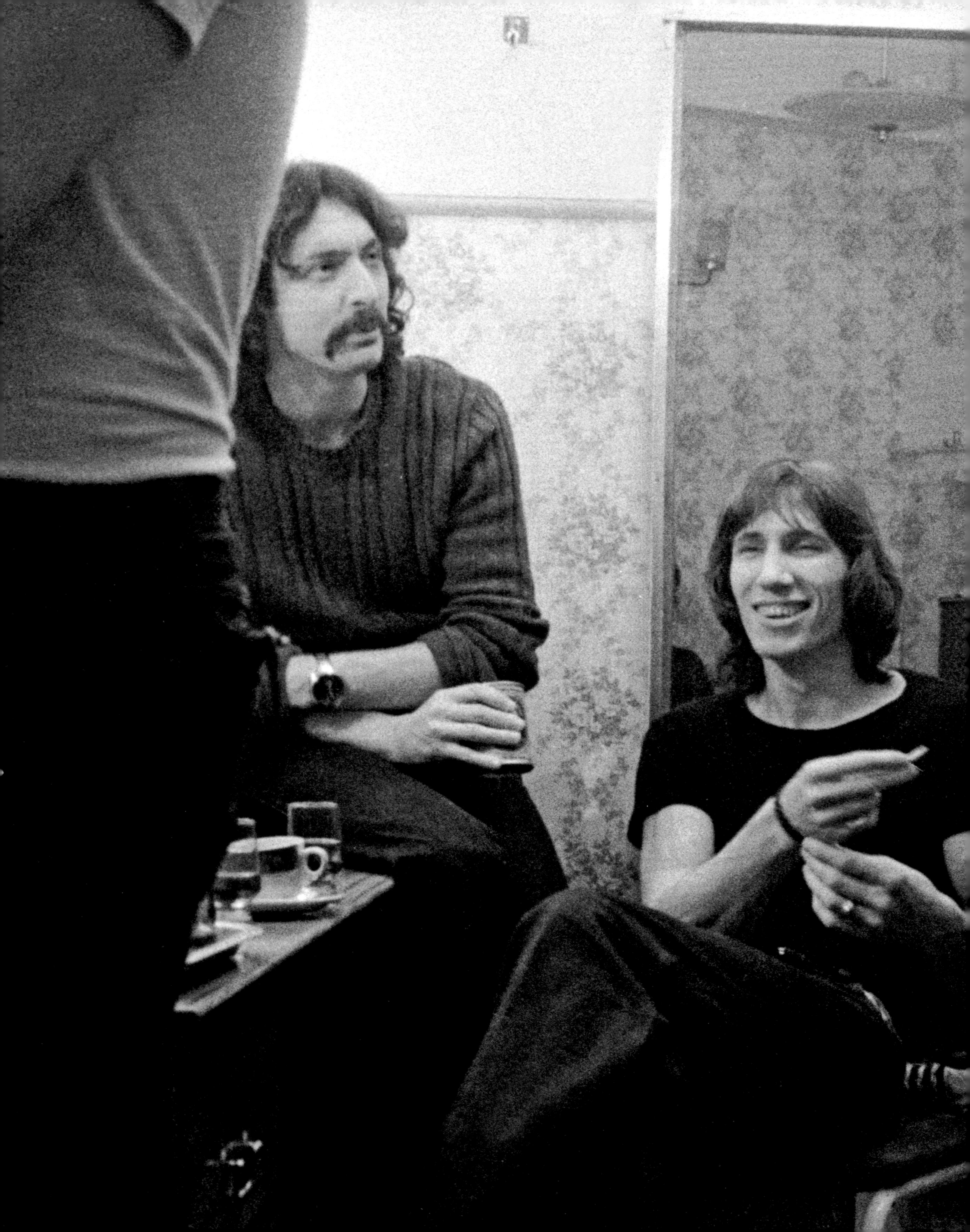

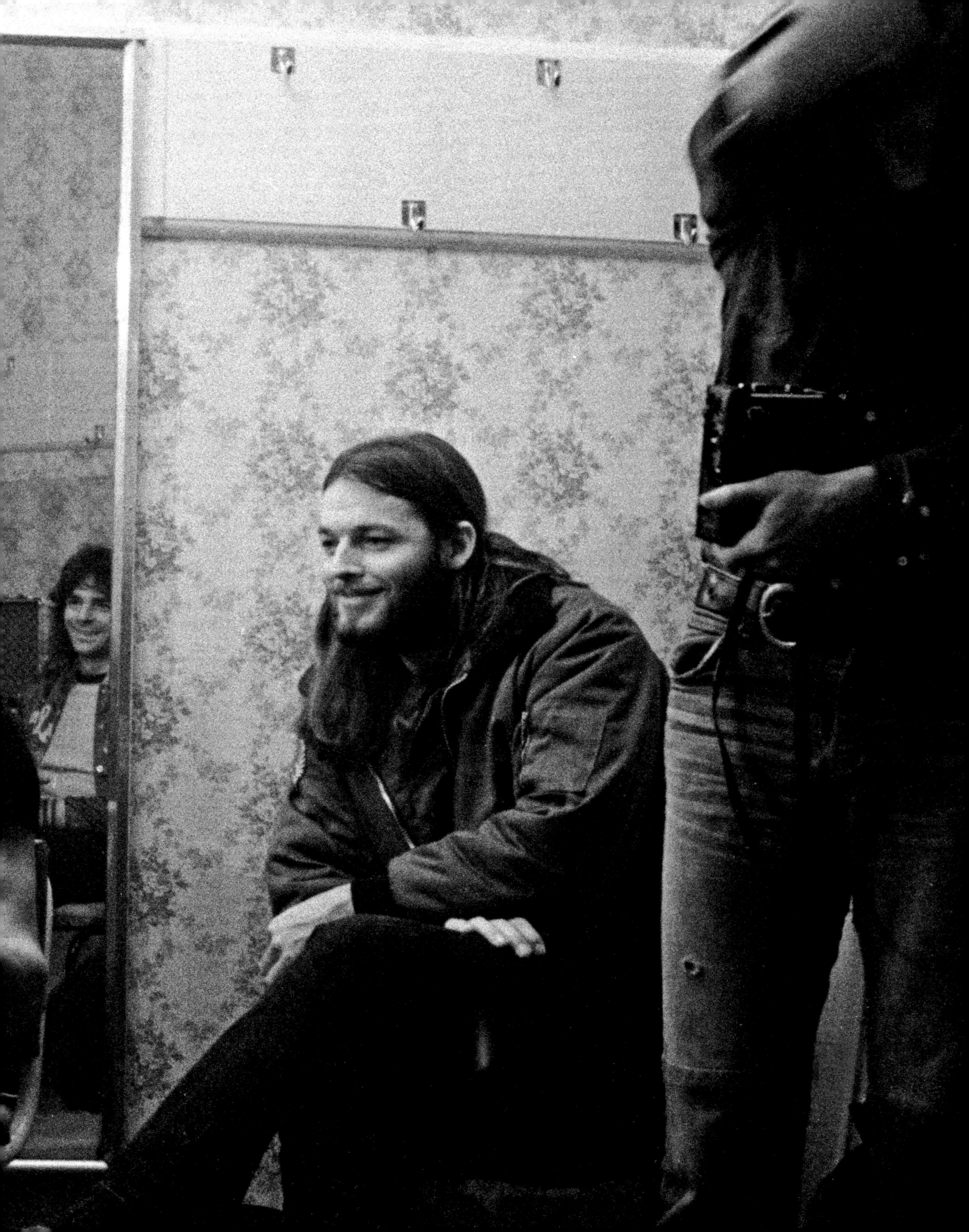

One further example of the long-form organization of harmony on *The Dark Side of the Moon* is illuminating. The bewitching sequence of four chords that underpin most of 'Us and Them', D (+ a suspended 2nd), E (+ a suspended 2nd), D minor (+ a sharpened 7th) and G (2nd inversion), all sit on top of what in classical music is termed a 'pedal' bass note, in this case D ('pedal' derives from the deep, underpinning root notes provided by the pedals on an organ, the favoured instrument in Bach's time, when modern harmony was being invented and perfected). Richard Wright's sequence, as we have seen, originally came from the unused portion of the soundtrack to *Zabriskie Point*. Because of the way that its chords progress against the rooting presence of the pedal D, it is a sequence that could theoretically continue indefinitely, since the tension between the upper movement and the lower root is self-perpetuating (that is, the four chords *seek* resolution in the way that a suspension seeks resolution by falling down to where the ear thinks it belongs). In the *Zabriskie Point* solo piano version, attractive though it undoubtedly is, there is more of a sense of inertia, of the pattern merely repeating without having an inner sense of direction. After just one round of the sequence, Wright heads down out of it to the new chordal destination of B minor for the second section. Moving to B minor from a D-based sequence is a perfectly respectable move, akin perhaps to the *Giuoco Piano* or *Giuoco Pianissimo* openings in chess, familiar and relatively passive. By the time, three years later, the piece has been transformed into 'Us and Them' on *The Dark Side of the Moon*, the move is utterly thrilling, one of the most dramatic and famous in popular music (it occurs at 2′47″ in the album version). How is this achieved, what has changed?

First, the tension has been increased by delaying the move considerably, from once through (about 30 seconds' duration) to four times through (over two and a half minutes' duration). Each pass adds new instruments or voices (for example, the saxophone and piano enter at the second pass, the voice at the third); the chords, in the earlier piano version, are played with a regular, slightly static right hand and a classical-style left hand rocking to and fro on the fifth, whereas in the later version a moving, arpeggiating guitar is featured from the start, intensifying the shifting relationship between the chords and setting up an expectation that we are heading somewhere. The addition of a vocal line, which follows the contour of the top of each chord, A to B to C sharp to B, descends initially back down to A at the end of the first sung verse, but the second time, instead of settling for a cadence, begins to head back up the scale again on the words, '*it's not what we would choose to do*', subtly alerting us to the possibility that the progression is not winding down but building upwards to some new chordal destination. As the voices appear to be indicating our direction of travel is upwards, the bass line, with great force, asserts in contrary motion a move in the opposite direction, downwards from D through C sharp to the new home of B. This effect, a simultaneous thrust in opposite directions, along with a huge, unstoppable crescendo sends us into the change to B minor expecting a dynamic pay-off, which comes in the form of a full-force opening up of the band's instruments and a huge multi-tracked, three-part harmony chorus on the moment of impact. The arrival on B minor is not interrupted, like the moments of release in 'Breathe' or 'Shine On You Crazy Diamond', but there is an unexpected interruption nonetheless shortly after, as the phrase, '*Forward, he cried from the rear/ And the front rank died*' reaches its conclusion, instead of landing back on the home key-chord ('tonic') of D, as one might expect, swerves and finds itself on the unsettling

59 · ABOVE · Recording session for *Wish You Were Here*, EMI Studio 3, Abbey Road, London, January–July 1975. Photograph by Jill Furmanovsky

usurper, the holding chord of C major. None of these chords is complex in itself, this is after all mainstream rock not bebop, but the subtle and knowing handling of their chemistry results in a highly sophisticated, gratifying musical journey.

If *The Dark Side of the Moon*'s emotional epilogue comes in Roger Waters' two-part hymn to Syd Barrett's mental instability and its fallout, 'Brain Damage / Eclipse', it did not, however, provide closure for the band members of this upsetting chapter in their lives. Far from it. It would take an entire album, *Wish You Were Here*, even to begin to seek answers to those questions. On a personal level, those answers may not have been forthcoming but the musical outcome of the anguish they provoked would prove to be superlative.

Wish You Were Here's running-time is dominated by the long-form Barrett tribute, 'Shine On You Crazy Diamond' (26 minutes of the total) but the title track's more straightforward country-blues lament is the lynchpin of the album's twin concerns, Barrett's absence and the band's anger at their experience of post-*Dark Side of the Moon* exploitation and cynicism by the music industry. Indeed, the vexed question of just one line of it, '*Did you exchange a walk-on part in the war for a lead role in a cage?*' condenses these two internal conflicts into one pithy conundrum. It goes without saying that most neutral observers would rather be part of the world's most successful rock band even if it involved sacrificing one's freedom and privacy. But Barrett was no ordinary, impartial observer, and the band's inner turmoil about his absence was clearly tinged with remorse, not to mention, dare one say, some nostalgia for an earlier, less complicated era

60 · ABOVE · Recording session for *Wish You Were Here*, EMI Studio 3, Abbey Road, London, January–July 1975. Photograph by Jill Furmanovsky

in their story, before world domination and all it entailed muddied the enjoyment of pure music-making. Examining the evidence of their pre-Floyd-mania days, however, it is hard not to conclude that there never was an uncomplicated, unconflicted period in the band's development, and the removal of the strife surrounding Barrett had merely been replaced by other tensions within the organism, tensions that were at a peak during the recording of *Wish You Were Here*. They were in a trap, of course, but they had a creative outlet and the layered richness of the album feeds off their sense of loss. *Wish You Were Here*'s mood, for all its sadness, is also full of affection, vulnerability and the memory of 'faraway laughter', in contrast to the bitter wrath of the album which followed it, *Animals*.

From *Animals* onwards, released in January 1977 as the music world was bracing itself for the ill-tempered spring-clean of Punk, Pink Floyd's music was as invigorating and as imaginative as it had always been at its best and the band's millions of fans were rarely disappointed by what they were offered. But the resentments and tensions within the group had reached a point where future releases, from the ferocious passion of Roger Waters' semi-autobiographical *The Wall* (1979) to the David Gilmour, Richard Wright-helmed contemplative late masterwork, *The Division Bell* (1994), had the character of solo efforts with band member support. That is not to say that the quality of output suffered accordingly, it did not, but by the 1980s Pink Floyd, still a huge force to be reckoned with, were not setting the pace others would follow, as they had in the '70s, but ploughed their own furrow, while fashions eddied around them.

The Band—Howard Goodall

The creation of *The Wall* may have been fraught with discord between band members but it proved that they were anything but spent as a musical entity, not to mention abreast of cutting-edge developments in multimedia presentation when it came to the accompanying tour. Roger Waters' searingly personal fable of alienation joined the – by then – distinguished roll call of previous rock operas, from James Rado, Gerome Ragni and Galt MacDermot's *Hair* (1967), The Who's *Tommy* (1969) and Andrew Lloyd Webber and Tim Rice's *Jesus Christ Superstar* (1970) to Paul Williams' *Phantom of the Paradise* (1974) and Jeff Wayne's *The War of the Worlds* (1978), not forgetting the flamboyant inventiveness of Queen's not-quite-a-rock-opera *A Night at the Opera* (1975), which featured the epic 'Bohemian Rhapsody'. There are even moments in *The Wall*, 'The Trial', for example, where the music-theatre resonance owes as much to Lionel Bart's *Oliver!* and Bertolt Brecht and Kurt Weill's *The Threepenny Opera* as to late '70s rock. The idea for the project is said to have come in a painful epiphany to Waters after a particularly unpleasant experience playing at a stadium concert in Montreal in July 1977. Ironically, the story motivated by the desire to tear down the (many different kinds of) walls that divide and alienate people came to fruition in recording sessions and a subsequent tour that marked a new, disastrously low point for the band's personal relationships.

There is tremendous authenticity in the anger and despair that Roger Waters breathes into his recollections of growing up, yet the collective will feels strangely absent from the resulting double album, as if the rest of the band were participating somewhat artificially, under duress, notwithstanding the producer credit accorded to David Gilmour and his pivotal role in creating the sound and structure of the iconic song 'Comfortably Numb'. The concept and content of the album's narrative could only have been written by a composer-lyricist of conspicuous sophistication and intelligence, who had learnt a great deal from the world of art, history, politics and literature around him, yet its monster hit, 'Another Brick in the Wall, Part 2', places Islington primary-school children centre-stage, with exaggerated Cockney accents singing '*We don't need no education*'. To conceive *The Wall*, alas, that's exactly what they would need. The breadth and challenge of the story's themes may have benefited from the piece being performed live before recording began, in the manner of *The Dark Side of the Moon*, allowing time to hone the material so that its dramatic flow is always forward-moving and its emotional punches strategically placed. But the financial, commercial and scheduling pressures being exerted on the group during its gestation were such that this luxury was for once foregone. Some of *The Wall*'s most memorably touching moments draw together the threads of loneliness and the need for common humanity ('*Hey you, would you help me to carry the stone?/ Open your heart, I'm coming home ... Hey you, don't tell me there's no hope at all/ Together we stand, divided we fall.*'), long-standing, underlying themes in much of the band's output over the previous decade and a half, yet here they were recording an album as tax exiles. They of all people will have recognized this irony.

The Wall is nonetheless a powerful, thrillingly theatrical and compelling endeavour, followed by what could be seen as its extended epilogue, the anti-war (specifically anti-Falklands War) *The Final Cut* (1983), since the latter was born out of material originally intended for the soundtrack of the 1982 film of *The Wall*. At times, *The Final Cut* assumes some of the slowly unfolding, minimalist calm of Gavin Bryars' haunting, melancholic 'Jesus' Blood Never Failed Me Yet' (1971), an instrumental work that underscores a looped tape of a homeless man singing the spiritual of its title. Overall the stinging anger of betrayal and deceit directed at political leaders, particularly Margaret Thatcher, is heartfelt, though the balancing temperaments and contributions of the other band members that would have characterized previous undertakings of this nature are mainly missing.

A Momentary Lapse of Reason (1987), by contrast, was characterized by musical collaborations that widened the net of previous Pink Floyd albums. Co-produced by David Gilmour and Bob Ezrin, and created with the committed support of Nick Mason and Richard Wright, the album also benefited from the contributions of lyricist Anthony Moore, instrumentalist Jon Carin and guitarist Phil Manzanera, among others. A non-momentary success in terms of record and box-office sales, the album and accompanying two-year world tour reassured fans that Pink Floyd were still a force to be reckoned with. The legal disputes and long-festering animosities that worsened after the release of *The Final Cut* found musical resolution a decade later in the restorative warmth of *The Division Bell*. Recalling Clare Torry's outstanding vocal contribution to 'The Great Gig in the Sky', one reason why *The Division Bell*'s tone is less sulkily morose than much that had preceded it may be the strong creative presence on it of a woman, in this case lyricist Polly Samson. Her piercing analysis of the acrimony that had shrouded so much of the band members' personal interactions in 'Lost for Words' prompted a majestic musical response from Gilmour. The album's concern is communication, or lack of it, perhaps not surprisingly, and at its heart lies a vintage Pink Floyd anthem, 'Keep Talking', wrapped around the voice of Professor Stephen Hawking, taken from a TV ad, 'For millions of years, mankind lived just like the animals. Then something happened which unleashed the power of our imagination: we learned to talk … It doesn't have to be like this. All we need to do is make sure we keep talking'. Using an effects unit called a TalkBox, even David Gilmour's guitar speaks.

Rather as *The Wall*'s sessions had spawned the by-product of *The Final Cut*, *The Division Bell* also contained enough material to support the evolution of a second project, *The Endless River* (2014), a mostly instrumental tribute to Richard Wright who had died in 2008. It may be one of the only posthumous artistic tributes in history in which he or she is a principal performer, since much of the ambient and instrumental music on it is derived from unused portions of Wright's work on *The Division Bell*. A particularly touching and unexpected moment is 'Autumn '68', a voiceless hymn built around Wright's playing the Henry 'Father' Willis Royal Albert Hall organ in 1968. *The Endless River* is a reminder, if one was needed, that Pink Floyd as a collective musical voice had so often moulded 'songs' from much longer instrumental meanderings even if individuals, especially Syd Barrett and Roger Waters, had advocated from time to time for an alternative approach led by meaning and lyrics. 'On Noodle Street' is the name of a track from *The Endless River* but it might also serve as the location of so much that had been fruitful in the band's career.

However, *The Endless River*'s primary purpose of celebrating the huge part Richard Wright had played in making the Pink Floyd sound results in it feeling, unintentionally of course, more like a solo album. If one were looking for a more all-embracing farewell to three decades of innovative, deeply felt and provocative music through albums and live shows that had brought immeasurable delight and solace to millions, the poignant closing song of *The Division Bell*, 'High Hopes', with lyrics by David Gilmour and Polly Samson, could hardly be bettered.

Beginning with the distant bells of an English rural landscape, summoning up Gilmour's Cambridge childhood, it seems to acknowledge that life does not, cannot, offer a perfect trajectory that answers or exceeds all our early aspirations. It is instead a muddling-through, a rambling scrapbook of fading, sepia photographs, a collage of sounds, songs, echoes and atmospheres. An unfinished symphony.

The grass was greener
The light was brighter
The taste was sweeter
The nights of wonder
With friends surrounded
The dawn mist glowing
The water flowing
The endless river
Forever and ever ...

61 · ABOVE · Recording session for *Wish You Were Here*, EMI Studio 3, Abbey Road, London, January–July 1975. Photograph by Jill Furmanovsky

62 · FOLLOWING SPREAD · Pink Floyd onstage, Seattle Center Coliseum, Seattle, 10 April 1975. Photograph by Storm Thorgerson

'Painters, Pipers, Prisoners': The Musical Legacy of Pink Floyd

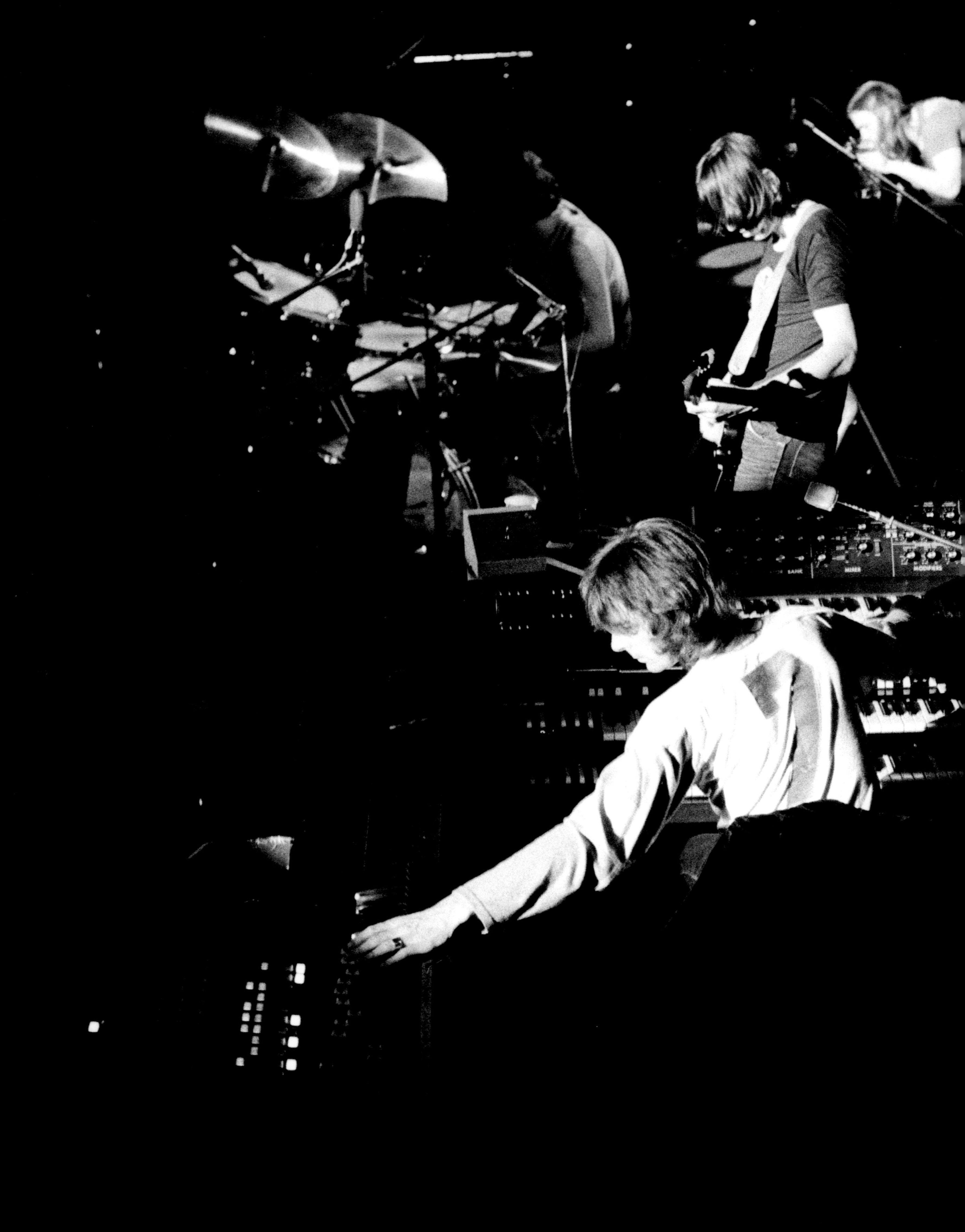

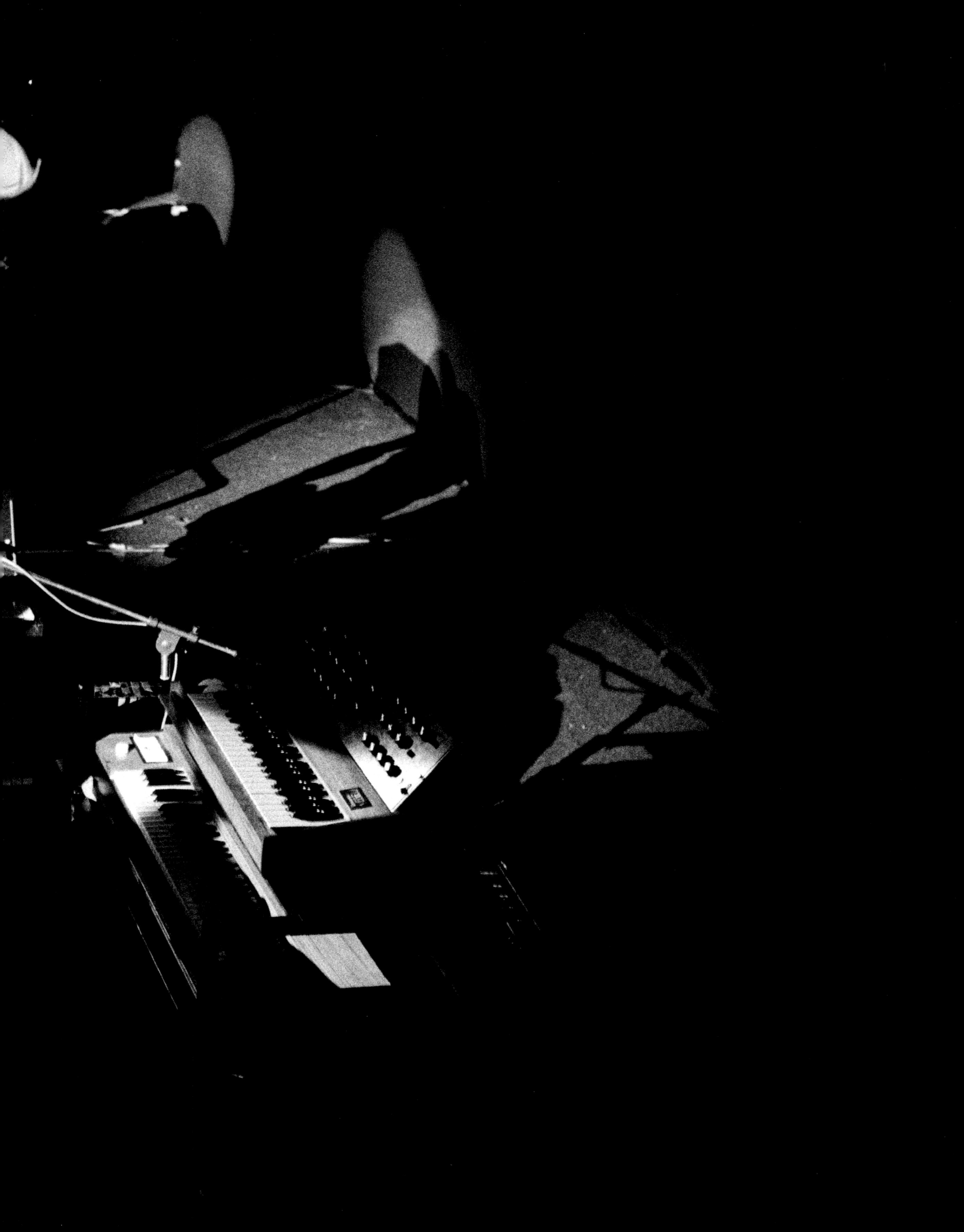

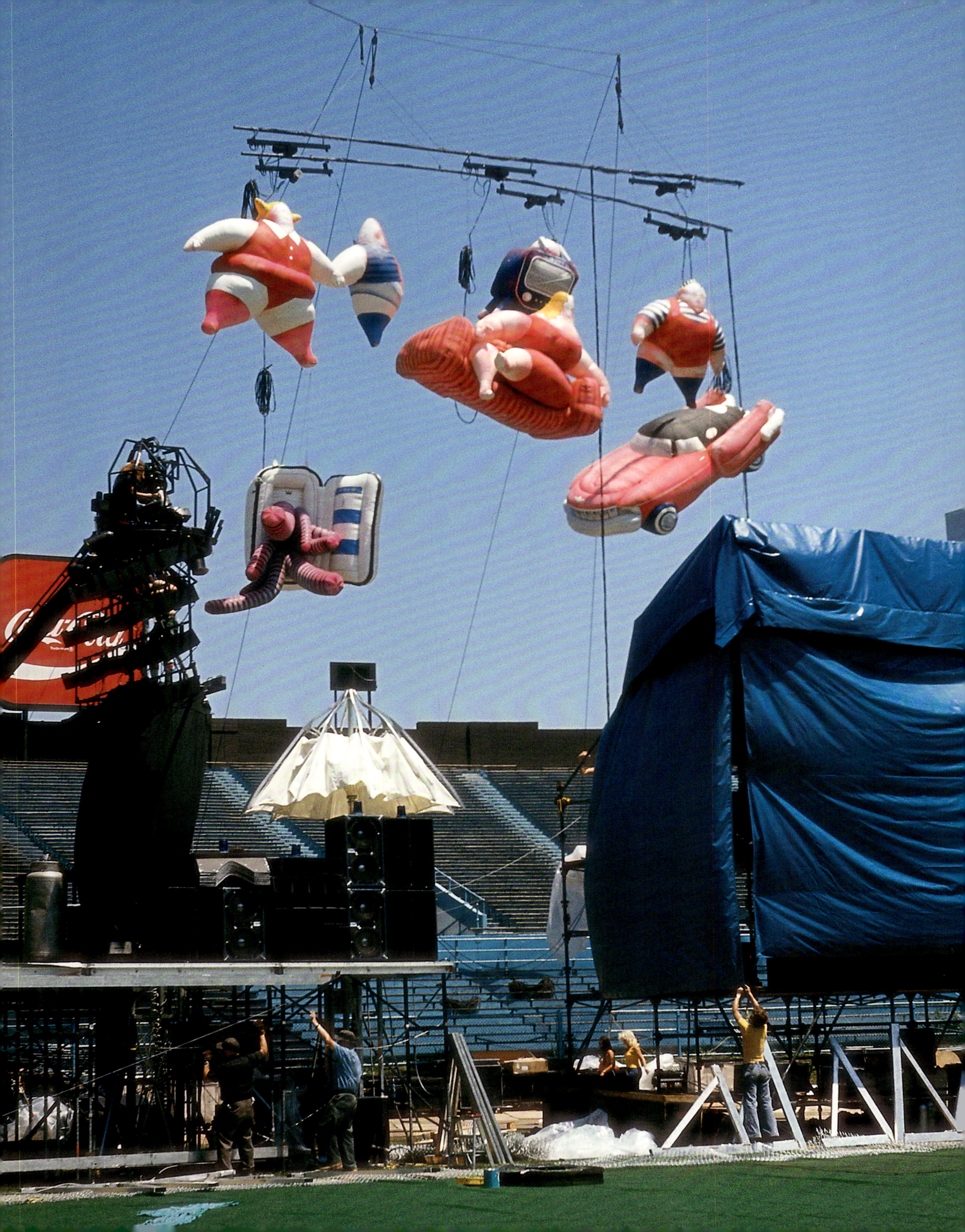

GREAT GIGS IN THE SKY

PINK FLOYD AND THE ARCHITECTURE OF ROCK

Victoria Broackes and Anna Landreth Strong

Conjure an image of 'Pink Floyd' in your mind. For many, this is more likely to prompt a vision of one of their great stage shows or iconic album covers than to evoke an image of the band members themselves. In comparison to groups of similar stature or longevity, there is an enigmatic quality to the Pink Floyd line-up. If you were to show someone a photograph of the individuals, they might struggle to identify them; however, show them a rainbow-refracting prism, a wall complete with marching hammers or a floating pig and they would get it in one.

63 · PAGE 112 · Stage set up for Pink Floyd's Animals / In the Flesh Tour, Cleveland Municipal Stadium, Cleveland, 25 June 1977. Photograph by Jonathan Park. Jonathan Park Collection

64 · BELOW · Pink Floyd performing under psychedelic lighting at the Student Christmas Carnival, Architectural Association School of Architecture, 16 December 1966. The band were booked by a committee of students including Mark Fisher. Photograph by Adam Ritchie

From the outset, visual experimentation and extravaganza have been at the centre of Pink Floyd's creative arsenal. The band, three of whom trained as architects, have always understood the importance of designing the environment in which their music would be heard. Over the years they have worked with many of the world's leading practitioners in rock 'n' roll staging. These partnerships comprise a roll call of industry greats: from designers Storm Thorgerson and Aubrey 'Po' Powell (founders of Hipgnosis),[1] to lighting pioneer Peter Wynne Willson, lighting and production designers Marc Brickman and Arthur Max, animator Ian Emes, satirical artist Gerald Scarfe and stage designer Paul Staples. From those mentioned, but including many others, Pink Floyd have worked with a long list of leaders in the field. As the band's live tours increased in scale, cost and ambition through the 1970s and beyond, the talented teams they assembled to create their tours also grew.

This chapter examines how Pink Floyd's ambitious staging concepts helped to move the entertainment architecture industry forward. It pays particular tribute to the late Mark Fisher, architect, innovator and pioneer of early stadium rock staging. Fisher was first approached by Pink Floyd while a Unit Master at the Architectural Association School of Architecture (AA). With colleague and leading engineer Jonathan Park, Fisher made possible the now well-known inflatables which flew over the band during their 1977 Animals / In the Flesh Tour. Fisher and Park then helped to realize the Roger Waters-designed *Pink Floyd The Wall* arena show, and Fisher worked together with Marc Brickman and Paul Staples on The Division Bell Tour in 1994. The text draws on interviews with Fisher's closest colleagues as well as those working with members of Pink Floyd today.[2]

The Band—Victoria Broackes and Anna Landreth Strong

65 · LEFT · Roger Waters and Nick Mason as architecture students at Regent Street Polytechnic, London, 1963. Pink Floyd Archive

The early Pink Floyd shows: sound and vision

Nick Mason, Roger Waters and Richard Wright met in 1962 on the Design and Architecture course at Regent Street Polytechnic, London (now the University of Westminster). After a few years and various line-ups they formed a band with another Roger, better known as 'Syd' Barrett, who was studying at Camberwell School of Arts. Fellow Cambridge boy David Gilmour joined Pink Floyd in 1968, establishing the line-up that would take the band forward to international fame.

From its inception, the group was at the central axis of art, music and architecture, and plugged into a network of architects, artists, academics, designers and engineers. As Nick Mason has commented, '[architecture provides] a really good training for rock and roll because it mixes the practical with fine art, drawing, three-dimensional thinking and structural engineering.'[3]

Pink Floyd staged early shows accompanied by theatrical lighting effects. Their liquid light shows, created using a combination of inks, chemicals, oil and water on a slide projector,[4] emitted amorphous and psychedelic waves of colour over the stage, the band and the audience, which for many seemed to evoke or augment the experience of taking LSD.

The band's interest in lighting effects was stimulated by one of their Regent Street Poly tutors, Mike Leonard, who also lectured at Hornsey College of Art in North London. Leonard was conducting experiments on the synthesis of lighting and sound and invited the band to musical 'improv' sessions, where visual effects would be improvised in accordance with the music they played.[5] Leonard and the band introduced these experiments during an episode of the BBC TV programme 'Tomorrow's World' in December 1967. The pre-professional Pink Floyd quickly incorporated light projections into their shows, with society magazine *Queen* reporting: 'Other groups have been dabbling with light and back projection, but the Floyd have gone into it in some kind of depth and their visuals make a reasonably logical connection with the music.'[6]

Great Gigs in the Sky: Pink Floyd and the Architecture of Rock

One of the greatest things about Pink Floyd was always the anonymity of the band. That they lived inside the experience, the music ... It wasn't about one person walking around the stage saying 'I'm the star'. It was really about the music and the lyrics.

—Marc Brickman, lighting and production designer

Most bands – if you were to put a prism up to their light – it would shine white in and white out. Right? But you know with Pink Floyd it is the full spectrum of colours that come out.

—Ray Winkler, CEO Stufish

66 · OPPOSITE · Pink Floyd onstage at the UFO club, London, February 1967. Photograph by Adam Ritchie

67 · ABOVE · Technician setting up Pink Floyd's projected light show at the *International Times* launch party 'All Night Rave', The Roundhouse, London, 15 October 1966. Photograph by Adam Ritchie

68 · LEFT · Rank Aldis Tutor (I) projector used for Pink Floyd's light shows 1966–7. Peter Wynne Willson Collection

Great Gigs in the Sky: Pink Floyd and the Architecture of Rock

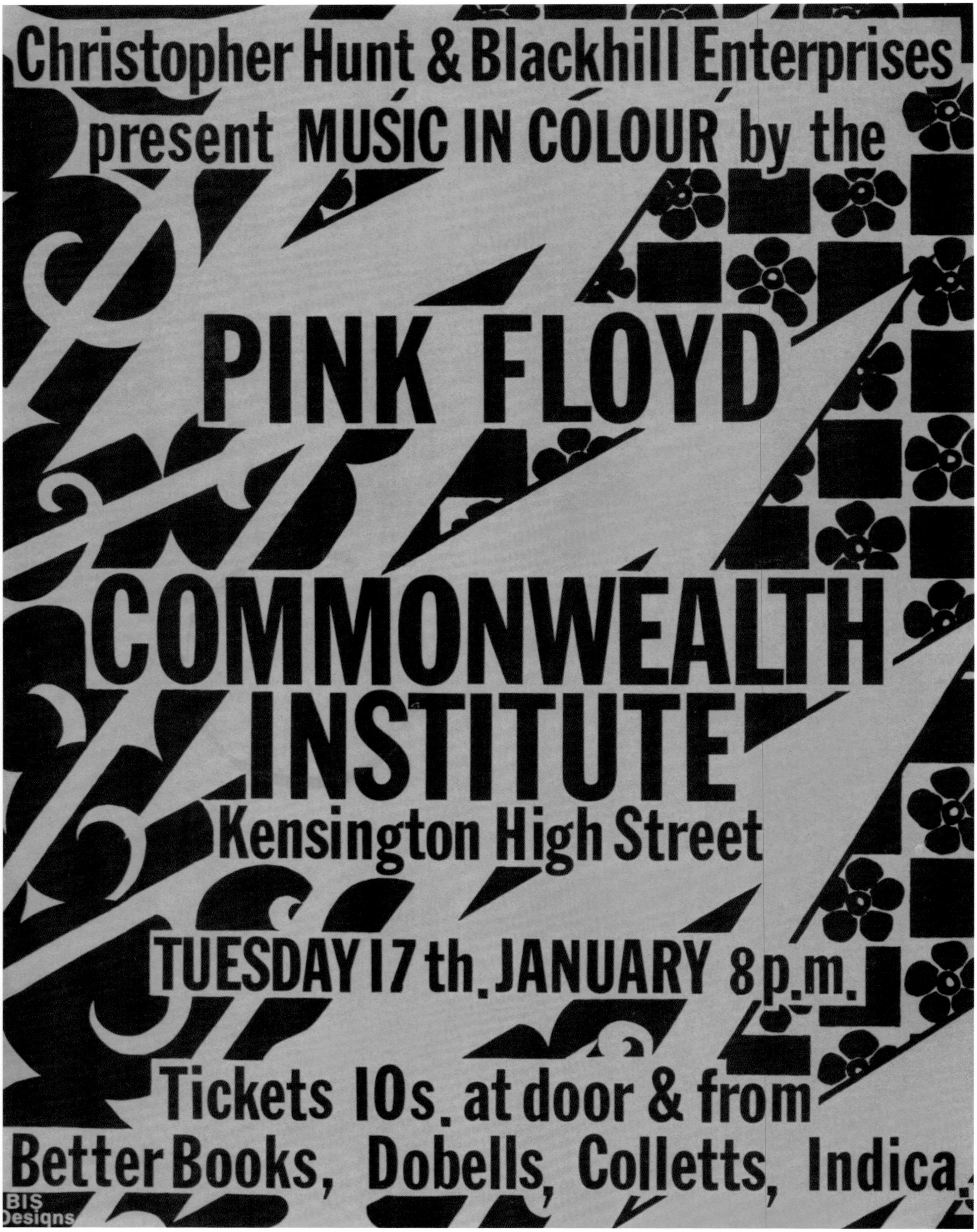
Christopher Hunt & Blackhill Enterprises
present MUSIC IN COLOUR by the
PINK FLOYD
COMMONWEALTH
INSTITUTE
Kensington High Street
TUESDAY 17 th. JANUARY 8 p.m.
Tickets 10s. at door & from
Better Books, Dobells, Colletts, Indica.
BIS
Designs

69 · OPPOSITE · Poster advertising 'Music in Colour by the Pink Floyd', Commonwealth Institute, Kensington, London, 17 January 1967. IBIS Designs. Pink Floyd Archive

70 · ABOVE TOP · Poster advertising Pink Floyd's concert at Hornsey College of Art, London, 18 November 1966. Designed by Diane Large. AlexandLiane Large Collection

71 · ABOVE BOTTOM · Poster advertising Pink Floyd's concert at the Marquee club, London, 22 and 29 December 1966. Designed by Wendy Gair. Collection of Lindy Mason

Great Gigs in the Sky: Pink Floyd and the Architecture of Rock

72–73 · ABOVE AND OPPOSITE · Back-projection tests for 'Games for May' by Pink Floyd, Queen Elizabeth Hall, London, 12 May 1967. Photographs by Nick Hale

Some of Pink Floyd's earliest gigs took place in Notting Hill at a series of 'social dances' – music events held to raise funds for the local London Free School, a community-focused, arts education centre for adults set up by a group including John 'Hoppy' Hopkins, Joe Boyd and the band's first co-manager, Peter Jenner of Blackhill Enterprises. Pink Floyd – still then relatively unknown – wowed the crowds at All Saints Church Hall with slide projections made for them by psychedelic light-show pioneers Joel and Toni Brown, an American couple and friends of Hoppy's who were visiting the UK from psychologist Timothy Leary's Castalia Institute in Millbrook, New York. *Melody Maker* reported: 'The slides were excellent – colourful, frightening, grotesque, beautiful, but all fall a bit flat in the cold reality of All Saints Hall.'[7]

As the light shows became a staple feature of Pink Floyd gigs their design was led by the band's resourceful managers Peter Jenner (with his wife Sumi) and Andrew King, and technician Joe Gannon, before passing into the creative hands of Peter Wynne Willson, a trained theatre lighting technician, who worked with Susie Gawler-Wright on psychedelic oil projections for the band. He was also assisted by technician John Marsh, who briefly took over responsibility for the band's lighting between late 1967 and June '68. Wynne Willson's DIY innovations included fashioning an oil slide from a condom stretched over a wire frame. He would later design psychedelic visual effects for the spectacular light show conceived by Marc Brickman for Pink Floyd's tour of *The Division Bell* in 1994.

The Band–Victoria Broackes and Anna Landreth Strong

In December 1966, Hoppy and Joe Boyd started a new venture in a more conveniently located London basement beneath the Berkeley Cinema on Tottenham Court Road. This became the UFO club, a short-lived but much-mythologized weekly underground haven for London's psychedelic scene. Pink Floyd were the UFO's first house band, playing 12 gigs there between December 1966 and July 1967. The revolutionary way they presented their music earned them a reputation among the underground network, and their audiences would spend hours bathed in a psyche-scape of sound and colour.

On 29 April 1967, Alexandra Palace in North London played host to 'The 14-Hour Technicolour Dream', a unique all-nighter billed as 'The Biggest Party Ever'. Within the huge Victorian hall, the audience (which included John Lennon) encountered a helter-skelter, a tent for smoking banana-skin 'joints' and performance artists alongside a 30-band line-up. Having played a gig in the Netherlands the night before, Pink Floyd arrived only at 3am and took to the stage as the sun began to rise, playing material from their forthcoming debut album *The Piper at the Gates of Dawn*. Film-maker Peter Whitehead captured the event in his film *Tonite Let's All Make Love in London*.

Two weeks later, the band's now legendary 'Games for May' concert took place in the Queen Elizabeth Hall at London's Southbank Centre, which had opened just two months earlier. Billed as 'space-age relaxation' with 'electronic composition, colour and image projections', the band's performance reached

74 · RIGHT · Azimuth Co-ordinator quadrophonic sound controller, 1969. Designed for Pink Floyd by Bernard Speight. V&A: s.294–1980

75 · OPPOSITE · Poster advertising 'The Massed Gadgets of Auximenies' (later: Auximines) by Pink Floyd, Royal Festival Hall, London, 14 April 1969. Designed by Storm Thorgerson / Aubrey Powell at Hipgnosis. V&A: s.295–1980

remarkable heights. Nick Mason later described the event as 'one of the most significant shows we have ever performed, since the concert contained elements that became part of our performances for the following thirty years'.[8] As well as using a quadrophonic speaker system and joystick for the first time (later to be called the Azimuth Co-ordinator), 'Games for May' broke new ground with a complex projector and light show. Soap bubbles were pumped through the air and daffodils were scattered over the seated audience. This radical multimedia performance helped pave the way for a new kind of rock theatre but, at the time, proved a step too far for the concert-hall's managers, who banned the group from future engagements on grounds of health and safety, and because the bubbles stained the venue's brand new seats.

Syd Barrett said later on in 1967, 'we think that the music and the lights are part of the same scene, one enhances and adds to the other ... But we feel that in the future, groups are going to have to offer much more than just a pop show. They'll have to offer a well-presented theatre show.'[9] Although Barrett parted from Pink Floyd in 1968, this vision and ethos were sustained in the band's future work. Back on the Southbank in April 1969, at the Royal Festival Hall, Pink Floyd introduced a new iteration of their sound-panner as the Azimuth Co-ordinator during 'The Massed Gadgets of Auximines', an event dubbed as 'More Furious Madness from Pink Floyd'. Featuring two extended musical suites, 'The Man' and 'The Journey', the performance also involved members of the band and crew constructing a table onstage and taking afternoon tea. Further theatrical enhancement was provided by way of performance art by Peter Dockley as the 'Tar Monster'. Dockley recalls one of the show's more invasive moments:

The Band—Victoria Broackes and Anna Landreth Strong

ROYAL FESTIVAL HALL

general manager:
j. denison c.b.e

THE MASSED GADGETS OF AUXIMENIES
MORE FURIOUS MADNESS FROM
PINK FLOYD
INTRODUCING
"THE AZIMUTH CO-ORDINATOR"

On April 14th 1969
At 8·00 pm
prices: 7/6 10/- 15/-
21/- 25/-

A
BRYAN MORRISON AGENCY
PRESENTATION

HIPGNOSIS

Printed at The Ranelagh Press, Hampstead, London

76 · ABOVE · Road crew lifting the circular screen during Pink Floyd's British Winter tour, Sophia Gardens Pavilion, Cardiff, 22 November 1974. Photograph by Storm Thorgerson

I would stand at the front of the stage between the band and the audience and produce my magic weapon, a large phallus, attached to the front of the suit, which was fitted with the biggest Sqezy bottle I could find, and this was filled with black liquid. I would arc sprays of this liquid over the front rows of the audience. At one performance it came into my head to spray the band in the same way. I had momentarily forgotten that they were connected to a trillion volts of electricity and turned the phallus towards them. For a brief moment they ducked back expecting to be soaked and then fried. Needless to say I didn't squirt. Just as well!

By the early 1970s, Pink Floyd were beginning to experiment with inflatables in their live performances and these went on to become one of their trademarks. Some of the band were inspired by the work of artist Jeffrey Shaw, whose performative art installation *Pneutube* they had seen on display at London's ICA in 1969. (Incidentally, it was at this event that Peter Dockley's Tar Monster costume made its debut, before it was adopted by Pink Floyd for 'The Massed Gadgets of Auximines' performances.) On 15 May 1971 Pink Floyd headlined The Garden Party at the Crystal Palace Bowl. Around 15,000 people endured the pouring rain to hear Pink Floyd top the bill; the band had now garnered a reputation for offering an impressive spectacle to intensify the experience of hearing their music live. 'They were certainly worth waiting for', wrote the *Croydon Advertiser*.[10] While the band played material from *Atom Heart Mother* through a quadrophonic sound system, a huge inflatable octopus, made by

Jeffrey Shaw and fellow artist Theo Botschuijver of Eventstructure Research Group, emerged from the depths of the lake surrounded by an orange mist. Entranced by the unlikely special guest, a group of hedonistic, and possibly tripping, fans jumped into the water and got caught up in its tentacles.

77 · **ABOVE** · Performance from Pink Floyd's British Winter tour, 1974. Photograph by Storm Thorgerson

The enormous success of *The Dark Side of the Moon* gave Pink Floyd the opportunity to re-develop their stage visuals in 1974. Significant improvements had already been made by Arthur Max, the award-winning production and lighting designer. Max created Pink Floyd's first complete lighting rig in 1972 and now, for the tour of *The Dark Side of the Moon*, he designed moveable light towers (later widely copied) and a 40-foot circular screen that formed a projection surface at the back of the stage. Dubbed 'Mr Screen', it became a defining feature of Pink Floyd shows, and appeared in live performances from the 1970s to the marathon world tours of *A Momentary Lapse of Reason* and *The Division Bell* between 1987 and 1994. Film and animation sequences to be projected onto the screen were commissioned from film-maker Peter Medak and animator Ian Emes. Emes had just created the award-winning film *French Windows*, inspired by 'One of these Days' from the Pink Floyd album *Meddle*. He would go on to design equally influential visuals for 'Time', while Medak, as the main film-maker, worked on sequences to accompany 'Money' and 'Us and Them'.

Pink Floyd and Fisher: 'Nice Ideas'

From 1967, as sales of albums outstripped those of singles for the first time, new creative possibilities opened up and rock music was taken increasingly seriously. The world it inhabited embraced a more avant-garde art spectrum, which was manifested in the cross-fertilization of genres, mixed-media mash-ups and 'happenings'. In 1968, choreographer Merce Cunningham, for example, was creating his piece *Rain Forest* (1968) utilizing Andy Warhol's air-art installation *Silver Clouds* – a series of inflatable silver pillows, which floated about the stage. Pink Floyd deepened their engagement with contemporary architectural theory and performance practice and, like others, were actively connected to the wider spheres of philosophy, art and design.

Adding to their register of notable collaborators, Pink Floyd developed ideas for a dance piece of their own with choreographer Roland Petit. Petit's non-narrative *Pink Floyd Ballet* premiered in November 1972 at Salle Vallier, Marseilles, with the band providing live accompaniment. Though talk of a new musical composition had been mooted in early discussions, the final work was choreographed to an existing Pink Floyd score which included 'Careful with that Axe, Eugene' and 'Echoes'. Blending classical dance and rock, the piece had a lighting design worthy of the band's touring shows.

Architectural developments in air-art and light structures found an important outlet in Pink Floyd's staging. After working in 1971 with Jeffrey Shaw and Theo Botschuijver, Pink Floyd commissioned them to create the first, and now infamous, escapee inflatable pig featured flying above Battersea Power Station on the *Animals* album cover shoot. Concurrently, Mark Fisher, an architecture student at the AA between 1965 and 1971, was developing his own practice specializing in pneumatics and temporary structures. Like Pink Floyd, he drew on a plethora of influences from the wider context of art, architecture and technology. In Fisher, the band found a collaborator who was equipped to help them create and realize their vision.

Fisher studied under Peter Cook of Archigram,[11] an avant-garde architectural collective founded at the AA whose mostly unrealized conceptual designs challenged the perceived need for architecture to be static, instead championing technologically driven, lightweight, mobile environments capable of enhancing human interaction. Archigram (from *archi*tecture and tele*gram*)[12] envisioned futuristic-looking, pop-up and, in some cases, floating cities, which were inspired by the pop art, science fiction and psychedelia of the period. Cook's vibrant collaged *Instant Cities* (1968) imagined a floating convoy of airships designed to deploy entertainment infrastructure – including lights, cranes and sound equipment – to underdeveloped residential towns in order to provide a simulated metropolis of concerts and festivals. Ray Winkler, now CEO of Stufish (formerly Mark Fisher Studio), studied under Cook at the Bartlett School of Architecture in the 1990s. He describes it as an 'an amazing frenzy of creativity where inhibitions were discarded', saying 'it was probably the most highly concentrated bunch of self-motivated people in a building. And with that comes a trajectory of innovation.'

As well as Archigram, a connection to the theoretical 'Fun Palaces' of architect Cedric Price and avant-garde theatre practitioner Joan Littlewood is also evident in Fisher's stage designs. Initially conceived in 1961, the Fun Palace was imagined as a flexible, performative 'building' – a utopian space for entertainment, the arts and societal interaction – which could learn from, respond to and transform for its audience, in order to best serve their needs. Its mechanical gantries, walls and containers were envisaged as a dynamic and ever-evolving meeting place for technology, discussion, leisure and creativity. Although never realized, the Fun Palace model was tested at two events in London: Bubble City (1968) and Stratford Fair (1975). It is also commonly cited as an influence on Renzo Piano and Richard Rogers' Pompidou Centre in Paris (1977).[13]

Developments in materials and technology during the Second World War had given rise to experimentation that made new inflatable structures conceivable. Fisher often spoke about the influence of post-war technology on the world of rock architecture, saying, 'I think that inflatables are the archetypical contribution of the sort of '60s architectural thoughts on this kind of [rock] show because they rely completely on post-war technology for their materials. The kind of materials that were being described by people like Archigram in the '60s which were being used in air-sea rescue and in safety clothing and things like that. These materials effectively make these constructions possible.'[14] Speaking of Fisher's work, his wife and fellow architect Cristina Garcia commented 'I think the idea of temporary architecture was very appealing to him; exploring new materials, new ways of living, that's why he got involved with inflatables and light structures.'

78 · ABOVE · Pink Floyd and choreographer Roland Petit rehearsing the *Pink Floyd Ballet* with the Ballet National de Marseille, 1972/3. Photograph by Thierry Boccon-Gibod. Pink Floyd Archive

Great Gigs in the Sky: Pink Floyd and the Architecture of Rock

79 · OPPOSITE · 'Personal Inflatable Suit', 1970s. Designed by Mark Fisher. Mark Fisher Collection, courtesy of Cristina Garcia

In 1968, *Architectural Design* magazine published a special edition, 'Pneu World', which was edited by Fisher's contemporaries at the AA and captured the experimental trend in inflatables and temporary structures. As well as Archigram in the UK, collectives of architects and artists were experimenting around the world: Haus-Rucker-Co in Austria; Superstudio and the political Archizoom Associati in Italy; and Ant Farm in San Francisco.

The development of geodesic domes, which had begun in Germany after the First World War, drew popular international recognition at both the New York World's Fair of 1964 and the 1967 Montreal Expo with the US Pavilion, designed by American inventor Richard Buckminster Fuller. Famed for their lightness to area ratio as well as their supposed relative ease of building, geodesic domes became a popular self-build dwelling during the back-to-the-land movement of the late 1960s. Like others at the AA, including engineer and soon-to-be collaborator Jonathan Park, Fisher was interested in the work of Buckminster Fuller and also that of German architect-engineer Frei Otto, whose pioneering experiments were often inspired by natural phenomena, utilising lightweight structures, tensile fabrics and adaptable architecture.

Fisher founded his first company Air Structures Design (ASD) in 1969.[15] In 1968 he had developed a transformable pneumatic structure 'Automat' with fellow AA student David Harrison. He later developed this work with his project 'Dynamat' (1971), a collaboration with colleague Simon Conolly. Automat and Dynamat were conceived as user-responsive pieces, which could transform to reflect the needs of their audience. Constructed in prototype form, these pneumatic structures could be programmed to morph into a variety of different rigid configurations to create a series of different user environments.[16]

Following his studies Fisher became a Unit Master, running the AA's 'Nice Ideas Unit' which emphasized the importance of innovative and experimental practice and, as Cristina Garcia puts it, 'encouraged students to approach projects in a completely different way'. At the same time, Jonathan Park directed the Diploma School Technical Studies Department. Park too had been creatively involved with pneumatics, having worked since 1969 on 'MoonRock' at the Roundhouse – an eclectic, multimedia gathering for children involving art, performance, music and inflatables.

It was in the AA office in 1976 that Fisher and Park received a call from Andrew Sanders asking whether they could collaborate on inflatable sculptures for Pink Floyd's Animals / In the Flesh Tour. While Fisher and Sanders focused on the design, Jonathan Park engineered a mechanical motorized system which would allow the structures to 'fly'. An automated programming system was not possible in 1977 so, as Park explains, 'it was all done by hand, eye and verbal communication, not by computerized cues'. This was, in Nick Mason's words, '[Pink Floyd's] first "branded" tour'; conceived specifically to promote the album *Animals*'.[17] As well as the emblematic inflatable pig, Fisher and Sanders expanded on the album's dystopian themes of a flawed capitalist society, designing a larger-than-life inflatable family (a business man and housewife and their 2.5 porky children), orbited by the accoutrements of their 'average' household: a fridge full-to-bursting, a television and a hot-pink Cadillac.

The Band—Victoria Broackes and Anna Landreth Strong

Mark's great success was that he could listen to everybody's ideas ... he understood that it was not just down to one single genius to lead the path to success. It was down to a lot of people with a lot of willpower to hack their way through people who had doubt.

—Ray Winkler

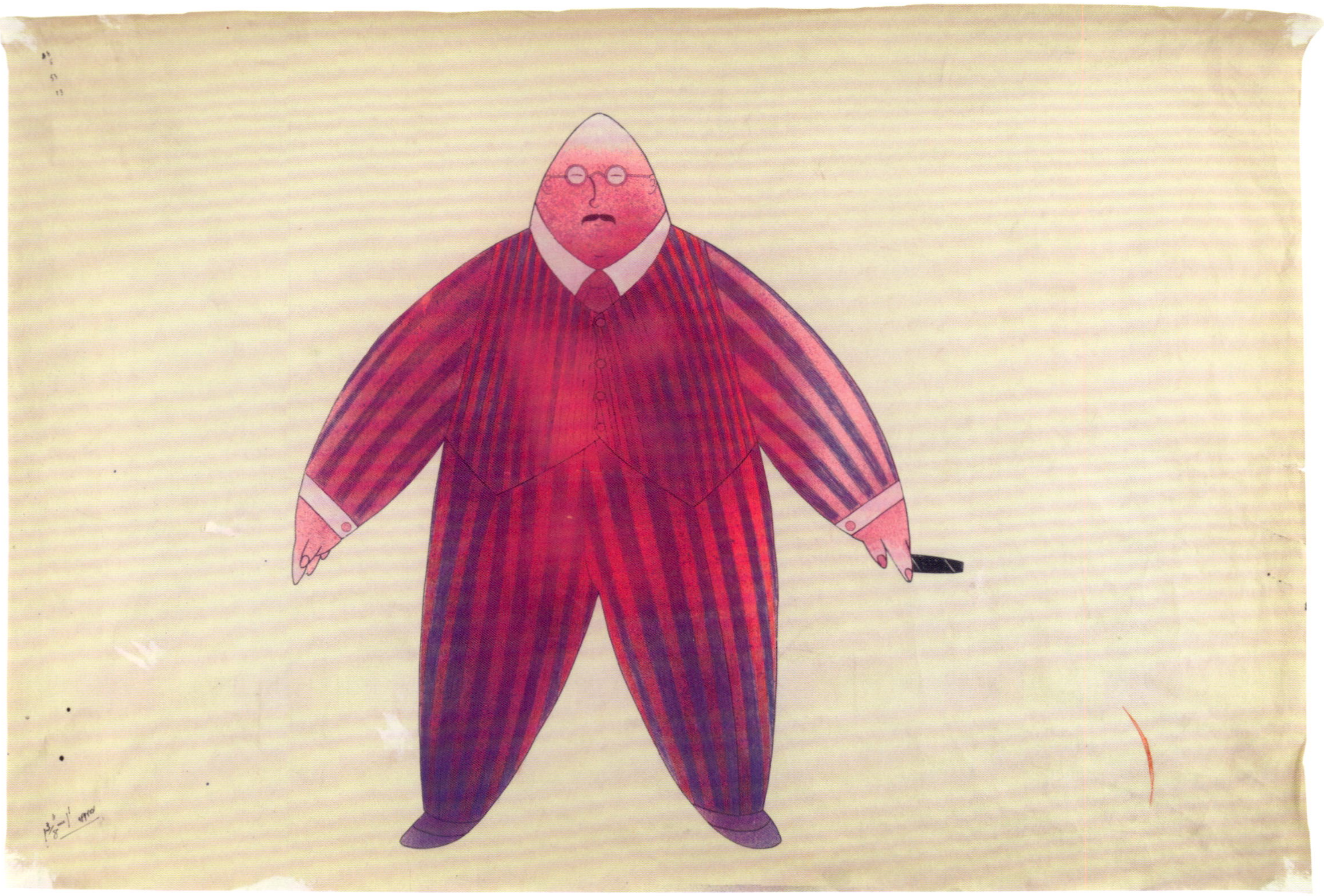

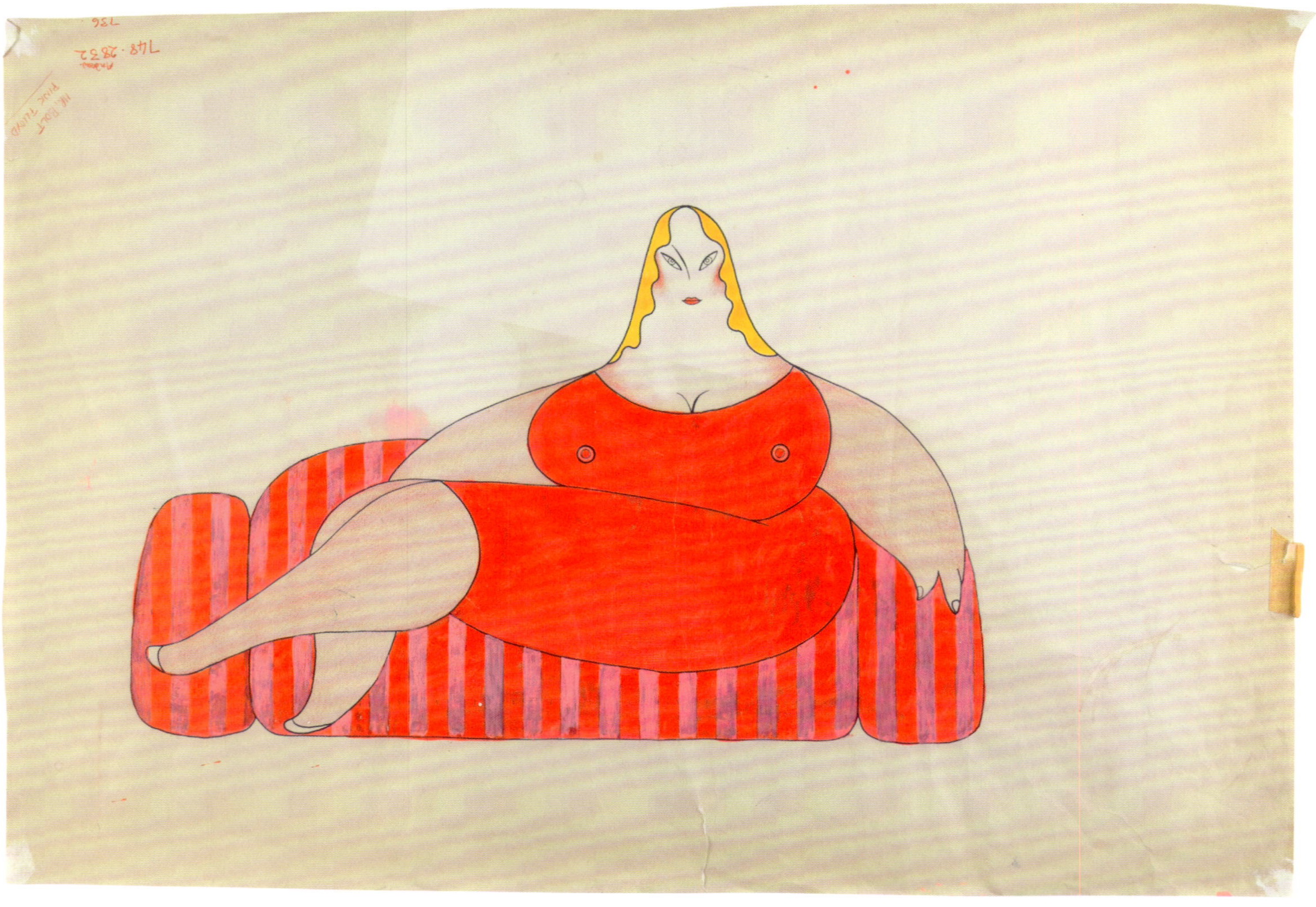

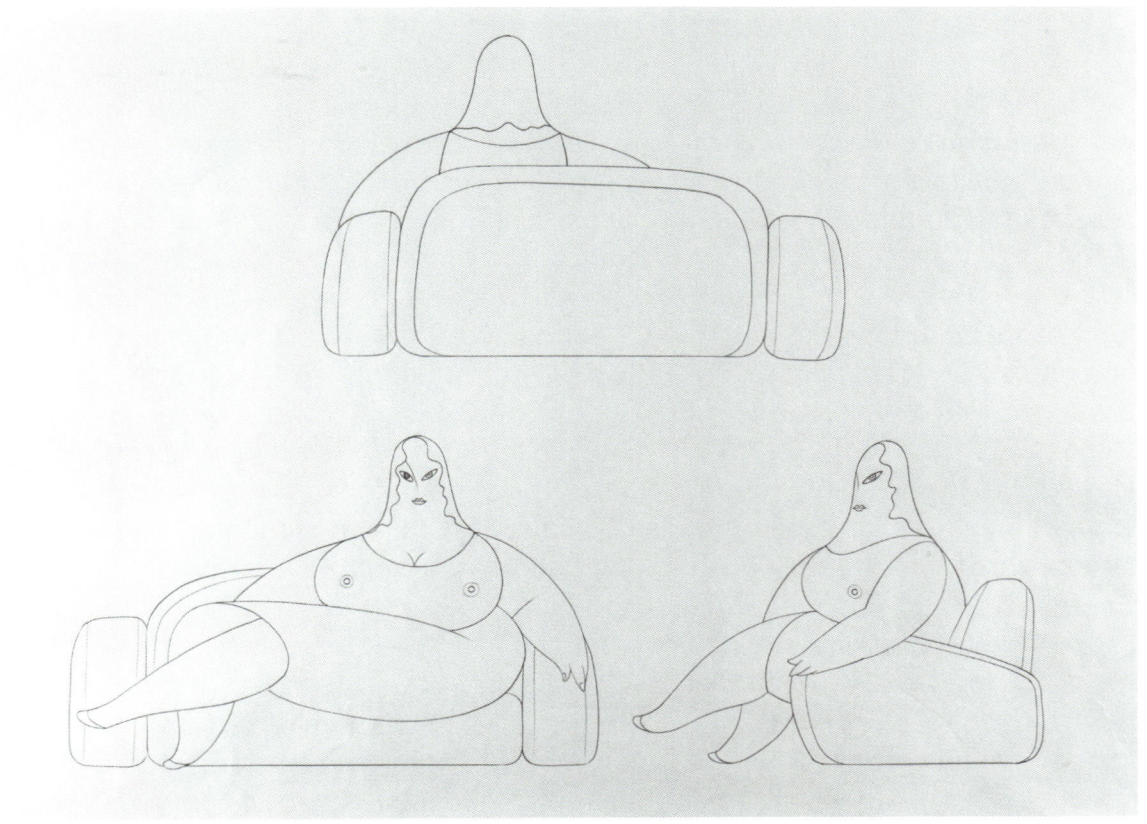

80–81, 83 · OPPOSITE TOP, OPPOSITE BOTTOM, BELOW LEFT · Concept drawings for inflatables commissioned by Pink Floyd for the Animals / In the Flesh Tour, 1977. Andrew Sanders. Collection of Andrew Sanders

82 · LEFT · Inflatables onstage during Pink Floyd's Animals / In the Flesh Tour, 1977. Photograph by Jonathan Park. Jonathan Park Collection

Pink Floyd's shows were second to none, they were the precursors to the MTV generation, where music and vision were inseparable.

—Ray Winkler

Great Gigs in the Sky: Pink Floyd and the Architecture of Rock

84 · OPPOSITE · (Detail) Panel 1 'Introducing Archigram', 1974. This collage features elements from 'The Instant City in a Field' by Peter Cook, 1969, and the 'Self Destruct Environ Pole' by Ron Herron, 1969. V&A: CIRC.472–1974

85 · FOLLOWING SPREAD · Fun Palace promotional brochure, 1964. Cedric Price and Joan Littlewood. Cedric Price fonds. Collection Centre Canadien d'Architecture / Canadian Centre for Architecture, Montreal

Pink Floyd and Fisher: the invention of an industry

In 2012, Mark Fisher gave the address at the Royal Designers for Industry Awards in London, where he was honoured for his pioneering work in the sector. Here, he explains the developments from the 1950s, that made the invention of the stadium tour possible:

> Fifty years of outdoor concerts have seen artists progress from performing in parking lots on the decks of flatbed trucks, to performing in modern sports stadiums on spectacularly elaborate custom-built stages. The positive reaction to Elvis Presley's performance at the Jacksonville Gator Bowl in 1955 marked the beginning of a trend towards larger and larger outdoor concerts that culminated with the half-million audience at Woodstock in 1969.
>
> This trend was made possible by the simultaneous development of four parallel phenomena: the emergence of artists with a massive audience of fans among the post-war 'baby boom' generation; the readiness of fans to see artists perform in non-traditional entertainment venues; the rise of a new generation of concert promoters who were prepared to gamble on bringing artists and audiences together in concerts of unprecedented size. [And] the construction of the Interstate Freeway System, described at the time [1956] as the largest public works programme since the Pyramids. The construction of the freeway system democratized freight movement in the continental USA … and this major investment in the USA made it possible for the invention of the rock 'n' roll tour. The first stadium concert that is really seen as the start of all of this was The Beatles in Shea Stadium in 1965 and it is very different to the way that concerts are done today.[18]

Like their predecessors in Archigram, Mark Fisher, Jonathan Park and their collaborators were working at the intersection of advanced technology and barely imaginable concepts. However, they realized that rock 'n' roll provided the ideal practical and real-world application for big ideas and flexible, portable environments. These ideas found traction with Pink Floyd's innovative approach to staging. As Ray Winkler notes: 'Fisher … could distinguish the important aspects from the unimportant ones and identify the path of getting to the end result – a commercially viable, sexy looking, but entirely practically workable tour.'

Propelled by the creative ambitions of bands and their designers, innovations in major staging components in the 1970s – rigging, trucking and automatic ticketing, as well as sound and video technology – changed the face of the rock 'n' roll tour forever. For the first time, shows were engineered to be able to migrate night after night to different cities, bringing bands' performances to ever larger audiences who began to expect a real spectacle. Unsurprisingly, with both the imagination to create the spectacular and the huge audience base to make it viable, Pink Floyd were at the vanguard of this innovation.

Aside from the memorable inflatables, the 1977 Animals / In the Flesh Tour brought about a significant development to the generic roof structure of rock architecture that had, since Woodstock, been a staple of the stadium show and had been used by Pink Floyd for their 1975 performances at Knebworth. Inspired by Frei Otto and Günter Behnisch's lightweight membrane tented roof structure

There was a connection between Mark and the band that made it possible to work together, because nearly all the band had trained as architects.

—Jonathan Park, engineer and co-founder of Fisher Park design studio

Great Gigs in the Sky: Pink Floyd and the Architecture of Rock

high-level site lighting

long-distance observation desk

circular theatre – part-enclosed

inflatable conference hall

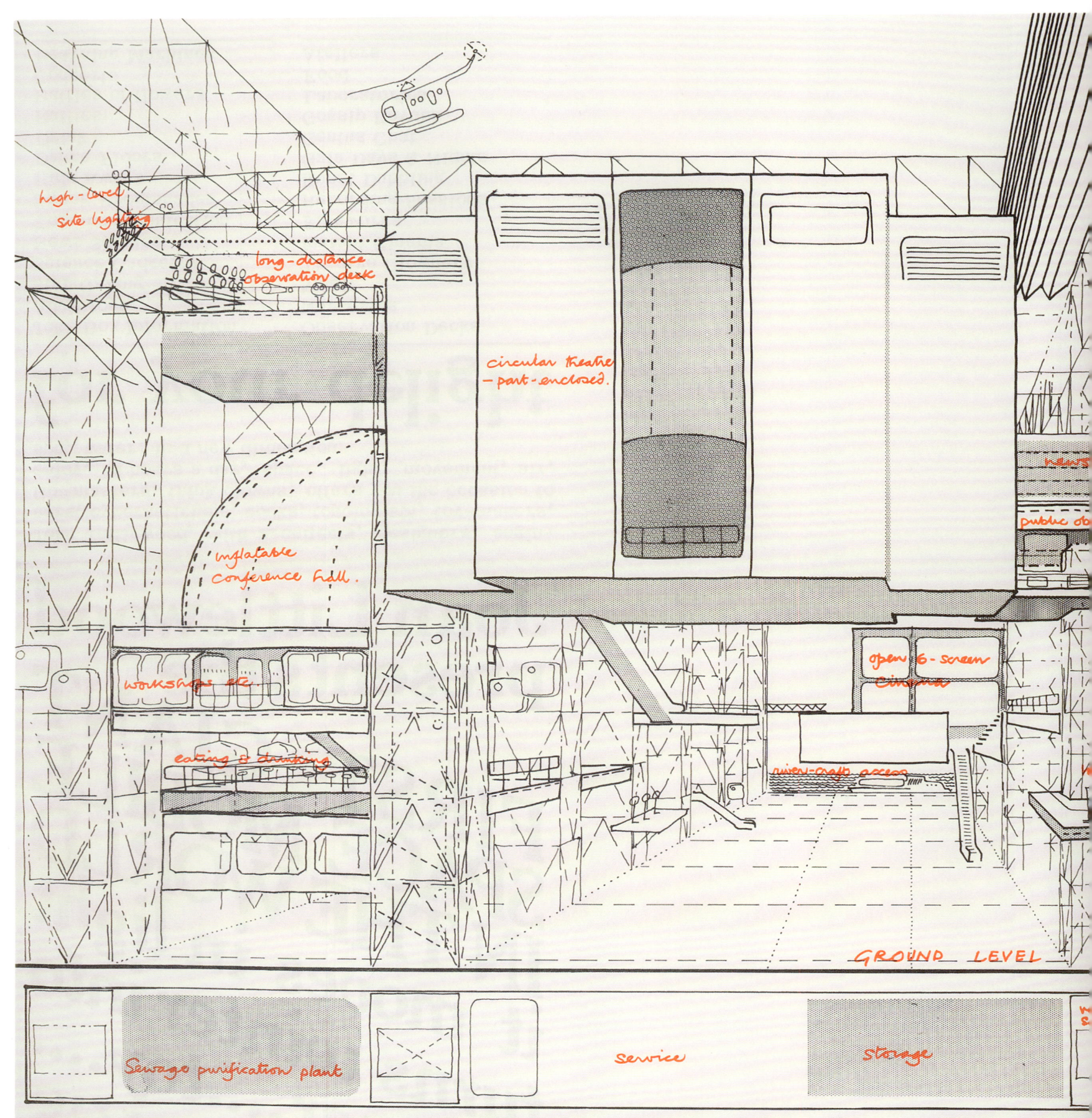

workshops etc.

eating & drinking

open 6-screen cinema

river-craft access

GROUND LEVEL

Sewage purification plant *service* *storage*

ARRIVE AND LEAVE by train, bus, monorail, hovercraft, car, tube or foot at any time YOU want to – or just have a look at it as you pass. The information screens will show you what's happening. No need to look for an entrance – just walk in anywhere. No doors, foyers, queues or commissionaires: it's up to you how you use it. Look around – take a lift, a ramp, an escalator to wherever or whatever looks interesting.

CHOOSE what you want to do – or watch someone else doing it. Learn how to handle tools, paint, babies, machinery, or just listen to your favourite tune. Dance, talk or be lifted up to where you can see how other people make things work. Sit out over space with a drink and tune in to what's happening elsewhere in the city. Try starting a riot or beginning a painting – or just lie back and stare at the sky.

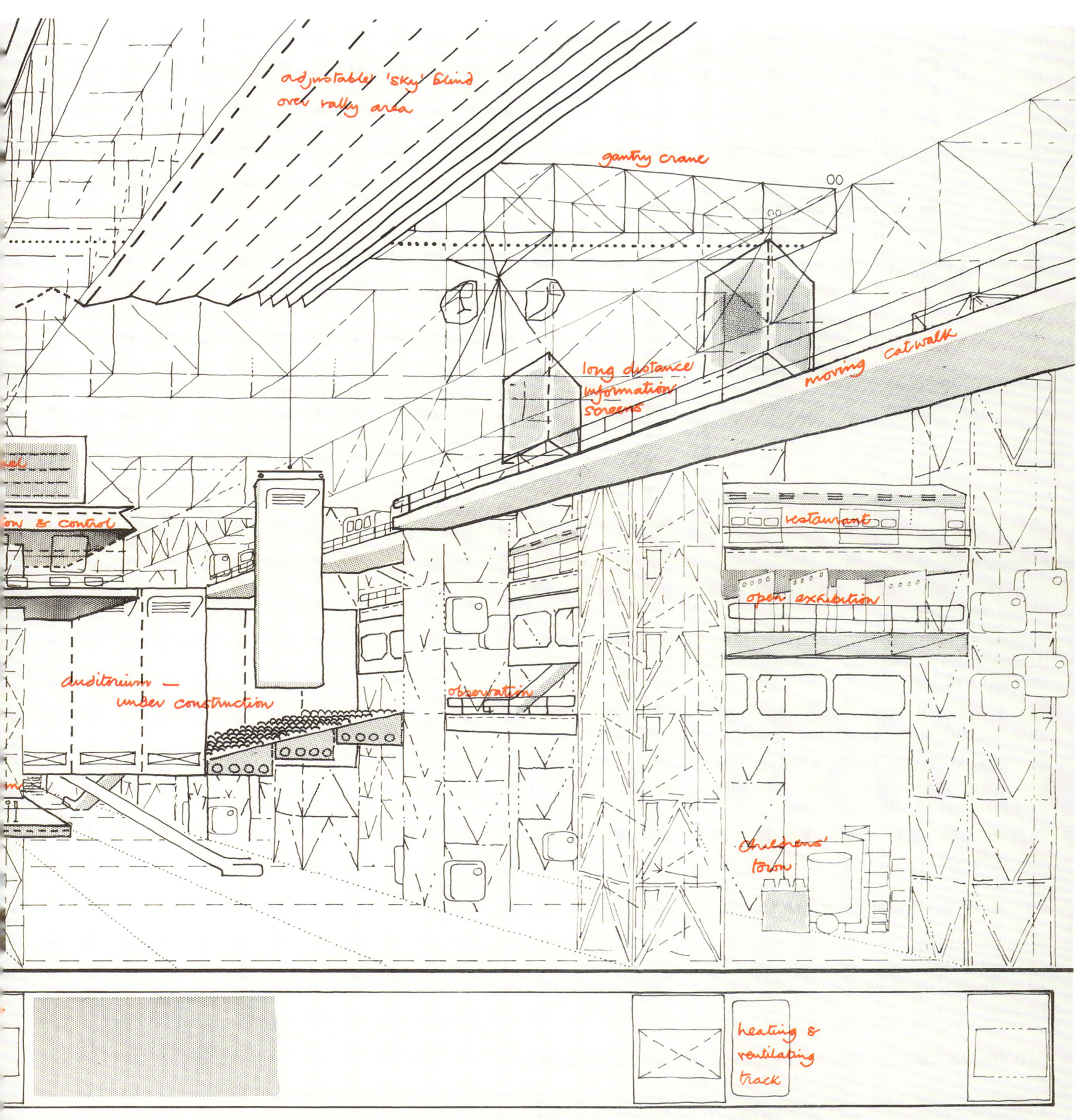

Labels on drawing:
- adjustable 'sky' blind over rally area
- gantry crane
- long distance information screens
- moving catwalk
- restaurant
- open exhibition
- auditorium — under construction
- observation
- childrens' town
- heating & ventilating track

WHAT TIME IS IT? Any time of day or night, winter or summer - it really doesn't matter. If it's too wet that roof will stop the rain but not the light. The artificial cloud will keep you cool or make rainbows for you. Your feet will be warm as you watch the stars - the atmosphere clear as you join in the chorus. Why not have your favourite meal high up where you can watch the thunderstorm?

WHY ALL THIS LOT? "If any nation is to be lost or saved by the character of its great cities, our own is that nation". - Robert Vaughan 1843

We are building a short-term plaything in which all of us can realise the possibilities and delights that a 20th Century city environment owes us. It must last no longer than we need it.

BILL GRAHAM PRESENTS
PINK FLOYD
OAKLAND COLISEUM
MAY 9 & 10, 1977
DESIGN R. TUTEN / W. BOSTEDT / © 1977 BILL GRAHAM / TEA LAUTREC LITHO SAN FRANCISCO

for the 1972 Munich Olympics and Otto's 'Large Umbrellas' at Cologne's Federal Garden Exhibition (1971), the band, working with Otto and engineer Ted Happold (of BuroHappold), sought to create a stage set which rather than being a displaced structure within the stadium was fully integrated with the wider space. They commissioned collapsible umbrellas which provided rain-cover for the stage in what Mark Fisher described as 'quite a subtle approach to the issue of presenting a show in a stadium because it showed an awareness of the existence of the stadium and did not choose to ignore its adjacent architecture'.[19]

Mark Fisher described the significance of the 1977 tour in his career:

> I realized that there was something going on in this business ... It was beginning to create an architecture which was consistent with what the band were trying to do – in the Floyd's case, particularly, developing ideas of a sort of dream world. And after I got back from that tour I did the sort of thing that one does of doing elaborate pictures of other ideas for even more crazy things which I could never get anybody to buy...[20]

The concept for the next Fisher Park–Pink Floyd collaboration came about during a well-documented performance at the Montreal Olympic Stadium at the end of the Animals / In the Flesh Tour, during which Roger Waters felt an escalating disconnect with the band's increasingly large audience. This sense of alienation and the presence of barriers, both imagined and literal, between the band and the audience became central to Pink Floyd's next album *The Wall*.

Fisher Park were approached to realize this concept in the live tour of *The Wall* – to find a spectacular but achievable solution to serve the narrative of the album. As Jonathan Park remarked, the show 'was actually a moving, mobile, theatrical musical'. It featured characters, a storyline, stage effects, puppetry, sleight-of-hand through a decoy band, projected films and an animated, sculptural stage set that evolved throughout the show as, brick by brick, the wall was built between the band and audience.

Not only was *The Wall* innovative in terms of concept and narrative – but the stage set itself broke new ground in terms of the logistics of rock touring to arena venues. As Mark Fisher explained:

> It was a piece of rock and roll touring theatre which was engaging with the [indoor] arena in the same way as I was interested in trying to deal with the stadium – it was actually taking the show and the arena and saying these things together are the experience of the evening – not just sitting looking at a proscenium stage.[21]

Explaining the important place that engineering played in the practical execution of this creative endeavour and its suitability to tour, Jonathan Park describes his work on the project:

> Roger and Mark had come up with the concept for *The Wall* and my contribution was to design everything to make it possible, buildable. I even went to Seattle for a month, working in the Director's Office of Genie Lifts [and] converted their equipment to make 'double lifts' to elevate the platform ... to

86 · OPPOSITE · Poster advertising Pink Floyd's concert at Oakland Coliseum, 9–10 May 1977. Designed by Randy Tuten and W Bostedt. Pink Floyd Archive

PINK FLOYD. THE FILM OF THE WALL. THE TEACHER. MARK FISHER . JONATHAN PARK & GREENWICH AUDIO SERVICES LTD. 1981.

allow the bricklayers to lay the bricks ... Because the bricks were made like boxes from heavy-duty cardboard, you could open them up and they would be rigid, but you could also fold the tabs back so they would lay flat and packable again ... Everything in the show was designed to be transportable, even the custom Genie lifts were designed so you could put two of them side by side in a truck.

The Division Bell Tour was Fisher's first collaboration with the post-Roger Waters era Pink Floyd and was, at the time, the highest-grossing rock tour ever. Fisher worked with lighting and production designer Marc Brickman (the pair had first worked together in 1980 when Brickman transformed the lighting design for The Wall Tour), and stage designer Paul Staples, to conceive and deliver The Division Bell Tour's spectacular set.

Both Staples and Brickman had previously worked together on the world tour of *A Momentary Lapse of Reason* from 1987 to 1988. Among other things, Staples had been the brains behind the *Momentary Lapse* tour's swiftly packable stage and lighting equipment. This development enabled the band to reach more stadiums in less time; a crucially enabling feature on a marathon tour which lasted for 199 performances. Brickman is well known for his acclaimed work with Pink Floyd, although his innovative lighting design spans many sectors including rock, theatre and the illumination of landmarks including the Empire State Building in New York.

87 · OPPOSITE · Illustration of the inflatable 'Teacher' puppet showing the engineering devised by Jonathan Park to make the puppet 'walk', January 1981. Mark Fisher. Jonathan Park Collection

88 · ABOVE · Mobile puppet 'Teacher' onstage during the tour of *The Wall*, Earl's Court, London, 6 August 1980. Photograph by Rob Verhorst/ Redferns

Great Gigs in the Sky: Pink Floyd and the Architecture of Rock

Mark was a great engineer as well as a great architect ... he was very interested in technical issues [and he] pushed the industry – he made the industry go that way. Nobody else had done it before and it changed the way that stages were built.

—Cristina Garcia, architect and wife of Mark Fisher

Other core members of The Division Bell touring team included engineer Neil Thomas, from Atelier One, who constructed the curved half-shell that towered over the stage in a manner reminiscent of the Hollywood Bowl, and production manager Robbie Williams, who joined the Pink Floyd crew in 1973 as an assistant on the *Pink Floyd Ballet* and worked on all of their subsequent tours. The bowl stage was conceptualized by Marc Brickman, and turned into reality by Fisher's architectural genius. Talking of the collaborative spirit that underpinned the design, Brickman said, 'once again we changed the way big shows and spectacles looked, all of us together'.[22]

Working with construction partners from the staging industry, the team sought to modify existing truss components to create a modular and, crucially, a replicable solution for the staging. Ray Winkler talks of the symbiosis between designers, engineers and production teams that bred this industry advancement:

> Mark Fisher pushed Stageco to use their trussing in a different way in order to create an arched roof. He used standard pieces of straight-run triangular trussing and introduced 'wedges' as keystones in the arch. If Mark had not convinced Stageco that this was possible, if Stageco had not had faith that the idea was actually practical, then The Division Bell Tour would not have happened the way it happened, and they would have never have gone on together to build the claw for U2's 360° Tour.

> The Division Bell design was configured to withstand the natural elements, with a base that also functioned as a water-ballast, a smaller secondary roof within the dramatic arch that kept the band and equipment dry, and two imposing towers of audio equipment, which were also used as support pillars. Fisher also conceived a series of high-tech capsule-like 'Band Environment Modules', each automated by scissor lifts.[23]

After the theatrical concept-led staging of The Wall Tour, The Division Bell Tour was, in part, a return to the non-narrative concerts of earlier Pink Floyd. The stage itself served as a backdrop to the band and their music, rather than as an additional cast member. The inclusion of Arthur Max's signature circular screen, initially hidden before being revealed as part of the show, enabled a sequence of films to be projected, enhancing the set-list and transporting the audience into other worlds. Some of the films were appropriated from and referred back to earlier shows, while others were new works by modern-day surrealist and long-time collaborator Storm Thorgerson. Combined with Brickman's design for high-tech gold lasers, colourful oscillating lights and projections of oil and water globules, the overall effect was an impressive, souped-up version of Pink Floyd's early psychedelic spectaculars.

By the time Pink Floyd staged *The Division Bell*, the logistics of stage-show touring had developed significantly. Back in 1980, the original tour for *The Wall* consisted of just 31 shows, although it was prominently restaged in Berlin in 1990 by Roger Waters to mark the fall of the Berlin Wall one year earlier and Waters, in collaboration with Artistic Director, Sean Evans, staged an epic world tour between 2010 and 2013. By the 1990s, rock shows could move more efficiently from audience to audience, reducing the turn-around time and increasing the frequency and speed at which live shows could take place. In his

89 · OPPOSITE · Stage truss tests for the tour of *The Division Bell*, 1993. Pink Floyd Archive

90 · OPPOSITE · Performance from the tour of *The Division Bell*, 1994. Photograph by Mark Fisher. Mark Fisher Collection, courtesy of Cristina Garcia

RDI address, Mark Fisher referred to the legacy of shows like The Division Bell Tour on future touring:

> The logistical and manpower aspects of large touring shows was settling into an operating pattern that prevails to this day. The driving force behind the operation is labour costs ... A typical large production aims to deliver between three and four shows per week in different cities to pay the bills. This is achieved by having three sets of the basic rental steel structure. On any day of the week, one structure is in use, one structure is being built in the next city and the other is being taken down and being moved from the previous city. A universal kit of parts, called the 'universal production' containing all the lights, video, sound and scenery, travels to every city accompanied by a specialist crew. It therefore arrives in the city when the substructure has been completed and has to be put up very fast. This arrangement maximizes the use of rental components, uses the crews efficiently and allows the artist to perform up to four times a week.[24]

Mark Fisher's collaborations with sector-leading peers, with Pink Floyd and other bands, including The Rolling Stones and U2, has contributed some of the most spectacular staging design to the rock 'n' roll industry. His pioneering practice, which married big ideas with only-just-possible technology, has left a legacy which will be felt for many years and seen by audiences the world over.

Finale

Working with artists, designers, photographers and film-makers, and alongside architects, technicians and engineers, Pink Floyd have matched their extraordinary musical catalogue with striking visual imagery that has forever changed the look and feel of rock 'n' roll shows.

The band's ability to interweave music, stagecraft and theatricality has always been evident: from the crumpled bedsheet which provided the canvas for their early liquid light shows, to the giant kinetic sets that thrilled thousands of fans from the late 1970s onwards. They have always been a band whose live performances are not to be missed, and provide audiences with an emotional experience far beyond that of listening to a record alone. Pink Floyd have left a lasting legacy as one of the biggest and most impressive touring bands in the world, who sought out and worked with the best creative teams and individuals in an industry that was itself innovative, new and evolving.

Without Pink Floyd and their creative teams, rock 'n' roll staging would not be the thrilling and inventive art form it is today. With their strong emphasis on visual communication, deep understanding of the multifaceted nature of live performance and ability to inspire and work with talented collaborators, Pink Floyd have been at the forefront of innovation in the rock industry for over 50 years, staging great gigs in the sky.

The way to end any good rock show ... is with some fireworks.[25]

—Mark Fisher OBE, MVO, RDI (1947–2013)

Some days I think, 'what have I done? I haven't built any bridges, I haven't built any huge skyscrapers', but then on the other hand you've designed stuff that is played before millions and millions of people all over the world and they have enjoyed it.

—Jonathan Park

There is no replacement for experiencing a live music event in a space with thousands of other people. Nothing comes close. Audiences expect to see something they have not seen before. They expect to be wowed.

—Sean Evans

91 · **ABOVE** · Drawing showing proposed preset for *The Wall* in Madison Square Garden, New York, June 1979. Mark Fisher. Mark Fisher Collection, courtesy of Cristina Garcia

92 · **OPPOSITE** · Pink Floyd rehearsing in the amphitheatre at Pompeii, Italy, October 1971. Photograph by David Gilmour. Pink Floyd Archive

There will always be a primal need for human beings to be entertained. Always. Whether you're in times of war, or no matter how poor a country is, people will want to be entertained. It is as important as bread, and water, and sleep. And so there will always be some form of entertainment architecture for us to engage with and indulge people with.

—Ray Winkler

THE ALBUMS

SCX 6157

THE PIPER AT THE GATES OF DAWN

SYD BARRETT—LEAD GUITAR & VOCALS
ROGER WATERS—BASS GUITAR & VOCALS
RICK WRIGHT—ORGAN/PIANO
NICKY MASON—DRUMS

SIDE ONE
1. **ASTRONOMY DOMINÉ**
   (Barrett)
2. **LUCIFER SAM**
   (Barrett)
3. **MATILDA MOTHER**
   (Barrett)
4. **FLAMING**
   (Barrett)
5. **POW R. TOC H.**
   (Barrett-Waters-Wright-Mason)
6. **TAKE UP THY STETHOSCOPE AND WALK**
   (Waters)

SIDE TWO
1. **INTERSTELLAR OVERDRIVE**
   (Barrett-Waters-Wright-Mason)
2. **THE GNOME**
   (Barrett)
3. **CHAPTER 24**
   (Barrett)
4. **THE SCARECROW**
   (Barrett)
5. **BIKE**
   (Barrett)

PRODUCED BY: NORMAN SMITH
Recording Engineer: Peter Bown
Front Cover Photo: Vic Singh
Rear Cover Design: Syd Barrett

℗ 1967

E.M.I RECORDS THE GRAMOPHONE COMPANY LTD
HAYES · MIDDLESEX · ENGLAND

Made and Printed in Great Britain

To play this **STEREO** record on a mono reproducer the reproducer should have either a stereo pick-up wired for mono or a suitable mono pick-up. Most pick-ups produced recently will be suitable for this purpose. If in doubt consult your dealer. True stereophonic reproduction will only be obtained from a complete stereo reproducer. To keep this record clean and dust free we recommend the regular use of **NEW EMITEX**.

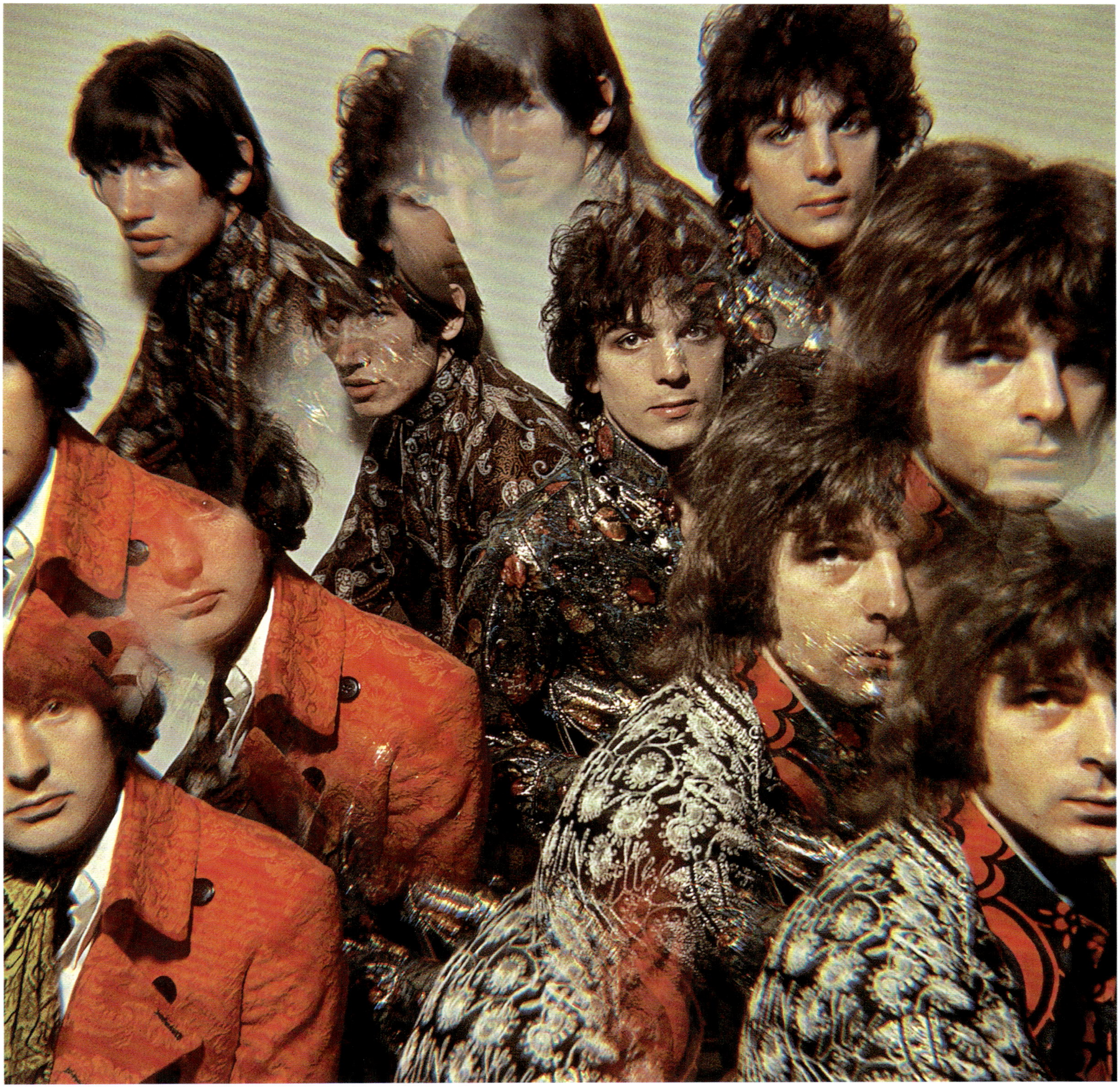

THE PIPER AT THE GATES OF DAWN

August 1967 • UK: Columbia EMI SX 6157 / SCX 6157

93–94 · **PREVIOUS SPREAD** · Album artwork, *The Piper at the Gates of Dawn*, 1967. Front cover: photograph by Vic Singh. Back cover: graphic illustration by Syd Barrett. Pink Floyd Archive

95 · **OPPOSITE** · Recording session for *The Piper at the Gates of Dawn*, EMI Studios, Abbey Road, June 1967. Photograph by Paul Berriff

Pink Floyd's debut album, *The Piper at the Gates of Dawn*, turns 50 in summer 2017. Released in the UK on 5 August 1967, and two months later in America, it gave the wider world an introduction to Pink Floyd and a fleeting glimpse of London's musical counter-culture.

Pink Floyd had been playing at the capital's hippest club, UFO, since its opening night in December 1966. It was here that their sound took shape: a unique synthesis of guitarist/vocalist Syd Barrett's abstract guitar playing, his unconventional songwriting and the whole band's flair for improvisation.

By the beginning of 1967, the English avant-garde's new group had come to the attention of several record companies. Pink Floyd signed with EMI in February 1967, and released their first single and Top 20 hit, 'Arnold Layne', a month later.

UFO co-founder and early Pink Floyd champion Joe Boyd produced the single but was replaced for the album by The Beatles' engineer, Norman Smith. Sessions for *The Piper at the Gates of Dawn* commenced in February at EMI's Abbey Road Studios and continued until June.

In March, the British style magazine *Town* reported on London's counter-culture, singling out UFO and Pink Floyd, 'the underground's house orchestra', for special praise. Onstage, Pink Floyd's signature instrumental 'Interstellar Overdrive', which sometimes lasted for 20 minutes, had become UFO's unofficial club anthem.

The band performed in semi-darkness, its members often obscured by a swirling, liquid light show created with coloured glass wheels, film projectors, slides, various liquids and on some nights chopped-up condoms stretched over the projector to enhance the effect. As primitive as it was, this light show, combined with Pink Floyd's freeform sound, created a multi-sensory experience for the audience.

The challenge facing Smith and EMI was to find the balance between the Pink Floyd that jammed for 20 minutes at a time and bombarded the senses with the Pink Floyd that had just had a hit single.

The group had recently recorded a version of 'Interstellar Overdrive' lasting over a quarter of an hour for the soundtrack to *Tonite Let's All Make Love in London*, advertised at the time as film-maker Peter Whitehead's 'definitive statement on the Swinging City'. On Norman Smith's watch, Pink Floyd compromised with a 9′41″ version for their own album.

150   The Albums

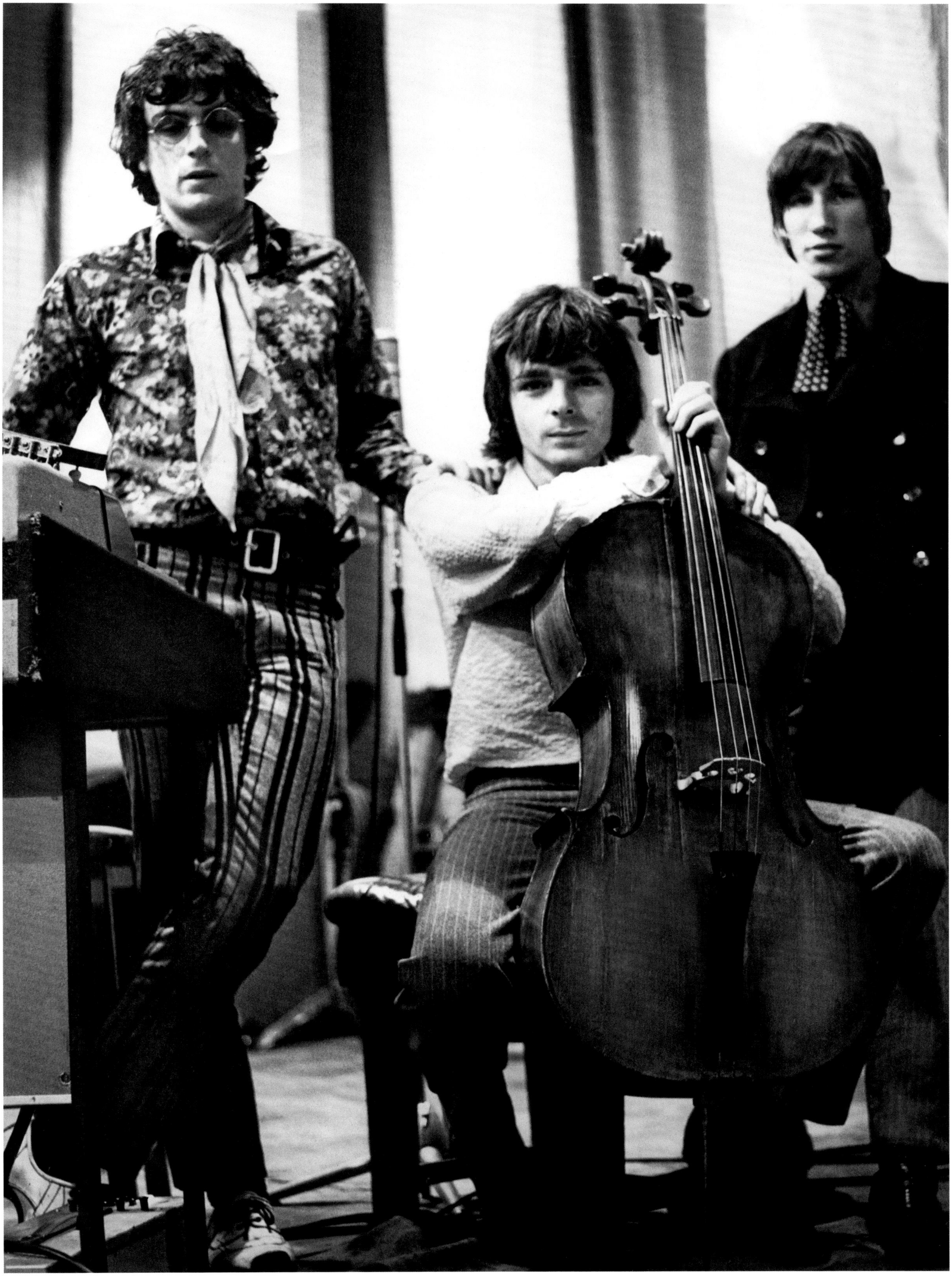

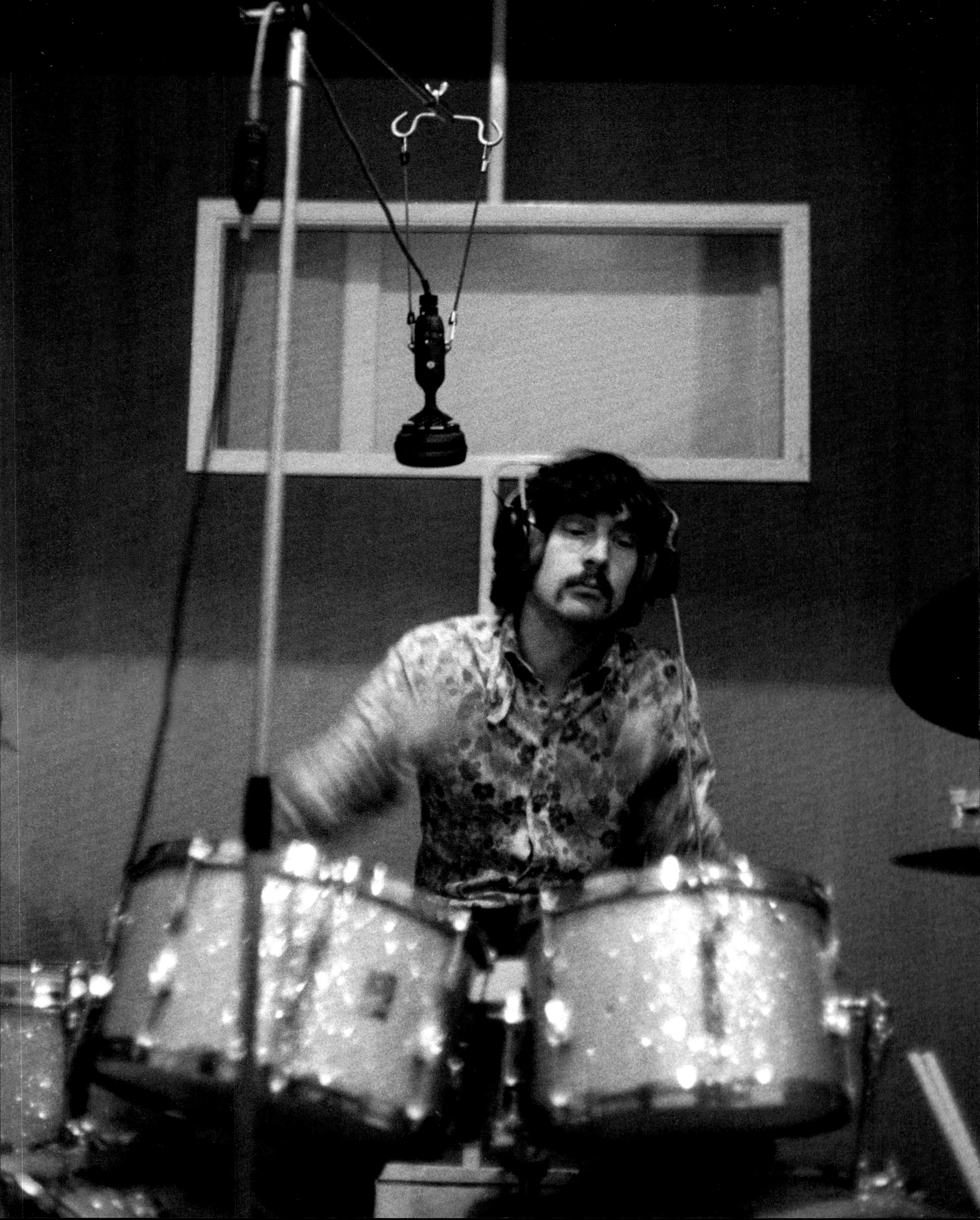

This need for compromise was to drive a wedge between Syd Barrett and the producer. Barrett proved to be a reluctant pop star, hated playing any song the same way twice and would soon start retreating from the group. In the meantime, though, EMI wanted another hit single and Pink Floyd obliged with 'See Emily Play' in June.

The Piper at the Gates of Dawn, while reining in Pink Floyd's onstage excesses, still demonstrated their experimentalism and breadth of sound. While the band made their first album in Abbey Road's Studio Three, The Beatles were crafting their eighth, *Sgt. Pepper's Lonely Hearts Club Band*, downstairs. One afternoon the members of Pink Floyd were ushered into Studio Two to hear an early version of the track 'Lovely Rita'.

The Beatles' album was released that summer and redefined pop music. But Pink Floyd showed a similar spirit of adventure; delving into Abbey Road's sound effects library and using the studio's harmonium, tubular bells, temple blocks and other exotic instruments alongside their traditional bass, guitar, organ and drums. Several songs on the album, including 'Interstellar Overdrive', also used the group's effects box, the Binson Echorec, which soon became part of their signature sound.

Pink Floyd's unorthodox approach began with songs that blurred the edges between pop, R&B, classical and even *musique concrète*. On 'Lucifer Sam' and Roger Waters' composition 'Take Up Thy Stethoscope and Walk', the group twisted R&B guitar riffs into peculiar shapes to create something entirely new.

Many of these songs also drew from Syd Barrett's childhood: the womb-like ambience of his family home, the books he'd read and the Cambridge countryside he'd explored as a boy. The LP's title is borrowed from Kenneth Grahame's *The Wind in the Willows*, and its opening song, 'Astronomy Domine', features the band's co-manager Peter Jenner reciting data from a book about the solar system.

'The Scarecrow', 'The Gnome' and 'Matilda Mother', the last with its references to dolls' houses and fairy stories, were flashbacks to childhood; to Hilaire Belloc's *Cautionary Tales for Children* and Lewis Carroll's *Alice's Adventures in Wonderland*. 'Chapter 24' lifted lyrics from a translation of the I Ching, the ancient Chinese Book of Changes, which Barrett pored over in his flat overlooking London's Cambridge Circus, where some of these songs were written.

The album ended with 'Bike', in which an Edward Lear-style nonsense lyric is spiked with a sound collage of bells, gongs and manic laughter. This was children's poetry meets 'psychedelia', a phrase which became used to describe any art form evoking the mind-altering experience of an LSD trip.

Although Pink Floyd never aligned themselves with the drug culture, Syd Barrett had taken LSD, and the group's lengthy improvisations and disorientating light show were embraced by the UFO audience and others as the ideal backdrop to an acid trip.

Pink Floyd's debut album came in a sleeve with kaleidoscopic band portraits shot by fashion photographer Vic Singh. 'I was introduced to Pink Floyd at a "happening" in Piccadilly near the statue of Eros,' recalls Singh. His first impression of *The Piper at the Gates of Dawn* was that it was 'completely alien and unlike any music I'd heard before'.

Singh wanted an image that complemented the music. He shot the cover photo at his studio near London's Bond Street, through a prism lens given to him by George Harrison. Like the music inside, its split imagery and Pink Floyd's hip boutique clothing, including Syd Barrett's silk Thea Porter shirt, reinforced their otherworldly image.

96 · OPPOSITE · Nick Mason recording at EMI Studios, Abbey Road, 1968. Pink Floyd Archive

The Piper at the Gates of Dawn 153

97 · ABOVE · Recording session for *The Piper at the Gates of Dawn*, EMI Studios, Abbey Road, June 1967. Photograph by Paul Berriff

98 · OPPOSITE · Promotional photographs of Pink Floyd, Ruskin Park, Camberwell, London, July 1967. Photographs by Colin Prime. Jill Furmanovsky Archive

The outlined photograph on this contact sheet is the basis for Syd Barrett's illustration of the group in silhouette on the back cover of *The Piper at the Gates of Dawn*. This was one of Pink Floyd's earliest promotional shoots and was commissioned by their management company, Blackhill Enterprises, to promote the band's first album.

But what was once the counter-culture's open secret had now reached the mainstream press. A *News of the World* 'exposé' about drug-taking at UFO led to the club being banished from its basement in Tottenham Court Road. It closed for good in October 1967.

The Piper at the Gates of Dawn arrived just as the musical underground went into decline, but Pink Floyd's debut would outlast the scene from which it came and, sadly, its principal songwriter Syd Barrett. Fifty years on, it remains a charming, strange and very English pop album: full of light and shade, poetry and whimsy.

The Albums

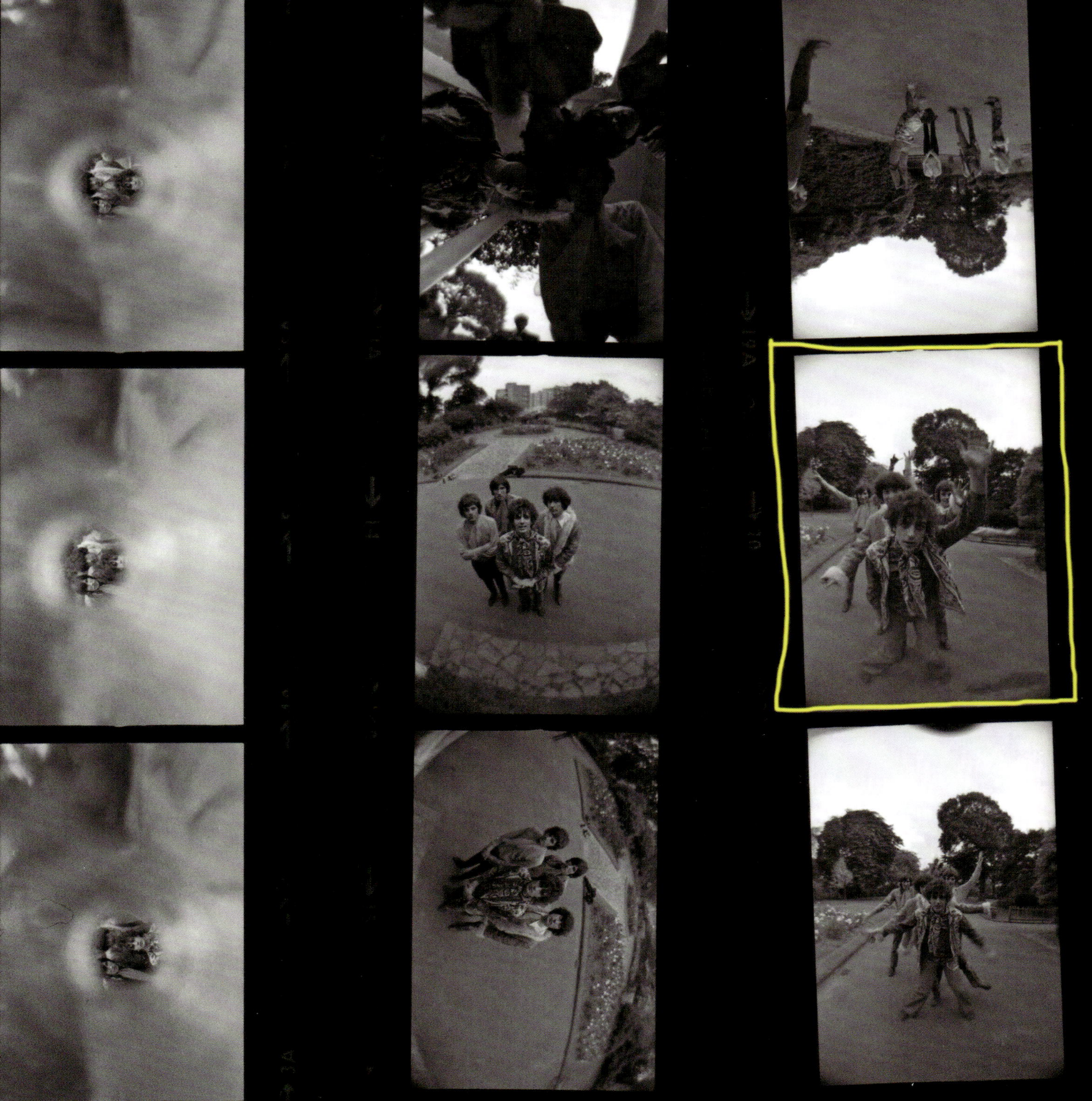

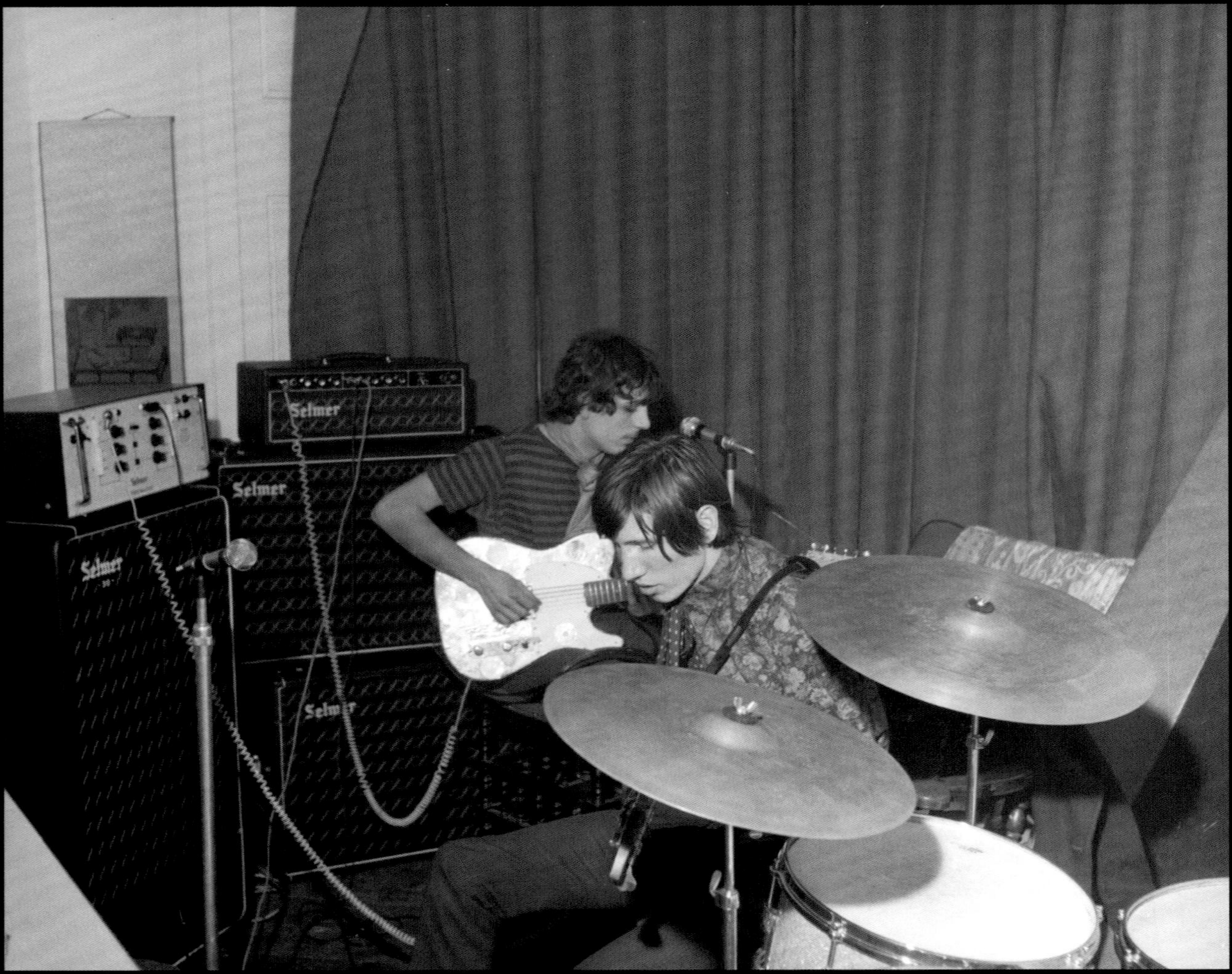
Selmer
Selmer
Selmer
Selmer

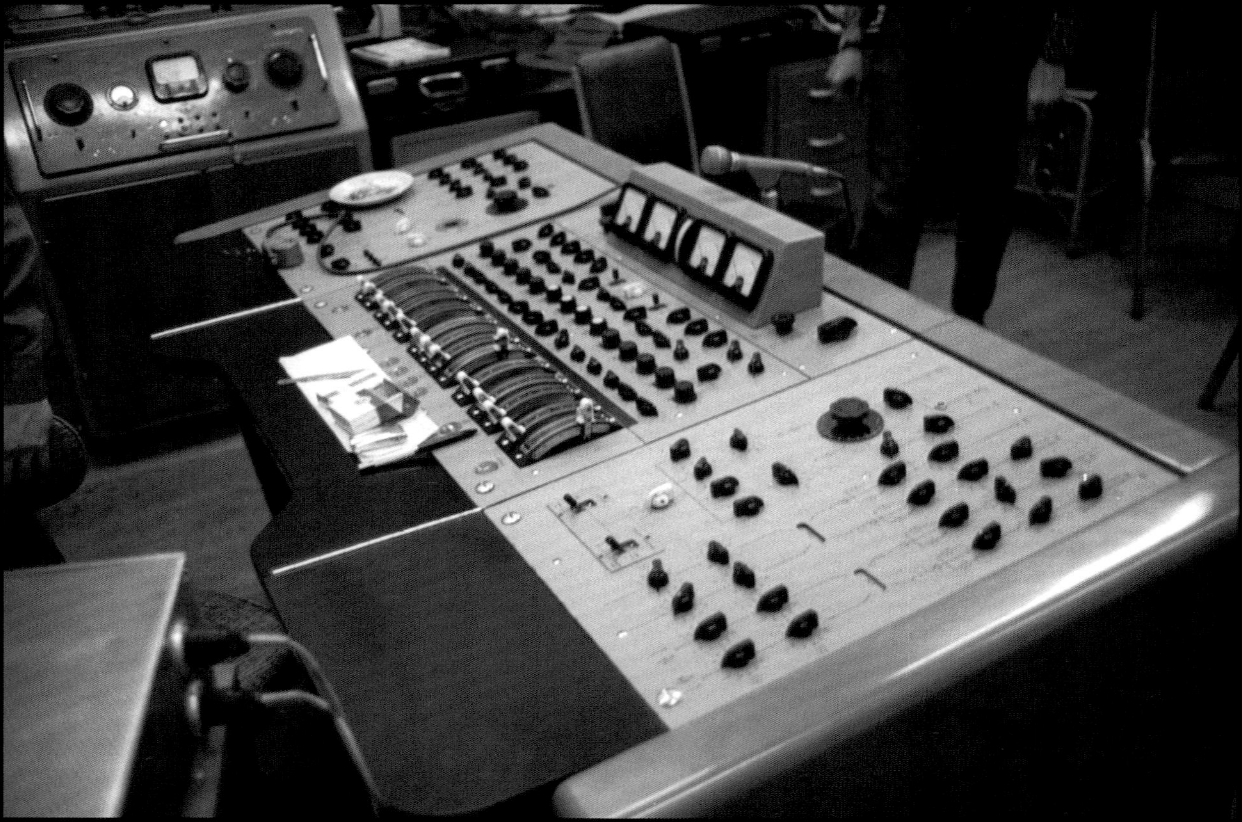

99 · OPPOSITE TOP · Roger Waters and Syd Barrett in rehearsal at the offices of Blackhill Enterprises, 41 Edbrooke Road, Maida Vale, London, January 1967. Photograph by Irene Winsby

Syd Barrett plays his mirrored Fender Esquire in this rehearsal session for 'Candy and a Currant Bun', the B-side of 'Arnold Layne'. Photographer Irene Winsby was called back for a second shoot by the band's co-manager Peter Jenner, who told her that the band would have 'tidied up' their appearance in the meantime.

100 · OPPOSITE BOTTOM · EMI REDD.51 'Stereosonic' four-track mixing console used for the recording of *The Piper at the Gates of Dawn*, EMI Studio 3, Abbey Road, London, about 1967. Designed by the Record Engineering Development Department (REDD) at Abbey Road, led by Len Page. Photograph by Nick Mason. Pink Floyd Archive

101 · RIGHT · Fender Esquire guitar with mirrored body. Replica of a 1960s guitar owned by Syd Barrett. Constructed by Phil Taylor, 2014. Pink Floyd Collection

Syd Barrett decorated his 1962 Fender Esquire guitar with silver Mylar reflective sheeting and polished metal circles. Its mirrored surface reflected and enhanced the mesmerizing effects of Pink Floyd's light show onstage. The original guitar is now lost.

The Piper at the Gates of Dawn

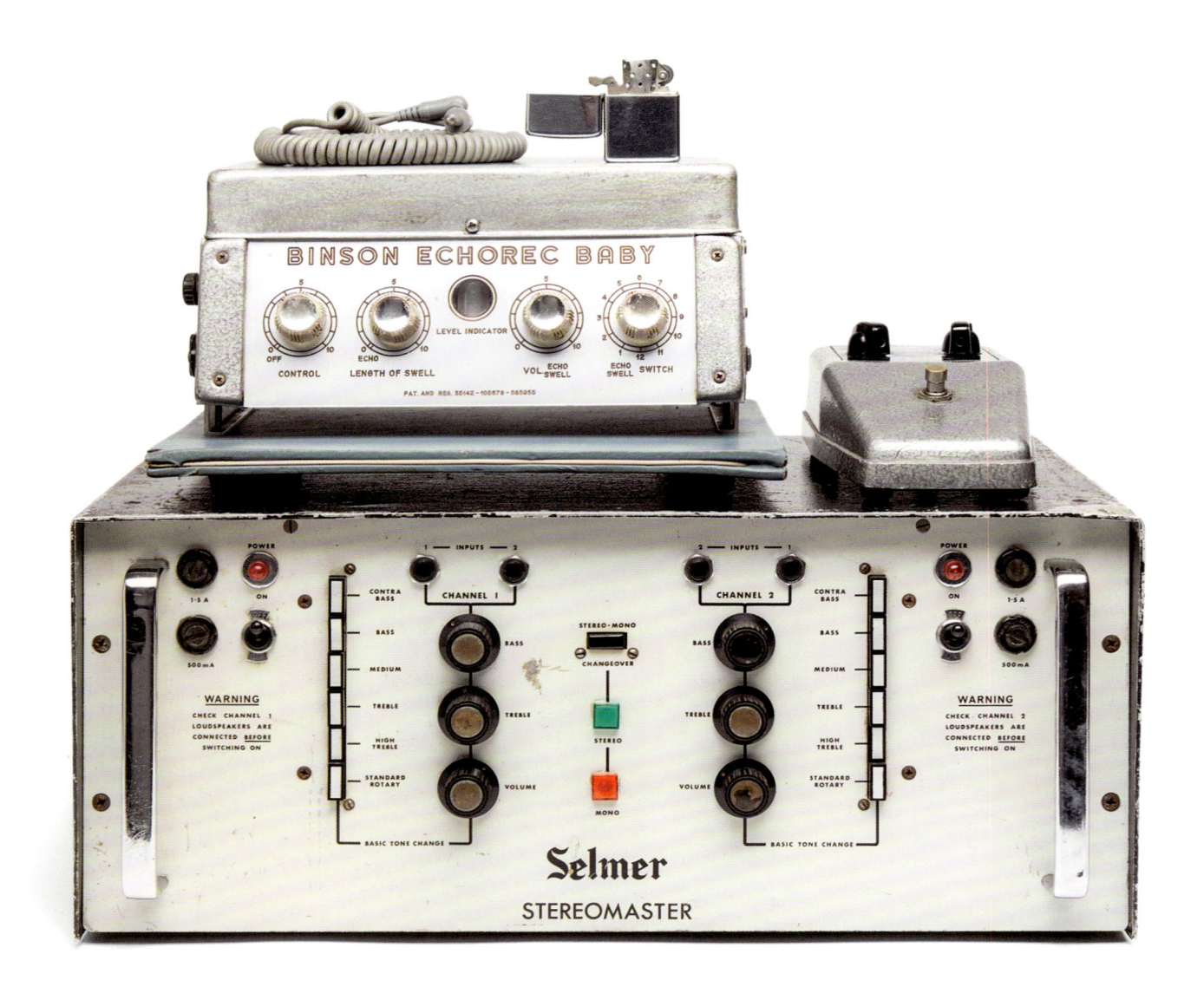

102 · ABOVE · Selmer Stereomaster amplifier, Binson Echorec Baby, 1967, Vox pedal and Zippo lighter, 1960s. Pink Floyd Collection

Selmer Stereomaster amps were used by members of Pink Floyd from 1966 onwards. Syd Barrett fed his guitar sound into a Binson Echorec Baby, an expensive and cutting-edge echo machine. Echorecs were central to the early Pink Floyd sound and the band used various models, including the Baby and the T5E. Syd also created experimental sounds by using his Zippo lighter as a guitar slide; a trick possibly inspired by Keith Rowe of the band AMM.

103 · OPPOSITE · Farfisa Compact Duo organ with power supply and gold Binson Echorec T5E, 1960s. Pink Floyd Collection

Richard Wright purchased this Farfisa Compact Duo organ in 1966 and played it as late as 2006. Its signal was passed into a Binson Echorec to create echo and delay sound. Nick Mason comments: 'Rick's Farfisa Duo – at a time when other keyboard players would probably have been using a Hammond organ or Vox Continental – was renowned for producing an extremely distinctive sound, which contributed to our overall sonic character.'

The Piper at the Gates of Dawn

104 · TOP · Peter Jenner, Peter Wynne Willson and audience watching Pink Floyd perform at the UFO club, London, December 1966. Photograph by Adam Ritchie

Pink Floyd played regularly at the short-lived but legendary counter-cultural venue, the UFO club, between 1966 and 1967. Their lengthy improvisations and swirling light show added to the club's otherworldly atmosphere. The band's co-manager, Peter Jenner, and lighting designer Peter Wynne Willson can be seen on the left in this photograph.

105 · BOTTOM · Entrance to the UFO club, London, December 1966. Photograph by Adam Ritchie

106 · OPPOSITE · Poster for *The Piper at the Gates of Dawn*, about 1967. Published by For Posters Ltd. V&A: E.31–1968

If we have to have some kind of definition you could say we are lights and sounds. The two mediums complement each other and we definitely don't use them together as a gimmick. Our aim is simply to make the audience dig the effect.

—Interview with Pink Floyd, *Record Mirror*, 25 March 1967

160   The Albums

DAWN PIPER AT THE GATES OF

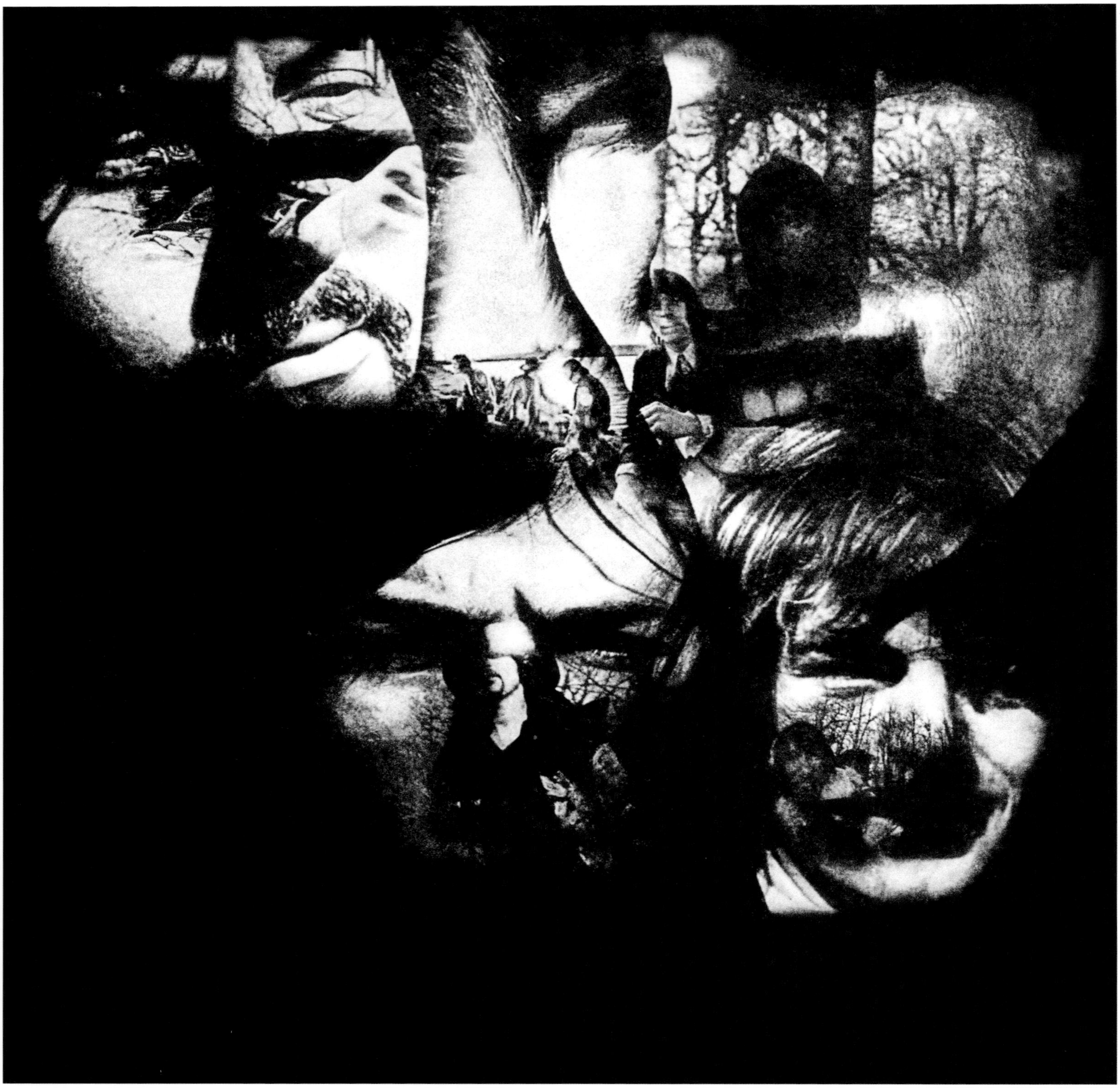

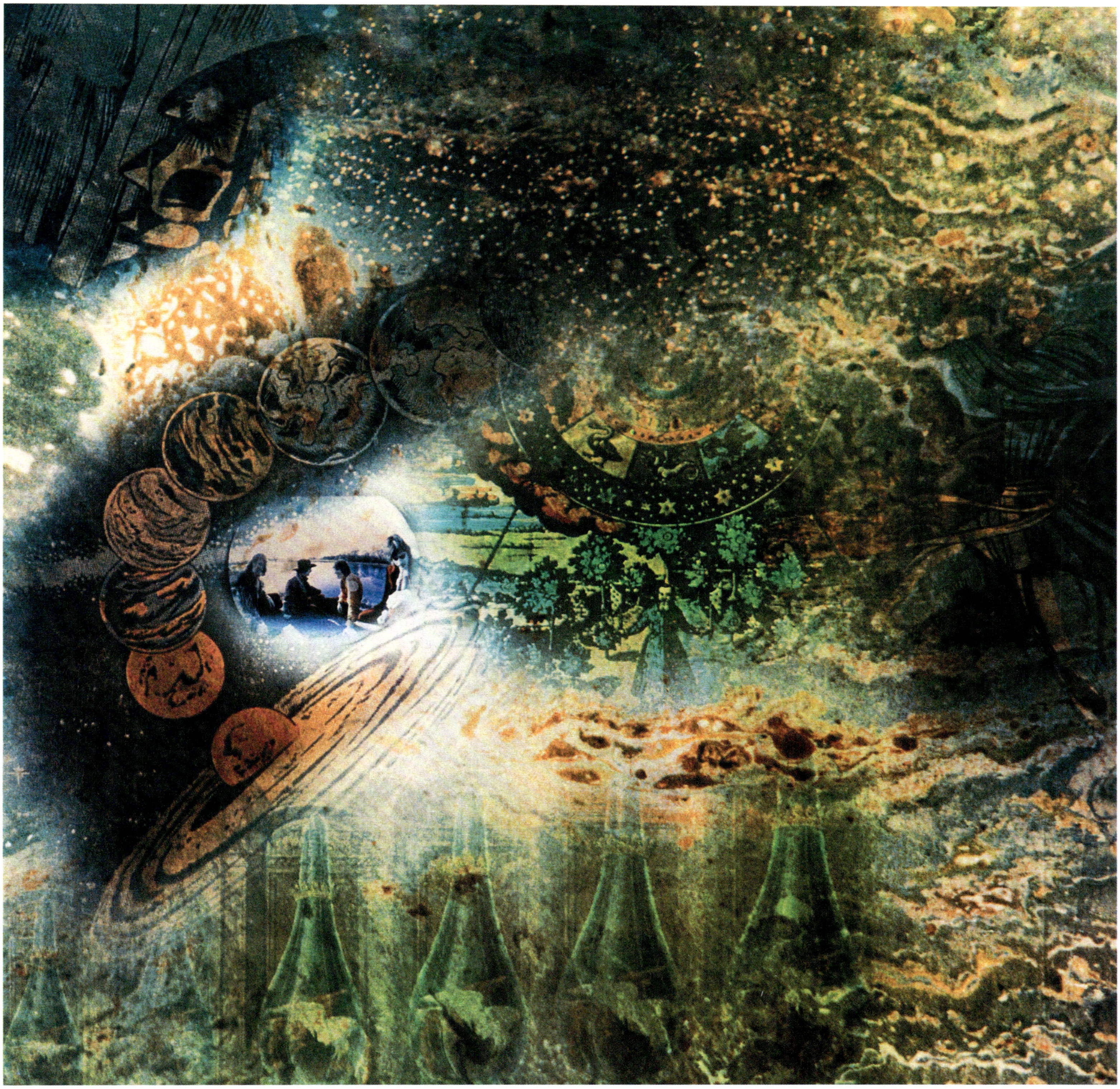

A SAUCERFUL OF SECRETS

June 1968 • UK: Columbia EMI SX 6258 / SCX 6258

107–108 · PREVIOUS SPREAD · Album artwork, *A Saucerful of Secrets*, 1968. Design and photographs by Storm Thorgerson / Aubrey Powell at Hipgnosis

109 · OPPOSITE · Sleeve photograph for *A Nice Pair* (double album re-release of *A Saucerful of Secrets* and *The Piper at the Gates of Dawn*), 1973. Photograph by Aubrey Powell at Hipgnosis. Pink Floyd Archive

This photograph shows Iain 'Emo' Moore, a friend of the band and sometime roadie, wearing a pair of 'psychedelic goggles' or 'cosmonocles' devised by Pink Floyd's first lighting designer Peter Wynne Willson: welder's goggles with coloured lenses and a glass prism inside each lens added to distort the view. The photograph was taken by Aubrey Powell in his own flat, reputedly without any extra set dressing.

A Saucerful of Secrets is a musical story of transition and change. The only Pink Floyd album to include both Syd Barrett and David Gilmour, it is the sound of a group in a state of flux but already finding a new direction.

The late Storm Thorgerson, who helped design the album artwork, once described its collage of superimposed images as 'indicating the lessening of boundaries between states'.[1] *A Saucerful of Secrets* is a collision of overlapping ideas and influences.

These are songs with themes, settings and characters as disparate as medieval Chinese poetry, outer space, the eleventh-century Saxon rebel Hereward the Wake and the fenlands surrounding Syd Barrett, David Gilmour and Roger Waters' home city of Cambridge.

However, by the time Pink Floyd's second LP was released in early summer 1968, Syd Barrett was no longer part of the group. Pink Floyd's frontman was a more fragile character than his bandmates, and this had only increased with the group's success. Barrett's use of LSD also contributed to his mental decline.

Syd was still there when Pink Floyd started recording *A Saucerful of Secrets* in August 1967, but only one of his compositions would survive. The song, 'Jugband Blues', included a Salvation Army marching band, instructed by Syd to play whatever they fancied, until producer Norman Smith intervened.

Yet the playfulness of nursery-rhyme-like songs such as 'Bike' from *The Piper at the Gates of Dawn* was replaced by lyrics that hinted at their composer's troubled mindset. *'What exactly is a dream./ And what exactly is a joke.'* sang Barrett at the end of 'Jugband Blues'. The question would remain unanswered.

'Apples and Oranges', a slight pop song and Syd Barrett's final Pink Floyd single, was released in November, but failed to match the success of 'See Emily Play'. Soon after, David Gilmour, another of Barrett's childhood friends from Cambridge, was invited to join the group, partly as a stabilizing influence for Syd. For a very short time, Pink Floyd performed as a five-piece. But Barrett's erratic live performances continued, and by the end of January 1968, the group decided to continue without him.

It was in this new and uncertain environment that much of *A Saucerful of Secrets* was created. With their principal songwriter gone, it was primarily Roger Waters, but also Richard Wright who filled the void. Between them, they composed songs that strove to replicate Barrett's very English style of writing, but which ended up exploring new musical ideas.

164   The Albums

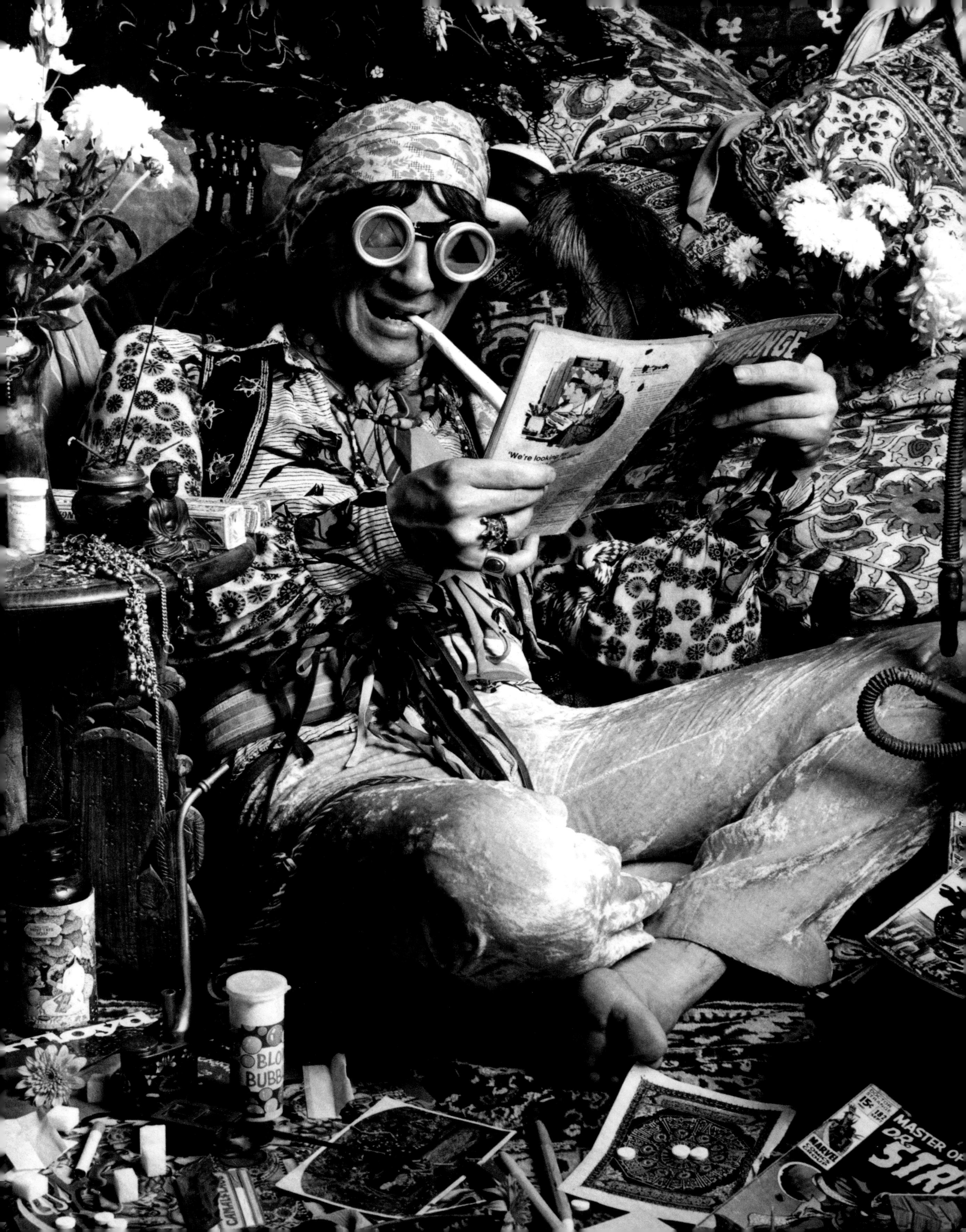
"We're looking
MASTER OF
MARVEL

FROM ENGLAND
PINK FLOYD
INITIAL SHOCK
A.B. SKHY BLUES BAND
JERRY ABRAMS HEADLIGHTS
SOUND FACTORY
AUGUST 16·17
1217 ALHAMBRA 9·1
$3.00 SACRAMENTO
TICKET OUTLETS: Sacramento - All Tower locations, Jack's House of Music, The Tape Shop, Village Records, Bruener's Box Office, The Eye, All College Hi Shops; Davis - U.C. Corner; Woodland - Bender's Music; Marysville - Sievwright's Music; Stockton - Weberstown Box Office, Miracle Music; Roseville - Roseville Records, Roseville Music.
PARK UNDER THE FREEWAY AT 29TH & L STREETS
san andreas fault · san francisco · 1968 ·

Richard Wright offered the delicate psychedelic pop of 'See-Saw' and 'Remember a Day'; Waters composed 'Corporal Clegg', a commentary on the brutality and futility of war, a theme he would return to many times as a writer.

In contrast, 'Let There Be More Light', with lyrics inspired by alien visitations, English history and the Cambridge fens, and 'Set the Controls for the Heart of the Sun' (with words borrowed from A.C. Graham's translated *Poems of the Late T'ang*) were more experimental works. The last is the only Pink Floyd song to feature both Syd Barrett and David Gilmour playing guitar. This experimentation peaked with the multi-part title track, composed by the whole group, in which dissonant special effects and feedback were deployed alongside conventional instruments.

It was this new music that would define Pink Floyd in 1968. 'Set the Controls for the Heart of the Sun' was among the new works performed by the group in May at the First European International Pop Festival in Rome. It was here on the continent, in underground music strongholds such as Paradiso in Amsterdam, that Pink Floyd found an audience eager to embrace their unconventional new sound.

A Saucerful of Secrets was released in June 1968 and reached the Top 10 in the UK. It was the first Pink Floyd album featuring artwork by Hipgnosis, a newly formed design studio launched by friends Storm Thorgerson and Aubrey 'Po' Powell.

Pink Floyd were adamant they didn't want their photograph on the cover, but EMI insisted otherwise. As a compromise, Powell shot the band in infra-red on London's Hampstead Heath but surrounded the picture with a collage of what he calls 'cosmic swirls'. 'Peter Blake's cover for *Sgt. Pepper* [in 1967] was a huge influence on us,' he says. 'It made us realize we could do something different, rather than a portrait of a group. We wanted to break away from the images of David Bailey or Gered Mankowitz's photographs of The Rolling Stones.'

Hipgnosis created a hand-tinted collage that reflected both theirs and Pink Floyd's fascinations at the time: 'Marvel comics featuring the wonderful stories of Stan Lee and the character Dr Strange, alchemy, flying saucers. It was the era of Druids, astrology, the author John Michell and his theories about ley lines [as explored in Michell's 1967 book, *The Flying Saucer Vision: The Holy Grail Restored*]. We wanted to blend all these elements together.'

A Saucerful of Secrets captured a moment in time; the music within as multi-layered as the image on the cover.

110 · **OPPOSITE** · Concert poster, Sound Factory, Sacramento, 16–17 August 1968. Designed by San Andreas Fault. Pink Floyd Archive

The best outdoor event that I've ever been to was the Pink Floyd concert in Hyde Park, when I hired a boat and rowed out [on the Serpentine], and I lay in the bottom of the boat ... and just listened to the band play, and their music then, as I think, suited the open air perfectly ... they just seemed to fill the whole sky.

—Interview with John Peel, 'The Pink Floyd Story', Capital Radio, 24 December 1976

111–114 · THIS SPREAD · Pink Floyd onstage at the 'Midsummer High Weekend', The Cockpit, Hyde Park, London, 29 June 1968. Photographs by Ray Stevenson

Pink Floyd headlined the first official free Hyde Park gig, which was organized by their management company Blackhill Enterprises. DJ John Peel was among the audience of thousands. Roy Harper, also on the line-up, joined Pink Floyd onstage to play cymbals on 'A Saucerful of Secrets', the title track from the album released on the previous day.

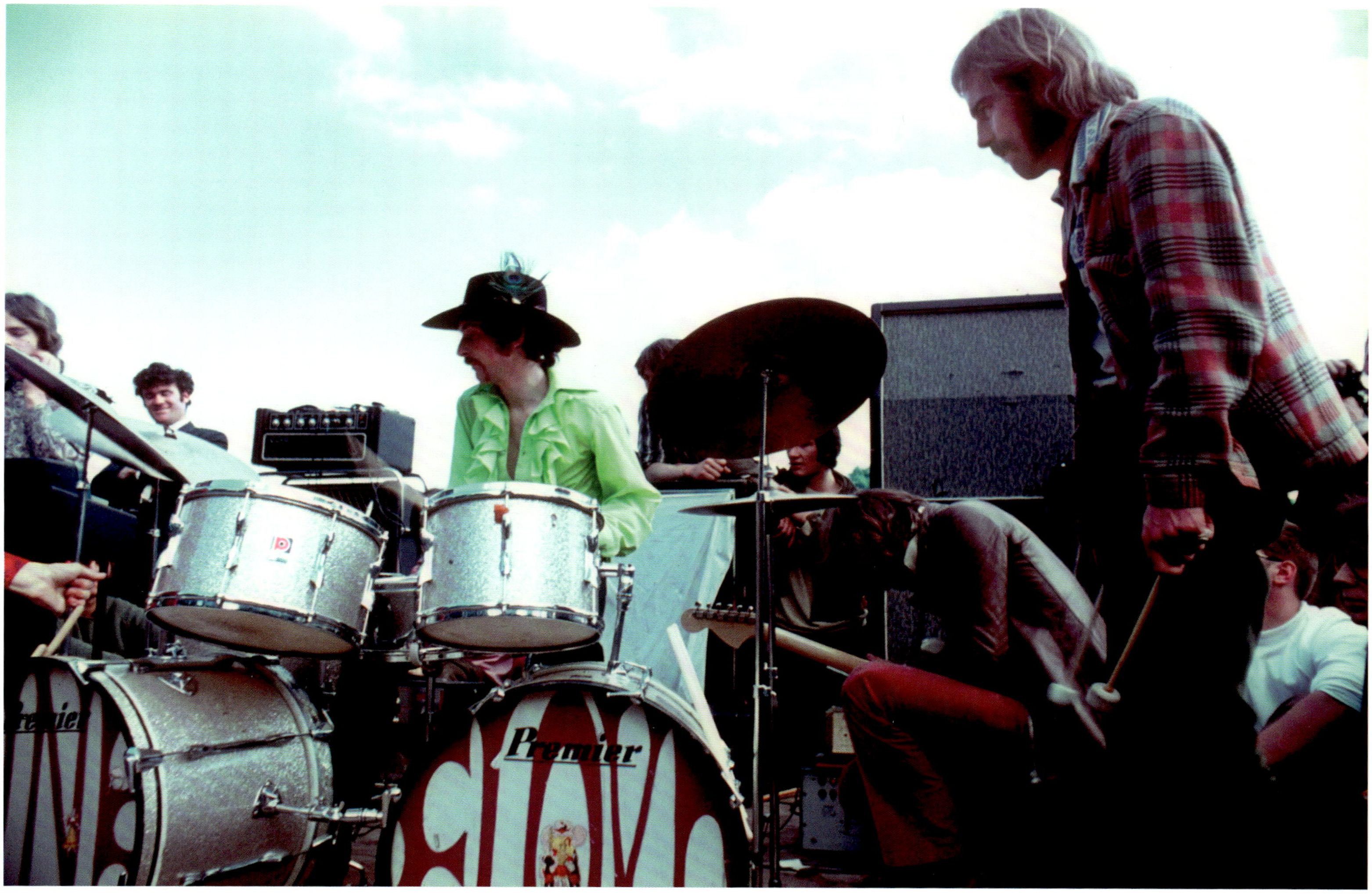
Premier

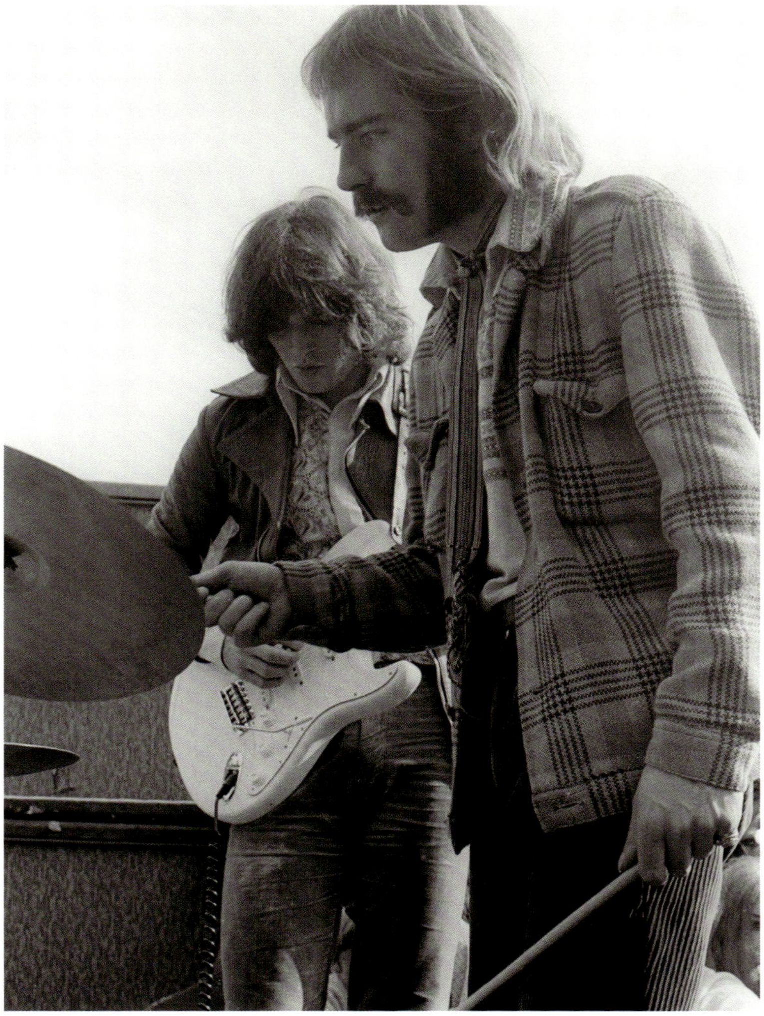

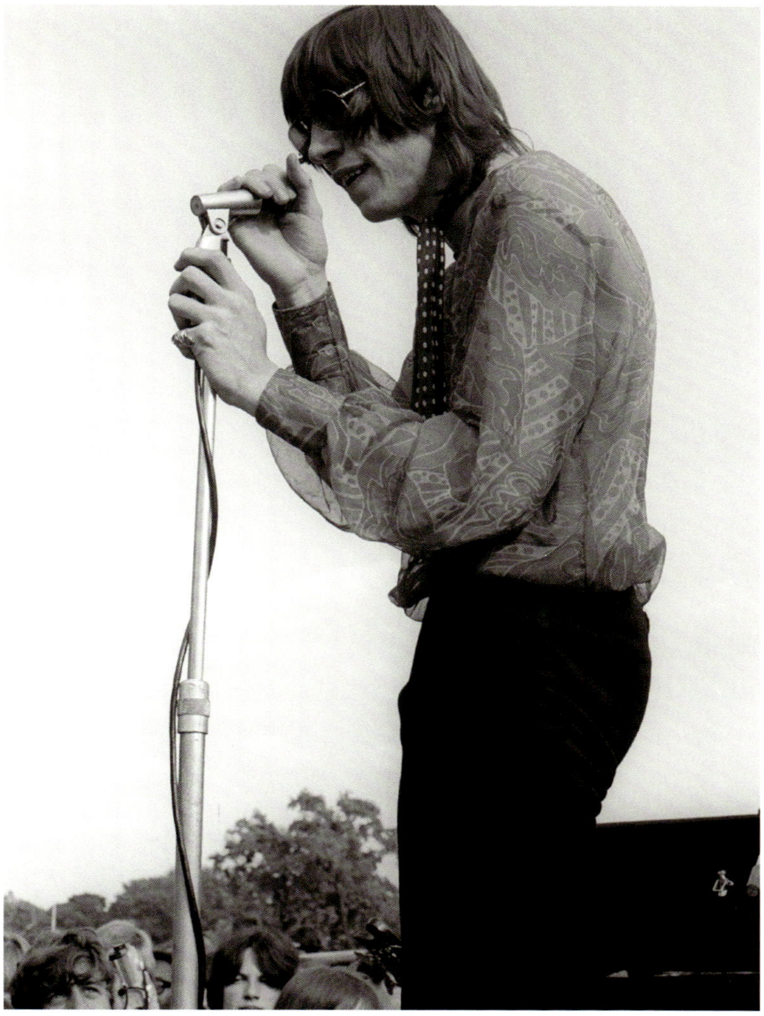

115 · ABOVE · Pink Floyd on Hampstead Heath, London, 1968. Photograph by Storm Thorgerson / Aubrey Powell at Hipgnosis

116 · OPPOSITE · Concert poster, Avalon Ballroom, San Francisco, 2–4 August 1968. Designed by Bob Schnepf and Jerry Wainwright. Pink Floyd Archive

Pink Floyd's second US tour coincided with the release in America of *A Saucerful of Secrets*. A review of the closing gig in Los Angeles described the band's 'wall of electronic gadgetry'. A brief recording session in Capitol Studios, LA, was also fitted into the tour but the tapes were never released. The band continued touring in the UK and Europe until recording sessions for *Ummagumma* began in mid-December 1968.

Unless you have a light show of your own – just close your eyes and turn your amplifier fully on, and your parents fully off, by putting A Saucerful of Secrets *on.*

—Pink Floyd gig review, *Fifth Estate*, July 1968

170   The Albums

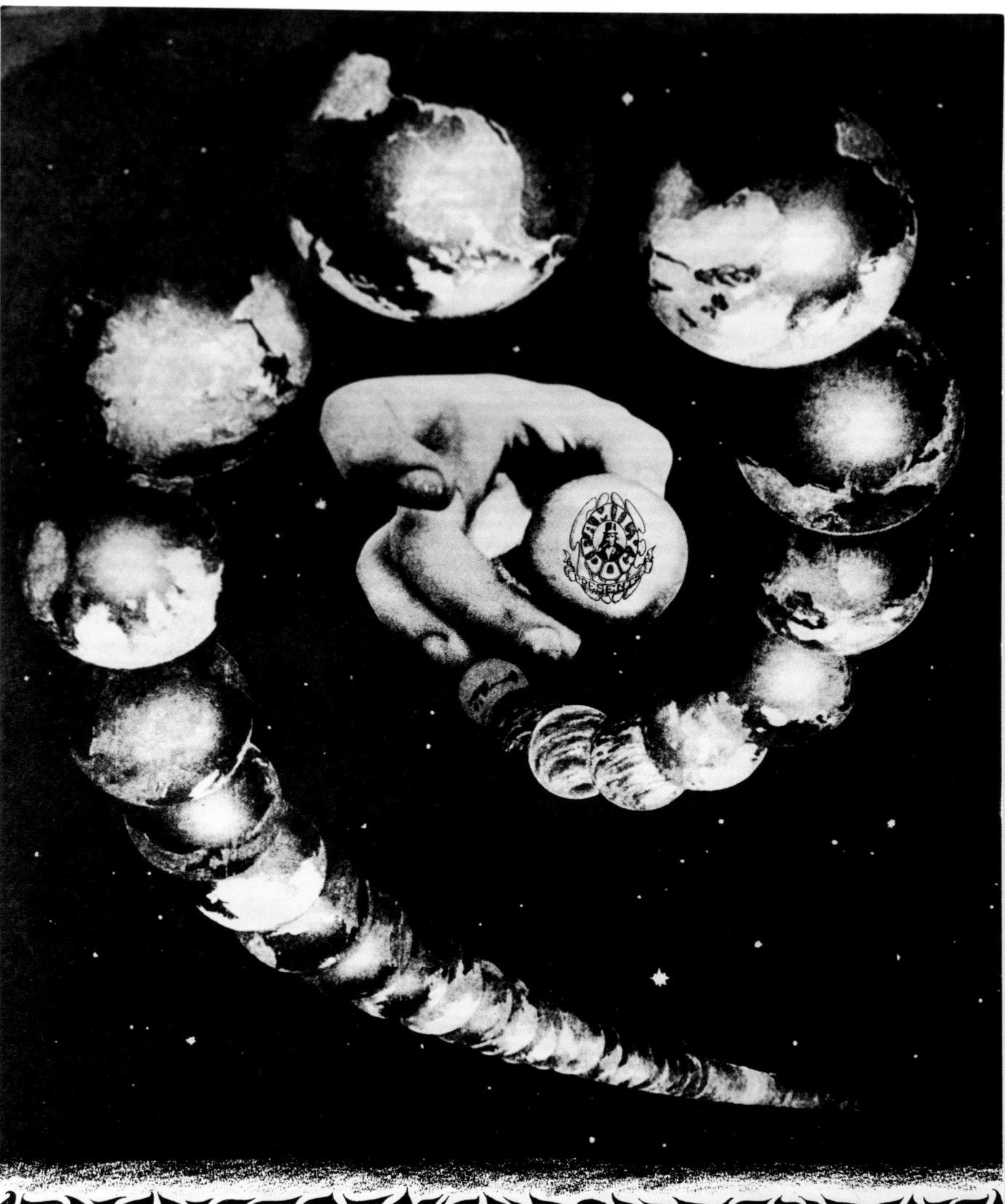

TICKET OUTLETS SAN FRANCISCO: TOWER RECORDS (COLUMBUS & BAY), GRAMAPHONE STORES (ALL), MNASIDIKA (HAIGHT ASHBURY), CITY LIGHTS BOOKS (NORTH BEACH), THE TOWN SQUIRE (1318 POLK). BERKELEY: DISCOUNT RECORDS. SAUSALITO: TIDES BOOKSTORE. REDWOOD CITY: REDWOOD HOUSE OF MUSIC (700 WINSLOW). SAN MATEO: LA MER CAMERAS & MUSIC (HILLSDALE AT 19TH). SAN RAFAEL: RECORD KING. MENLO PARK: KEPLER'S BOOKS & MAGAZINES (825 EL CAMINO). PALO ALTO: EAST FARTHING TRADING CO. (616 COWPER). SAN JOSE: DISCORAMA (235 SO. FIRST ST.) FAMILY DOG LISTENS TO FAMILY RADIO - KSAN 95

© 1968 FAMILY DOG, INC. 639 GOUGH ST. SAN FRANCISCO, CALIF. 94102   # 131   TEA LAUTREC LITHO

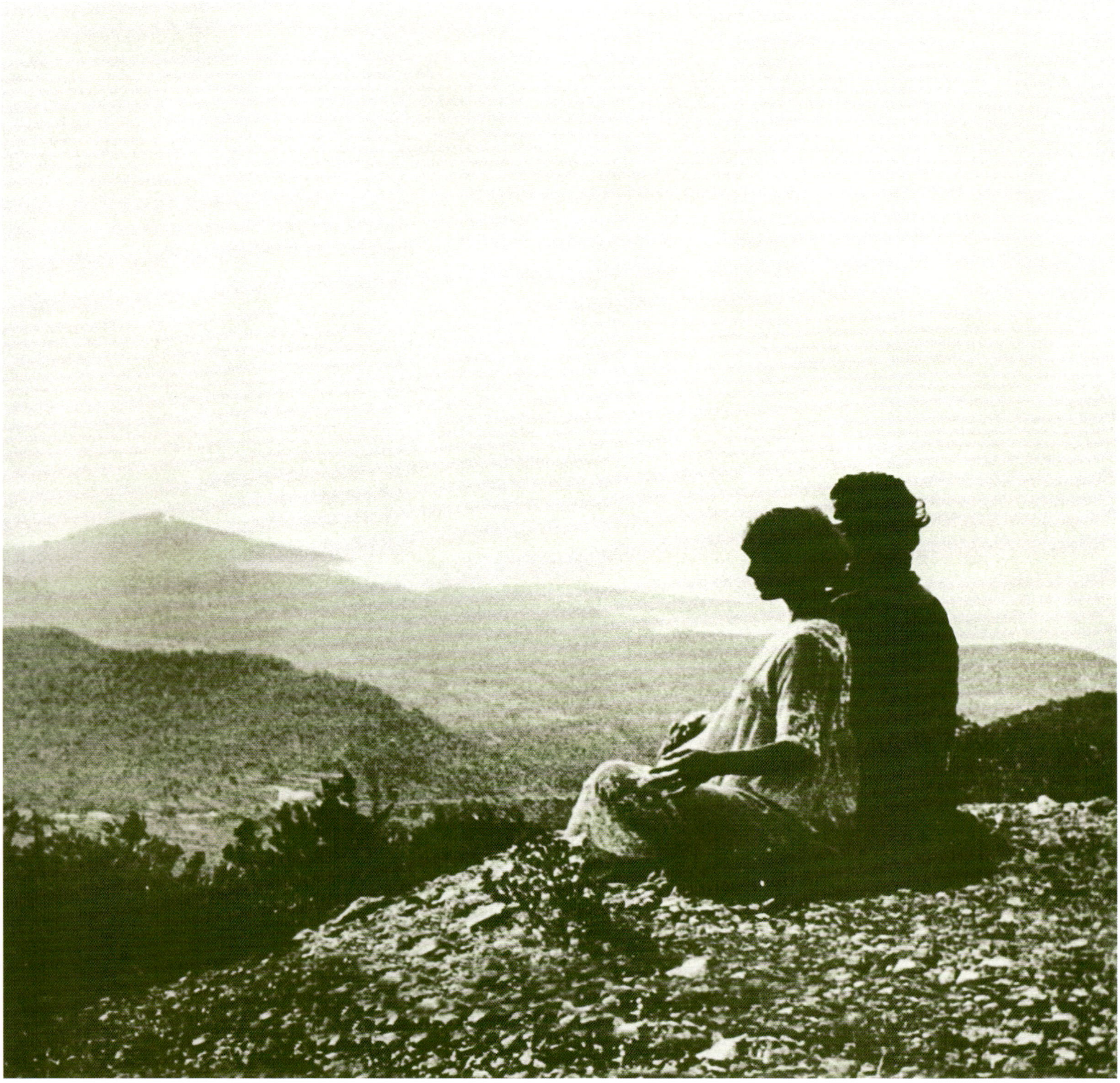

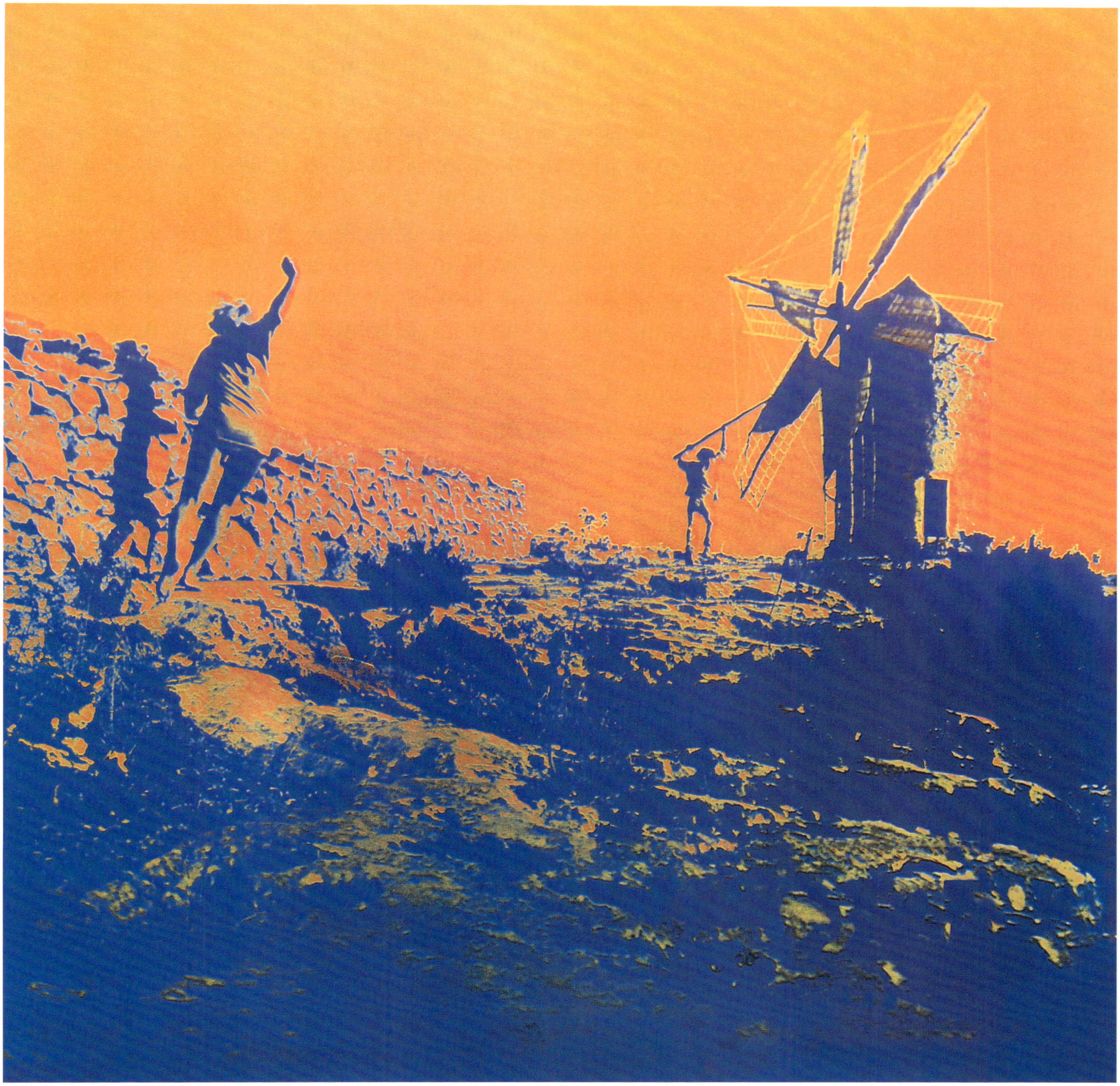

SOUNDTRACK FROM THE FILM MORE

June 1969 • UK: Columbia EMI SCX 6346

117–118 · PREVIOUS SPREAD · Album artwork, *Soundtrack from the film More*, 1969. Based on stills from the film *More*, directed by Barbet Schroeder. Design by Storm Thorgerson / Aubrey Powell at Hipgnosis

119 · OPPOSITE · Still from the film *More,* featuring Klaus Grünberg and Mimsy Farmer, directed by Barbet Schroeder, 1969

In the 1960s, the Balearic Islands of Ibiza and Formentera, and the village of Deia on Majorca, offered a refuge and playground for many poets, writers, artists and musicians. Syd Barrett fled to Formentera for a short time after leaving Pink Floyd in 1968. Other members of the group and their friends at Hipgnosis were regular visitors throughout the '60s and beyond.

The cover of Pink Floyd's first soundtrack album, *More*, shows one of Formentera's centuries-old windmills, between the main towns of San Fernando and San Francisco. And the atmosphere and mood of the island suffuses the music.

Barbet Schroeder, an up-and-coming Iranian-born new-wave film-maker and former assistant to Jean-Luc Godard, had been fascinated by *The Piper at the Gates of Dawn* and *A Saucerful of Secrets*. 'I thought Pink Floyd's music was the most extraordinary thing I had ever heard.' He asked the group to contribute the soundtrack to his first film, *More*.

It was a timely commission. The band's last single, 'Point Me at the Sky', released in November 1968, hadn't charted. Pink Floyd had now abandoned the idea of releasing further singles and saw film soundtracks as another possible artistic outlet. In 1967, the group had composed a soundtrack for the conceptual artist John Latham's short movie, *Speak*. A year later they'd done the same for director Peter Sykes' film-noir drama *The Committee*.

More, a tale of young thrill-seekers in Ibiza, was told with a generous amount of nudity and drug-taking, and chimed with the times. However, Schroeder didn't want Pink Floyd to compose an incidental soundtrack. Instead, the music would be heard playing at a party, in a bar or on the radio.

The nature of the commission meant the band had to work quickly, removing any temptation for self-indulgence. They composed and recorded a bespoke soundtrack in a little over a week, working with engineer Brian Humphries at London's Pye Studios.

Pink Floyd's soundtrack touched on pop, jazz, folk, electronic sounds and, on 'The Nile Song', punishingly heavy rock. But there was also a conciseness to much of this new music. 'Cirrus Minor', 'Cymbaline' and 'Green is the Colour' pushed David Gilmour's voice to the fore, and had simpler melodies that hinted at the sound Pink Floyd would eventually arrive at on *The Dark Side of the Moon*.

Aubrey 'Po' Powell photographed the windmill on the set of *More*. Hipgnosis then solarized the picture, reversing the tone of the image and creating a wash of blue and orange on the final sleeve. 'We were influenced by many jazz LP covers from the time,' Powell recalls, 'and particularly the jazz covers Andy Warhol drew for the Blue Note label, which had these wonderful splashes of bright colour on them.'

    More premiered at the Cannes Film Festival in May 1969. Pink Floyd's soundtrack was released two months later and became another UK Top 10 hit. The music complemented Schroeder's movie, but has also endured in its own right. Though nobody knew it at the time *More* would point the way forward for much of Pink Floyd's output in the next decade.

Soundtrack from the film *More*

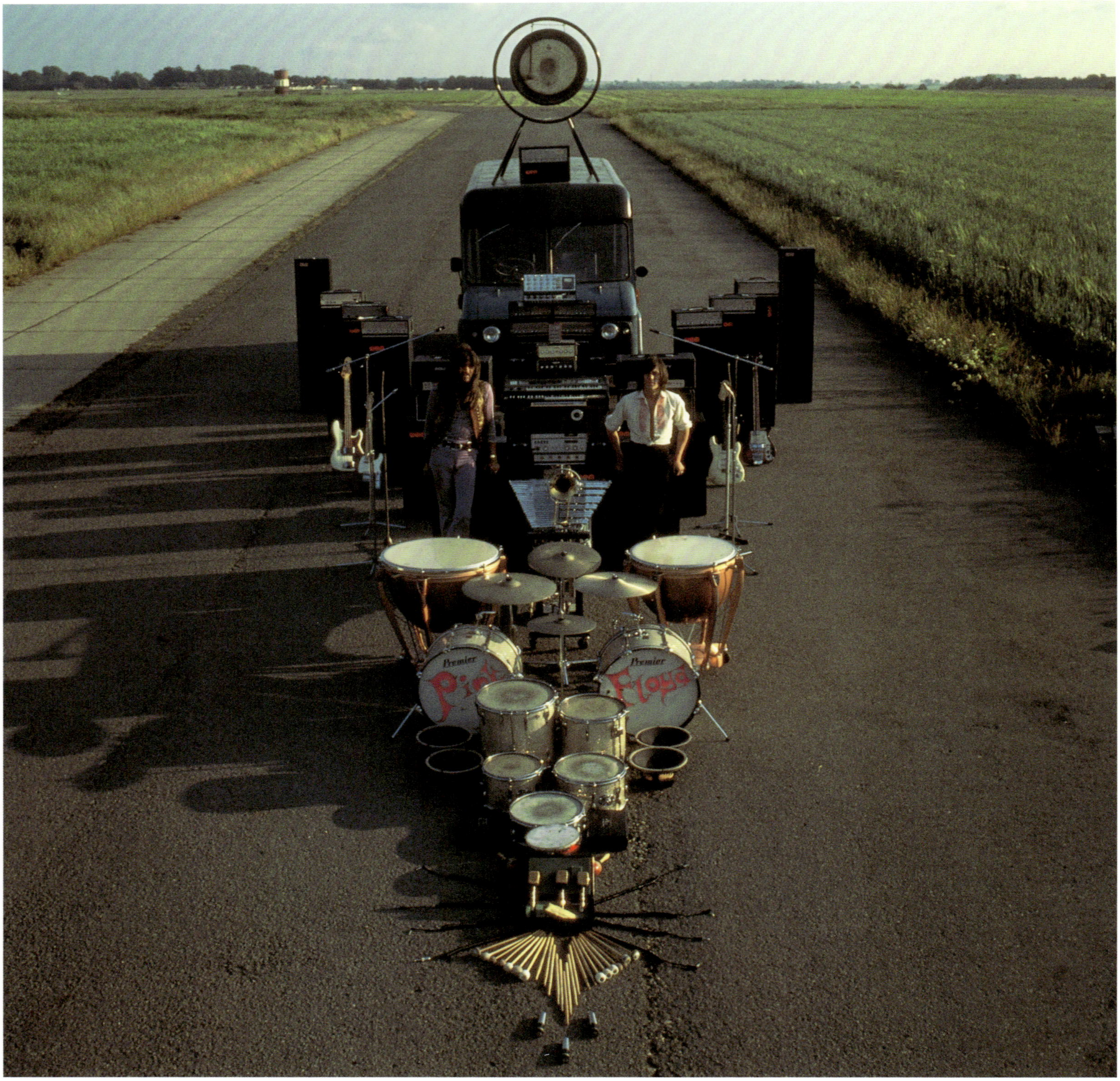
Premier
Premier
Floyd

PINK FLOYD

UMMAGUMMA

November 1969 • UK: EMI Harvest SHDW 1/2

120–121 • PREVIOUS SPREAD • Album artwork, *Ummagumma*, 1969. Design and photographs by Storm Thorgerson / Aubrey Powell at Hipgnosis

122 • OPPOSITE • Cover photo session for *Ummagumma*, 1969. Design and photographs by Storm Thorgerson / Aubrey Powell at Hipgnosis. Aubrey Powell Collection

Ummagumma is the perfect snapshot of Pink Floyd at the end of the 1960s: a double LP documenting the group live and in the studio. It is also that rarest of Pink Floyd artefacts, an album with a group photograph on the sleeve, before the band members disappeared from their covers forever.

Pink Floyd's fourth album was the result of a shift in pop music and its surrounding industry. In 1967, the band's improvisational approach often alienated audiences on the traditional ballroom circuit, where people came to dance and hear the 'hits'. However, two years later EMI's Harvest imprint, on which Pink Floyd's music was released, was regarded as the home of 'serious' album music. The group were regulars on a booming circuit of college halls and underground venues; a new world where the LP was king and audiences sat rapt and cross-legged on the dancefloor, immersed in the music.

Ummagumma's live versions of 'Astronomy Domine', 'Careful with that Axe, Eugene', 'Set the Controls for the Heart of the Sun' and 'A Saucerful of Secrets' were recorded on that circuit: at Manchester's College of Commerce and Mothers in Birmingham (the Midlands successor to London's UFO and Middle Earth clubs).

Meanwhile, Pink Floyd pieced together *Ummagumma*'s studio sides at Abbey Road Studios in between live dates. Each band member had a quarter of the LP to use as they saw fit. Their subsequent solo compositions illustrate how distanced Pink Floyd had become from the mainstream. Without record-company pressure to produce singles, they were free to experiment.

Richard Wright's 'Sysyphus' was a keyboard concerto in four movements; Nick Mason's 'The Grand Vizier's Garden Party' a filmic, three-part suite for percussion and woodwind; while the track by Roger Waters, 'Several Species of Small Furry Animals Gathered Together in a Cave and Grooving with a Pict', used found sounds, treated voices and special effects. In contrast, Waters' wistful 'Grantchester Meadows' and the acoustic sections of David Gilmour's 'The Narrow Way' were more melodic and direct.

Ummagumma's studio compositions also contained traces of what could have become Pink Floyd's first concept album. Throughout 1969, the group performed two musical suites, 'The Man' and 'The Journey' (telling the story of one man's day in the life, broadly described as 'Sleep, Work, Play, Start Again'), at venues including London's Royal Albert Hall and Royal Festival Hall.

'The Man' and 'The Journey' evolved over the course of the year to include visual effects and elements of performance art. Played live through a quadrophonic sound system, the music became all-encompassing as Richard Wright controlled its direction with the Azimuth Co-ordinator, a device that panned the sound via a joystick around any given venue.

178 The Albums

PINK
FLOYD
PINK
FLOYD
PINK
FLOYD
PINK
FLOYD
PINK
FLOYD
PINK
FLOYD
PINK
FLOYD
PINK
FLOYD
PINK
FLOYD
PINK
FLOYD
PINK
FLOYD
PINK
FLOYD

123 · ABOVE · Pink Floyd tour booklet, 1969. Illustrations by Nick Mason. Design by Storm Thorgerson / Aubrey Powell at Hipgnosis. Pink Floyd Archive

124 · OPPOSITE · Pink Floyd and band equipment at Biggin Hill Airport, from the back album cover shoot for *Ummagumma*, 1969. Design and photographs by Storm Thorgerson / Aubrey Powell at Hipgnosis

This photo session was inspired by a magazine image, spotted by Nick Mason, of the armaments for a Phantom bomber. The impressive amount of band equipment, arranged in formation, reflects the increasing scale and ambition of Pink Floyd's performances. While the band are pictured here, the back cover photograph features road manager and sound engineer Peter Watts, and roadie Alan Styles.

The show's visual spectacle was provided by the band members and road crew sawing wood and drinking tea onstage. While offstage their art-school friend, Peter Dockley, dressed in a grotesque rubber suit as the 'Tar Monster', dashed around terrorizing members of the audience.

Although neither piece was recorded in full in the studio, 'The Man' and 'The Journey' borrowed from parts of the *More* soundtrack and from 'Grantchester Meadows', 'The Narrow Way' and 'The Grand Vizier's Garden Party'. In that sense, *Ummagumma* captured the sound of Pink Floyd in 1969 in greater detail than many realized.

Released in October that year, the album reached Number 5 in the UK charts — proof that Pink Floyd's non-pop music had a following among those uninterested in singles or the traditional hit parade. This multi-dimensional music was echoed in the cover image: a picture within a picture continued ad infinitum.

'We used the "Droste Effect"', explains Aubrey 'Po' Powell, referring to the Dutch brand of cocoa powder whose packaging shows a woman holding a box of the same product on a tray, thereby creating a picture within itself. 'Up until now, Pink Floyd were so mysterious they were unknown. This time they wanted to be seen on an album cover, but in a radically different way.'

The 'Droste Effect' was applied to a set of band photographs taken in the house of Storm Thorgerson's girlfriend in Cambridge. But there were other influences at work, not least from Hipgnosis' favourite surrealist artists: Salvador Dalí, René Magritte and Man Ray. 'Pink Floyd's music was inward-looking,' offers Aubrey Powell. 'In many ways, the cover of *Ummagumma* was a psychological reflection of the band.'

180   The Albums

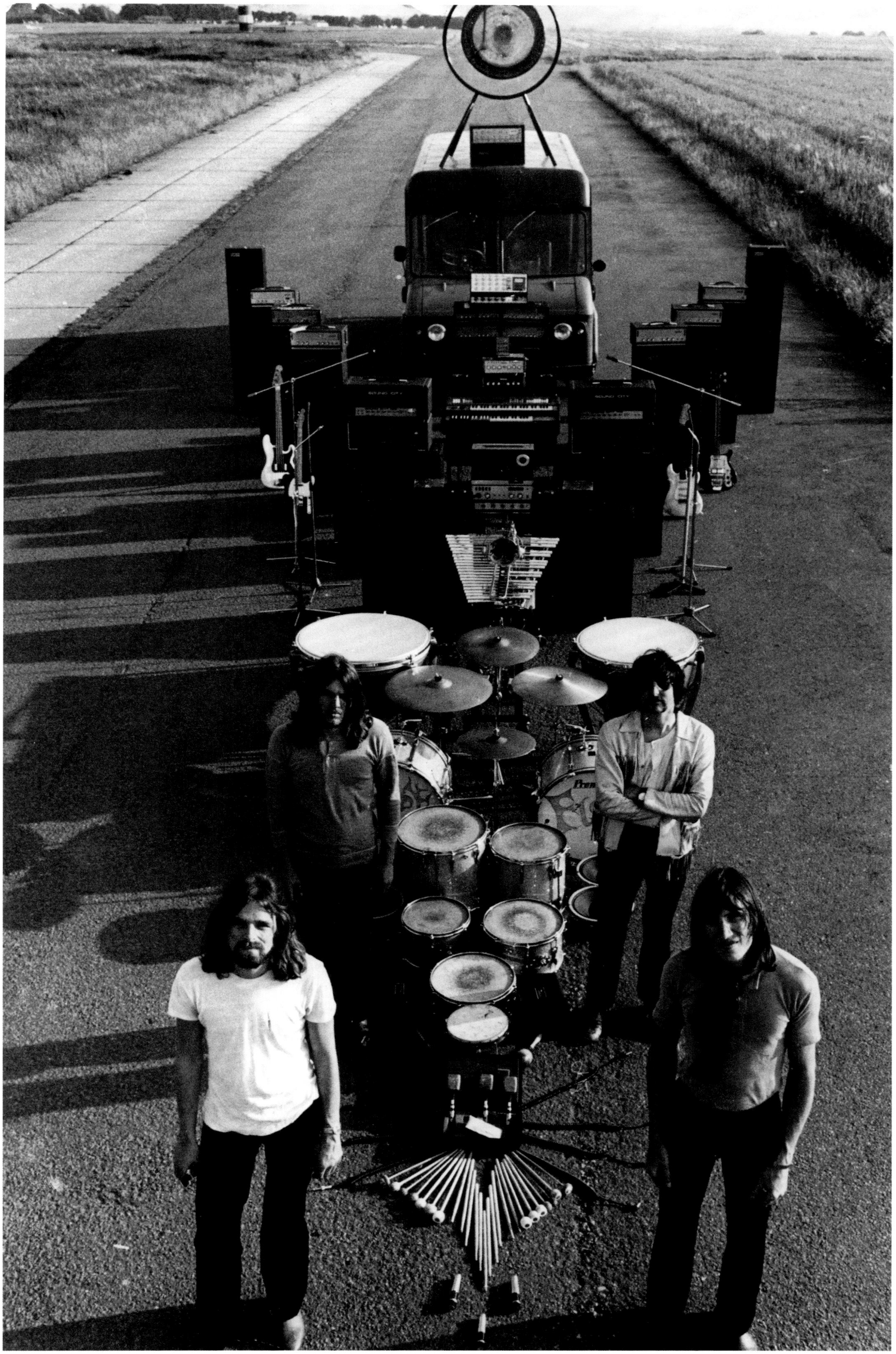

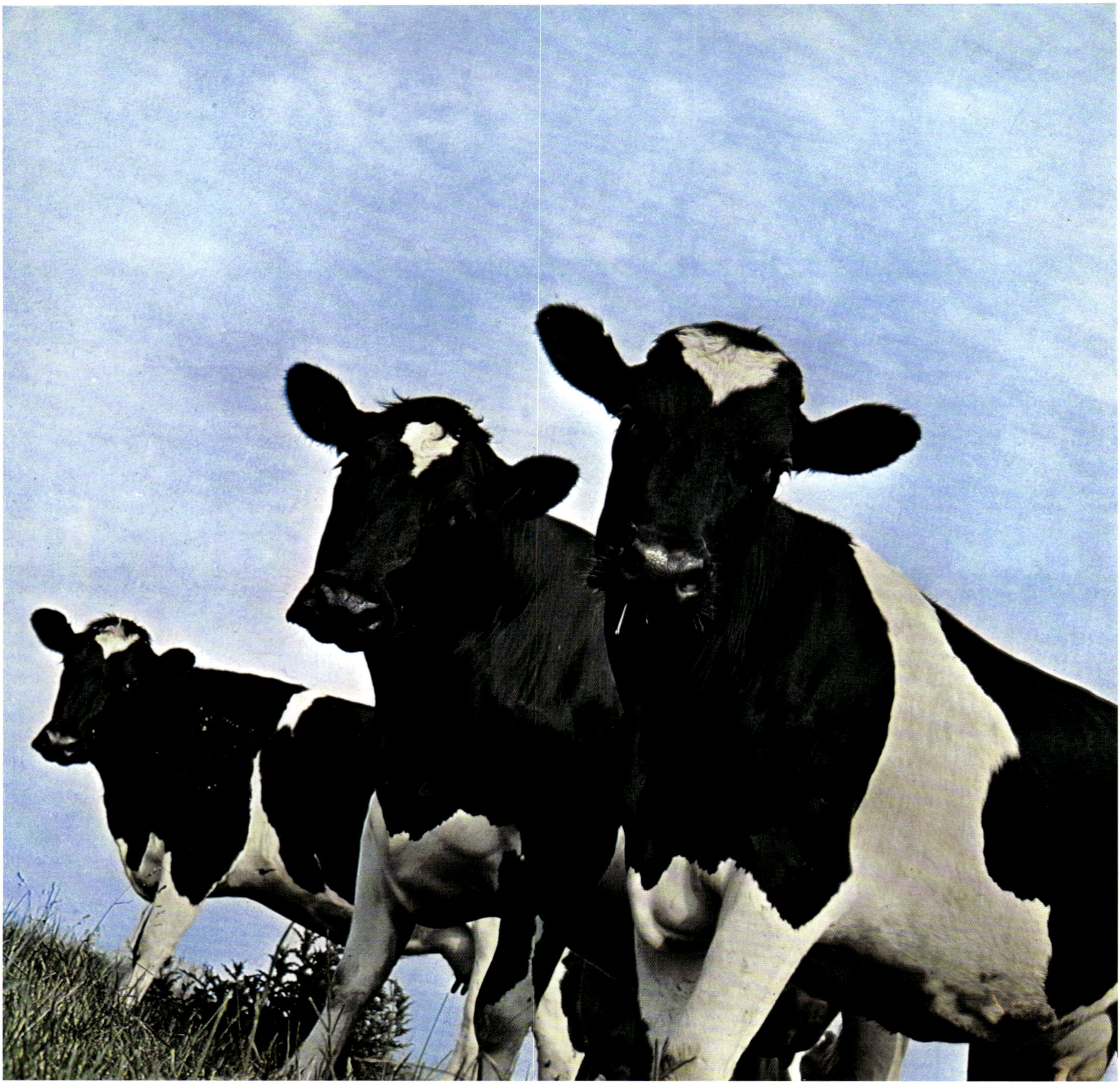

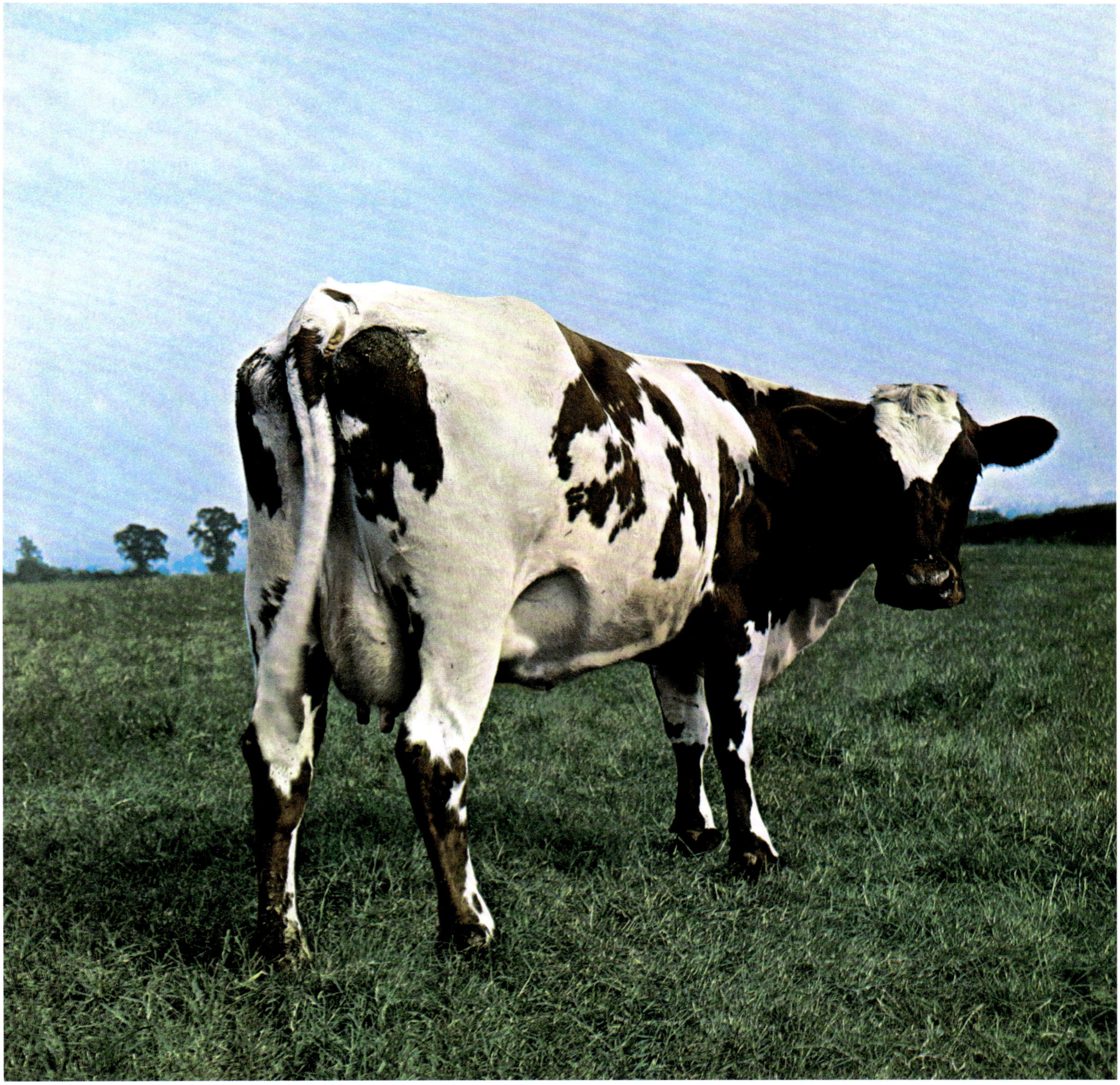

ATOM HEART MOTHER

October 1970 • UK: EMI Harvest SHVL 781

125–126 · PREVIOUS SPREAD · Album artwork, *Atom Heart Mother*, 1970. Design and photographs by Storm Thorgerson / Aubrey Powell at Hipgnosis

127 · OPPOSITE · Blackhill's Garden Party, Hyde Park Free Concert, London, 18 July 1970. Pink Floyd Archive

128–129 · FOLLOWING SPREAD · Vocal and instrumental arrangements for *Atom Heart Mother*, 1970. Ron Geesin. Collection of Ron Geesin

In October 1970, Pink Floyd welcomed the new decade with an album that bemused their critics and record company, but which became their biggest hit so far. The sounds on *Atom Heart Mother* were created by Pink Floyd, a choir, a brass ensemble, dripping taps, frying bacon and whistling kettles. And they were sold to the world with a photograph of a cow in a field.

Throughout 1969, Pink Floyd performances such as 'The Massed Gadgets of Auximines' at London's Royal Festival Hall had pushed the boundaries of what constituted a rock concert. The group brought a similar sense of adventure to the studio for *Atom Heart Mother.*

The album's roots can be traced to a recording session in Rome in November 1969. Pink Floyd had been approached by the Italian film director Michelangelo Antonioni (of *Blow-Up* fame) to provide the soundtrack to his forthcoming counter-culture drama *Zabriskie Point*. But Antonioni was dissatisfied with most of the music they produced and the band returned home. Among the rejected pieces was a guitar figure, redolent of a cinematic Spaghetti-Western theme, which would become the starting point for *Atom Heart Mother*'s side-long suite.

This untitled 20-minute piece, with the working title 'Epic', was performed live before the group decided to add brass and a choir. At the time, Roger Waters and the Scottish-born composer, poet and arranger Ron Geesin were working on a parallel project. This was the soundtrack for a scientific documentary, *The Body*, for which they were creating music with conventional instruments and 'human noises' including breathing, talking and a beating heart. *Atom Heart Mother* would use a similar mix of conventional and unconventional sounds.

Geesin's background in jazz and classical music made him an obvious choice to compose Pink Floyd's orchestral score. However, the recording session with the EMI Pops Orchestra, a group of seasoned, hard-bitten Abbey Road session musicians, was problematic. Choral scholar John Alldis eventually replaced Geesin to conduct both the orchestra and his own choir, which contributed the suite's celestial, wordless vocals.

With its brass overture, choral voices and special effects, including the sound of gunshots and whinnying horses, there was a cinematic quality to Pink Floyd's new composition. The piece, still referred to as 'Epic' and, later, 'The Amazing Pudding', was performed live that year at the Bath Festival of Progressive Music and at a free concert in London's Hyde Park. Its final title only

The Albums

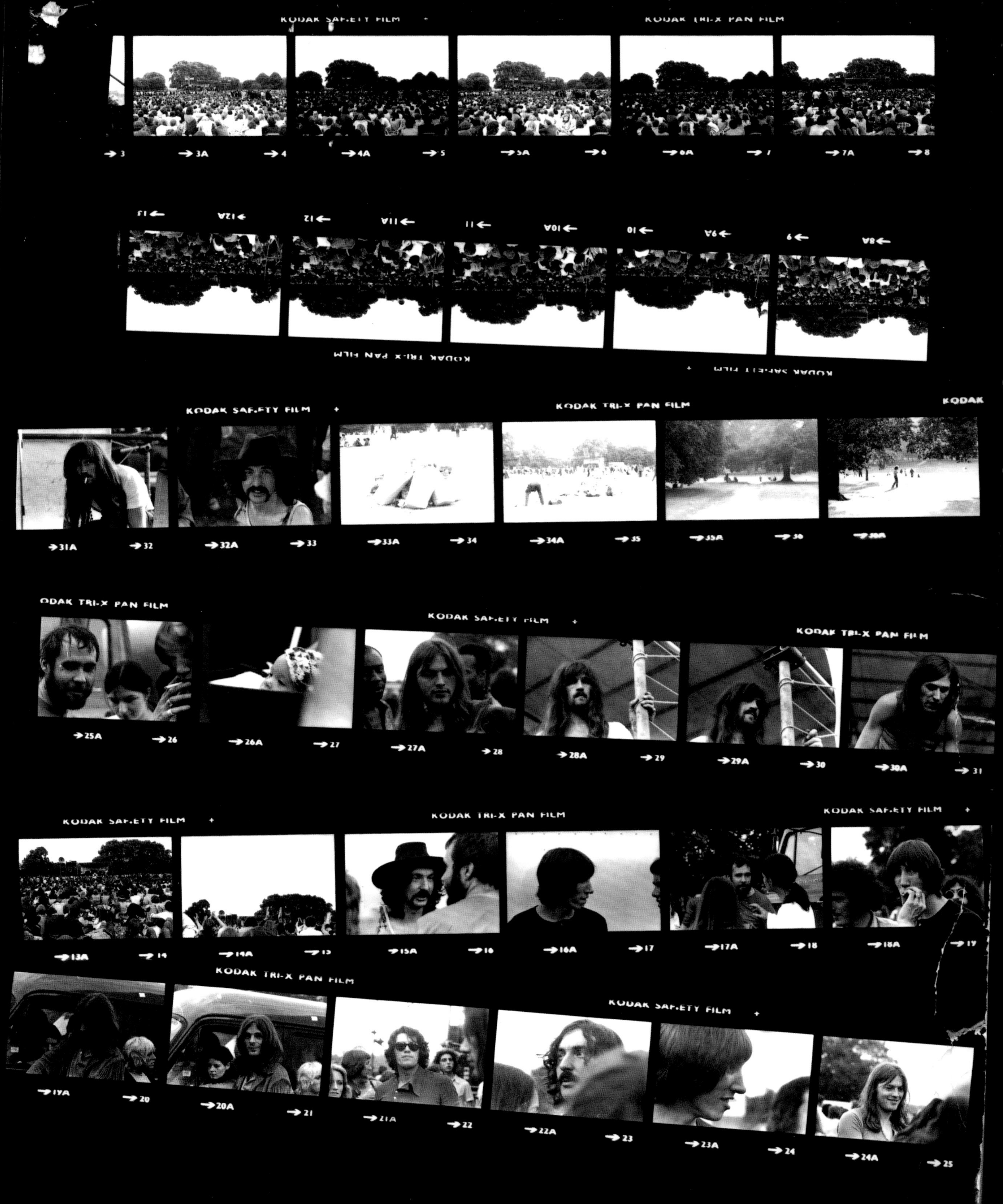
KODAK SAFETY FILM
KODAK TRI-X PAN FILM

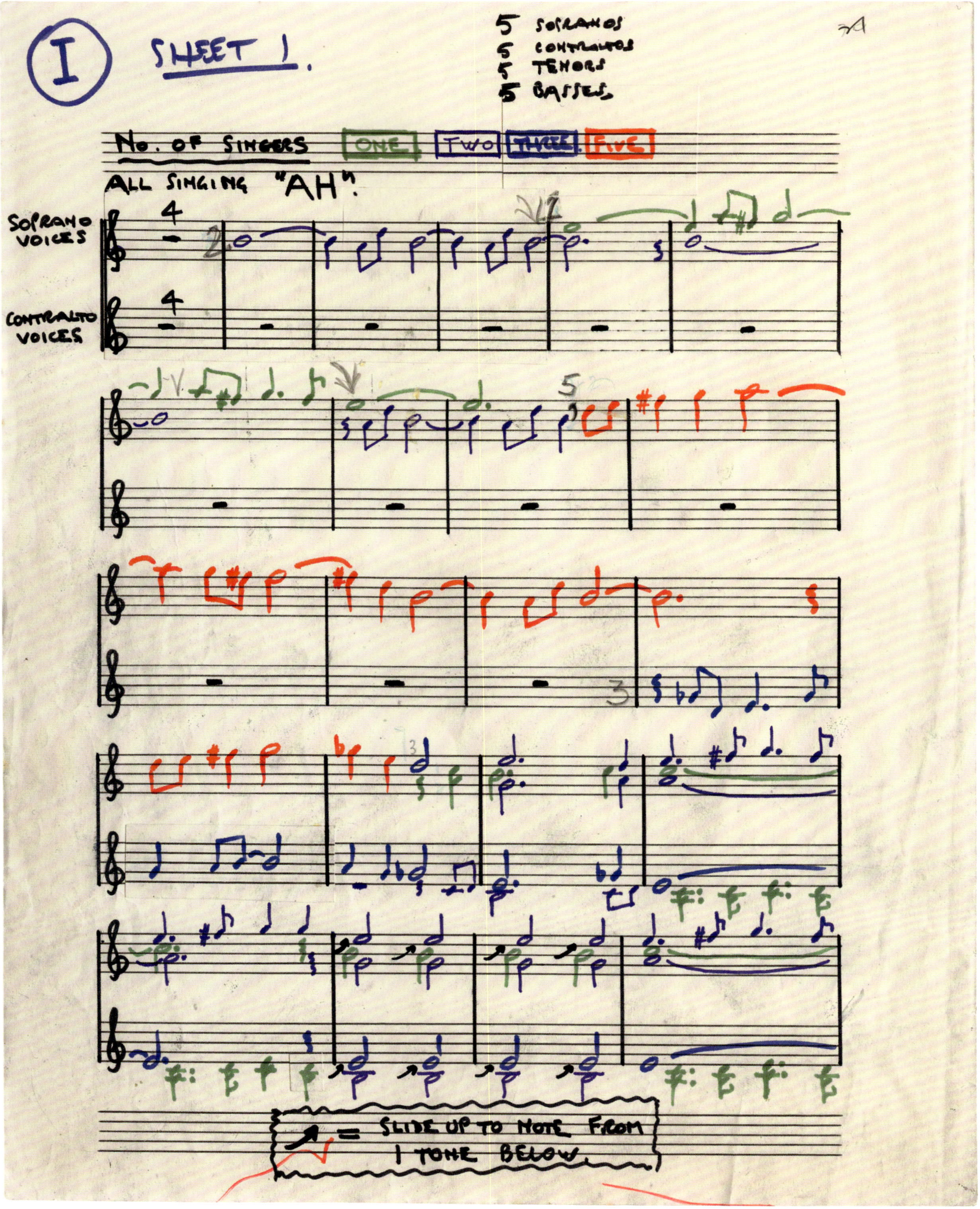
I
SHEET 1.
5 SOPRANOS
5 CONTRALTOS
5 TENORS
5 BASSES
NO. OF SINGERS
ONE
TWO
THREE
FIVE
ALL SINGING "AH".
SOPRANO VOICES
CONTRALTO VOICES
= SLIDE UP TO NOTE FROM 1 TONE BELOW.

A. INTRO.

130 · RIGHT · Pink Floyd onstage at Blackhill's Garden Party, Hyde Park Free Concert, London, 18 July 1970. Photograph by Michael Putland

Blackhill Enterprises organized successive free gigs in Hyde Park after 1968. Pink Floyd previewed music from the forthcoming album *Atom Heart Mother* in 1970, including the 25-minute-long title track, for which a brass section and choir were brought onstage. Although Ron Geesin was unhappy with the orchestra's performance, *Disc and Music Echo* reported enthusiastically: 'The Pink Floyd gave an hour of beautifully mature music, soothing and inspiring to listen to.'

131 · OPPOSITE · Fender Sunburst Stratocaster, 1959, with rosewood neck, 1963. Peter Barnes Collection

David Gilmour used this guitar to play 'Atom Heart Mother' at the Hyde Park Free Concert, 1970. It was given to him by Steve Marriott, guitarist for Humble Pie and Small Faces. The rosewood neck, a favourite of Gilmour's, was swapped on to his Black Fender Stratocaster between 1974 and 1977.

came after Roger Waters spotted a headline in the *London Evening Standard* above a story about a woman fitted with a plutonium pacemaker.

The remainder of the album was, like its predecessor *Ummagumma*, largely given over to solo compositions. However, Roger Waters' 'If', Richard Wright's 'Summer '68' and David Gilmour's 'Fat Old Sun' shunned *Ummagumma*'s dense experimentation for more orthodox rock and folk influences.

The only anomaly was the group-composed 'Alan's Psychedelic Breakfast', which decorated its gentle instrumental jazz with the sound of Pink Floyd's roadie Alan Styles cooking his morning meal. *Atom Heart Mother* was mixed for four-channel quadrophonic sound as well as stereo, reproducing the noises of cracking eggs, sizzling bacon and popping toast with incredible clarity.

Pink Floyd's experimental music came with a cover that also challenged expectation and commercial wisdom. Hipgnosis' cow was photographed in a farmer's field in Potters Bar, north of London, and owed something to conceptual artist Marcel Duchamp, who used everyday objects as symbols of art.

With Pink Floyd's blessing, Hipgnosis defied EMI and also refused to include the band name or the album title anywhere on the sleeve. It was a minimalist approach partly inspired by the pop artist Richard Hamilton's stark design for The Beatles' *White Album* and Andy Warhol's 'banana' artwork for *The Velvet Underground and Nico*.

'The cow had nothing to do with the music or the album title,' says Powell. 'It was lateral thinking in the extreme, but in a world where things like the band's name and the album title would be as big as possible, and the hardest sell imaginable.'

The band's and Hipgnosis' truculence paid off. *Atom Heart Mother* gave Pink Floyd their first UK Number 1 hit, and one of their most enduring artworks. 'It's art that's all about nothing and yet all about everything,' says Powell. 'It has an essence to it and a gravitas.'

The Albums

Atom Heart Mother

132–133 · ABOVE AND LEFT · Drum heads with 'Star Head' design, 1970. Original artist unknown. Image by Matthew Rich, Jealous / Kate Hepburn / Peter Curzon. Pink Floyd Archive

These intricately painted drum heads were given by the artist to Nick Mason and appeared onstage at the Hyde Park Free Concert, 1970. The full symbolism of the design is lost, along with the identity of the original artist, but it incorporates the Renaissance figure of the Vitruvian Man and the Egyptian Eye of Horus, a symbol of protection. Two further sets were gifted to Nick Mason at a later date.

190   The Albums

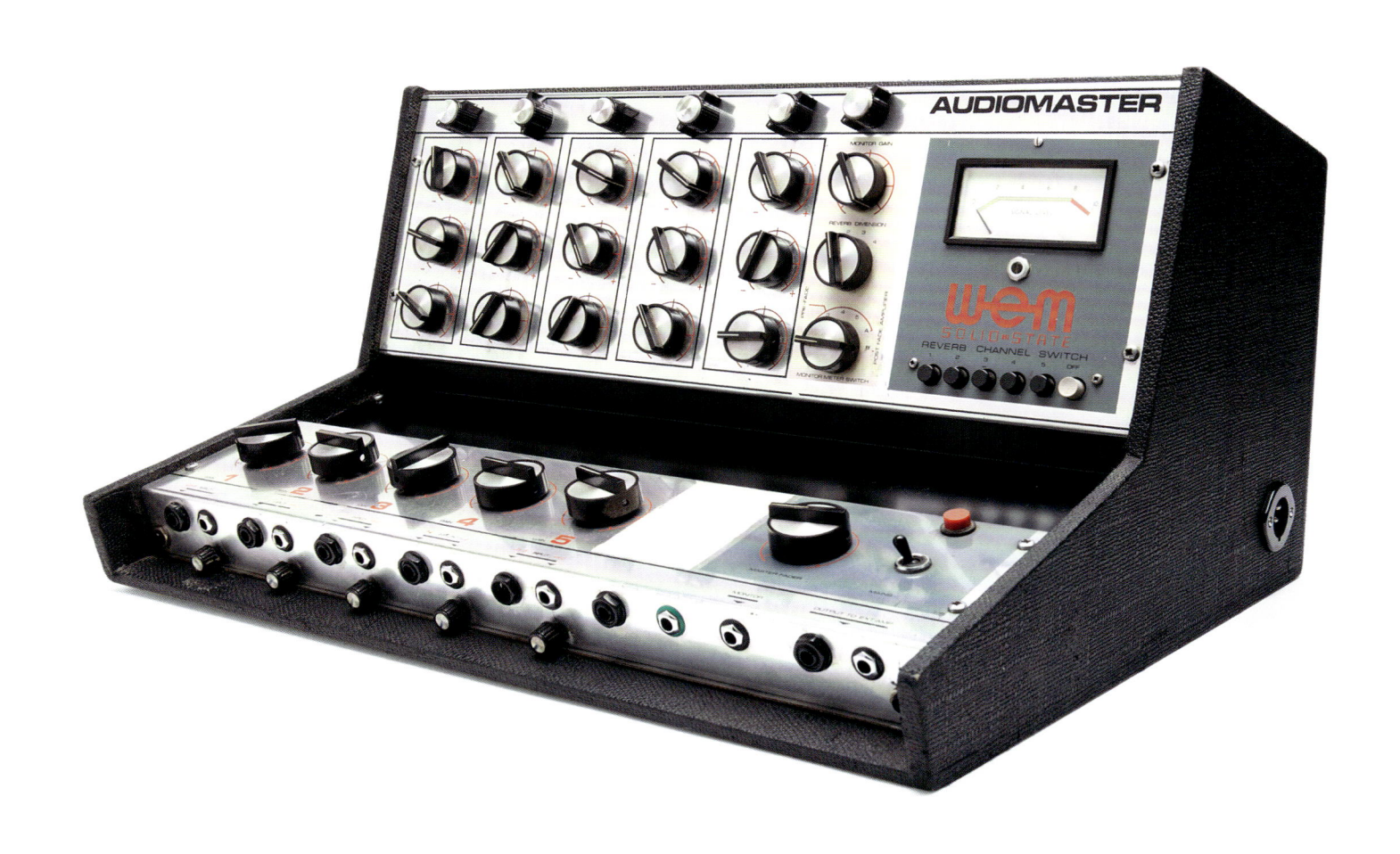

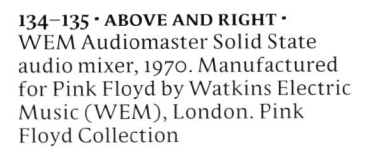

134–135 · ABOVE AND RIGHT ·
WEM Audiomaster Solid State audio mixer, 1970. Manufactured for Pink Floyd by Watkins Electric Music (WEM), London. Pink Floyd Collection

Charlie Watkins of WEM and Pink Floyd road manager Peter Watts developed a customized system of four connected Audio Masters. The resulting 20 audio inputs could accommodate the band and the extra choir and brass sections brought onstage for 'Atom Heart Mother'. Watts mixed the sound for the audience from the side of the stage. Watkins described the band's system as, 'the most sophisticated PA in the country'.

Atom Heart Mother   191

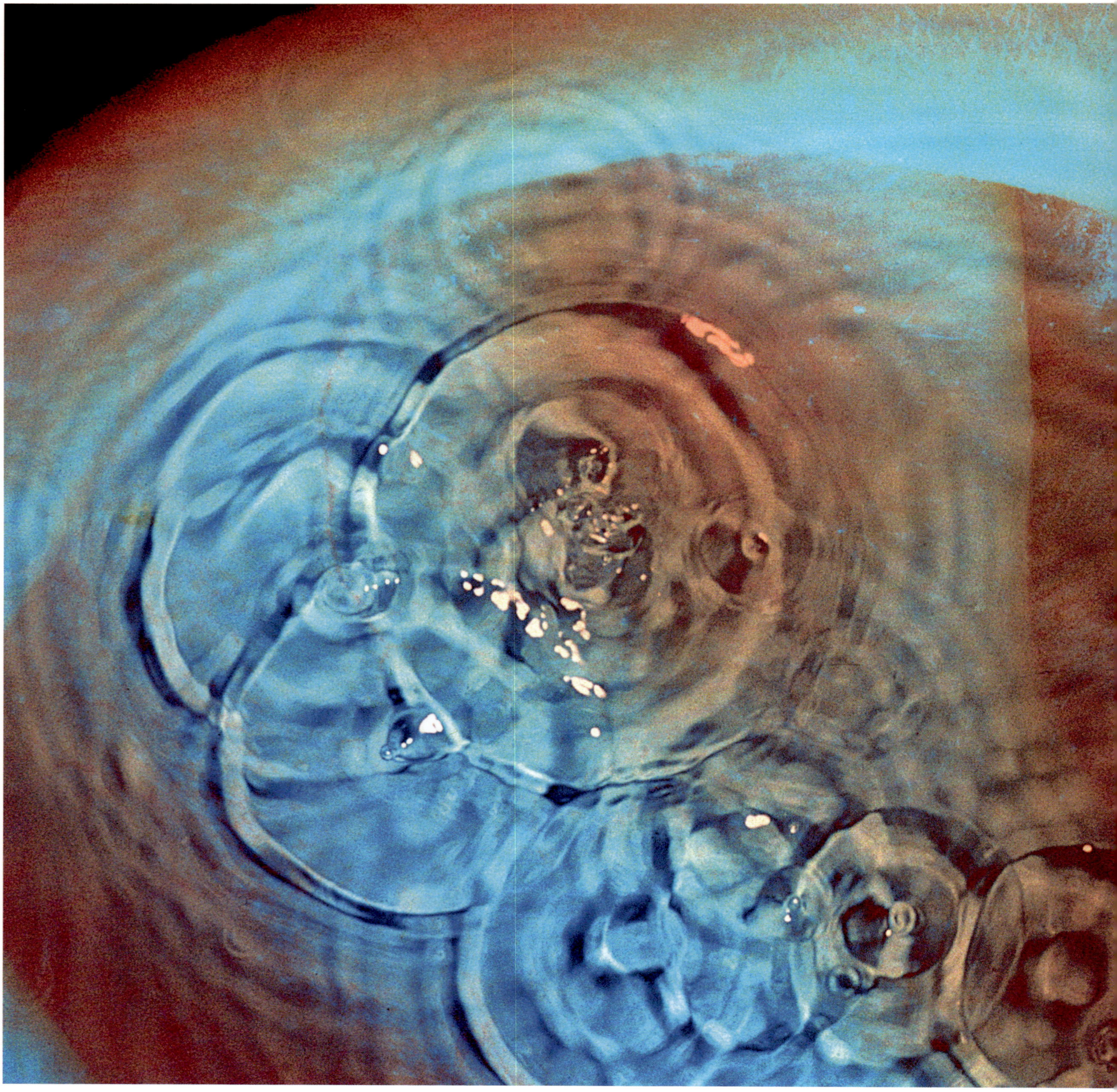

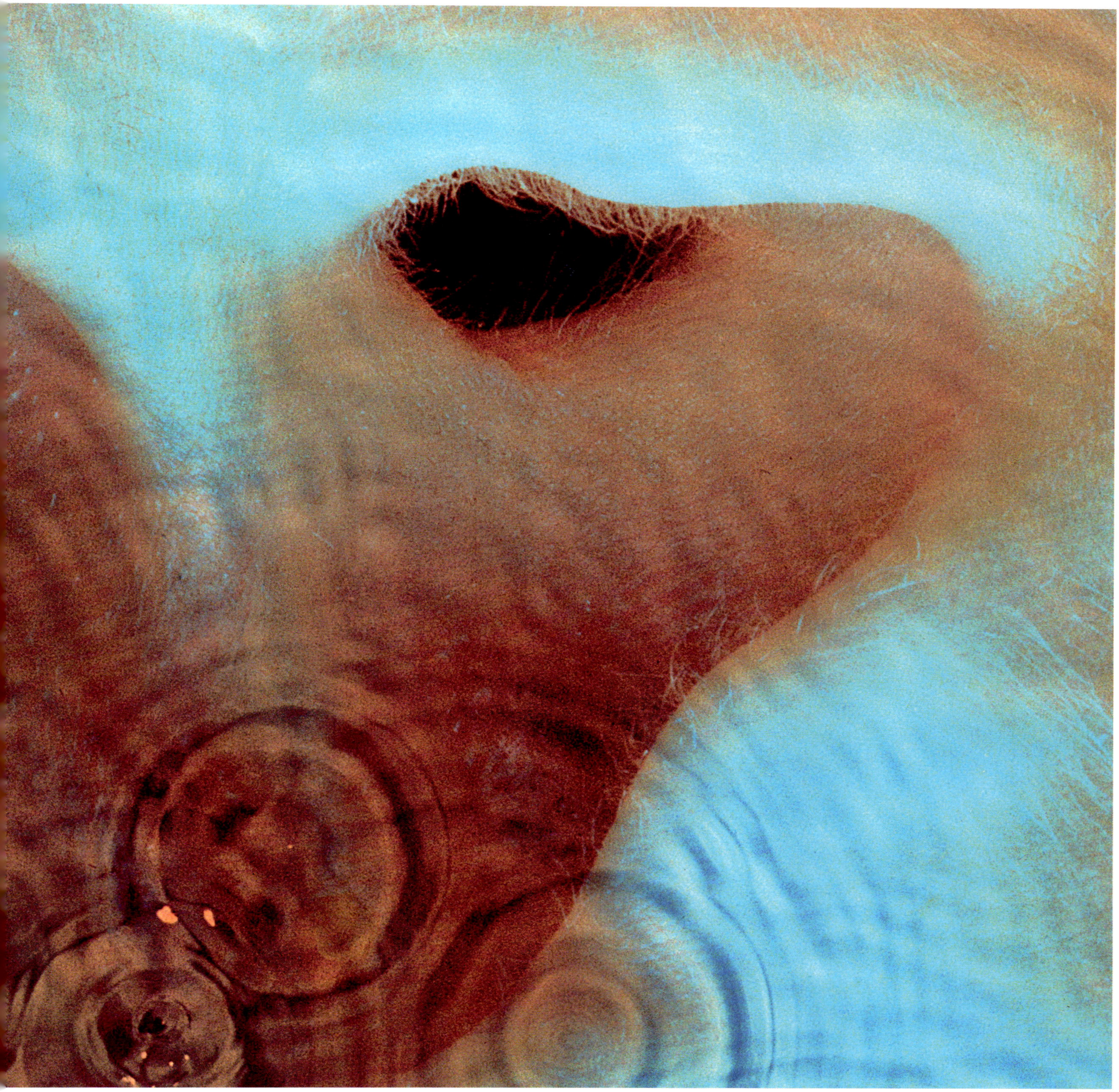

MEDDLE

November 1971 • UK: EMI Harvest SHVL 795

136 · PREVIOUS SPREAD · Album artwork, *Meddle*, 1971. Photograph by Bob Dowling. Design by Storm Thorgerson / Aubrey Powell at Hipgnosis

137 · OPPOSITE · Phase Linear 400 PA amplifier, 1970s. Pink Floyd Collection

Improvements to Pink Floyd's PA system were made in 1971 by Peter Watts in collaboration with audio pioneers Bill Kelsey and the late Dave Martin. This powerful American amplifier was incorporated into the band's live touring equipment at the time.

Pink Floyd's sixth album, *Meddle*, was the precursor to *The Dark Side of the Moon*. But what became a collaborative group effort after the band's solo adventures on *Atom Heart Mother* and *Ummagumma* started off very differently.

Pink Floyd convened at Abbey Road Studios in January 1971, intending to take an unconventional approach to making their next album. It was decided that each band member should play on a track but not be allowed to hear what the others had played first. This musical 'cut-up' approach was eventually abandoned, but not before the group had amassed a collection of random sounds and scraps of ideas which were catalogued 'Nothing 1' up to 'Nothing 36'.

Among these musical 'Nothings' was a sound resembling the 'ping' of a ship's sonar hunting for submarines. It was a happy accident, which occurred when Richard Wright played a note on the piano fed through a rotating Leslie speaker cabinet. Another musical mishap occurred when David Gilmour's effects pedal was wired incorrectly and created a screaming effect, similar to the noise of crying seagulls. Both sounds were used on a new side-long composition, initially known as 'The Son of Nothing' and later, 'Return of the Son of Nothing' before finally becoming 'Echoes'.

Pink Floyd road-tested this new work ahead of the album's release. An early performance of 'Echoes' took place at their May 1971 concert at London's Crystal Palace Bowl, an event which saw their artist-friend Peter Dockley's latest creation, a giant inflatable octopus, rise from the lake in front of the stage.

Meddle was pieced together in the studio between live dates, and finally completed in August. Like the 'Atom Heart Mother' suite, the 23′31″ 'Echoes' took up a whole side of the original vinyl. But unlike that earlier instrumental, 'Echoes' showcased David Gilmour and Richard Wright's lead harmony vocals and the same sweeping grandeur that later informed multi-part Pink Floyd compositions, including 'Shine On You Crazy Diamond' and *The Dark Side of the Moon*. 'Echoes' took its own time and switched between moods and tempos, but it was more focused than the band's earlier epic experiments.

'Echoes' was also a turning point for Roger Waters' lyrics. It explored a theme he'd touched on in the *Atom Heart Mother* track 'If': the need for communication. For some time, Waters had noticed a procession of weary commuters trooping past his Islington house on their way to and from work. He was struck by the daily grind and repetition, but also the lack of communication. The lyrics to 'Echoes' centred on the idea of strangers making a connection; a theme Roger Waters would return to again and again in his work.

The rest of the album was given over to individual songs, most of which, unusually, were credited to more than one band member. *Meddle* was a truly collaborative effort. 'A Pillow of Winds' and 'Fearless' were folk-rock songs written

194   The Albums

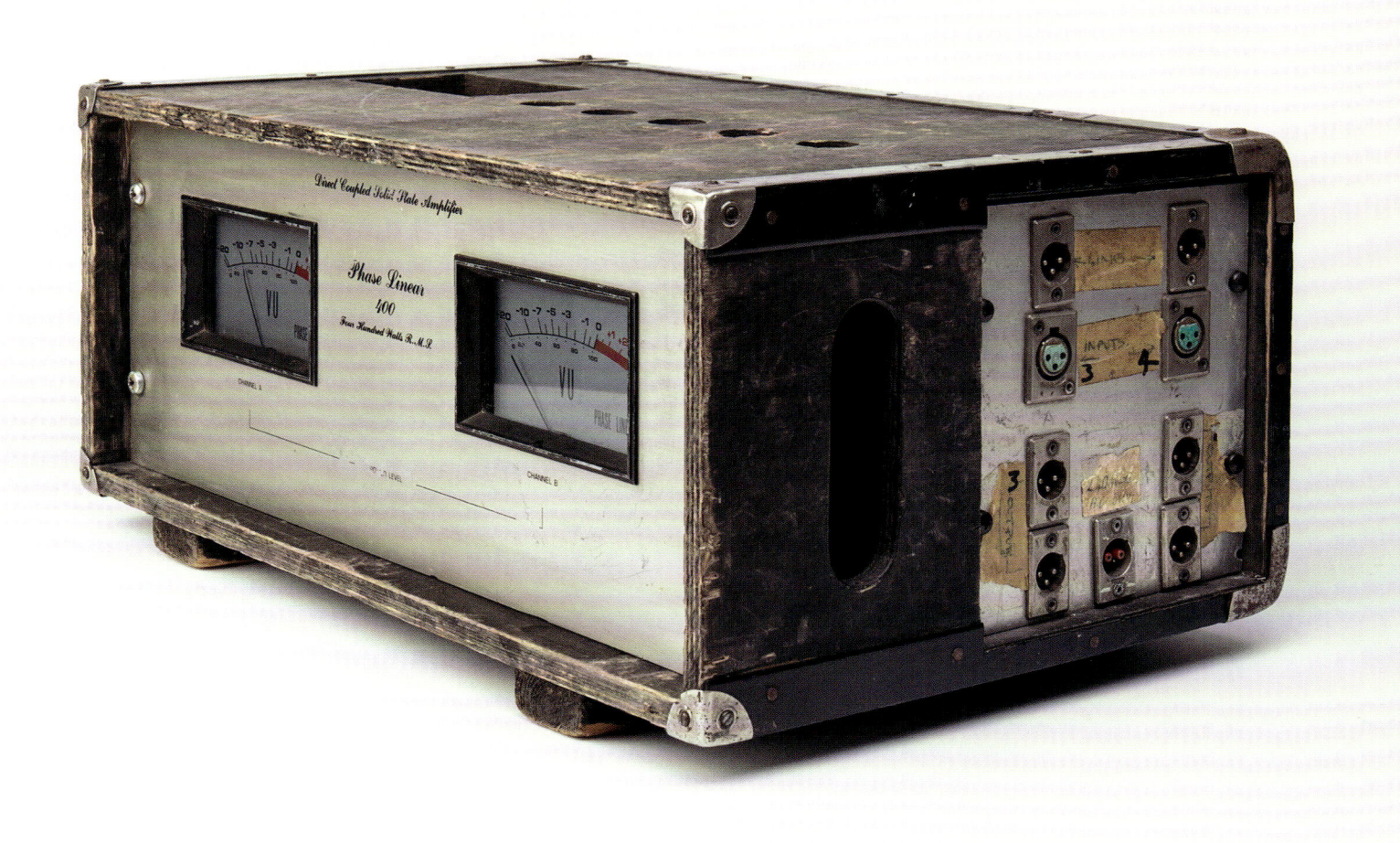

by David Gilmour and Roger Waters together. The first borrowed its title from a scoring system in mahjong, of which some band members were avid players; the second featured a sample of Liverpool Football Club supporters singing 'You'll Never Walk Alone'. Elsewhere, there was the sleepy jazz number, 'San Tropez', and 'Seamus', a tongue-in-cheek blues starring Small Faces/Humble Pie frontman Steve Marriott's titular dog howling along to the music.

In stark contrast to these gentler moments was *Meddle*'s opening track. 'One of these Days' paired Nick Mason's treated vocal with a thunderous bassline fed through Pink Floyd's favourite effects unit, the Binson Echorec. *Meddle* was a perfect union of experimental sounds, focused songwriting and cerebral lyrics.

'Echoes' and its ghostly 'ping' also inspired Hipgnosis' artwork: a human ear photographed underwater in a style that borrowed from the surrealist artist Man Ray and the British photographer Bill Brandt, known for his unique studies of the human body. 'We'd heard "Echoes" and Floyd's music had that fluid quality,' says Aubrey 'Po' Powell, who cites *Meddle* as his least favourite Floyd artwork. 'The cover has an abstract element to it … But I don't think it works as a piece of art.'

Despite its impenetrable artwork *Meddle* became a Top 5 hit in October 1971. The feverish experimentation and solo excursions of the late 1960s had been replaced. *Meddle* sounded like Pink Floyd's future.

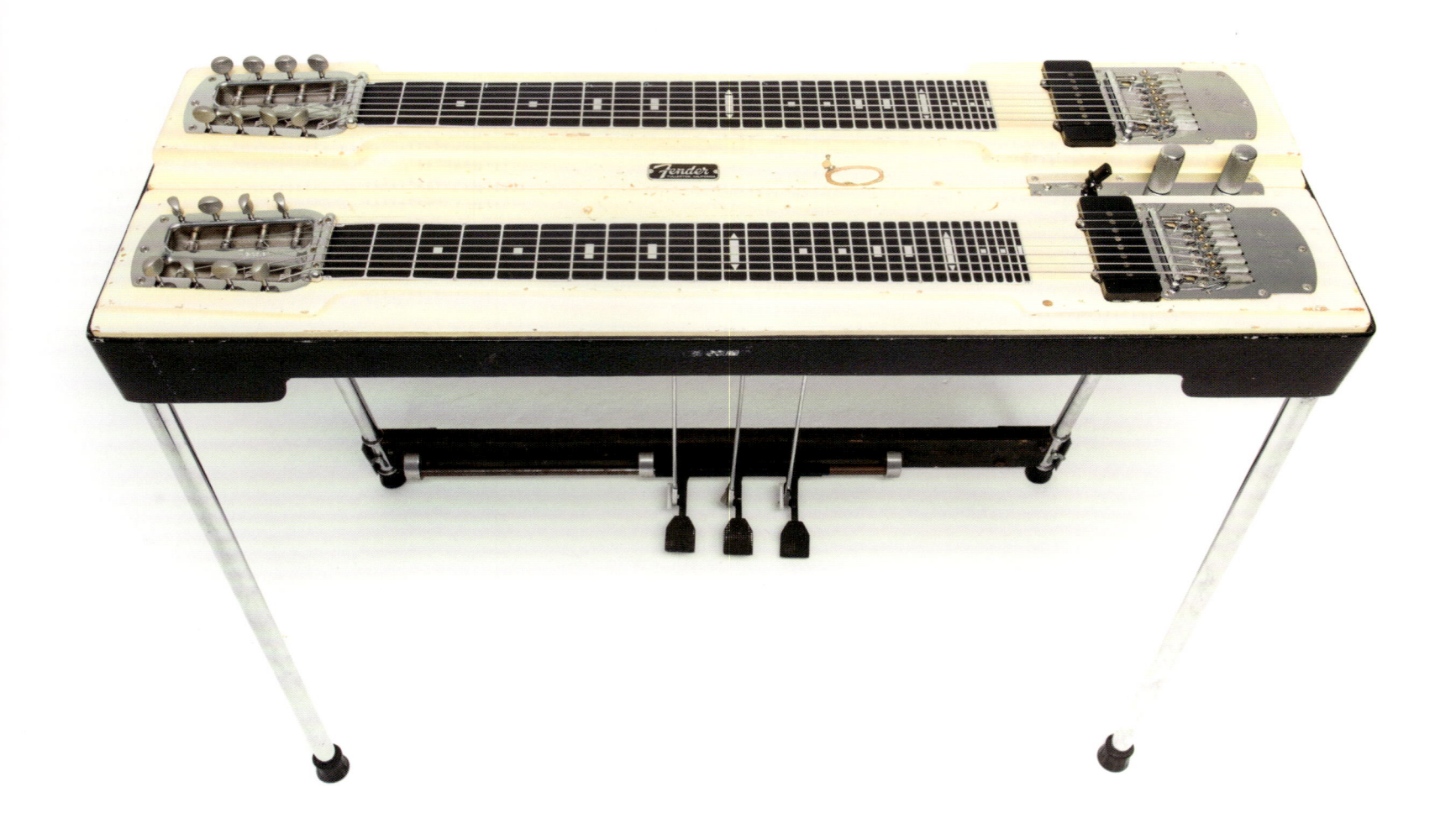

138 · ABOVE · Fender Duo 1000 Pedal steel guitar, 1962. Pink Floyd Collection

David Gilmour bought this guitar in Seattle during the band's October 1970 tour of America. Soon after, he used it on the recording of 'One of these Days' from *Meddle*. It can also be heard on the studio recordings of 'Breathe' and 'Great Gig in the Sky' from *The Dark Side of the Moon* as well as 'Shine On You Crazy Diamond' from *Wish You Were Here*.

139 · LEFT · David Gilmour playing a Jedson Blonde lap steel guitar on tour, 1974. Photograph by Storm Thorgerson

'One of These Days' and 'Echoes' from *Meddle* remained on Pink Floyd's set list during the 1970s. Gilmour's Jedson Blonde lap steel was purchased by guitar technician Phil Taylor: 'one of the first jobs I had to do was to go out and buy two lap steel guitars for the different tunings needed on 'Great Gig in the Sky' and 'One of These Days'.'

140–141 · ABOVE AND RIGHT ·
Drum heads with 'Expanding Circles' design, 1971. Original artist unknown. Image by Matthew Rich, Jealous / Kate Hepburn / Peter Curzon. Pink Floyd Archive

These drum heads, believed to be by the same artist as the 'Star Head' set, were given to Nick Mason as a replacement pair and appear in the film *Pink Floyd Live at Pompeii* (1972). Director Adrian Maben filmed Pink Floyd performing a set in the empty Roman amphitheatre, a few weeks before the release of *Meddle*.

Meddle 197

142 · ABOVE · Pink Floyd, Kodalith print featured on the inner sleeve of *Meddle*, 1971. Photograph by Storm Thorgerson / Aubrey Powell at Hipgnosis

The band arrived at different times to the photo shoot and this image is consequently a montage of two photographs: one of Richard Wright and Roger Waters, and another taken later of David Gilmour and Nick Mason. Kodalith photographic printing paper gives a high contrast print with very dense blacks when processed in Kodalith developer.

Meddle

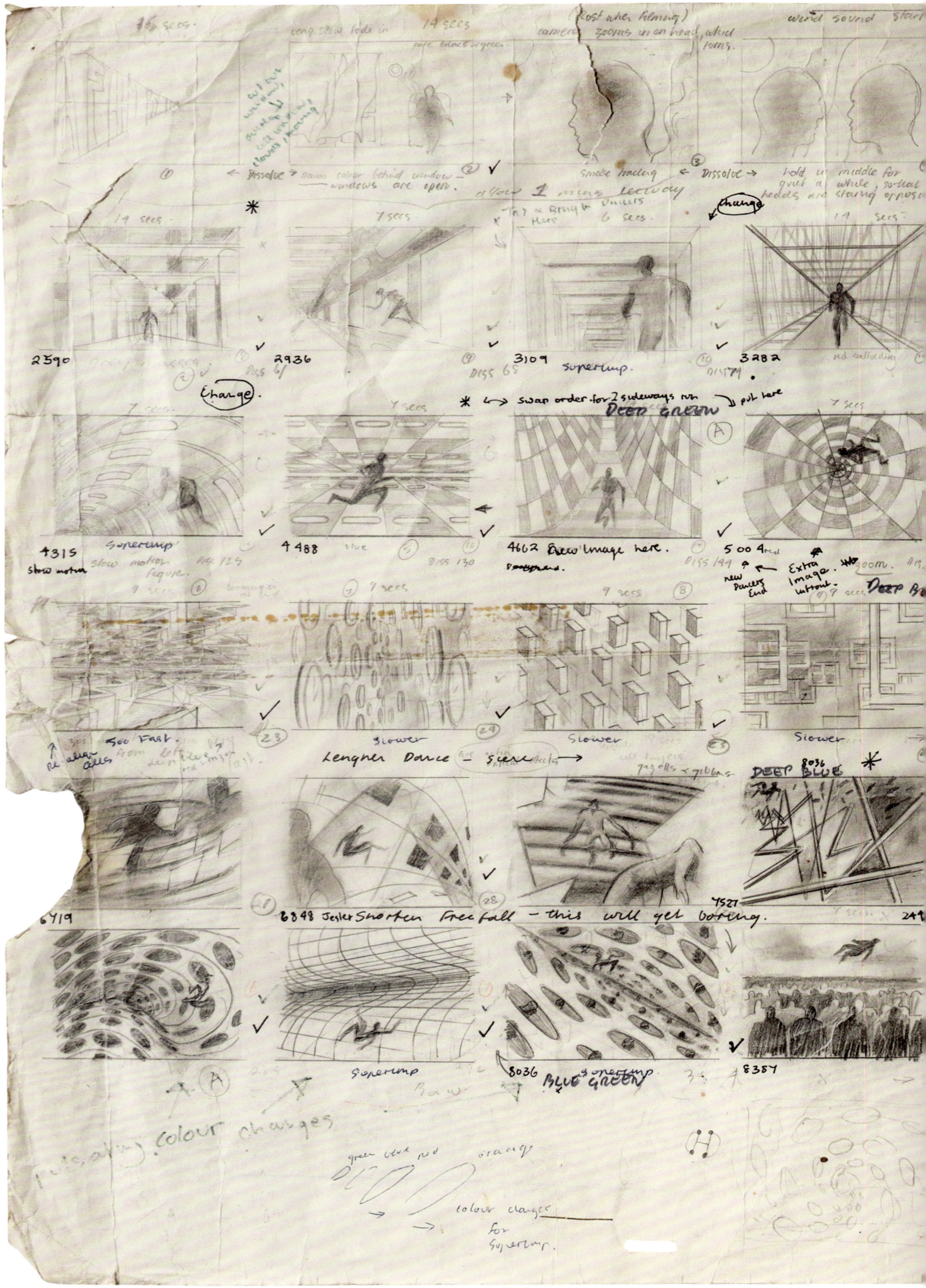

14 secs
camera zooms in on head which turns.
Dissolve
Dissolve
Change
2590
2936
3109
Superimp.
3282
Change
swap order for 2 sideways run
DEEP GREEN
4315
Superimp
slow motion figure.
4488
4662
5004
Extra image
zoom.
Too Fast.
Slower
Slower
Slower
Lengner Dance – scene
DEEP BLUE
8036
6419
6848 Jester Shorten Free fall – this will get boring.
7527
Superimp
8036
Superimp
BLUE GREEN
8357
colour changes
green blue red orange
colour changes
for
superimp.

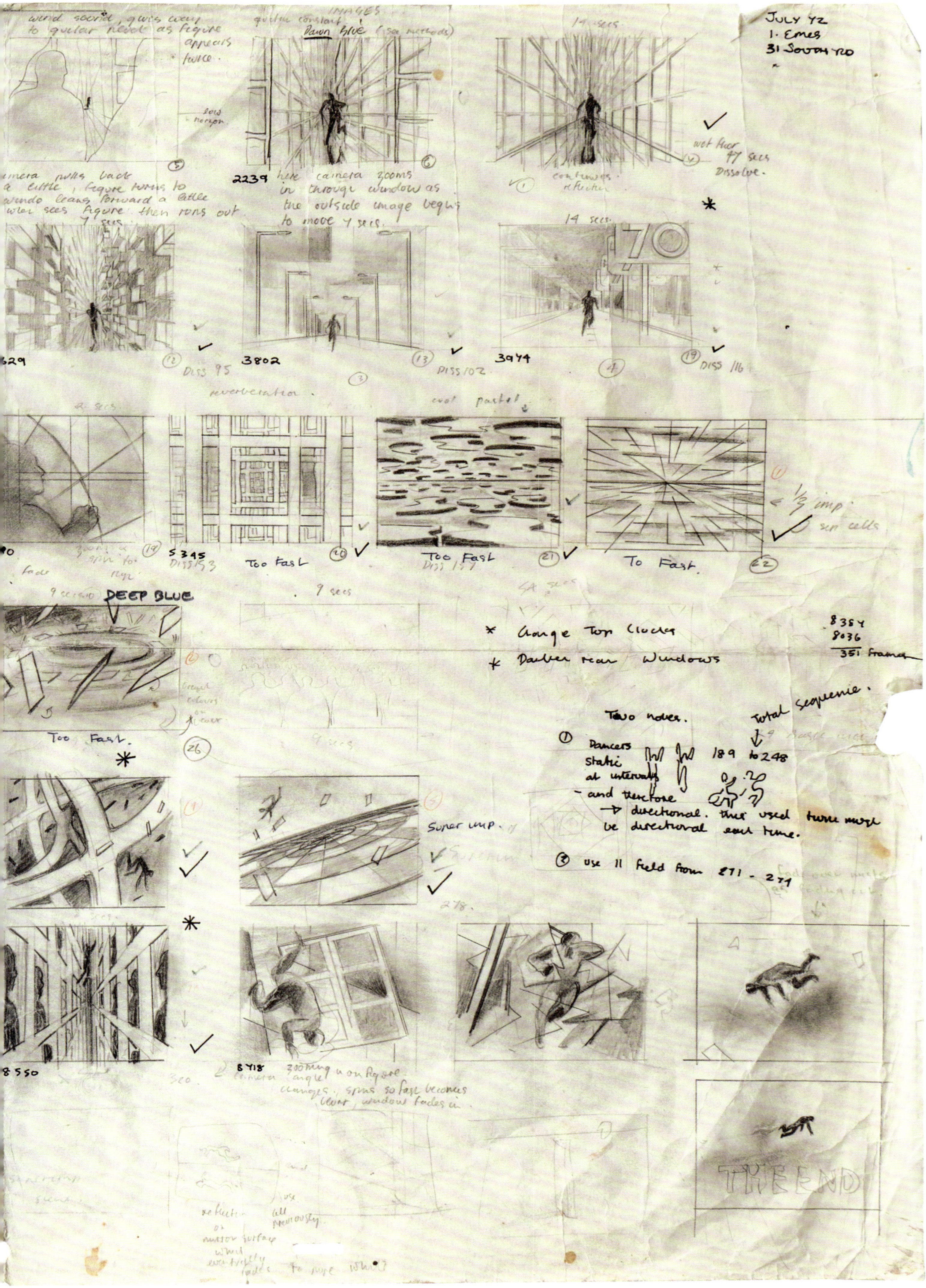

JULY 72
DEEP BLUE
Too Fast
Too Fast
To Fast
Too Fast.
Two notes.
Total sequence.
Super imp.
THE END

143 · PREVIOUS SPREAD · Storyboard for *French Windows*, an animated film set to 'One of these Days' from *Meddle* by Pink Floyd, 1972. Ian Emes

Ian Emes describes the origins of *French Windows* on his personal website: 'This film was a continuation of my body of work as a painter and kinetic artist [... made for] the joy of making it. I was a self-taught animator, inventing my own techniques through trial and error. The film went on to win awards across the world and led to an invitation to work with Pink Floyd.'

144–145 · ABOVE AND OPPOSITE · 'Whirlpool/Maelstrom' and 'Neons' from *French Windows*, painted on celluloid acetate, 1972. Ian Emes

Ian Emes used the traditional, hand-drawn animation technique of painting objects onto transparent sheets of celluloid acetate. With the rapid growth of the animation industry and computer-assisted animation production, this earlier process has been largely abandoned.

202   The Albums

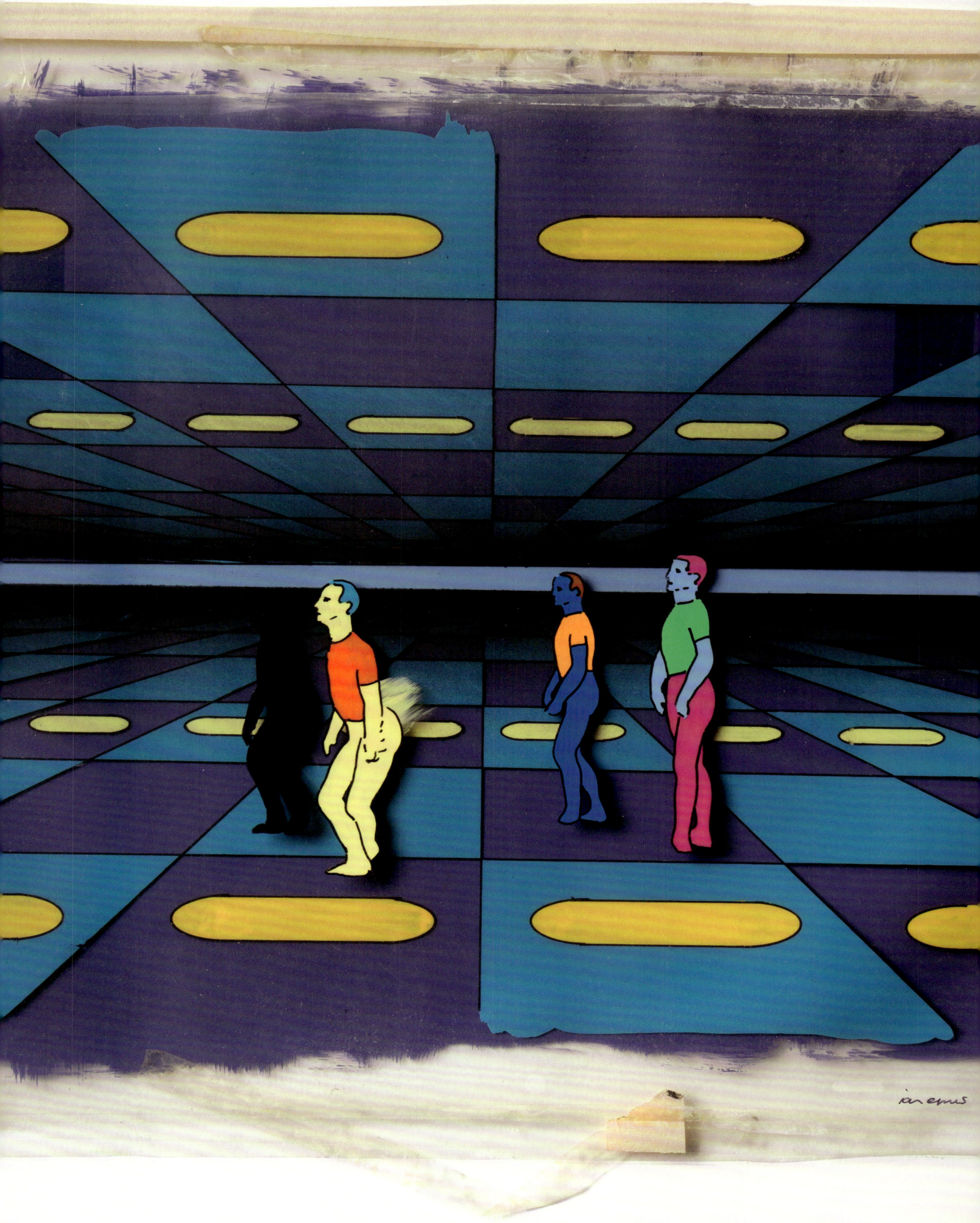

SHSP 4020
(1E 062 ○ 05054)
stereo

Obscured by Clouds
Music from La Vallée

Side 1. Obscured by Clouds *(Waters, Gilmour).* When You're In *(Waters, Gilmour, Mason, Wright).* Burning Bridges *(Wright, Waters).* The Gold it's in the ... *(Waters, Gilmour).* Wot's ... uh the deal *(Waters, Gilmour).* Mudmen *(Wright, Gilmour).*

Side 2. Childhood's End *(Gilmour).* Free Four *(Waters).* Stay *(Wright, Waters).* Absolutely Curtains *(Waters, Gilmour, Wright, Mason).*

La Vallée directed by Barbet Schroeder with Bulle Ogier, Jean Pierre Kalfon and Michael Gothard. Produced by Les Films de Losange. Album Cover by Hipgnosis.

Music Composed and Produced by Pink Floyd.

℗ 1972

EMI
E.M.I RECORDS (The Gramophone Company Ltd)
HAYES · MIDDLESEX · ENGLAND

This STEREO record can be played on mono reproducers provided either a compatible or stereo cartridge wired for mono is fitted. Recent equipment may already be fitted with a suitable cartridge. If in doubt consult your dealer.

Regd Trade Mark
The Gramophone
Company Ltd
HARVEST
A COMPANY OF
THE EMI GROUP

Made and Printed in Great Britain

7206 TPS Printed and made by Garrod & Lofthouse Ltd SHSP 4020   File under POPULAR : Pop Groups

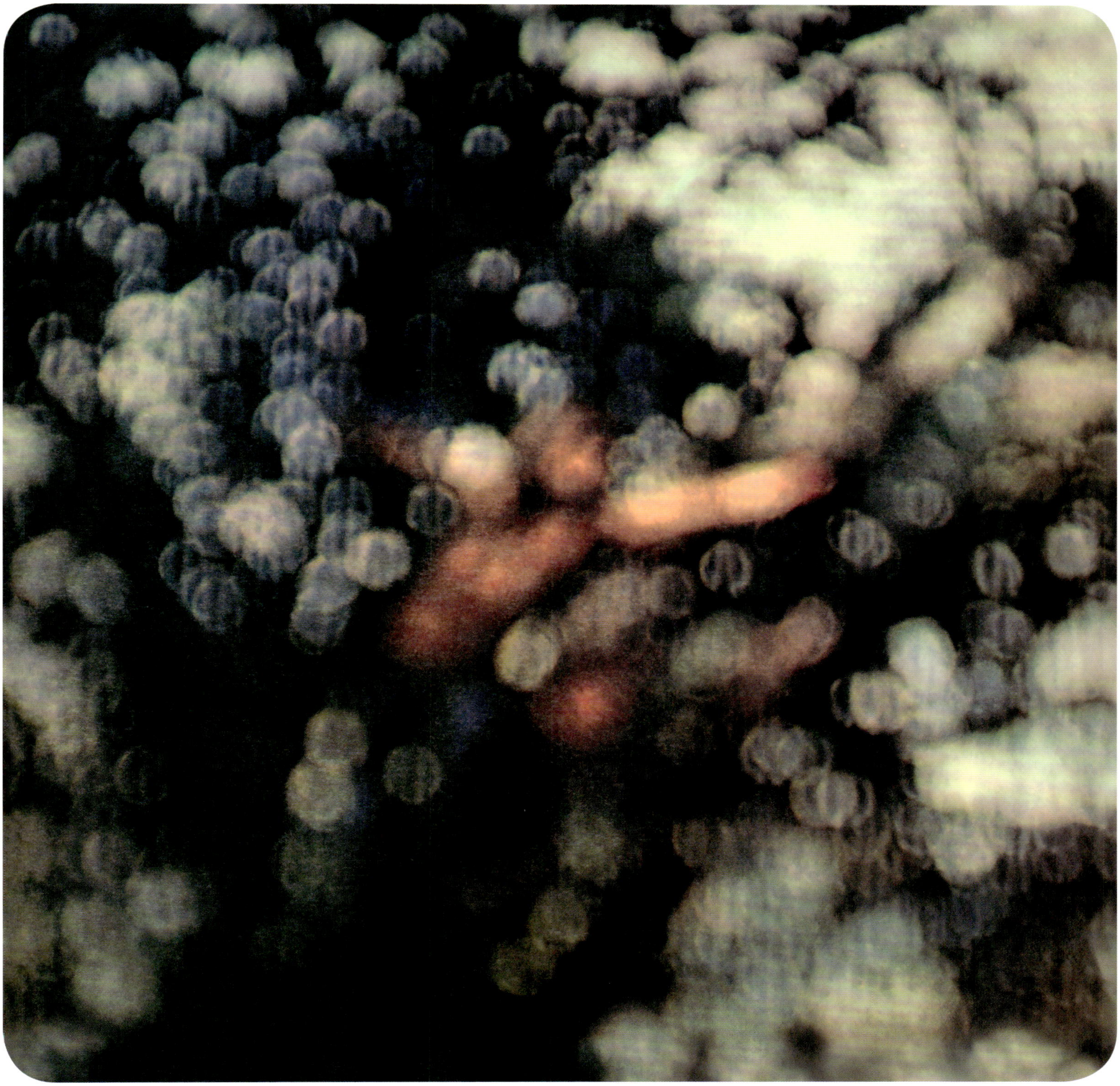

OBSCURED BY CLOUDS

June 1972 • UK: EMI Harvest SHSP 4020

146–147 · PREVIOUS SPREAD · Album artwork, *Obscured by Clouds*, 1972. Back cover features stills from the film *La Vallée*, 1972, directed by Barbet Schroeder. Design and photographs by Storm Thorgerson / Aubrey Powell at Hipgnosis

148 · OPPOSITE · Richard Wright and David Gilmour experimenting with EMS synthesizers (VCS3 and Synthi A), Strawberry Studios, Château d'Hérouville, France, 1972. Photograph by JD Mahn

For a group who'd later take 20 years between albums, Pink Floyd's work ethic in 1972 was remarkable. In those 12 months, they played the UK, Europe, the United States, Australia and Japan; released a concert movie, *Pink Floyd Live at Pompeii*; provided music for choreographer Roland Petit's ballet company; recorded most of *The Dark Side of the Moon*; and somehow found time to score *More* director Barbet Schroeder's latest movie, *La Vallée*.

La Vallée told the story of a French diplomat's wife who joins a party of explorers in Papua New Guinea; the physical quest soon becoming a metaphor for her journey of spiritual self-discovery.

As with *More*, Floyd recorded the music in a fraction of the time taken on their regular albums. Instead, it was created in two week-long sessions during February and March 1972 in Strawberry Studios at Château d'Hérouville near Paris.

The collaborative approach that defined *Meddle* continued in this new work. Pink Floyd crafted 10 songs (mostly credited to more than one band member), beginning with the title track, a baleful sounding instrumental with Nick Mason playing primitive electronic drums.

As with *More*, the soundtrack offered an eclectic mix. There was West-Coast-inflected pop (Richard Wright's ballad, 'Stay') and sturdy blues rock ('The Gold it's in the...', 'Childhood's End') alongside the wistful, folky 'Wot's ... Uh the Deal?' and the closing 'Absolutely Curtains', which included the voices of the New Guinean Mapuga tribe.

Although Pink Floyd scholars would later pore over the tracklisting searching for hidden meanings, song titles such as 'Wot's ... Uh the Deal?' and 'When You're In' were taken from catchphrases used by the band's roadie Chris Adamson.

Lyrically, however, one song explored what would become familiar Pink Floyd territory. Roger Waters' 'Free Four' smuggled its bleak subject-matter – mortality, old age and the aftermath of war – in an upbeat, almost country-rock song. '*I am the dead man's son*', sang Waters, alluding for the first time in song to his father, Eric Fletcher Waters, a member of the 8th Royal Fusiliers, who died in combat when Roger was just five months old.

Pink Floyd's soundtrack was released a month before the film, in June 1972. Barbet Schroeder later described their score as 'the best possible present for my movie'. However, a dispute with the film company saw the group change the album's title to *Obscured by Clouds*.

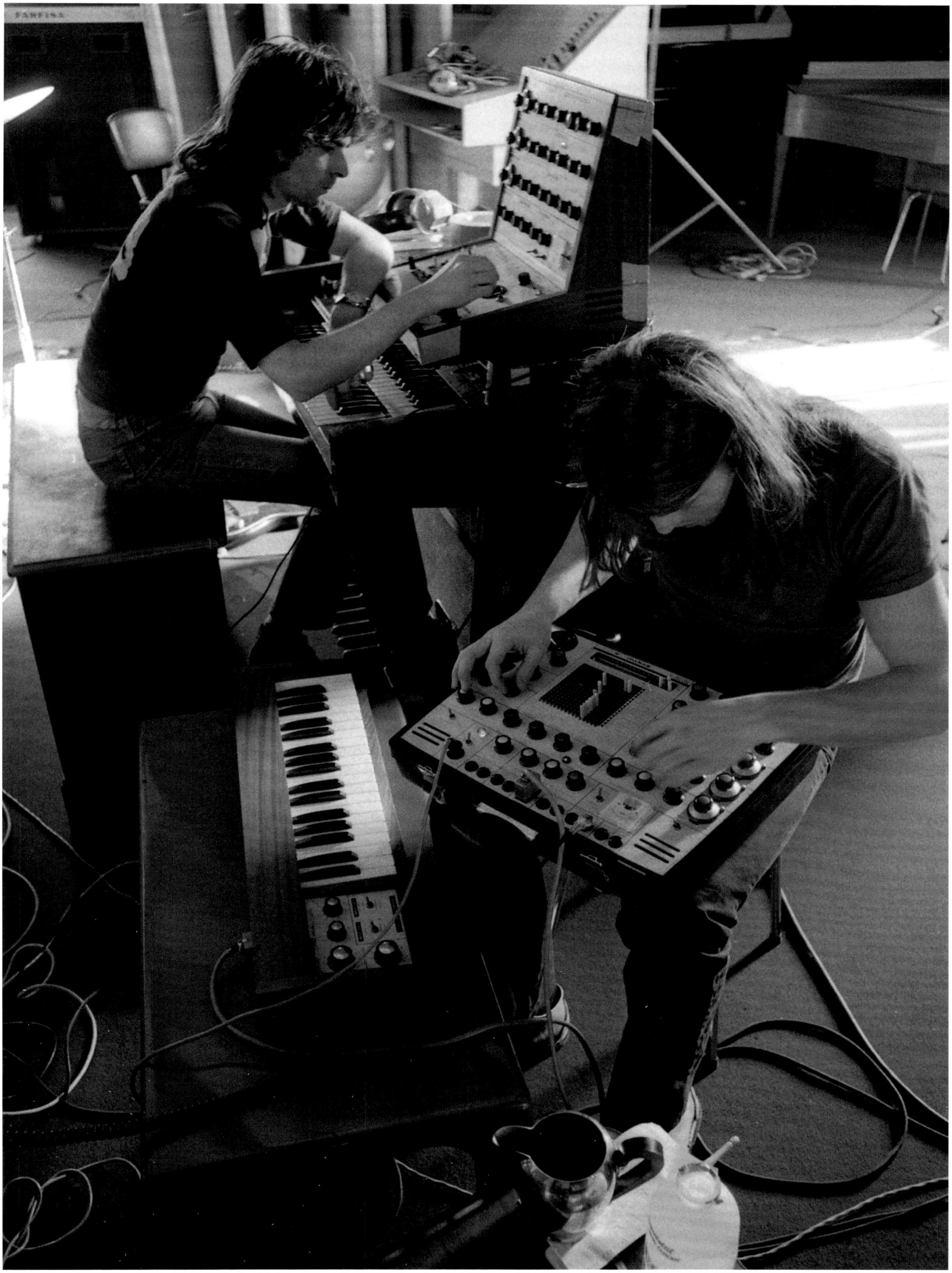
FARFISA

LA SOCIÉTÉ NOUVELLE DE CINEMATOGRAPHIE PRÉSENTE

la vallée

un film de Barbet Schroeder

avec **Bulle Ogier** / **Jean-Pierre Kalfon** / **Michael Gothard** / et **Valérie Lagrange**   musique **Pink Floyd**

adaptation et dialogues Paul Gegauff et Barbet Schroeder / images : Nestor Almendros / sons : Jean-Pierre Ruh / montage : Denise de Casabianca

PRODUCTION LES FILMS DU LOSANGE - S.N.C.

INTERDIT AUX MOINS DE 18 ANS

Like the music, Hipgnosis' artwork was created to a strict deadline. Without time for a photo shoot, Schroeder supplied Storm Thorgerson and Aubrey 'Po' Powell with stills from the film. 'Storm and I began experimenting in the darkroom, and throwing the stills out of focus, just to see what would happen,' recalls Powell.

One blurred image caught their attention: a man in a tree (in a scene edited out of the final film). Its indistinct appearance suited the album title and now reminds Aubrey Powell of the work of Georges Seurat, the French Post-Impressionist known for his use of pointillism (in which tiny dots are used in a pattern to create an image). 'It had that same abstract, painterly quality – especially when we blew it up full size,' he says.

Having found their image, Hipgnosis decided to reverse the packaging. This meant the outer sleeve on which the picture was printed had a matt finish and the inside sleeve a glossy finish. 'We flipped the cover inside out,' says Powell, 'which was a most unusual thing to do.' Finally, Hipgnosis insisted on rounding off the edges of the LP sleeve to ensure it stood out from everything else in the shop and most people's record collections.

Pink Floyd's soundtrack became a British Top 10 hit and even snuck into the US Top 50. Besides being recorded around the same time, there are musical parallels between *Obscured by Clouds* and *The Dark Side of the Moon*. In some ways, the band's score was a dummy run for many of the ideas explored in greater depth on their biggest selling album of the 1970s. Both records share a widescreen, cinematic quality. But if *The Dark Side of the Moon* is the main event, then *Obscured by Clouds* plays like its supporting feature.

149 · OPPOSITE · Promotional poster for the film *La Vallée*, 1972, directed by Barbet Schroeder. Design and photographs by Nestor Almendros / Denise de Casabianca. Pink Floyd Archive

150 · ABOVE · Pink Floyd taking a brief break from recording *Obscured by Clouds*, Strawberry Studios, Château d'Hérouville, France, 1972. Photograph by JD Mahn

Obscured by Clouds 209

151 · ABOVE · Auto Rhythm De-luxe drum machine, 1960s. Manufactured by Delsonics Ltd., UK. Pink Floyd Collection

This is the drum machine heard on 'Childhood's End', and the instrumental title track for *Obscured by Clouds*. Pink Floyd first used it live at the Royal Festival Hall in 1969. Drum machines were originally designed to imitate the sound of percussion instruments but became part of the fabric of popular music when bands like Pink Floyd started to exploit their distinctive, synthetic, sonic character.

152 · LEFT · Blue Fuzz Face pedal, 1968. Manufactured by Dallas Arbiter England, USA. Pink Floyd Collection

153–154 · OPPOSITE · Recording session and equipment at Strawberry Studios, Château d'Hérouville, France, 1972. Photographs by JD Mahn

Two classic guitar effects are pictured on the studio floor in this photograph taken during recording sessions for *Obscured by Clouds*: a Fuzz Face pedal, and a Univox Uni-Vibe, which creates a warm, smooth sound. Both effects were popularized by American musicians including Jimi Hendrix. David Gilmour was introduced to the Fuzz Face by the guitarist of Blue Cheer when they shared a stage in LA in 1968.

The Albums

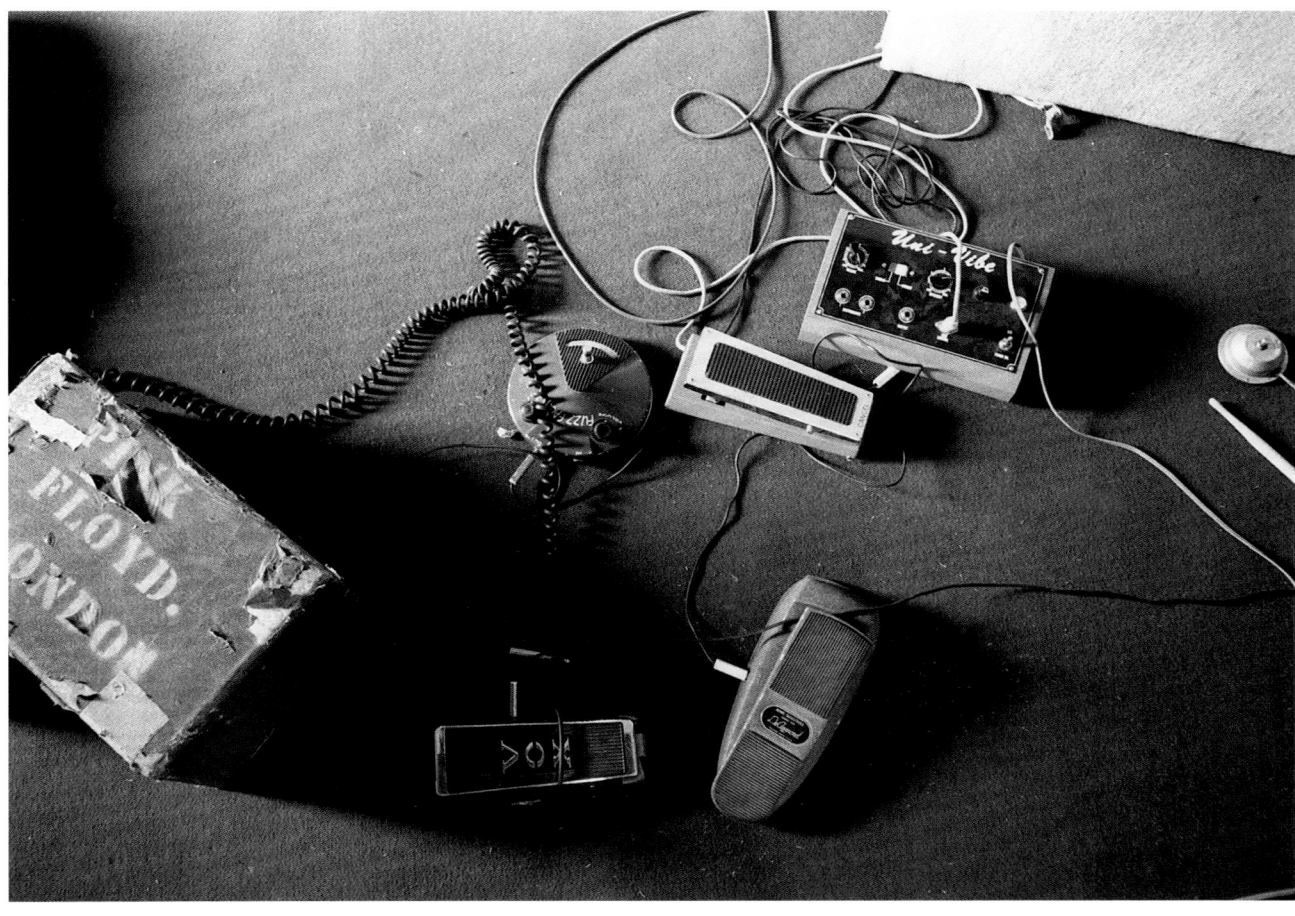

Obscured by Clouds

155 · ABOVE · EMS Synthi VCS3 synthesizer, 1969. Designed by Peter Zinovieff, David Cockerell and Tristram Cary of Electronic Music Studios (EMS), London. Collection of Roger Waters

The intensive recording session for *Obscured by Clouds* took place in the middle of *The Dark Side of the Moon*'s much lengthier development phase. The distinctive sound of the VCS3 synth can be heard on both albums. This ground-breaking portable modular synthesizer was developed by electronic music pioneers who were also involved in the influential BBC Radiophonic Workshop. Alongside the VCS3, Pink Floyd owned more than one EMS Synthi A, which consisted of the VCS3 technology packed into a briefcase design.

212   The Albums

156 · ABOVE · M-102 Hammond organ, 1960s. Pink Floyd Collection

Richard Wright played this electric organ onstage and used it in the studio for *Obscured by Clouds*. It also features in the film *Pink Floyd Live at Pompeii* (1972). Modifications were made so that it could be toured in two halves, with multi-pin audio connectors in the middle and EP6 cannon connectors for the accompanying Leslie 145 speakers. Wright used Hammonds, including C3 and B3 models, throughout his career.

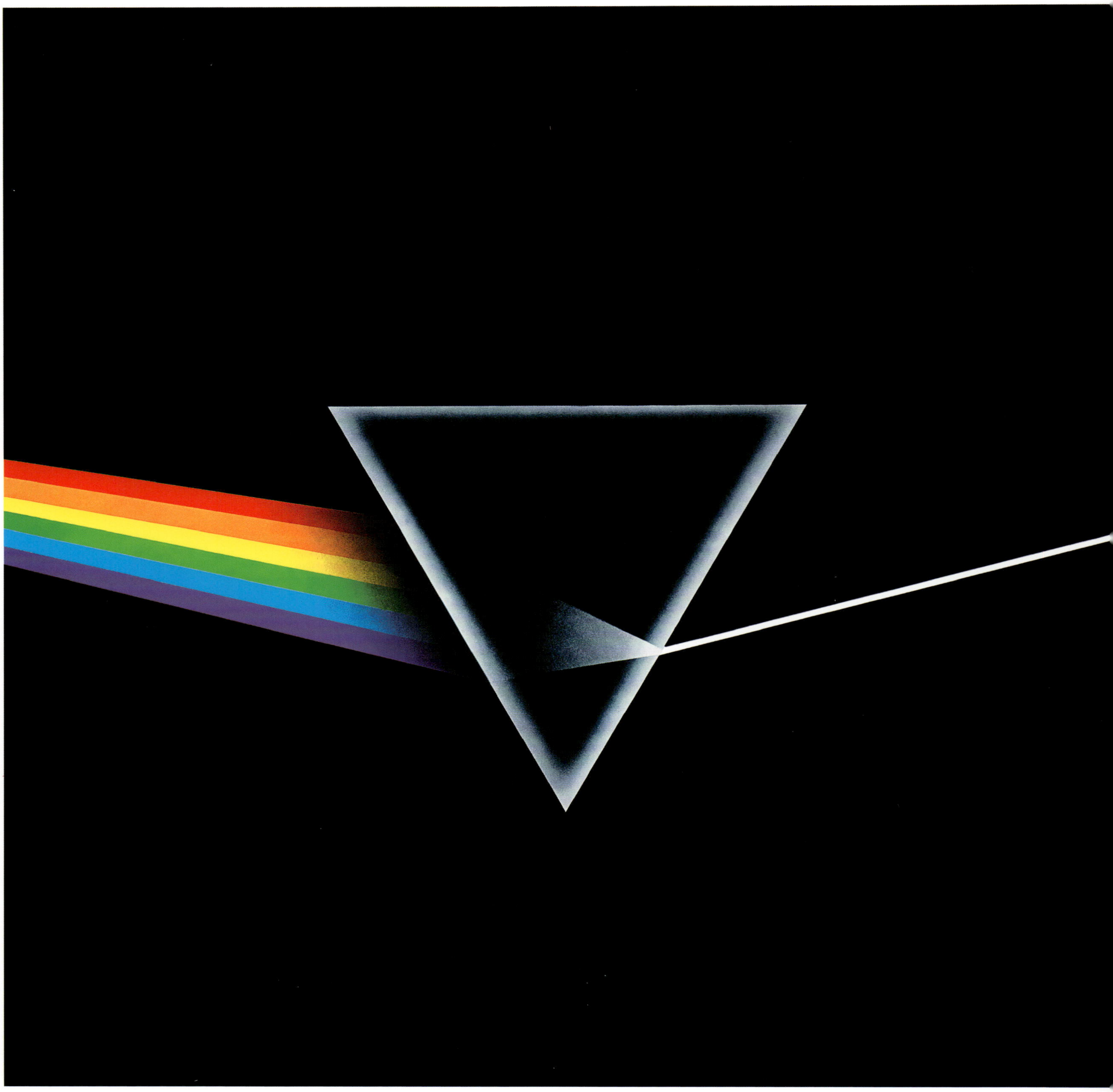

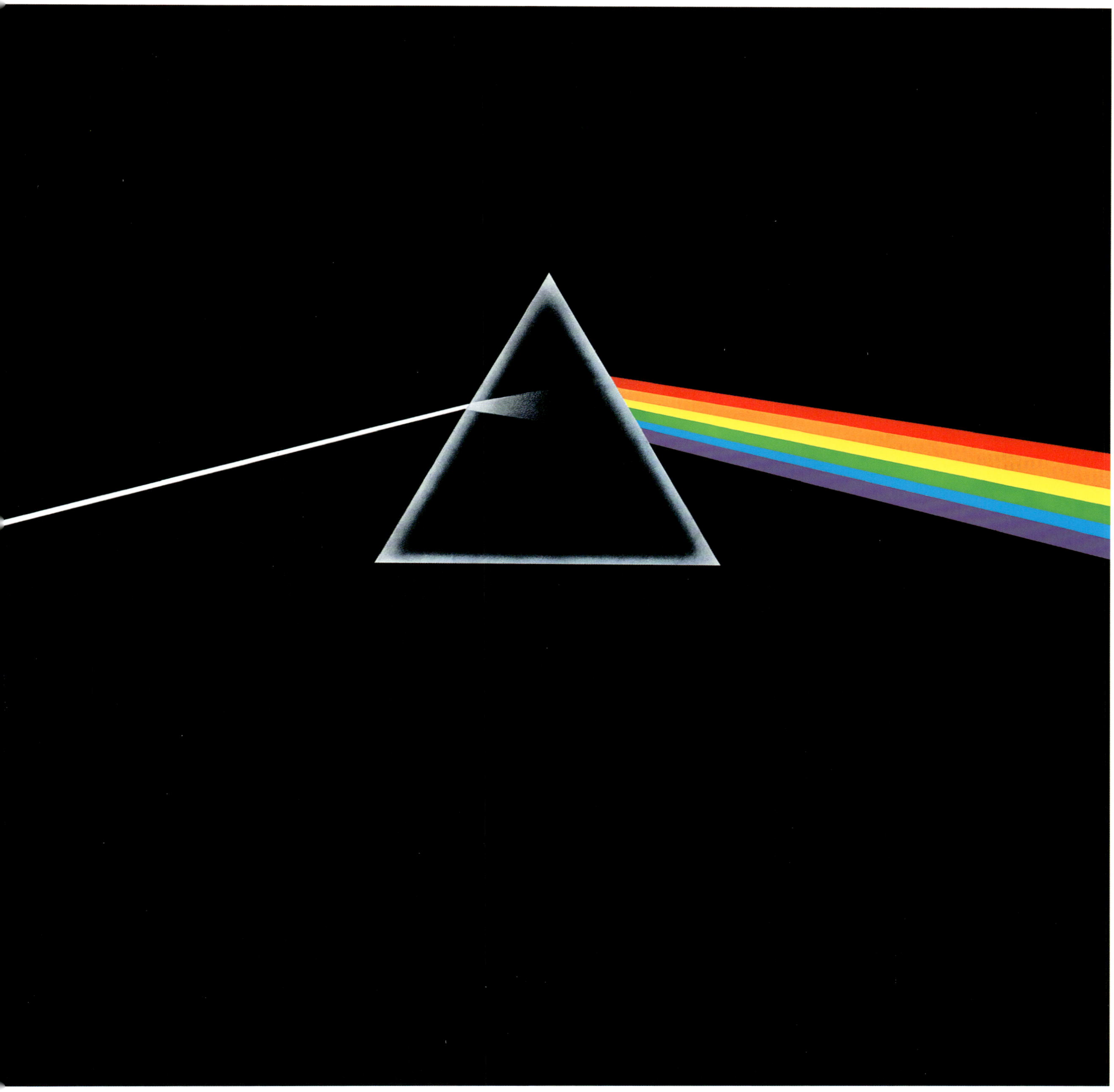

THE DARK SIDE OF THE MOON

March 1973 • UK: EMI Harvest SHVL 804

157 · PREVIOUS SPREAD · Album artwork, *The Dark Side of the Moon*, 1973. Designed by Storm Thorgerson / Aubrey Powell at Hipgnosis

158 · OPPOSITE · Audience members making the 'prism' shape with their hands during a performance of *The Dark Side of the Moon*, 1974. Photograph by Storm Thorgerson

The making of Pink Floyd's *The Dark Side of the Moon* officially began in November 1971 at Decca Studios in West Hampstead. However, the theme of the album had been developing in Roger Waters' mind long before then. On the brink of turning 30, he later revealed, he had begun to look at the world with deeper concern. It was at a band meeting in Nick Mason's house that he proposed an album that addressed the pressures of modern life and posed some philosophical questions. The idea was fleshed out over the coming months, and soon encompassed broader concerns: greed, insanity, religion, war and the fear of dying. Tellingly, *The Dark Side of the Moon* would be the first Pink Floyd album to have its lyrics printed on the sleeve.

The album was recorded between May 1972 and January '73 with sound engineer Alan Parsons at Abbey Road. Sessions were fitted around live dates and a trip to France to make the *La Vallée* soundtrack. As on *Meddle*, previously discarded ideas were repurposed. A piano theme rejected by film director Michelangelo Antonioni for *Zabriskie Point* found a home on 'Us and Them'. Elsewhere, Pink Floyd's new song 'Breathe' borrowed a title from a track on Roger Waters' and Ron Geesin's 1970 documentary soundtrack album, *Music from The Body*.

Meddle's side-long 'Echoes' was a musical and lyrical reference point. But while *The Dark Side of the Moon* contained two continuous suites of music of five songs each, it had a greater focus and sense of direction than anything that came before.

Incredibly, for an album that has since sold more than 50 million copies worldwide, the material was performed live in the year leading up to its release, and heavily bootlegged. Pink Floyd first attempted to play their new work when it was still in its infancy at the Brighton Dome in January 1972. That night, their equipment malfunctioned and they gave up. It was performed in full for the first time the following night at Portsmouth Guildhall. Later, at the end of February, 'Dark Side of the Moon – A Piece for Assorted Lunatics' made its London debut at the Rainbow Theatre.

By playing the piece live, the band discovered what worked and what didn't, and so were able to amend and finesse the material on their next studio visit. However, when the folk-rock group Medicine Head released an album with the same title in summer 1972, *The Dark Side of the Moon* briefly became 'Eclipse', until its earlier namesake failed to sell.

216   The Albums

Pink Floyd's *The Dark Side of the Moon* finally appeared in March 1973. Even at the time, it sounded like the apotheosis of all the restless experimentation that had defined the band's music during the previous six years. The album was ethereal and otherworldly but unequivocally rooted on Planet Earth, with lyrics about the human condition and music that borrowed liberally from the blues, rock 'n' roll and pop that its composers had grown up with.

The Dark Side of the Moon began with 'Speak to Me' and the pulse of a human heartbeat, before seguing into 'Breathe'. Here, David Gilmour voiced Roger Waters' lyrics about the frantic pace of everyday life and the need to savour the moment. In stark contrast, 'On the Run', a frantic instrumental inspired by the fear of dying in a plane crash, was created on the band's new toy, the EMS Synthi A, a synthesizer small enough to fit into a briefcase.

Many songs were interspersed with spoken-word segments. Waters asked Pink Floyd's roadies and the Abbey Road doorman a list of questions (When had they last hit someone? Were they afraid of dying? Of going insane?) and taped the responses. These fleeting, unidentified voices proclaiming 'I've been mad for fucking years' and 'there is no dark side of the moon ... in fact, it's all dark', created an atmospheric sub-plot to the music.

Ultimately, one of *The Dark Side of the Moon*'s great strengths was its fusion of cutting-edge technology and elements of *musique concrète* with traditional blues guitar, pop choruses and female backing vocals. The cacophony of alarm clocks at the beginning of 'Time' is deposed by Gilmour's howling Fender; the rattle of cash registers creates the syncopated rhythm on 'Money' before

THE SEQUENCE

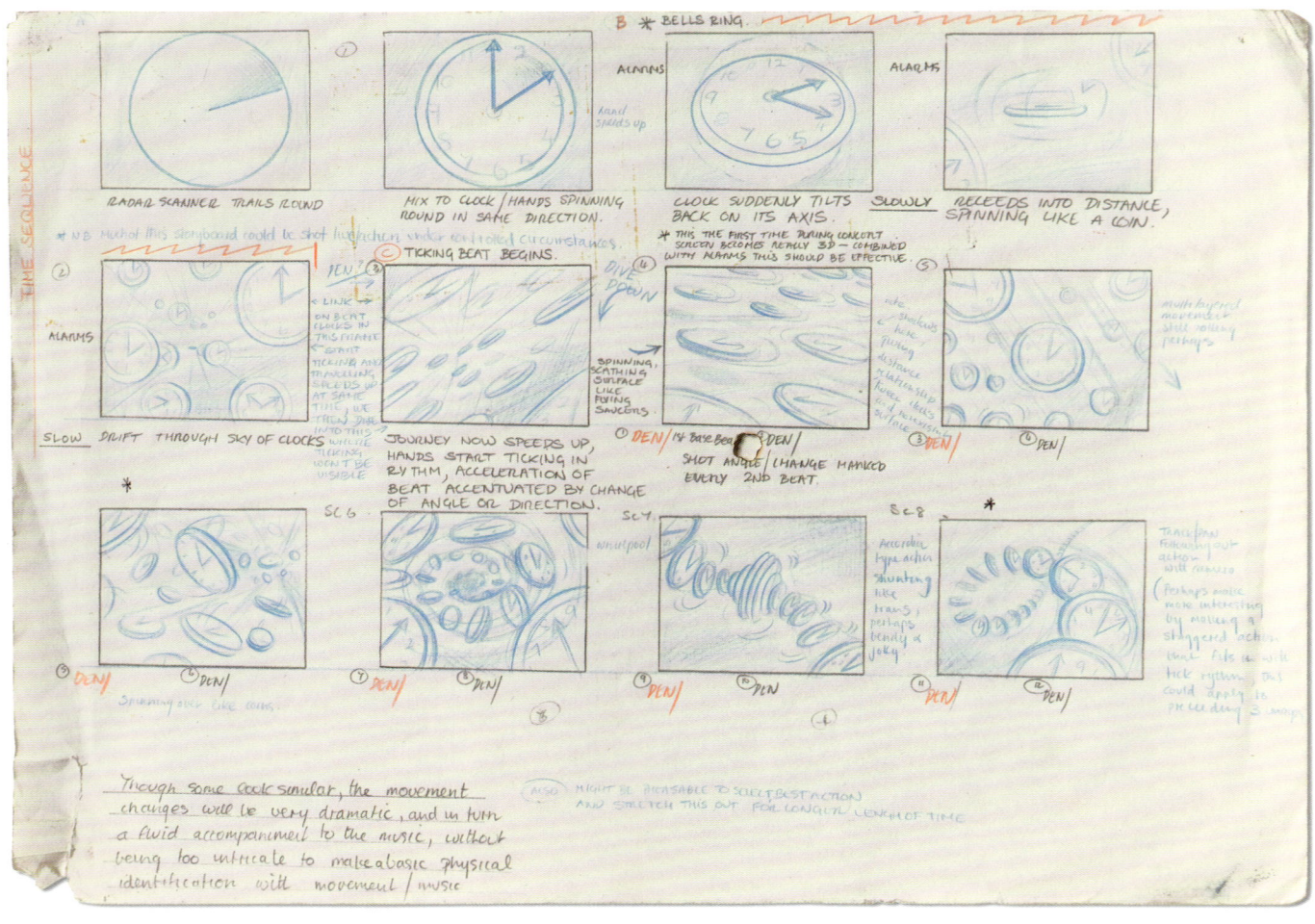

B * BELLS RING

		ALARMS	ALARMS
RADAR SCANNER TRAILS ROUND.	MIX TO CLOCK / HANDS SPINNING ROUND IN SAME DIRECTION.	CLOCK SUDDENLY TILTS SLOWLY BACK ON ITS AXIS.	RECEEDS INTO DISTANCE, SPINNING LIKE A COIN.

* NB Michael this storyboard could be shot live/action under ideal circumstances.

© TICKING BEAT BEGINS.

* This the first time that the concept screen becomes really 3D – combined with alarms this should be effective.

SLOW DRIFT THROUGH SKY OF CLOCKS

JOURNEY NOW SPEEDS UP, HANDS START TICKING IN RYTHM, ACCELERATION OF BEAT ACCENTUATED BY CHANGE OF ANGLE OR DIRECTION.

1st Bar Beat — SHOT ANGLE / CHANGE MAN/CCD EVERY 2nd BEAT.

SC 6   SC 7 whirlpool   SC 8

Though some clock similar, the movement changes will be very dramatic, and in turn a fluid accompaniment to the music, without being too intricate to make a basic physical identification with movement / music

ALSO MIGHT BE ADVISABLE TO SELECT BEST ACTION AND STRETCH THIS OUT FOR LONGER LENGTH OF TIME

saxophonist Dick Parry's jazz solo takes precedence. And only a few minutes separate 'On the Run's robotic synth and Richard Wright's mellow piano and session singer Clare Torry's wordless vocals on 'The Great Gig in the Sky'.

For all its experimentation and daring, there was an everyman quality to this music: the questions it asked connected with those who'd grown up with Pink Floyd since the 1960s, but also with those coming of age in the mid-'70s. And, inevitably, with the band itself. Roger Waters' lyrics on the subject of madness were seen as at least partly referring to Syd Barrett's mental instability. The album connected with audiences worldwide, becoming a Number 2 hit in the UK and Number 1 in the US.

Contributing to its global success was Hipgnosis' now world-famous artwork. When Storm Thorgerson and Aubrey 'Po' Powell visited Abbey Road during the final album sessions, Richard Wright suggested they break with tradition on their next cover design. 'Rick said, "For God's sake, let's not have another one of your surreal ideas",' recalls Powell. 'He also told us how much he liked the packaging on a box of Black Magic chocolates – just black and white. He considered that a great piece of simple product design. Storm and I left the studio rather depressed.'

Feeling starved of inspiration, Powell leafed through a physics textbook and stopped at a drawing of a glass paperweight on a piece of sheet music, with light streaming through a window to create a rainbow effect on the paper: 'Storm saw it, clicked his fingers and said, "That's it".'

159–160 · **OPPOSITE** · Storyboard and cell for 'Time' animation, 1974. Designed by Ian Emes. Ian Emes Collection

161 · **ABOVE** · 'Time' animation by Ian Emes projected onstage, Royal Albert Hall, London, 2016. Photograph by Ian Emes. Ian Emes Collection

Ian Emes had impressed Pink Floyd with an animated sequence inspired by 'One of these Days' from *Meddle*. He was commissioned to design further animations for the tour of *The Dark Side of the Moon*, as part of an overall enhancement of the band's stage visuals. The 40-foot circular screen designed by acclaimed lighting and production designer Arthur Max became a signature feature of subsequent Pink Floyd shows.

The Dark Side of the Moon

The Floyd are one of the few groups who can appreciate that electric instruments are more than just ordinary instruments with amplification.

—Peter Jenner interviewed by David Hughes,
  Disc and Music Echo, 22 July 1967

Hipgnosis' simple design of a prism dispersing light into colour on a black background met with the whole band's approval. 'We presented them with other ideas, but as soon as they saw the prism they were unanimous,' says Powell.

At the time record companies were experimenting with giving away lyric sheets and posters inside LPs. Hipgnosis extended the imagery on the sleeve by photographing the pyramids in Cairo for a poster and including further pyramid-related imagery on two postcard-sized stickers. 'There was no great hidden meaning to the prism or the pyramid,' admits Powell, 'only that they were the perfect shape.'

The artwork for *The Dark Side of the Moon* is so synonymous with the music that it's now impossible to think of one without the other. Both remain timeless: still connecting with new generations and new audiences. Strangely, in a world moving at an even faster pace than in 1973, Pink Floyd's commentary on the pressures of modern life and encroaching mortality has never grown old.

162 · **OPPOSITE** · EMS Synthi VCS3 II, 1973. Designed by Peter Zinovieff, David Cockerell and Tristram Cary of EMS (Electronic Music Studios), London. Pink Floyd Collection

163 · **ABOVE** · DK1 keyboard controller for VCS3 synthesizer, 1970s. Designed by EMS (Electronic Music Studios), London. Pink Floyd Collection

VCS3 synthesizers were primarily used to generate sound effects because, lacking a keyboard, they were not instinctively easy to use as melodic instruments. To help overcome the problem, keyboard controllers like the DK1 were designed to be plugged into the VCS3. The DK1, first launched in 1969, also had an internal oscillator and amplifier.

The Dark Side of the Moon

CONTROLLERS
OSCILLATOR BANK
MIXER
MODIFIERS
OUTPUT
moog
minimoog

SERIAL NO.

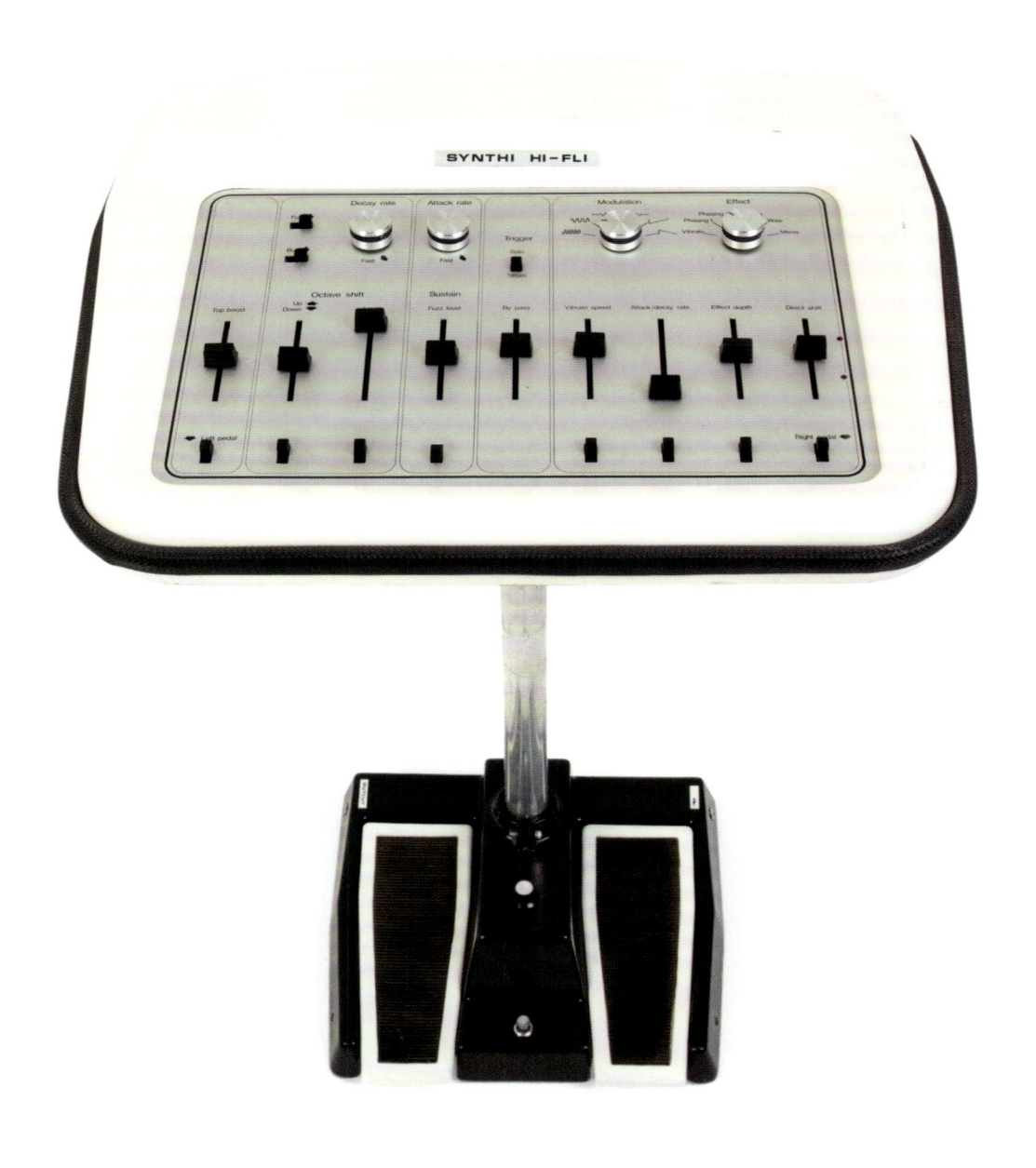

164 · OPPOSITE TOP · Mini-Moog synthesizer, 1970s. Designed by Bob Moog and manufactured by Moog Music. Pink Floyd Collection

Richard Wright used the Mini-Moog in 1973–7, mainly as a solo lead instrument. It was first played on 'Any Colour You Like' from *The Dark Side of the Moon*, and features on *Wish You Were Here* and *Animals*. Moog Music in America and the London-based EMS were leading the invention of functional, sophisticated electronic instruments. Pink Floyd, always tuned into the latest advances in music technology, were clients of both studios.

165 · OPPOSITE BOTTOM · 'Quadpot' quadrophonic sound machine, about 1974. Probably designed by Ivor Taylor with Peter Watts. Pink Floyd Collection

Pink Floyd pioneered live quadrophonic sound with the 'Azimuth Co-ordinator'; a device invented and built by Bernard Speight, a technical engineer at EMI Studios, Abbey Road. The same technology was built into a smaller format that could be operated with one hand, known as the 'Quadpot'. This model sat on the Hammond organ and was operated by Richard Wright during tours of *The Dark Side of the Moon* and *Wish You Were Here* from 1974 to 1975.

166 · ABOVE · EMS Synthi Hi-Fli, 1972. Designed by David Cockerell. Pink Floyd Collection

David Gilmour bought this 'very, very expensive' Synthi Hi-Fli prototype in 1972. Only 350 were ever made. It functions as an analogue multi-effect processor, which can be applied to vocals, guitars and organs. With no memory to record settings, the sliders must be manually tweaked for each tone change. This Synthi Hi-Fli was used onstage in 1972–3 and during recording sessions for *The Dark Side of the Moon*.

167 · PAGE 224 · Multimedia planning chart for *The Dark Side of the Moon* live performances, 1974. Nick Mason. Pink Floyd Archive

Pink Floyd devised a sophisticated stage show for live performances of *The Dark Side of the Moon* in 1974, with animations, lighting and sound effects specific to each track. Synchronizing the sound and visuals required careful planning and rehearsal. Nick Mason's notes capture the process and list some of the show's sound effects, film and classic tracks.

168 · PAGE 225 · Draft artwork with working album title 'Eclipse' (later *The Dark Side of the Moon*), 1972. Pink Floyd Archive

The Dark Side of the Moon

Pink Floyd · Dark Side of the Moon

Time	Film	Tape	Music	Time	Notes
0	Moon Approach	Heartbeat pulse		0	
	Pulsing Globe Forms	Drones			
	Heartbeat oscilloscope	Build up to chord			
5			Breathe, Breathe in the air.....	5	
10	Take off	Organ Leslie swish	VCS 3 pattern	10	
	Clouds + Lightning	footsteps			
	Earth Approach				
	Explosion	Explosion			
	Clocks	Alarm	Bass + Rototoms		
15	Pendulums			15	
	Fade		Ticking away the moments.....		
20			Home home again.....	20	
	Waves. low		Piano Intro		
	Waves. faster		Girls solo		
25	Fade	Collection Register rhythm		25	
	Money sequence	Fade	Bass lead in		
			Money......		
30	Fade			30	
			Us + Them.....		
35	Zabriskie Point		} Sax solo	35	
	slowed explosions				
40			Instrumental Section	40	
			} Girls		
			The lunatics.....		
45	Politicians	Laughter		45	
	Sun Prominances Blue Red Natural		All that you.....		
	Dissolve to Corona on Sun	Tolling Bell Fade			

The Dark Side of the Moon

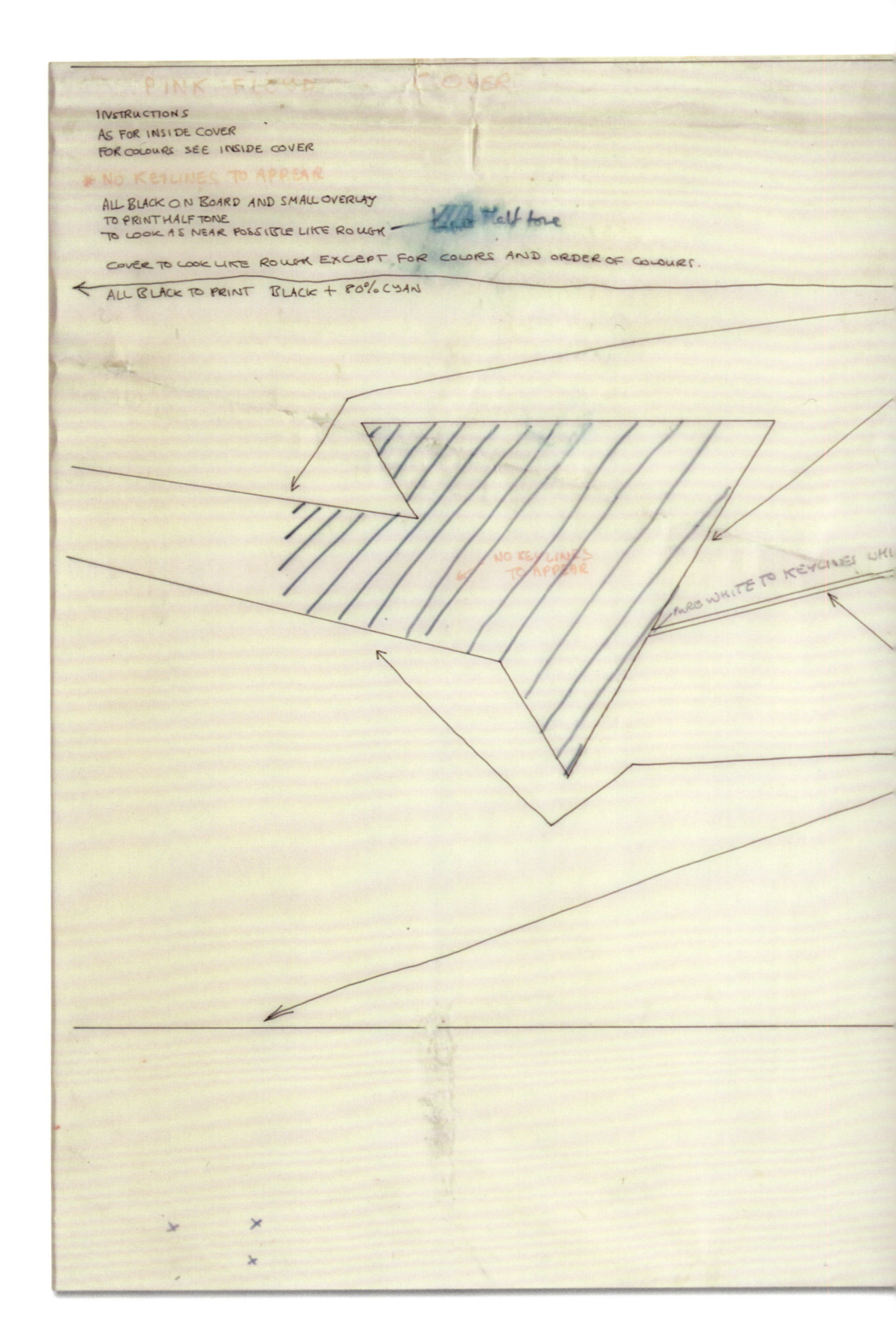

169 · RIGHT · Line-drawn artwork for *The Dark Side of the Moon* album cover, 1973. George Hardie. Collection of George Hardie

Most Hipgnosis album cover designs centred on a photographic image, but *The Dark Side of the Moon* was an exception. Hipgnosis called on the graphic design skills of George Hardie, a friend from the Royal College of Art who had recently worked on Led Zeppelin's first album cover. His mechanical line drawing showed the printers where to apply colour to create a scientifically precise image. No-one knew quite how the final image would look until it came off the press. The result was surprising and, in this case, masterful.

226 The Albums

SOLID BLACK
TO KEYLINES

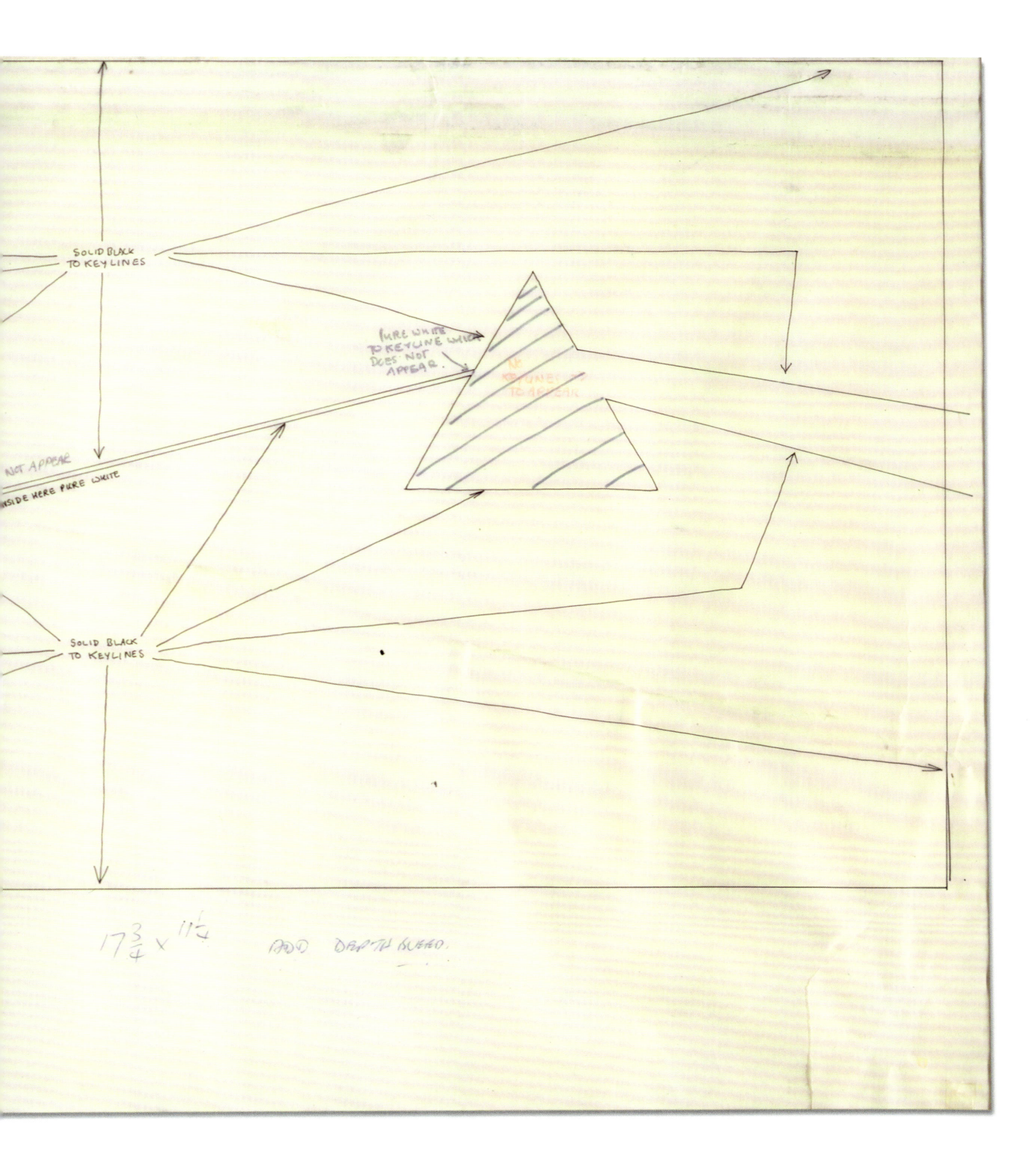

PURE WHITE
TO KEYLINE WHICH
DOES NOT
APPEAR.

NOT APPEAR
INSIDE HERE PURE WHITE

SOLID BLACK
TO KEYLINES

$17\frac{3}{4} \times 11\frac{1}{4}$ ADD DEPTH BLEED.

The Dark Side of the Moon

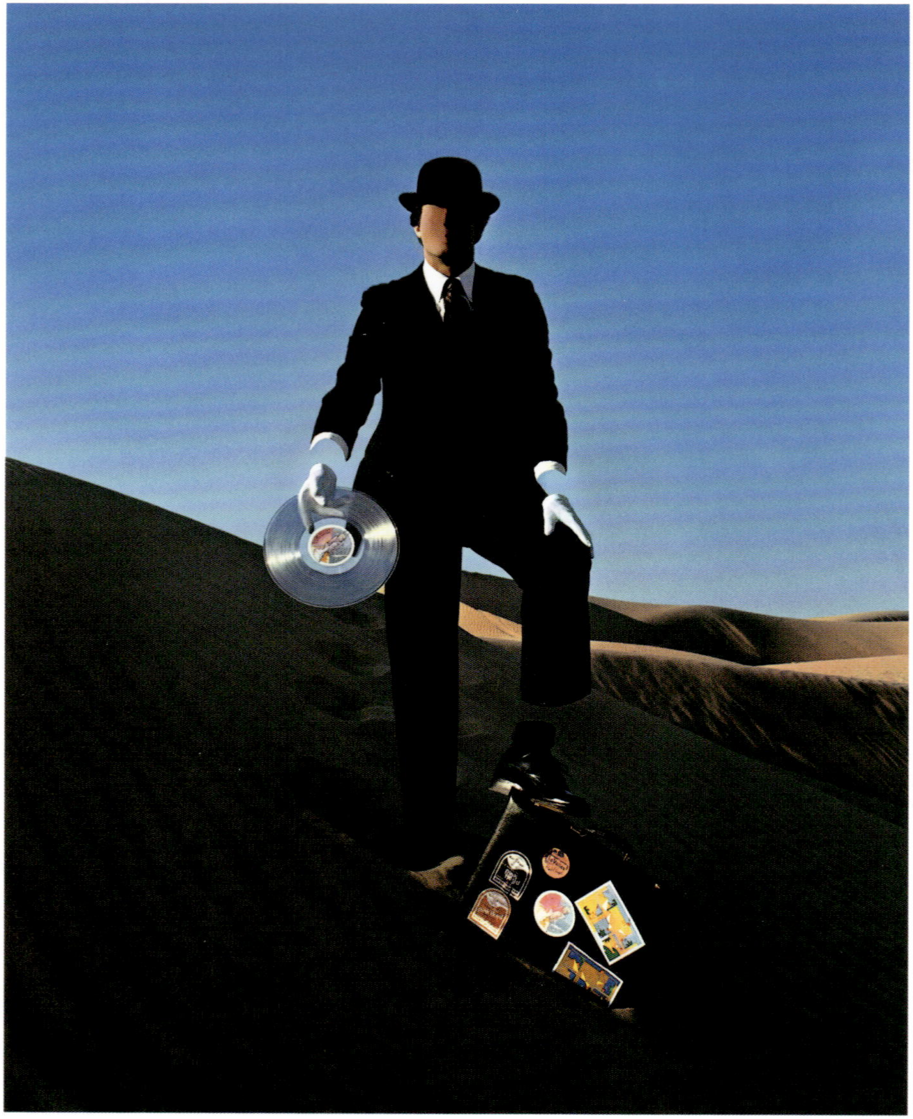

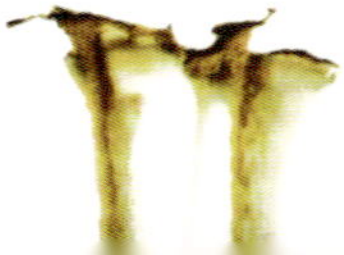

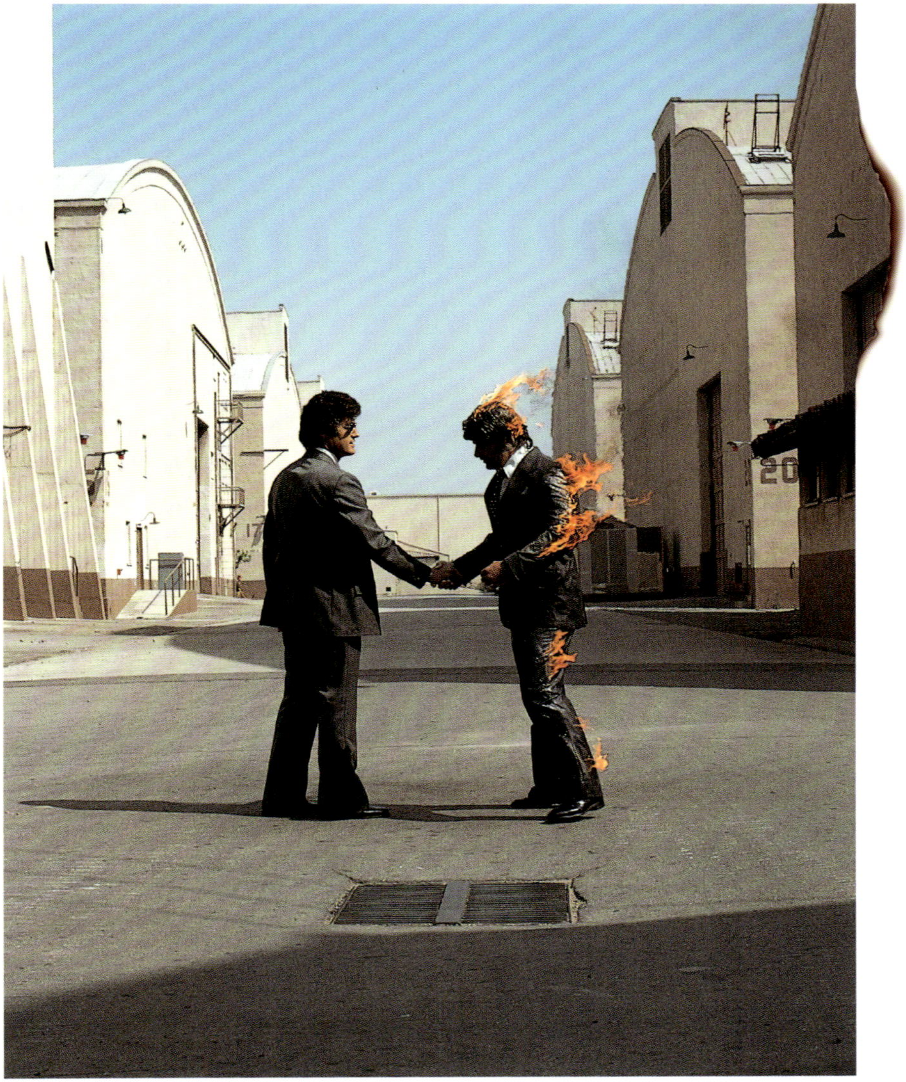
20

WISH YOU WERE HERE

September 1975 • UK: EMI Harvest SHVL 814

170–171 · PREVIOUS SPREAD · Album artwork, *Wish You Were Here*, 1975. Designed by Storm Thorgerson / Aubrey Powell at Hipgnosis

172–175 · OPPOSITE · Cover photo shoot for *Wish You Were Here* with stuntmen Ronnie Rondell and Danny Rogers, Warner Brothers film studios, Burbank, 1975. Photographs by Aubrey Powell at Hipgnosis. Aubrey Powell Collection

Hipgnosis famously shot their album covers 'for real' rather than creating a digitally manipulated image. These images show stuntman Ronnie Rondell covered in flames, while assistants stand by with fire extinguishers. For Storm Thorgerson, the handshake captured the play of absence and presence in the album: 'An ordinary handshake – definite, but often as meaningful as flyshit.'

The Dark Side of the Moon turned Pink Floyd from a hugely successful, but nevertheless cult band, into one of the best-selling rock groups on the planet. Global success came at a price, though. The follow-up, *Wish You Were Here*, was a response to their new-found fame and wealth that initially saw them struggling for inspiration.

The album that now contains that evergreen title track and 'Shine On You Crazy Diamond' began life as a series of sounds, created using a range of everyday items ranging from cigarette lighters to elastic bands, and aerosol cans to wine glasses.

The 'Household Objects' project had been mooted in the early stages of recording *Meddle*. Pink Floyd revived the idea in winter 1973, spending weeks at Abbey Road in which they shunned conventional instruments, using elastic bands to create a bassline and striking a piece of wood with an axe to replicate a drum sound.

They soon gave up. By January 1975, they'd begun making music by conventional means, but progress was slow. Pink Floyd had performed three new songs – 'Gotta Be Crazy', 'Raving and Drooling' and 'Shine On You Crazy Diamond' – on their 1974 UK and European tour. But once in the studio there was an overwhelming mood of inertia. The band's members were now all in their thirties, had wives or girlfriends and, in some cases, children to occupy their time outside the group. Furthermore, *The Dark Side of the Moon* had been so successful, they weren't entirely sure how they could follow it up.

After six arduous weeks at Abbey Road Studios, Roger Waters called a meeting and suggested they start again. 'Gotta Be Crazy' and 'Raving and Drooling' were dropped (though both would reappear, as 'Dogs' and 'Sheep' respectively, on 1977's *Animals*), while 'Shine On You Crazy Diamond' was split into two sections to open and close the album.

Waters composed two new songs, 'Welcome to the Machine' and 'Have a Cigar', while he and David Gilmour co-wrote what would become the title track, 'Wish You Were Here'. There was a theme of regret and disillusionment running through 'Shine On You Crazy Diamond' and this new material. The mood of the songs matched the mood in the studio.

The lyrics to 'Shine On You Crazy Diamond' were partly a eulogy to Syd Barrett, who made an unexpected appearance at Abbey Road while the group were recording. 'Welcome to the Machine' and 'Have a Cigar' saw Roger Waters

230   The Albums

Wish You Were Here

176 · OPPOSITE · René Magritte with his painting *The Great War*, 1966 (photographed), 1976 (printed). Photograph by Bill Brandt.
V&A: PH.95–1978

Hipgnosis were inspired by surrealist artists including René Magritte, Salvador Dalí and Man Ray. The image of a faceless bowler-hatted man on the back cover of *Wish You Were Here* pays homage to Magritte, who repeatedly painted bowler hats and – as Bill Brandt's arresting photograph shows – often wore them himself.

railing against the music industry. The former's baleful robotic rhythm was created by the EMS Synthi A and suggested a huge mincing machine chewing up the artistic 'talent' before spitting it out. Meanwhile, the lyrics to 'Have a Cigar' were inspired by Pink Floyd's past US tours where back-slapping record executives told them how wonderful they were and then asked 'Which one's Pink?' Both songs signposted ideas and sentiments that would later be fully explored on *The Wall*. Yet, despite several attempts, neither Waters nor Gilmour were comfortable with their voices on 'Have a Cigar'. In the end, fellow Abbey Road client, singer-songwriter Roy Harper, recorded the final vocal.

An air of melancholy suffuses the title track and the multi-part 'Shine On You Crazy Diamond'. The latter is the album's centrepiece. It begins with the sound of a tuned wine glass, left over from the 'Household Objects' project, contains one of David Gilmour's most enduring guitar motifs, and ends with the nostalgic sound of Richard Wright playing the refrain from 'See Emily Play'.

'Wish You Were Here', another song partly about Barrett, brought melodic folk-rock and a more sympathetic lyric to the mix. An alternative take featuring jazz violinist Stéphane Grappelli was recorded, and finally appeared on the 2011 remastered version of the album.

For Hipgnosis, the overriding theme was absence; the absence of Syd Barrett and, for a time, the absence of inspiration and communication within the group. 'We'd heard the record and read the lyrics,' says Aubrey 'Po' Powell. In contrast to their simple design for *The Dark Side of the Moon*, Powell and Storm Thorgerson created a set of images tipping a nod to the surrealist artists Man Ray and René Magritte, and to Roger Waters' lyrics.

'The front cover picture of two businessmen shaking hands, with one of them catching fire, was one of Storm's visual puns,' explains Powell. 'It was a '70s expression – "Man, I've been burned" – as in ripped off.' The photograph showed two seasoned Hollywood stuntmen, Danny Rogers and Ronnie Rondell, at the Warner Brothers film studios in Burbank. Rondell was set alight 15 times until Powell was satisfied with the picture. 'It was,' he admits, 'incredibly dangerous.'

The faceless businessman in a Magritte-style bowler hat on the back cover referenced both 'Welcome to the Machine' and 'Have a Cigar', while the theme of what Powell calls 'non-permanence' was explored in the sleeve's other images and its accompanying postcards. The picture of a floating diaphanous red veil suggested 'transience and a sense of uncertainty'. The same idea drove the images of a man 'swimming' through the sand dunes in Arizona's Yuma Desert and a diver upside down in California's Mono Lake.

The model for the Mono Lake shoot was a yoga-trained diver, able to hold his breath for a minute and a half underwater. The photograph showed the lower half of his body protruding from a perfectly still lake. Powell: 'Storm and I wanted a natural action – a man diving into water – but without any after effects, with the absence of any ripples.'

With the images complete, Hipgnosis chose to conceal the whole sleeve in black shrink-wrap. EMI insisted the band's name and album title appear somewhere. Hipgnosis compromised by producing a front-cover sticker, showing the band's name and the album's title alongside an illustration by artist George Hardie of two robotic hands clasped together.

The imposing, black-shrink-wrapped sleeve arrived in the shops in September 1975. *Wish You Were Here* became the first Pink Floyd album to reach Number 1 in both the UK and the US. If *The Dark Side of the Moon* marked the beginning of a new phase in the group's sound, *Wish You Were Here*

The Albums

Wish You Were Here 233

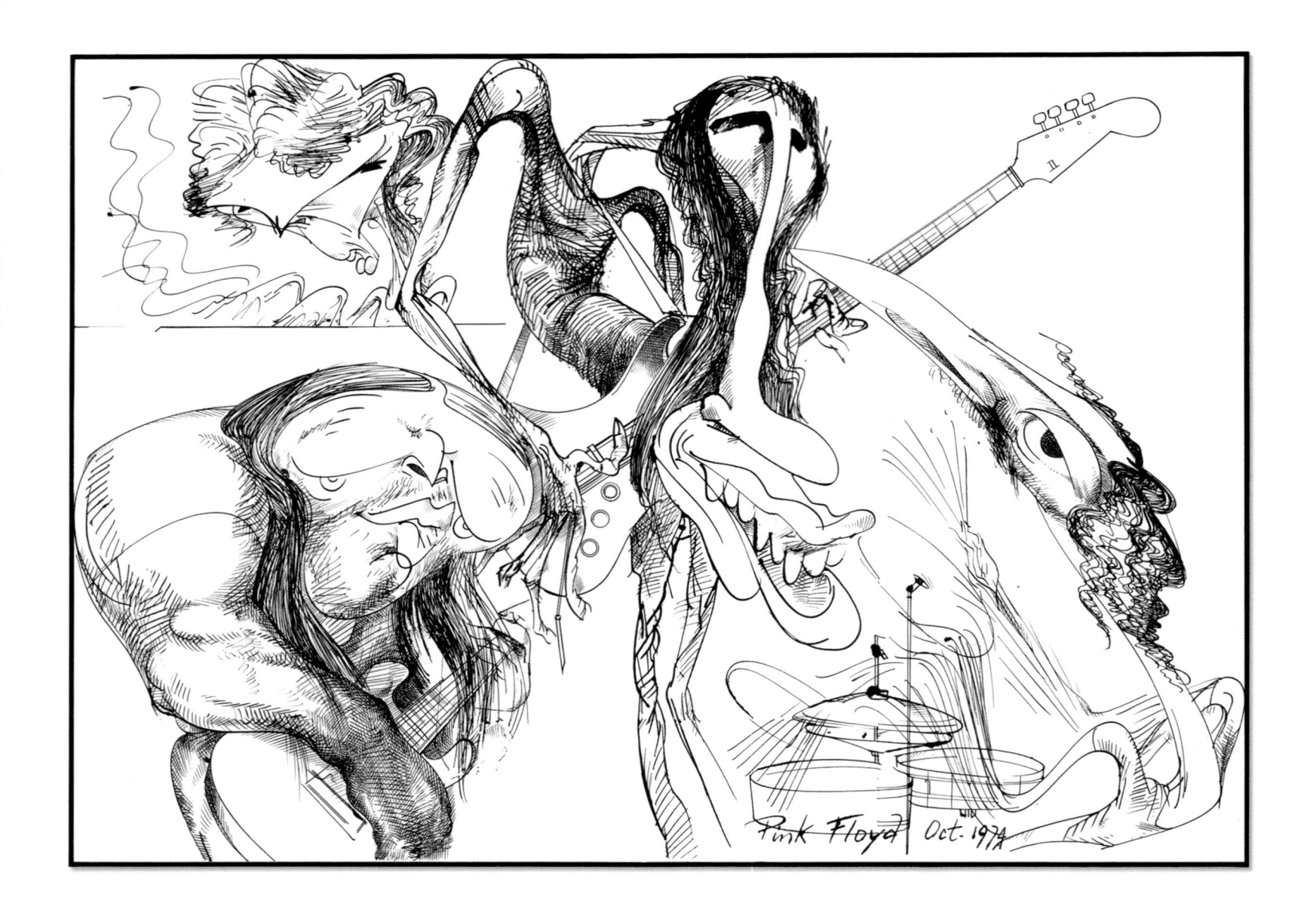

177 · ABOVE · Cartoon of Pink Floyd, 1974. Gerald Scarfe. Pink Floyd Archive

Gerald Scarfe's cartoon of the four band members was printed in the tour booklet for their 1974 UK shows. They played *The Dark Side of the Moon* and performed songs that were still works-in-progress and would later be released on *Wish You Were Here*. Scarfe famously collaborated with the band again on *The Wall* stage show and film.

178 · OPPOSITE · Artwork for the inner sleeve of *Wish You Were Here*, 1975. Designed by Storm Thorgerson / Aubrey Powell at Hipgnosis

acknowledged both Pink Floyd's past and present. Its lyrics addressed very human emotions, but the cinematic grandeur of 'Shine On You Crazy Diamond' was a partial flashback to the epic Pink Floyd of 'Atom Heart Mother' and 'Echoes'.

With over 40 years' hindsight, the abstract nature of some of the album has become one of its great strengths. It's about anything and *everything* its listeners want it to be. For music created in such difficult circumstances and with such downbeat subject-matter, *Wish You Were Here* remains oddly timeless and strangely uplifting.

Wish You Were Here

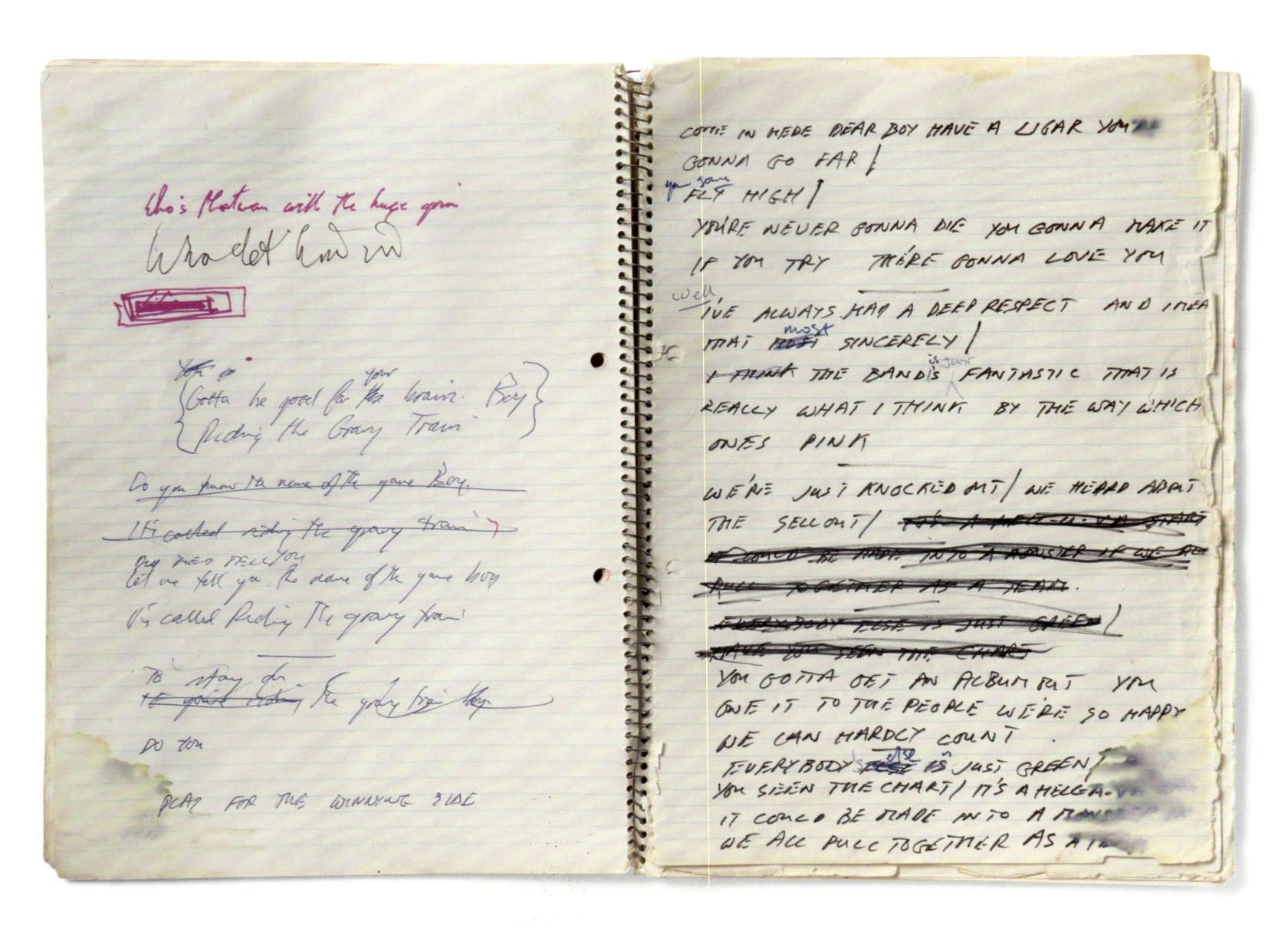

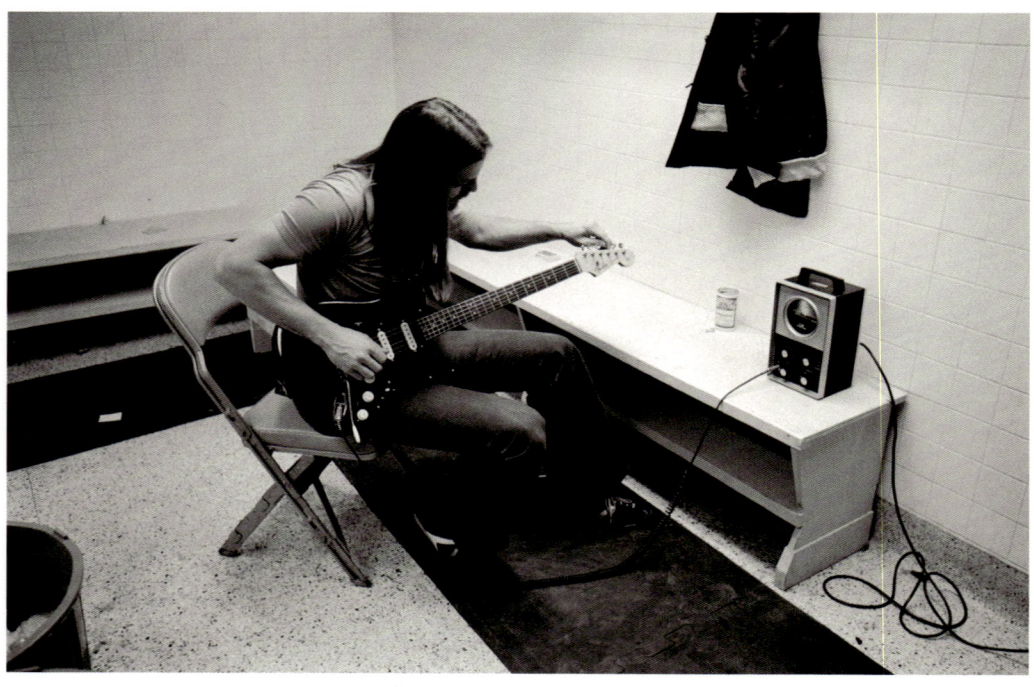

179 · ABOVE · Hand-written lyrics for 'Have a Cigar' from *Wish You Were Here*, 1975. Roger Waters. Collection of Roger Waters

The lyrics of 'Have a Cigar' express Waters' growing distaste for the hit-making, money-making 'gravy train' of the music industry. The lyric, '*By the way, which one's Pink?*', was a question often asked of the band by those who expected to meet 'Pink Floyd', the frontman, rather than four reticent band members. Waters gave life to the non-existent 'Pink' when he created the rock star anti-hero of *The Wall*.

180 · LEFT · David Gilmour tuning the Black Fender Stratocaster during the tour of *Wish You Were Here*, 1975. Photograph by Storm Thorgerson

This legendary guitar was purchased at Manny's guitar store in New York at the end of Pink Floyd's 1970 North American tour. David Gilmour used it on all Pink Floyd albums and live shows until the mid-1980s, as well as for Live 8 (2005) and *The Endless River* (2014). Over the years it has had many different necks, pickups and custom features.

181 · OPPOSITE · Black Fender Stratocaster, purchased May 1970. Pink Floyd Collection

The Albums

Wish You Were Here

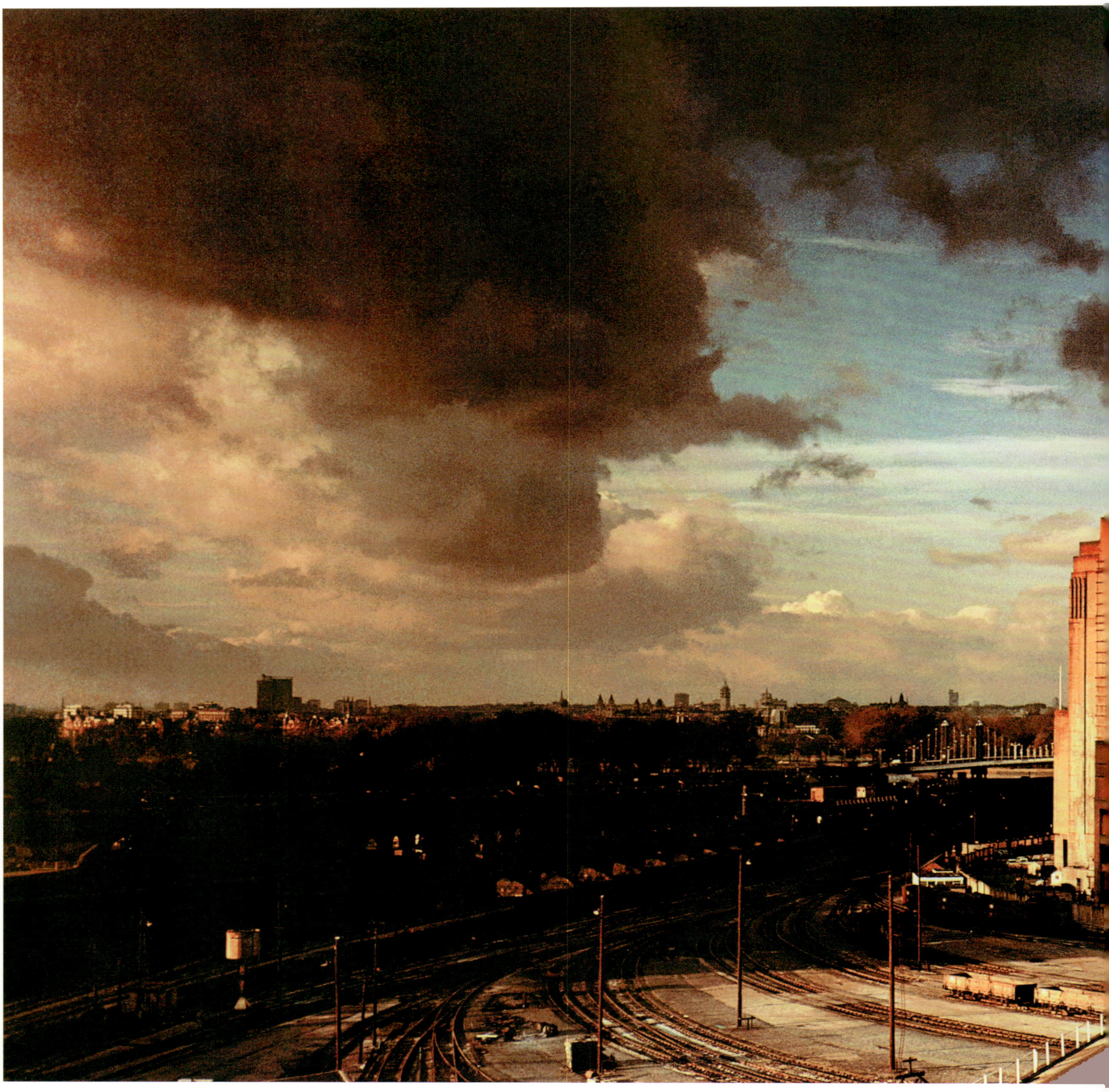

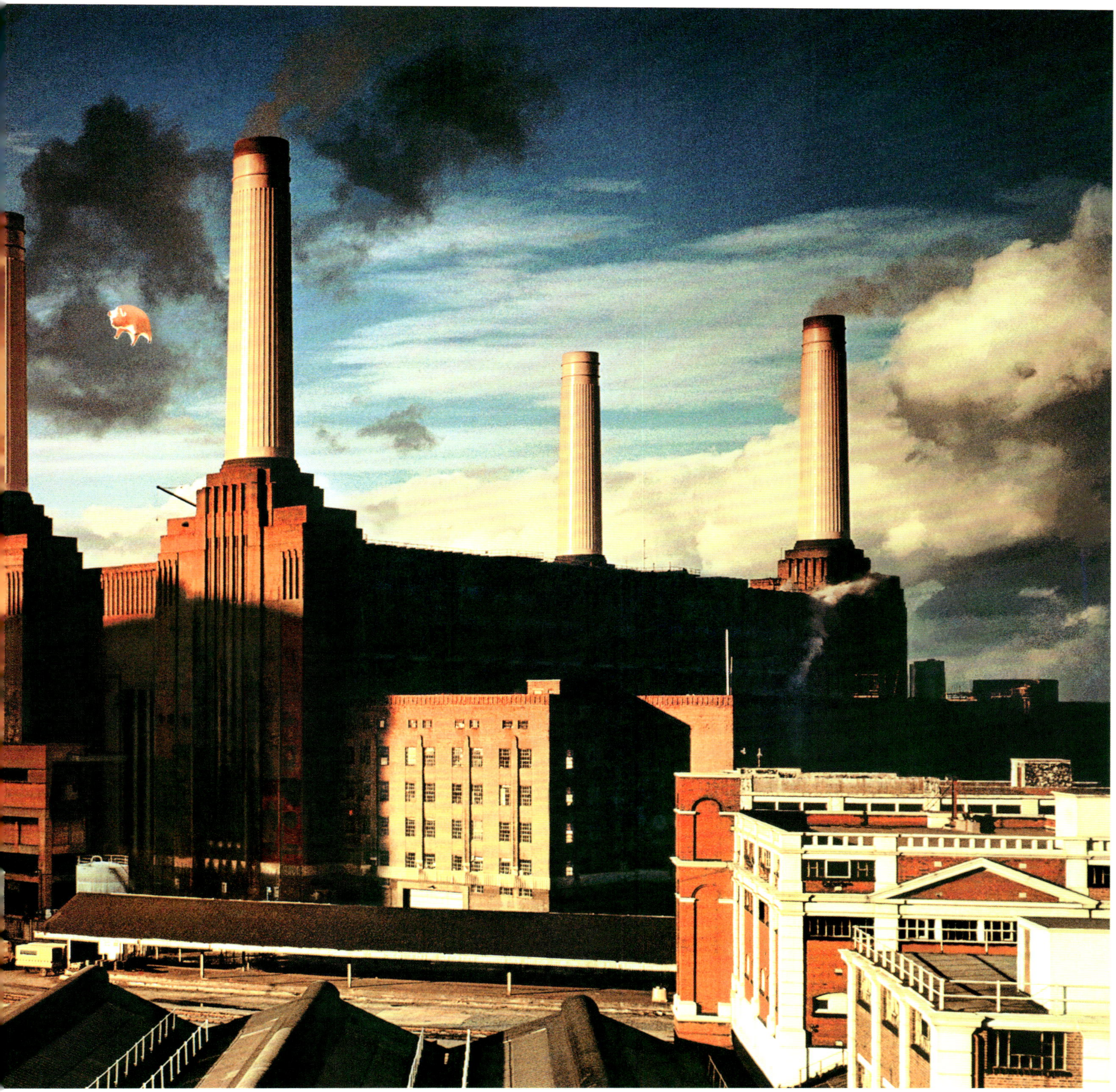

∆NIM∆LS

January 1977 • UK: EMI Harvest SHVL 815

182 · PREVIOUS SPREAD · Album artwork, *Animals*, 1977. Design by Roger Waters. Graphics by Nick Mason. Production and art direction by Storm Thorgerson / Aubrey Powell at Hipgnosis

The cover of Pink Floyd's *Animals* shows an inflatable pig drifting between the chimneys of Battersea Power Station. This striking image would become a familiar band motif; visual shorthand almost as recognizable as *The Dark Side of the Moon*'s prism and rainbow. Yet the photographs inside the sleeve, of barbed wire, iron gates and scrawled graffiti, also reflect the sombre tone of Pink Floyd's tenth album.

In 1975, the band purchased a block of church buildings in Britannia Row, Islington, which they converted into a studio and storage facility. *Animals* was recorded there between April and December 1976 with engineer Brian Humphries, returning from the *Wish You Were Here* sessions, making it the first non-soundtrack Pink Floyd studio album not to be created, even partly, at Abbey Road.

The songs 'Gotta Be Crazy' and 'Raving and Drooling', rejected from *Wish You Were Here* as they didn't fit the concept, were re-worked for *Animals*, and their titles changed to 'Dogs' and 'Sheep'. This new album was conceived as a critique of capitalism but also of society as a whole. The lyrics to 'Dogs', 'Pigs (Three Different Ones)' and 'Sheep' compared human behaviour to that of beasts, suggesting the human race comprised three sub-species: tyrannical pigs, aggressive dogs and mindless sheep.

In many ways *Animals* caught the fractious mood of Britain in the late 1970s: an era of industrial action, economic strife and racial tension. 'Pigs (Three Different Ones)', a barely veiled attack on Mary Whitehouse, head of the National Viewers' and Listener's Association and an outspoken campaigner against sex and violence on TV, contained Roger Waters' most scathing lyrics yet.

Equally, most of the music on *Animals* was a shift away from the lavish soundscapes of 'Shine On You Crazy Diamond'. Instead, David Gilmour and Richard Wright's wall of ominous-sounding guitars and synths seemed to mimic the dark lyrics. Only one song, the Waters/Gilmour composition 'Dogs', featured Gilmour's vocals. Roger Waters wrote everything else alone and sang most of it himself.

There were just two moments on *Animals* that suggested some hope for humanity. The romantic, acoustic 'Pigs on the Wing 1' and 'Pigs on the Wing 2' were from the same song, but with the verses split in two to open and close the album.

The idea for the now-famous pig came from Roger Waters rather than Hipgnosis. The band had been unimpressed by Hipgnosis' original ideas for the artwork. Waters had commissioned a huge inflatable pig as a stage prop for their next tour, and told Aubrey 'Po' Powell he wanted it pictured on the sleeve floating above Battersea Power Station.

Waters and Powell visited the site one Sunday afternoon. The inspiration for those dour inside cover shots was obvious. 'It was a very disenfranchised

240 The Albums

and impoverished area,' explains Powell. 'You had this wonderful old working power station but the grounds were a dump.'

Pink Floyd's 30-foot pig, nicknamed 'Algie', was manufactured by the same German company that had produced the original Zeppelin airships. Aubrey Powell had arranged for 14 photographers in different locations to shoot the airborne beast. However, on the day of the shoot, the pig refused to inflate.

A second attempt the following day was successful. But no sooner was it airborne, than the hawser snapped, the pig broke free and was soon drifting towards 10,000 feet. 'I had to call 999 from a phone box and tell the police,' recalls Powell. 'They stopped all flights in and out of Heathrow, as pilots had reported seeing the pig. A helicopter and two RAF jets were sent up to look for it. Warnings were issued on TV and radio along with requests for the public to report any sightings.'

Powell was escorted by the police to Hipgnosis' Denmark Street studio, where he was instructed to wait by the phone. At 9pm, a farmer in Kent called to complain that the pig had landed on his property and was scaring his cattle. Pink Floyd's road crew retrieved the deflated animal.

183, 185–187 · **ABOVE AND PAGES 243–245** · Cover photo shoot for *Animals*, Battersea Power Station, London, 2–4 December 1976. Inflatable pig designed by Jeffrey Shaw and Theo Botschuijver at Eventstructure Research Group. Photographers: Storm Thorgerson / Aubrey Powell at Hipgnosis, Peter Christopherson, Howard Bartop, Nic Tucker, Bob Ellis, Rob Brimson, Colin Jones

Animals

184 · ABOVE · Remo Weather King Coated Ambassador Drum Head, USA (split), 1970s. Pink Floyd Collection

Nick Mason often wrote gig notes on his drum heads, and used gaffer tape to dampen the sound. This snare drum head from the 1977 USA Animals / In the Flesh Tour shows city names with numbers agreed by the band: 'Atlanta 32', 'Phoenix 36' and so on. These were location codes and would be called out onstage so that illegal bootleg recordings could be traced back to a particular show.

The shoot went ahead again the following day. This time there was a heavy police presence and a marksman on standby. The pig became airborne, and the shoot went off without a hitch. Unfortunately, what Aubrey Powell now calls 'the pristine blue sky' that day didn't suit the mood of their intended cover.

Fortunately, the Hipgnosis team had also photographed the sky on the first day. Using a dye-transfer print Powell and Storm Thorgerson stripped out the pig from the final shoot and superimposed it in the sky from two days earlier. Powell: 'That first sky had this wonderful, broody Turner-esque quality to it, which suited the mood of the picture and the music.'

Animals was released in January 1977. Its pessimistic worldview proved no obstacle to sales, as it reached Number 2 in the UK; 3 in the US and Number 1 in several European countries. The troublesome inflatable pig joined Pink Floyd on tour in 1977, and variations of the animal have appeared on subsequent Pink Floyd and Roger Waters solo tours. 'The pig has become synonymous with Pink Floyd,' concurs Aubrey Powell. 'It's one of their great brand symbols.'

242   The Albums

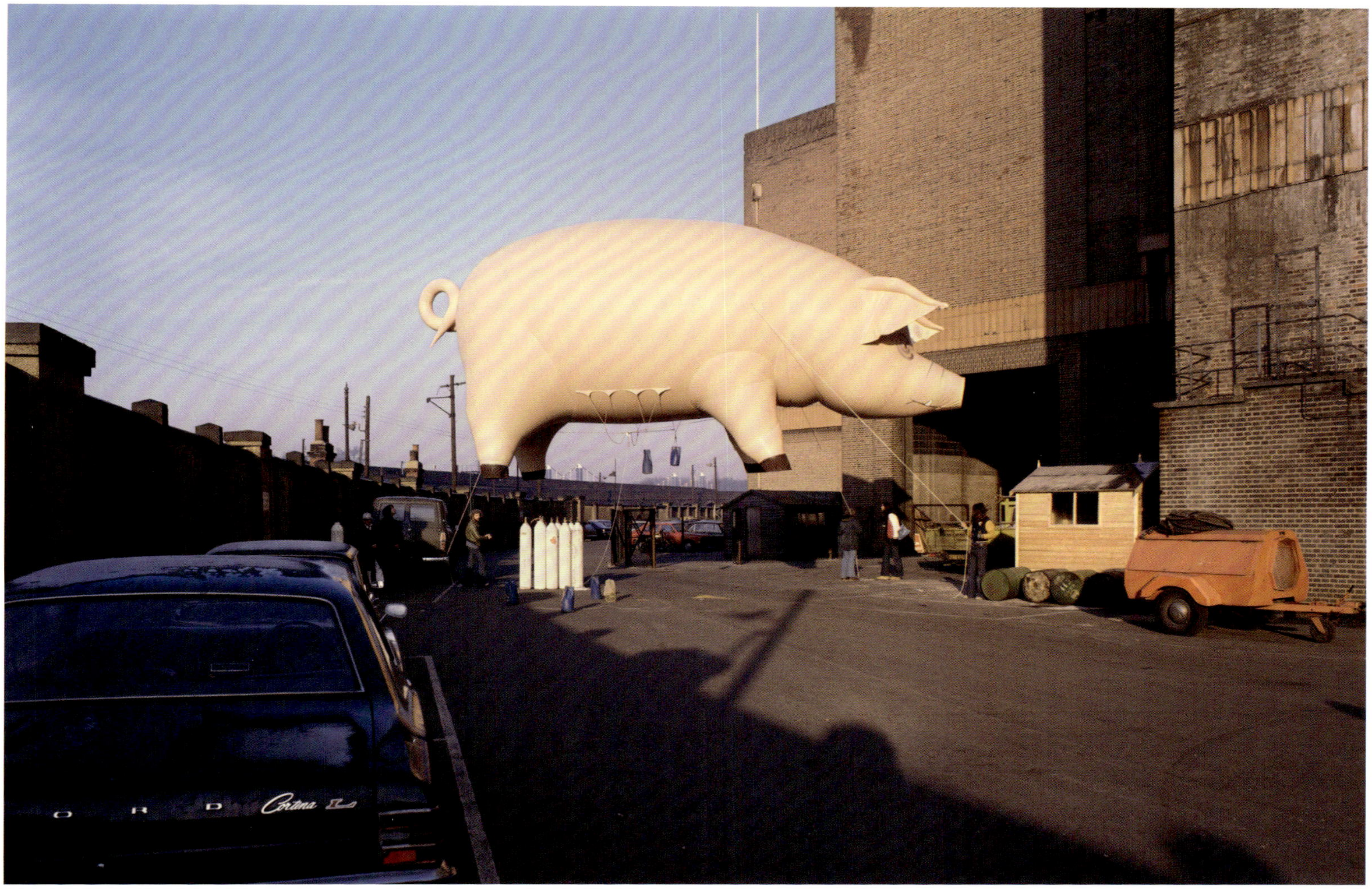
Cortina L

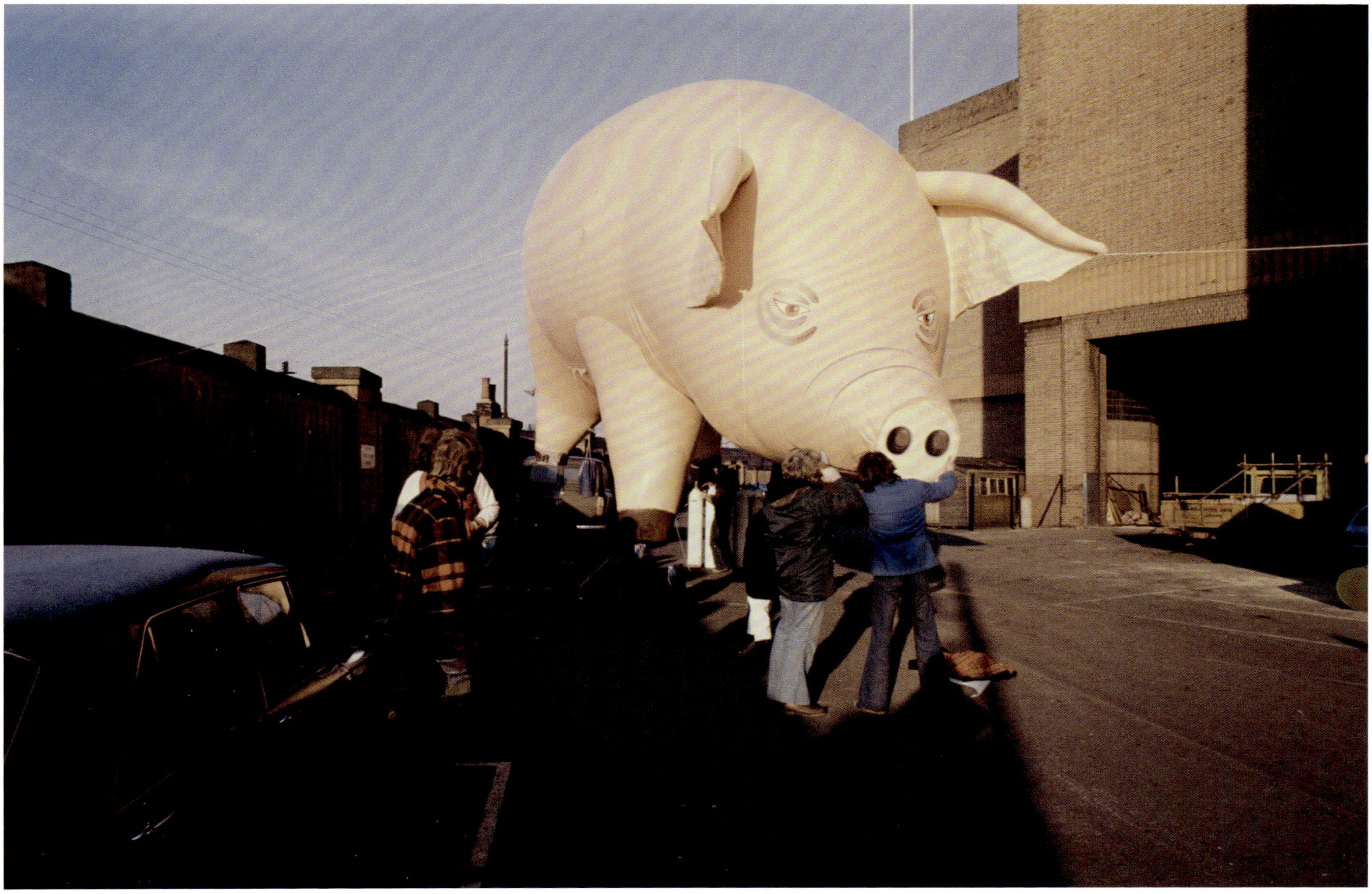

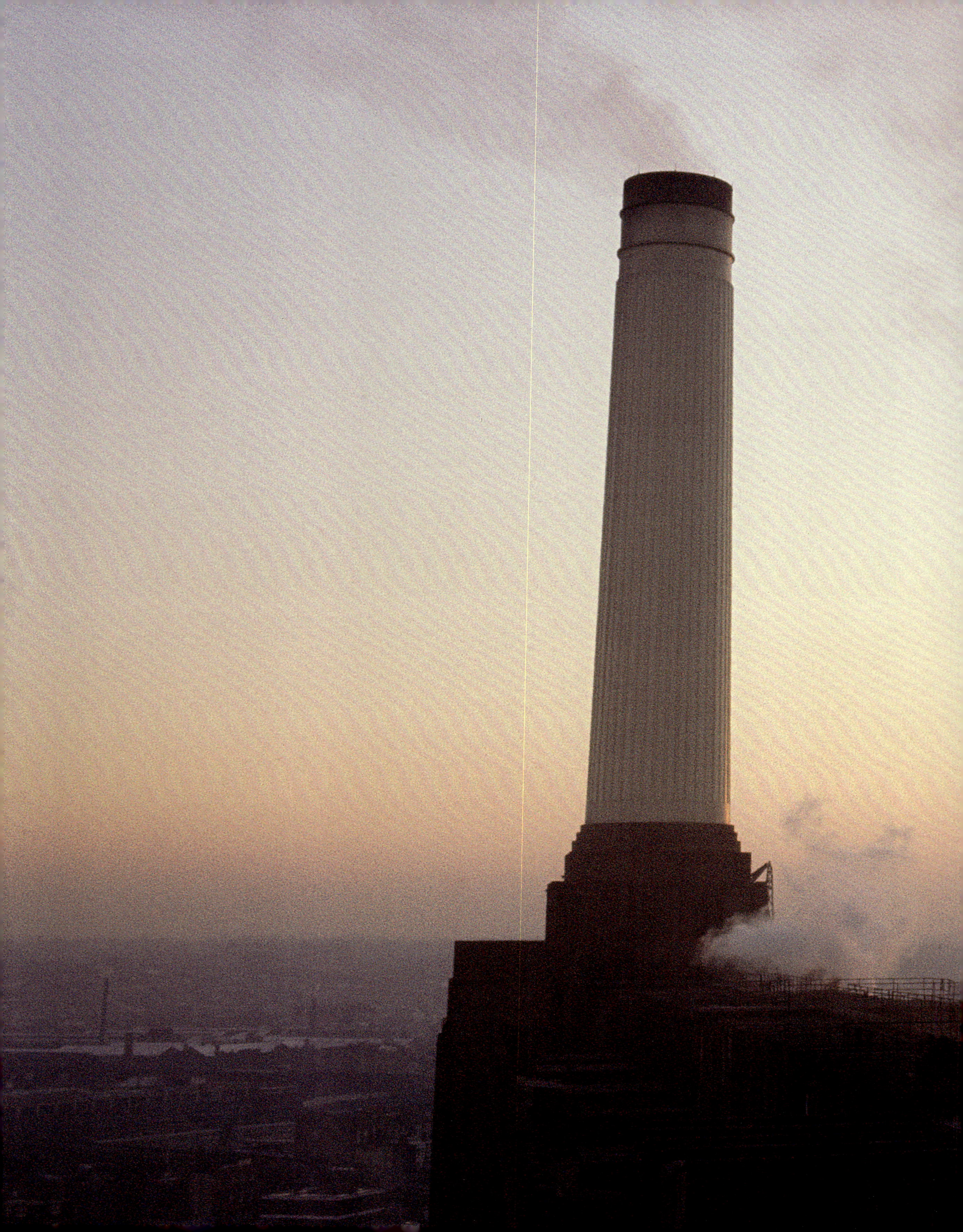

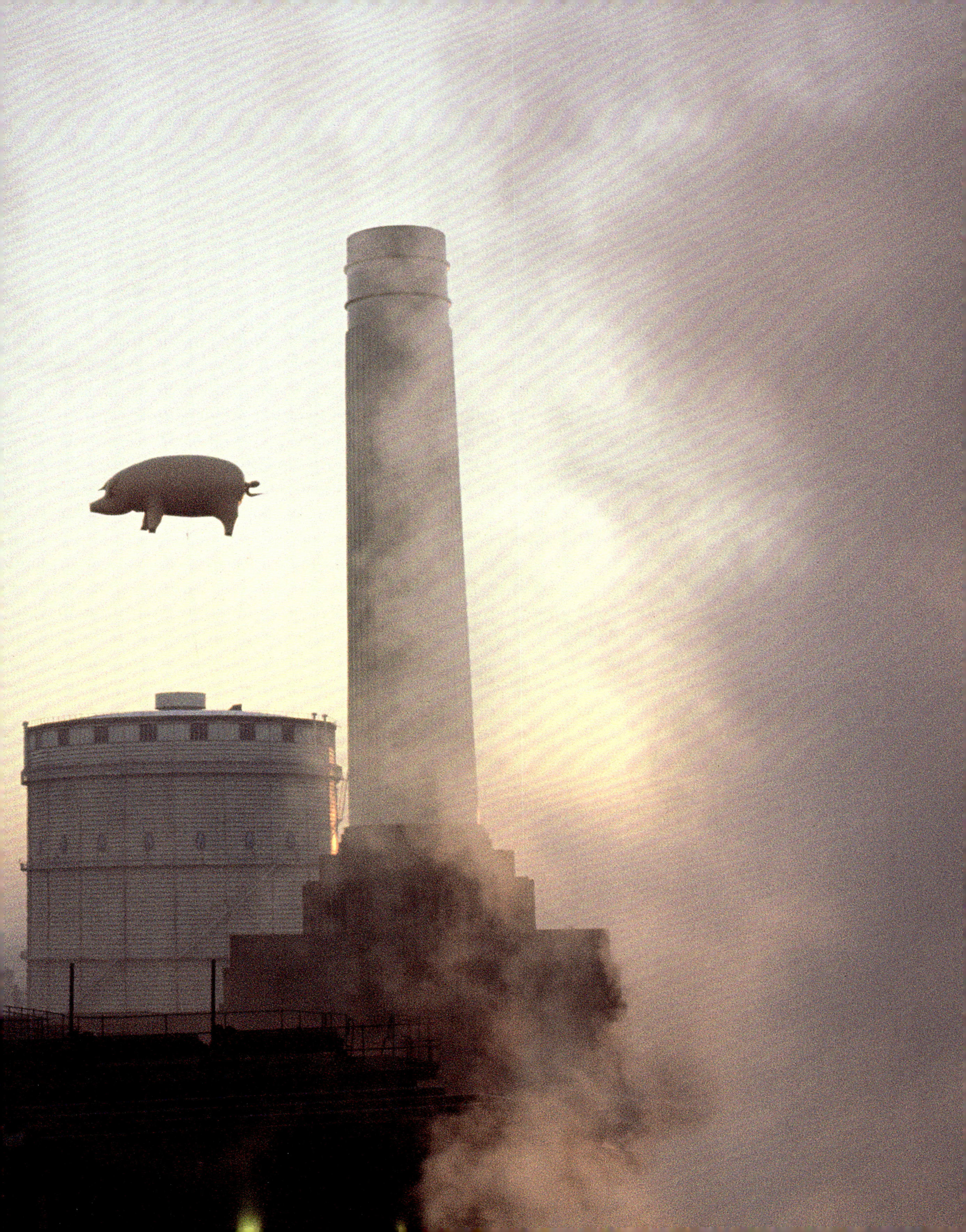

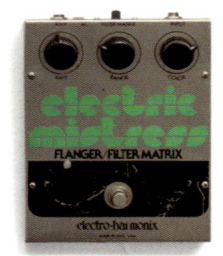

188 · ABOVE · Customized guitar effects pedal board with: Electric Mistress and Big Muff pedals; Morley EVO-1 echo unit; and foot speed switch for Yamaha RA200 rotating speaker, 1977 (set up). Board designed by Phil Taylor and David Gilmour, built by Pete Cornish, 1976. Pink Floyd Collection

189 · OPPOSITE · Fender Custom Telecaster, 1962. Pink Floyd Collection

When Pink Floyd toured in November 1974, they premiered a new song, 'You Gotta Be Crazy', later released as 'Dogs' on *Animals*. David Gilmour performed and recorded the song using this 1962 Fender Custom Telecaster.

246   The Albums

Animals

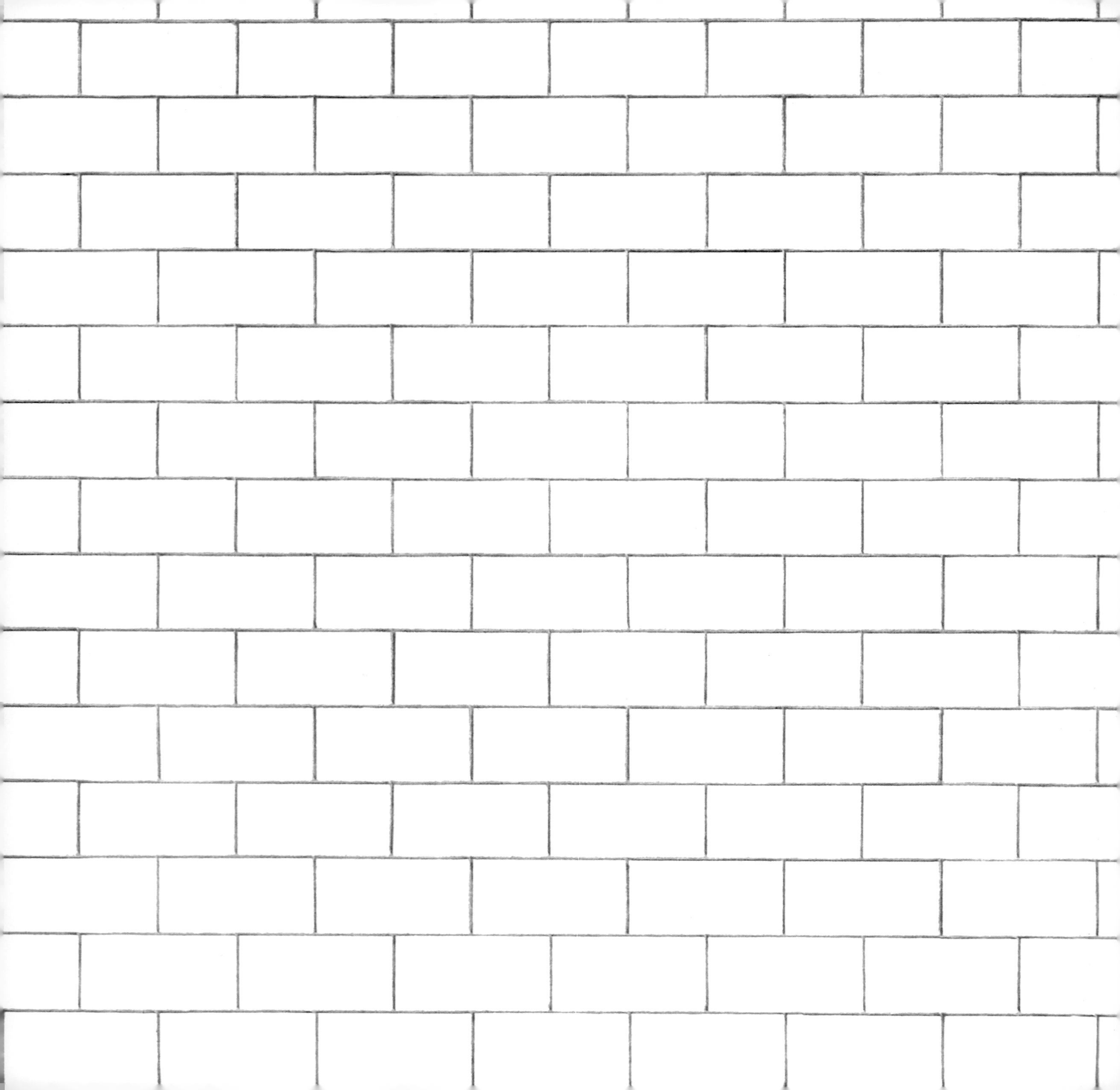

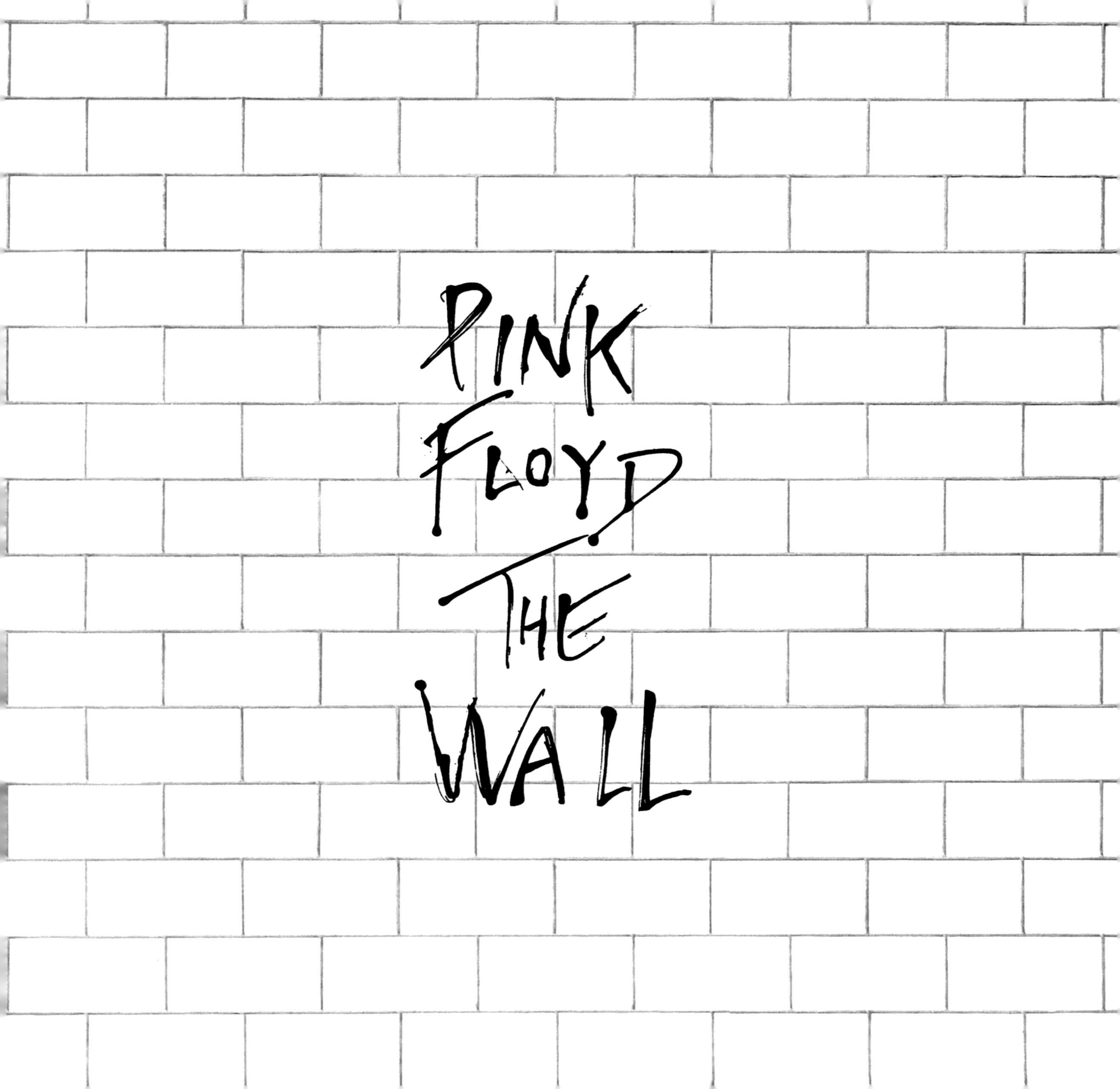
PINK
FLOYD
THE
WALL

THE WALL

November 1979 • UK: EMI Harvest SHVL 822

190 · PREVIOUS SPREAD · Album artwork, *The Wall,* 1979. Design by Gerald Scarfe and Roger Waters

191 · OPPOSITE · Prophet-5 synthesizer keyboard, 1978. Designed and manufactured by Sequential Circuits Inc. Pink Floyd Collection

Technological breakthroughs by American electronic music pioneers led to the invention of the Prophet-5: a legendary polyphonic analogue synthesizer with five voices and memory capacity for multiple settings. Richard Wright's model was painted black for the live shows of *The Wall*. His hand-written show notes, taped above the keyboard, also refer to his Hammond electric organ, 'Quadra' (short for 'quadraphonic') and Wurlitzer EP-200 electric piano.

The first brick in Pink Floyd's wall was put in place during the final dates of their 1977 North American tour. The band had been playing increasingly large venues since *The Dark Side of the Moon*, culminating that year with a show at Montreal's 78,000-capacity Olympic Stadium.

Roger Waters was unhappy. He loathed the impersonal nature of these cavernous venues, but also those members of the audience who didn't care what Pink Floyd played or only wanted to hear the hits. In Montreal, Waters lost his temper and spat at a particularly vocal fan. He regretted his actions, but vowed never to play stadiums again. What Waters wanted, he said, was to build a wall between Pink Floyd and their audience.

The Wall is one of the few Pink Floyd albums for which artwork and imagery were created while the music was still being composed. Newspaper cartoonist and illustrator Gerald Scarfe already knew the group and had made short films for their 1975 tour. Waters played him some rough demos of what was still being called 'Bricks in the Wall' before revealing his grand plan. 'He had it all mapped out in a very meticulous way,' says Scarfe today. '"The Wall" was going to be an album, a stage show and a movie.'[2]

The Wall would become all three. But the album came first, and was a collaborative effort between Roger Waters, the rest of Pink Floyd and their co-producer, Bob Ezrin. Over time, the concept was reworked until it became the tale of a disenfranchised rock star named Pink and the metaphorical walls created by events in his life.

Many aspects of Pink's story, among them the death of his father in the Second World War, his troubled schooldays and conflicted relationship with his mother, drew on Waters' own experience. Other events, including Pink's withdrawal and growing isolation, owed much to Syd Barrett's story.

Each of these experiences would create another metaphorical brick, with the wall 'demolished' during the album's grand finale. Pink's story mirrored the fears and insecurities of many rock stars, but also those of their audience. There was an everyman quality to the issues it addressed.

Gerald Scarfe's task was to turn Waters' characters into illustrations, in the same style as his brutal depictions of famous politicians. 'What Roger wanted from me as a political cartoonist was for my political side to come across,' he says. 'These characters had to be bizarre and memorable and bear repetition.'

Aptly, for an artist who would go on to draw Margaret Thatcher as a dominatrix and a pterodactyl, Scarfe's characters, including the overbearing mother and sadistic schoolmaster, had a striking, grotesque quality.

Scarfe also helped create the wall itself. 'Roger wanted to keep it simple,' he explains. 'We experimented with black bricks and white lines and different

250   The Albums

shaped bricks, until we decided on the image you see today on the cover – an unadulterated, pure work.'

In the meantime, financial mismanagement and stringent tax laws led to Pink Floyd recording *The Wall* overseas. In January 1979, the band and Bob Ezrin, co-producer, relocated to the south of France to start work at Super Bear Studios, near Nice. But there was growing tension between Roger Waters and Richard Wright, who was contributing little to the project. Wright was distracted by personal issues, but admitted he was also struggling to come up with ideas.

By the time the sessions moved to Los Angeles in September, Wright's position in the band had become untenable. Under great pressure from Waters, Wright agreed to leave Pink Floyd, but to perform in the subsequent live shows as a salaried musician.

Despite its troubled development, *The Wall*, released as a double LP in November 1979, was a tribute to Pink Floyd's collaborative efforts. It told Pink's story with great empathy, melodrama and some of the best, and best-selling, music of Pink Floyd's career. The album reached Number 3 in Britain, and Number 1 in the US and across Europe.

The album was trailered by Pink Floyd's first UK single since 1968, 'Another Brick in the Wall Part 2', which went to Number 1 in 16 countries including the UK and the US. It was a startling fusion of children's voices (an ad hoc 'choir' of pupils from Islington Green School, chanting *We don't need no edu-cation*'), David Gilmour's sinuous guitar solo and a four-to-the-floor disco rhythm.

The Wall 251

192 · RIGHT · Performance of *The Wall*, Earl's Court, London, June 1981. Photograph by Jill Furmanovsky

193 · OPPOSITE · Performance notes for live shows of *The Wall*, 1980. Roger Waters. Pink Floyd Archive

The scope and ambition of the album's music matched the story. *The Wall* wove together spartan ballads, bombastic hard rock and bleak electronica with the sound of crying babies, dive-bombing aeroplanes and a hotel room being vandalized. It had its roots in *The Dark Side of the Moon* but also reached further back to the soundtracks for *La Vallée*, *More* and beyond. *The Wall* was widescreen and panoramic; the soundtrack to a movie still to be made.

One song on the album, 'Comfortably Numb', seemed to distil every element of Pink Floyd's trademark sound since the late 1960s, with Roger Waters' affecting lyric and David Gilmour's climactic guitar accessorized by Hollywood film-score composer and arranger Michael Kamen's sweeping strings. 'Comfortably Numb' perfectly demonstrated Waters and Gilmour's ability to create together, in spite of the personal chaos surrounding the band. It remains one of Pink Floyd's most popular and enduring songs.

Pink Floyd's subsequent tour of *The Wall* ran to just 31 shows between spring 1980 and summer '81. Waters' original idea for the band to perform completely hidden from their audience behind the wall was vetoed by David Gilmour and Richard Wright. Instead, the 40-foot-high wall was slowly assembled from cardboard bricks, as they performed the album, and then destroyed towards the end of the show. Gerald Scarfe's illustrations were recreated as animations and grotesque, 50-foot puppets. It was a wildly ambitious and striking piece of theatre, but it was too expensive and unwieldy to take on a world tour.

As predicted by Roger Waters, the shows were followed a year later by director Alan Parker's film version of *The Wall*, which combined Pink Floyd's music and Gerald Scarfe's animations with real-life rock star Bob Geldof of The Boomtown Rats in the role of Pink.

In 1990, Roger Waters performed the album with special guests, including Sinéad O'Connor and Van Morrison, for charity on the site of the former Berlin Wall. Ten years later, he embarked on a hugely successful world tour, which saw him perform a new version of *The Wall* in the United States, Europe, Australia and South America.

'*The Wall* fits all walls,' offers Gerald Scarfe. 'From the wall in China, to the wall in Israel to Donald Trump's wall. It's always been about the wall between people.' Its message is as relevant now as it was in 1979.

The Albums

2a

Preliminaries.

In the streets surrounding the venue we will place buskers
playing tunes from the show to the punters as they arrive
and queue.

Inside the stadium, scattered, there will be aural tricks
and jokes, e.g., locked road boxes with taped laughter issuing.

The teacher's voice shouting in lavatories, "You there!
Put that away and get back inside this minute."

Monotonous piped selling of "Britro Brick-a-Brac."
       "Britro Brick Co. proudly present Brick Sunglasses.
       Do you have trouble looking blank? Be the first
       one on your block to develop wall eyes with
       Britro Brick Shades."

For an hour before the show starts, throughout the venue,
we will run a tape of tunes, all with some connection
with the war.
       The Green Beret, Vera Lynn's Hits from the Blitz,
       Don't Take Your Love to Town, Glenn Miller,
       assorted Dylan, Over the Sea to Sky, et al,
       finishing up with We'll Meet Again.
At the end of We'll Meet Again an M.C. will come forward in
a tuxedo and announce:

       "Ladies and gentlemen, here they are, the one
       and only, the unbelievable PINK FLOYD.

The Albums

194 · OPPOSITE TOP · Solina String Ensemble synthesizer keyboard played on live shows of *The Wall*, 1975. Collection of Roger Waters

195 · OPPOSITE BOTTOM · Front stage guitar and bass pedal board built for the tour of *The Wall*, 1979. Designed by Phil Taylor. Pink Floyd Collection

This compact board incorporates guitar effects for the songs performed from a small stage area in front of the 'Wall'.

196 · ABOVE · Megaphone used onstage by Roger Waters, The Wall Live Tour, 2010–13. Collection of Roger Waters

The Wall Tour in 1980–1 was the only Pink Floyd show in which the band were costumed and acted in character. Waters devised an even more theatrical staging for his subsequent solo tours. This megaphone is part of his costume for a sequence in which the troubled rock star Pink is transformed, in his hallucinating mind, into a neo-fascist demagogue. The album's dramatic narrative is fully told in the 1982 film *Pink Floyd – The Wall*, in which Bob Geldof plays Pink.

The Wall

197 · ABOVE · Performance of *The Wall* featuring Pink Floyd and musicians Willie Wilson, Andy Bown, Peter Wood and Snowy White, USA, 1980. Photograph by Bob Jenkins. Pink Floyd Archive

198 · LEFT · Performance of *The Wall* featuring 'Pink's motel room', Westfalenhalle, Dortmund, February 1981. Photograph by Bob Jenkins. Pink Floyd Archive

As the show progressed, more and more 'bricks' (made from collapsible cardboard box structures) were removed from the wall onstage. Scenes from the story were gradually revealed; including a 'motel room' from which Roger Waters, in the character of Pink, sang 'Nobody Home'. At the show's finale the wall appeared to be in ruins.

199 · OPPOSITE · Concept sketch of 'Pink's motel room' for the tour of *The Wall*, 1979. Mark Fisher. Mark Fisher Collection, courtesy of Cristina Garcia

256   The Albums

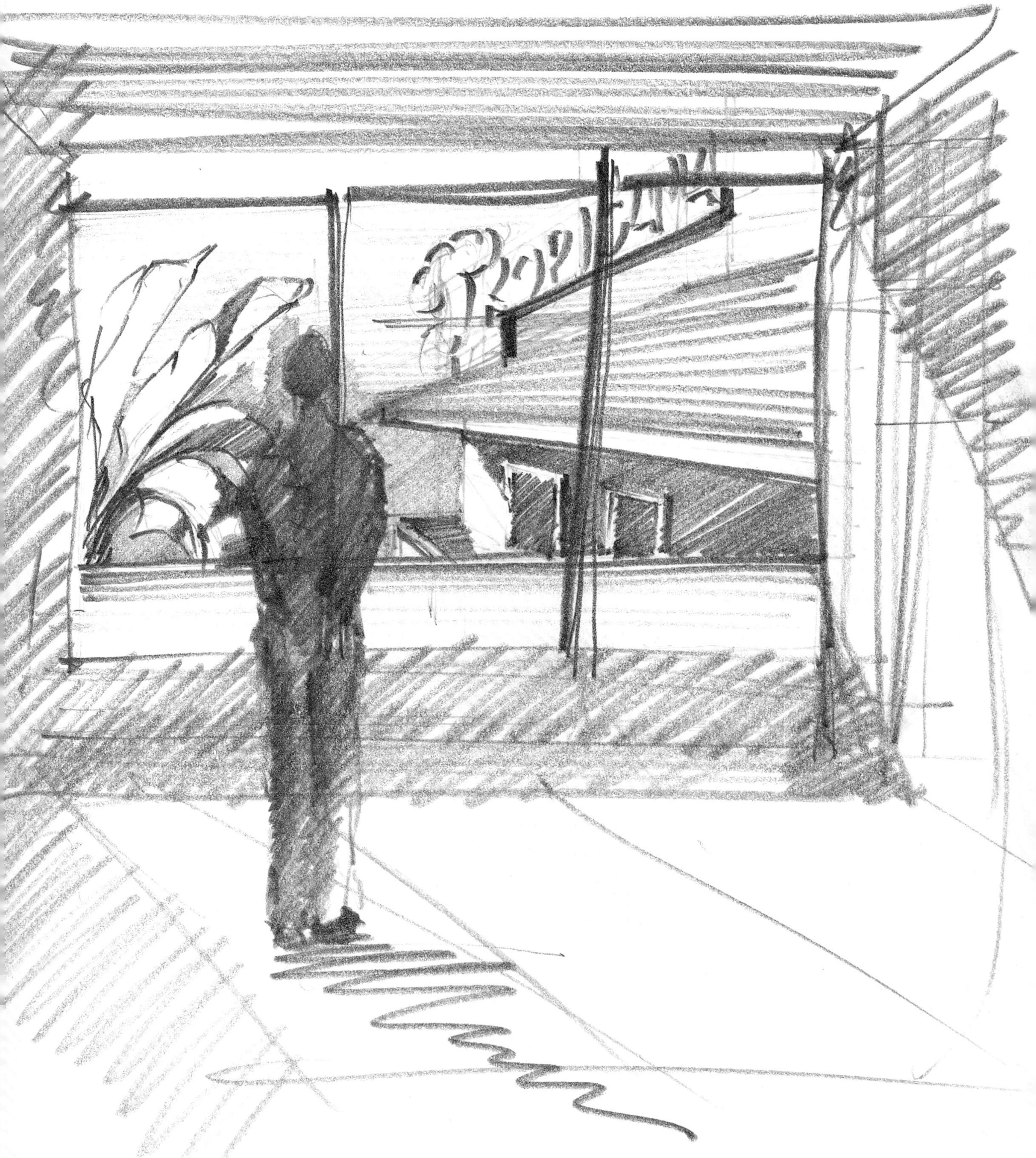

200 · RIGHT · White Fender Stratocaster (serial number #0001), 1954. Signed by Tadeo Gomez and 'Mary', possibly Fender employee Mary Lemus. Pink Floyd Collection

David Gilmour played this precious and collectable guitar on the recording of 'Another Brick in the Wall, Part 2'. It is one of the earliest Fender Stratocasters and the handiwork of revered craftsman Tadeo Gomez.

201 · OPPOSITE · Gibson Les Paul Goldtop, 1955. Pink Floyd Collection

This rare, all-gold model can be heard on David Gilmour's guitar solo in 'Another Brick in the Wall, Part 2' and was played live during the tour of *The Wall*.

258   The Albums

The Wall

202 · RIGHT · Ovation 12-string guitar, 1978. Designed by Charles Kaman, manufactured by KMC Music. Collection of Roger Waters

Roger Waters played this guitar live during The Wall Tour. Ovation acoustic guitars, designed by the aeronautical engineer and entrepreneur Charles Kaman, featured a semi-parabolic body made of synthetic composite material called Lyrachord. Unlike a more traditional wood body, the synthetic bowl helped to avoid feedback problems at high volume and made Ovations a popular choice for live shows.

203 · OPPOSITE · Ovation bass guitar, 1978. Designed by Charles Kaman, manufactured by KMC Music. Collection of Roger Waters

204–205 · FOLLOWING SPREAD · Hand-written notes and sketches for performances of *The Wall*, 1978. Roger Waters. Collection of Roger Waters

The Albums

The Wall

FILM.

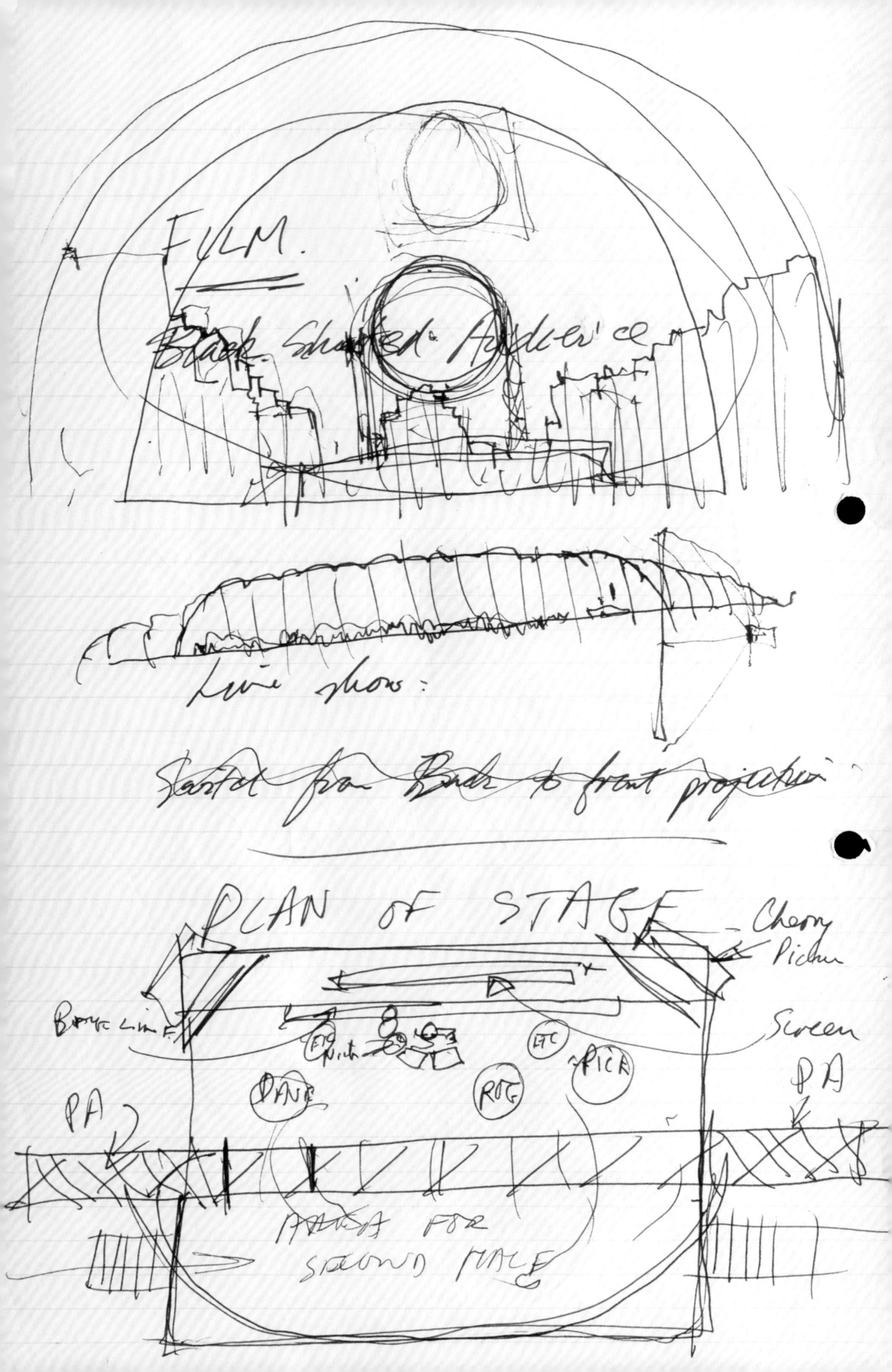

Black Shorted Audience

Live show:

Started from Back to front projection

PLAN OF STAGE — Cherry Picker

Bryce Line   Screen

PA   DAN?   ROG   PICK   PA

AREA FOR
SOUND MALE

Put the cars on the guitars.
Put the lo fi amps.

people holding cards.
car crashes / suicides / lumi bar
entrys

ANOTHER BRICK IN THE WALL

I don't need no education.
I don't need no rising water.
I don't need no high rise building
I don't need no spreading mildew.
All in all its just another brick in the wall.

We don't need your cold invective
We don't need your flecks of foam
Your dark sarcasm in the classroom
Teacher leave the kids alone
Cos All in All yave just another brick in the wall.

We don't need your silver lining
We don't need your heart of stone
We don't need your lonesome something
We don't want your crowd contract.
All in All its just another brick in the wall.

We don't need repatriation
We don't got no starry eye
We don't want a sullen losers
Can't use your patronising smiles
All in all its just another brick in the wall

I don't need your drugs to calm me down
I don't need your hands to push me down.
I don't need your tongue to put me down
I don't need your ashes to cough me.
All in all its just another brick in the wall

Don't need your feet walking on me
I don't need your fist to feed me
I don't need your eyes to con me me
don't think I need you at all.
All in All you're just another brick in the wall

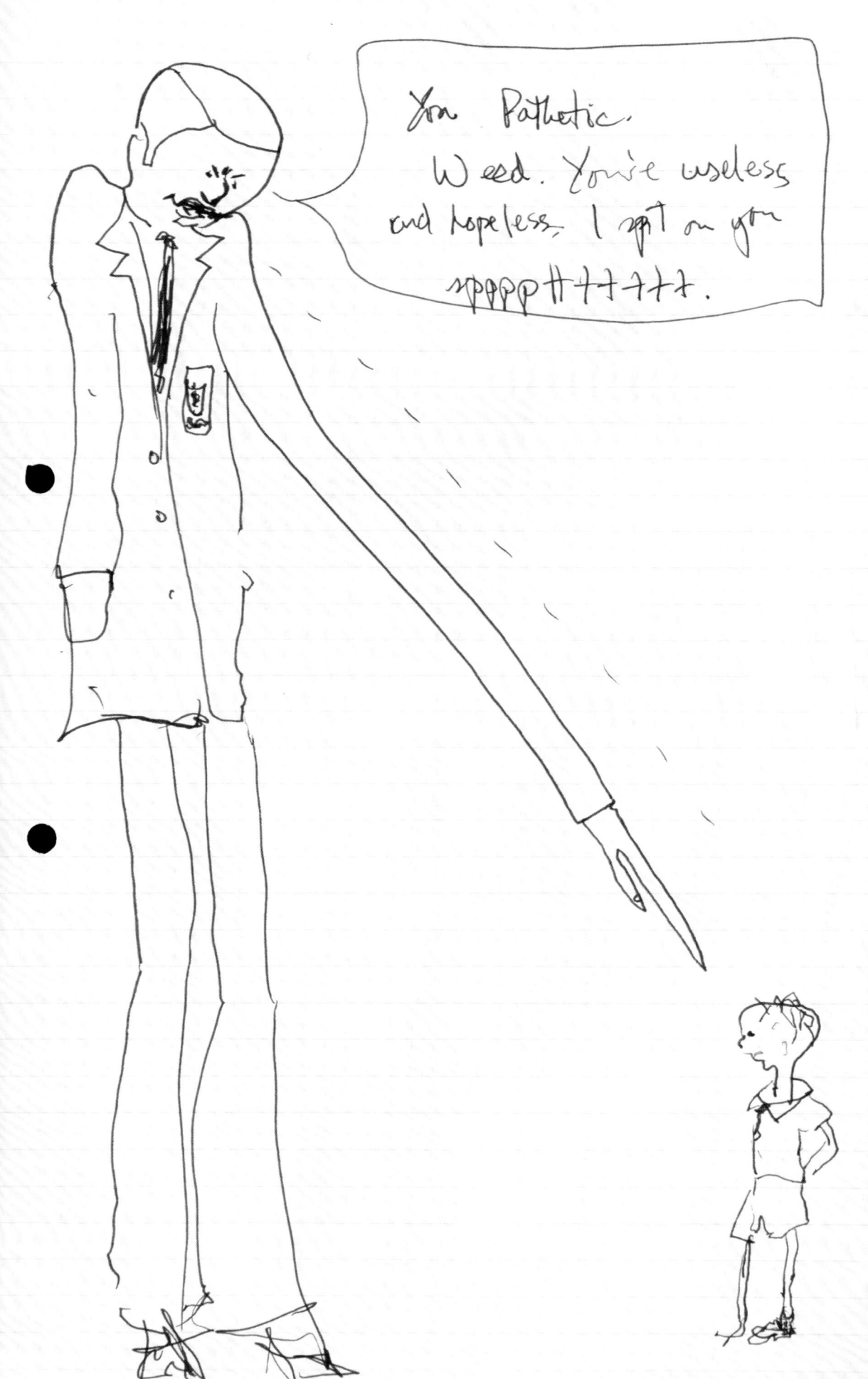

EDUCATION

> You Pathetic Weed. You're useless and hopeless. I spit on you ppppttttt.

The Albums

206 · PAGE 264 · Hand-written lyrics for 'Another Brick in the Wall'', 1978. Roger Waters. Collection of Roger Waters

207 · PAGE 265 · Satirical drawing titled 'Education' in notes for *The Wall*, 1978. Roger Waters. Collection of Roger Waters

208 · OPPOSITE · Cane and punishment book, Cambridgeshire High School for Boys, Cambridge, 1950s. Hills Road Sixth Form College

The demonic figure of the 'Teacher' in *The Wall* was inspired by Roger Waters' memories of harsh school discipline. This punishment book records the canings given to boys including Waters, Syd Barrett and Storm Thorgerson for misdemeanours such as playing truant and 'cutting P.T. [physical training]'. Corporal punishment was banned from UK state schools in 1986 and subsequently from all schools in the country.

209 · ABOVE · Clay models of the 'Teacher', 'Wife' and 'Mother' inflatables for *The Wall* tour and film, 2010. Designed and painted by Gerald Scarfe. Sculpted by Jacqueline Pyle. Photograph by Julie Davies. Mark Fisher Collection, courtesy of Cristina Garcia

The Wall 267

210 · ABOVE TOP · Conceptual painting depicting the Judge and Marching Hammers for *The Wall*, 1979. Gerald Scarfe. Collection of Gerald Scarfe

211 · ABOVE · Stage design proposal for *The Wall* at Nassau Coliseum, featuring inflatable hammer spotlights, August 1979. Mark Fisher. Mark Fisher Collection, courtesy of Cristina Garcia

212 · OPPOSITE · Paiste 36" Symphonic Gong with stand and mallet, 1969–80. Pink Floyd Collection

This gong had been part of Pink Floyd's equipment for some time before it was incorporated into live shows of *The Wall* and later the film *Pink Floyd – The Wall*. During live shows in America it burst into flames when struck by Roger Waters, performing in the character of Pink.

213 · FOLLOWING SPREAD · Inner sleeve album artwork for *The Wall*, 1979. Design by Gerald Scarfe and Roger Waters

268   The Albums

The Wall 269

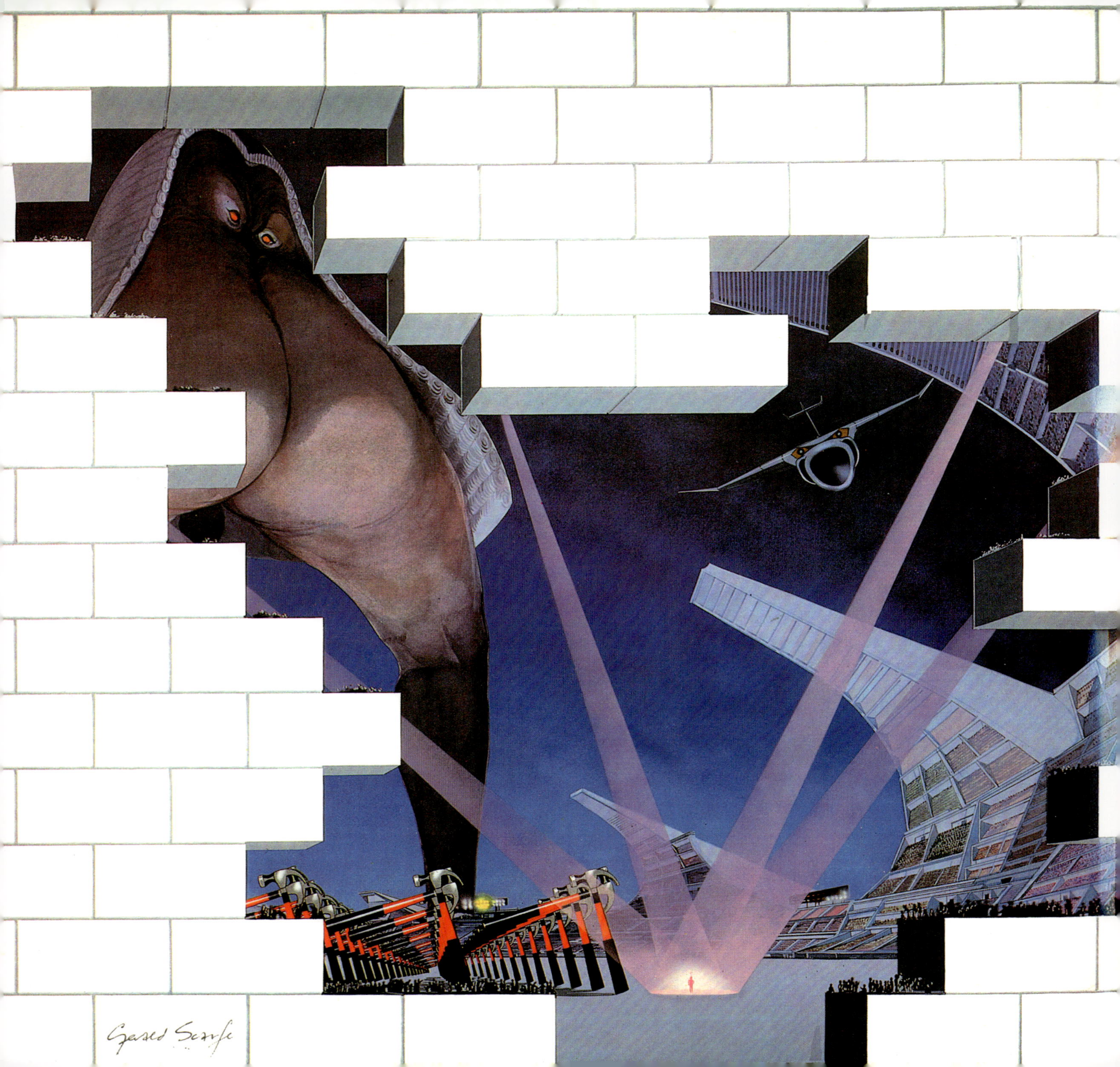
Gerald Scarfe

PRODUCED BY
DAVID GILMOUR
BOB EZRIN
ROGER WATERS

WORDS AND MUSIC
ROGER WATERS
EXCEPT
YOUNG LUST (WATERS GILMOUR)
COMFORTABLY NUMB (GILMOUR WATERS)
RUN LIKE HELL (GILMOUR WATERS)
THE TRIAL (WATERS EZRIN)

CO-PRODUCED AND ENGINEERED BY
JAMES GUTHRIE

OTHER ENGINEERS
NICK GRIFFITHS
PATRICE QUEF
BRIAN CHRISTIAN
JOHN McCLURE RICK HART

SOUND EQUIPMENT
PHIL TAYLOR

ORCHESTRA ARRANGED BY
MICHAEL KAMEN
AND
BOB EZRIN

BACKING VOCALS
BRUCE JOHNSTON
TONI TENNILLE
JOE CHEMAY
JOHN JOYCE
STAN FARBER
JIM HAAS
ISLINGTON GREEN SCHOOL

SLEEVE DESIGN BY
GERALD SCARFE
AND
ROGER WATERS

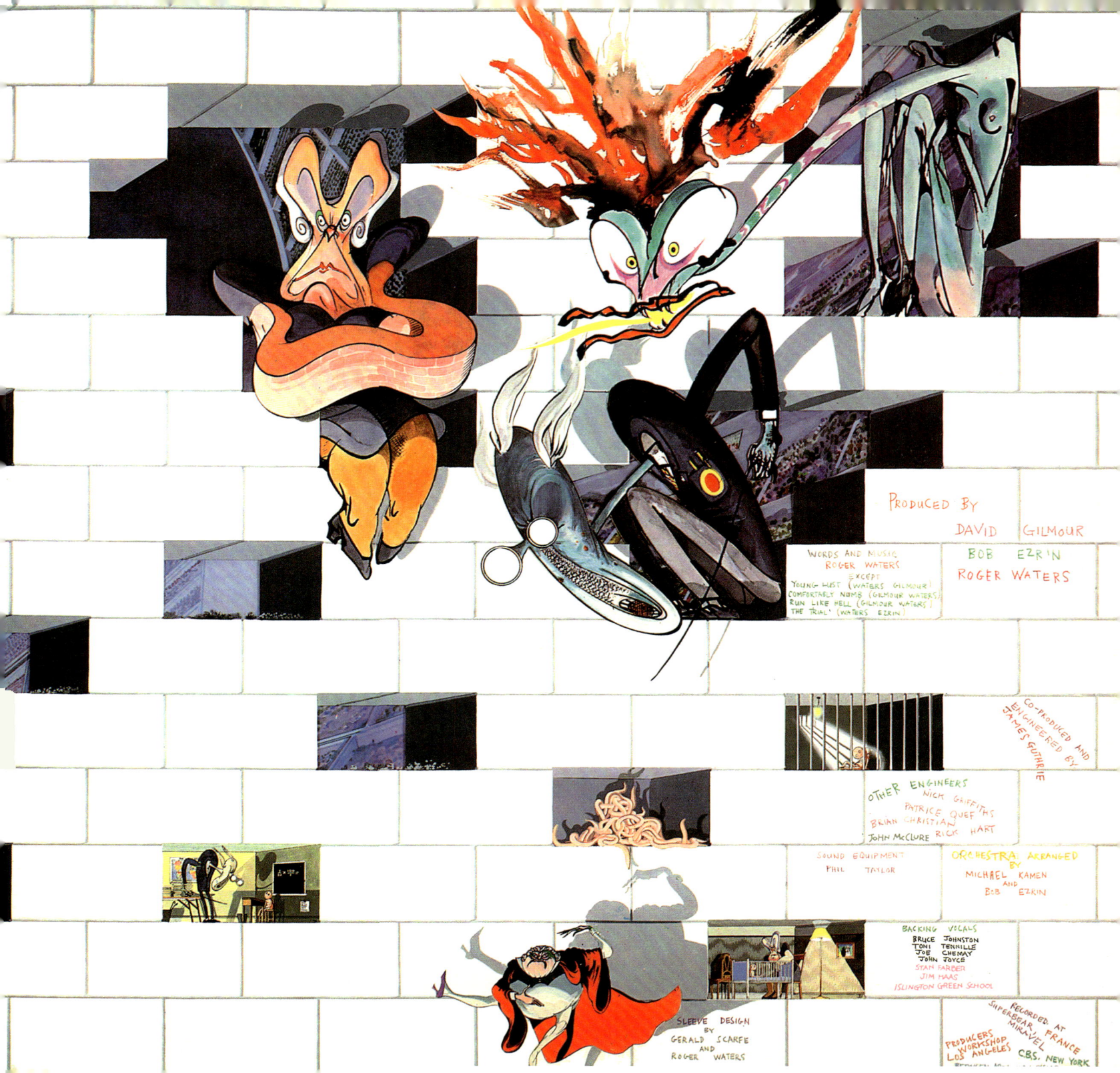

RECORDED AT
SUPERBEAR, FRANCE
MIRAVEL
PRODUCERS WORKSHOP
LOS ANGELES   CBS, NEW YORK

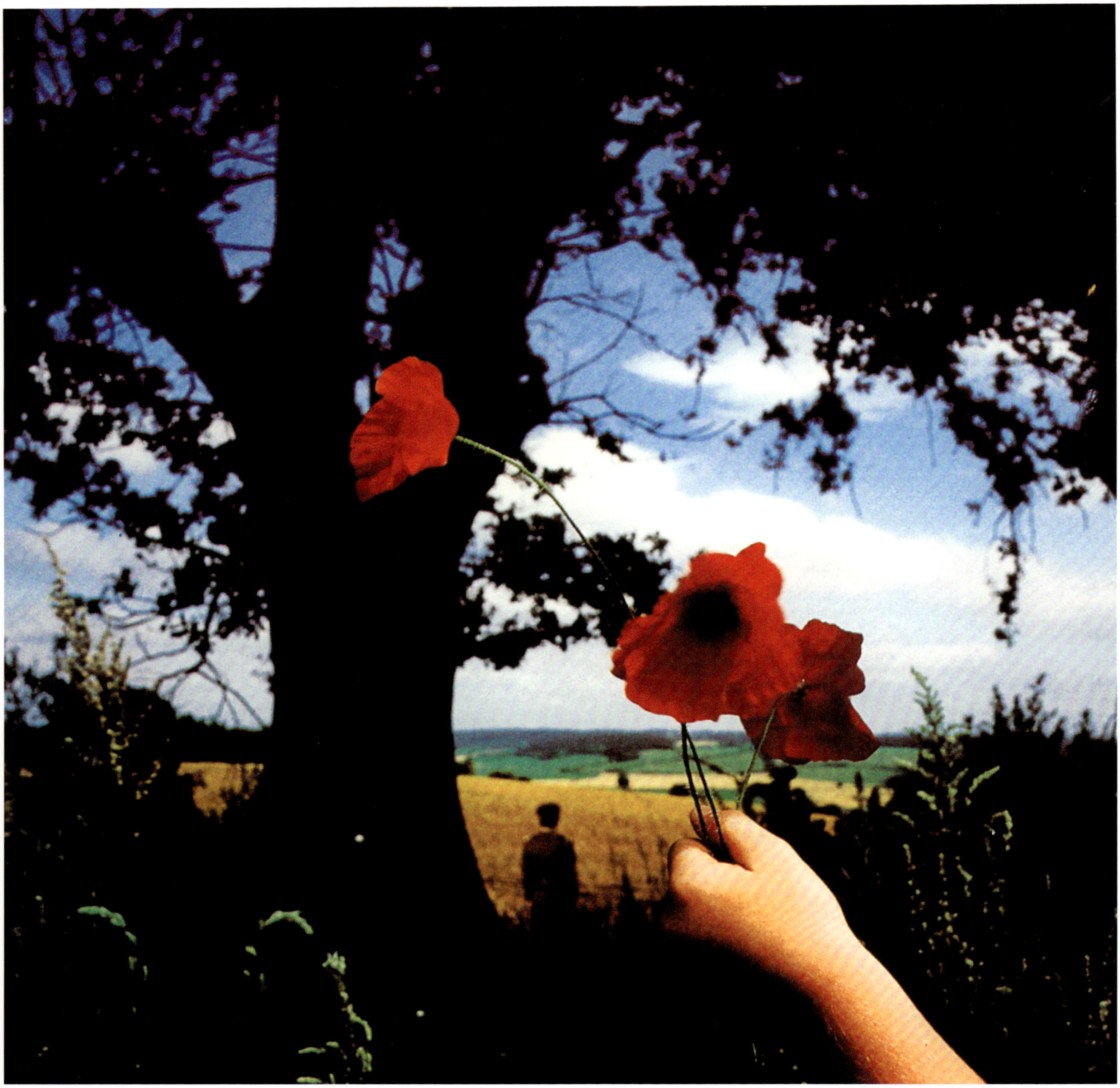

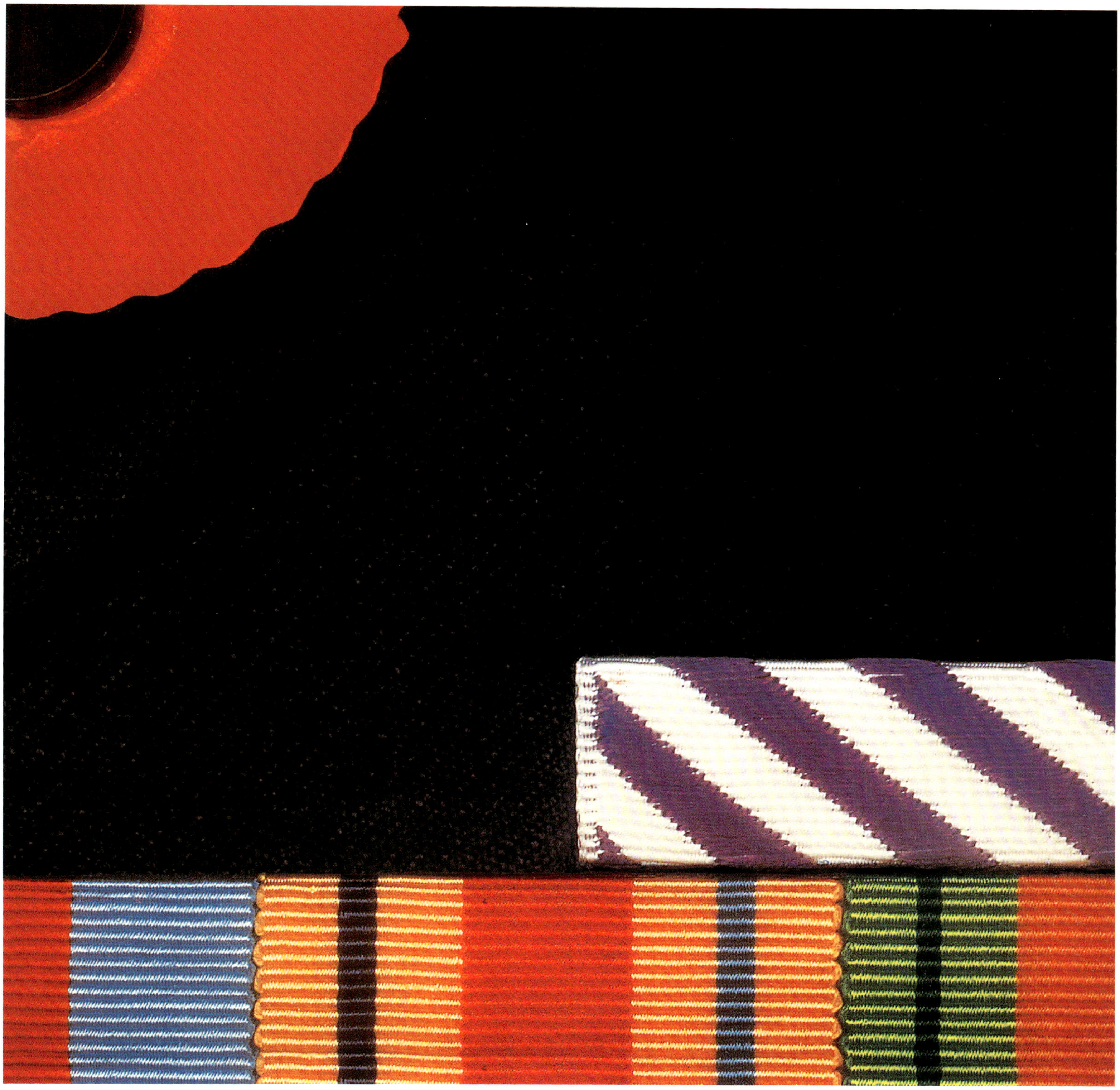

THE FINAL CUT

March 1983 • UK: EMI Harvest SHPF 1983

214–215 · PREVIOUS SPREAD · Album cover and centrefold artwork for *The Final Cut*, 1983. Design by Roger Waters. Photographs by Willie Christie. Artwork by Artful Dodgers

216 · OPPOSITE · Hand-written lyrics for 'The Post-War Dream' from *The Final Cut*. Roger Waters. Collection of Roger Waters

The theme of war first appeared in Roger Waters' songwriting as far back as 'Corporal Clegg' on *The Piper at the Gates of Dawn*. Ever since, the ghost of his father, Second Lieutenant Eric Fletcher Waters, killed in combat in Italy in 1944, had periodically surfaced in his lyrics.

Following Alan Parker's movie adaptation of *The Wall*, Pink Floyd mooted the idea of 'Spare Bricks', an album of collected out-takes from *The Wall* and material recorded for the film. The first taste came in July 1982 with the single, 'When the Tigers Broke Free'.

The song's unflinching lyrics addressed Eric Waters' death directly: name-checking his regiment, the Royal Fusiliers; the place of his death, Anzio; and how '*kind old King George sent mother a note, when he heard that father was gone...*'

'When Tigers Broke Free' felt like the beginning of something bigger than a movie soundtrack. Soon after, the out-takes album idea was abandoned, and Roger Waters proposed a new Pink Floyd record, initially known as 'A Requiem for the Post-War Dream', later re-titled *The Final Cut*. It would be Roger Waters' most personal album yet.

The Final Cut, was the first Pink Floyd album recorded without Richard Wright, and was created at several studios including Roger Waters' own, between July and December 1982. Waters' new songs were especially topical. The Falklands War had just come to an end. This brief but bloody conflict between Britain and Argentina over the sovereignty of the South Atlantic Islands had seen casualties on both sides and British prime minister Margaret Thatcher was accused of jingoism and warmongering.

Roger Waters' requiem was dedicated to his father and all casualties of war, but also to the welfare state, the National Health Service and British industry, which Waters regarded as further casualties of Margaret Thatcher's divisive government policies.

The Final Cut began with 'The Post-War Dream' and the sound of a car radio scrolling between stations. A newscaster is heard discussing a planned nuclear fallout shelter in Cambridgeshire; another explains that the replacement for a ship lost in the Falklands War will be built in Japan. Waters had established the theme of *The Final Cut* in less than 30 seconds, even before his questioning opening lyric – '*Tell me true, tell me why was Jesus crucified, is it for this that Daddy died?*'. Seconds later, he tackled what he considered Thatcher's betrayal of British industry by giving lucrative shipbuilding contracts to the Japanese, '*If it wasn't for the nips being so good at building ships, the yards would still be open on the Clyde*'. The later line, '*What have we done? Maggie what have we done? What have we done to England?*', drove the message home to any listener still uncertain about his sentiments.

The Post War Dream

Tell me true tell me why was Jesus crucified.
Is it for this that daddy died?

War it you was it me? Did I watch too much T.V.
Is that a hint of accusation in your eyes.

If it wasn't for the nips.
Being so good at building ships
The yards would still be open on the Clyde
And it can't be much fun for them beneath
the rising sun,
With all their kids committing suicide.

What have we done Maggie what have we done

What have we done.   To England.

Should we shout should we scream.

"What happened to the post war dream?"

Oh Maggie.   Maggie what have you done?

217 · OPPOSITE TOP LEFT · Back cover inset photograph for *The Final Cut*, 1983. Design by Roger Waters. Photographs by Willie Christie. Artwork by Artful Dodgers

218–219 · OPPOSITE TOP RIGHT AND BOTTOM · Centrefold artwork for *The Final Cut*, 1983. Design by Roger Waters. Photographs by Willie Christie. Artwork by Artful Dodgers

Elsewhere, Roger Waters sang about absent fathers on 'Southampton Dock'; soldiers mentally scarred by war on 'The Hero's Return' and took verbal pot-shots at world leaders, including US president Ronald Reagan, in 'The Fletcher Memorial Home'. Waters sang everything himself, only sharing lead vocals with David Gilmour on 'Not Now John', a stinging commentary on the decline of British industry.

Waters' then brother-in-law, fashion photographer Willie Christie, helped create *The Final Cut*'s military-themed artwork. At the time, Christie was living with his sister Carolyne and Waters. 'I'd heard some of the album being made', he recalls, 'Roger had discussed his politics with me. The jingoists were all for the Falklands War, and Roger and co were not.'

Waters wanted the cover to show a remembrance poppy and medal ribbons. Christie photographed the 1939–1945 Star, the Africa Star, the Defence Medal and the Distinguished Flying Cross, and took the pictures used elsewhere on the cover, including a field of poppies near Henley and his photographer's assistant dressed as an army officer with a knife protruding from his back: 'A very striking image.'

Sadly, the turmoil and conflict informing the artwork and the music matched the mood in the studio. Waters clashed with his bandmates, who felt side-lined and relegated. Making *The Final Cut* was, they admitted, an unhappy experience for all. While David Gilmour's howling lead guitar buoyed up many of the songs, he was dissatisfied with much of *The Final Cut*. Although he and Roger Waters set out to produce the album collaboratively, the final production credits were in Waters' name only. Pink Floyd had thrived for years on the creative tension between Waters and his bandmates. But the relationship had broken down for good.

Finally released in March 1983, *The Final Cut* gave the band their first UK Number 1 since *Wish You Were Here*, but it was a pyrrhic victory. Within months, Roger Waters announced his decision to leave the group. Waters' most personal Pink Floyd album would turn out to be his last.

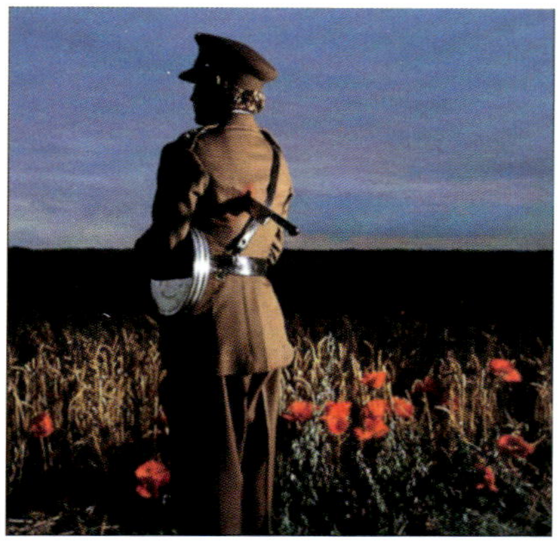

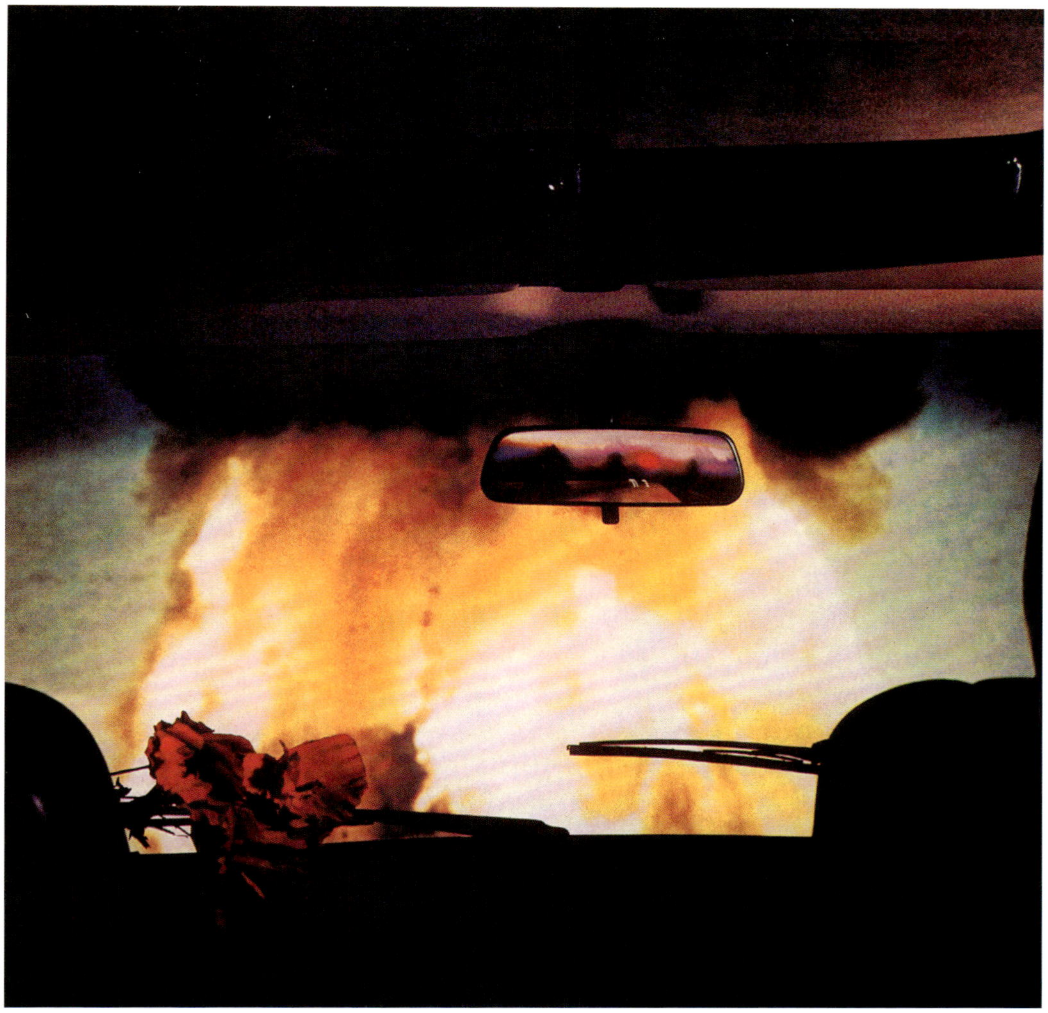

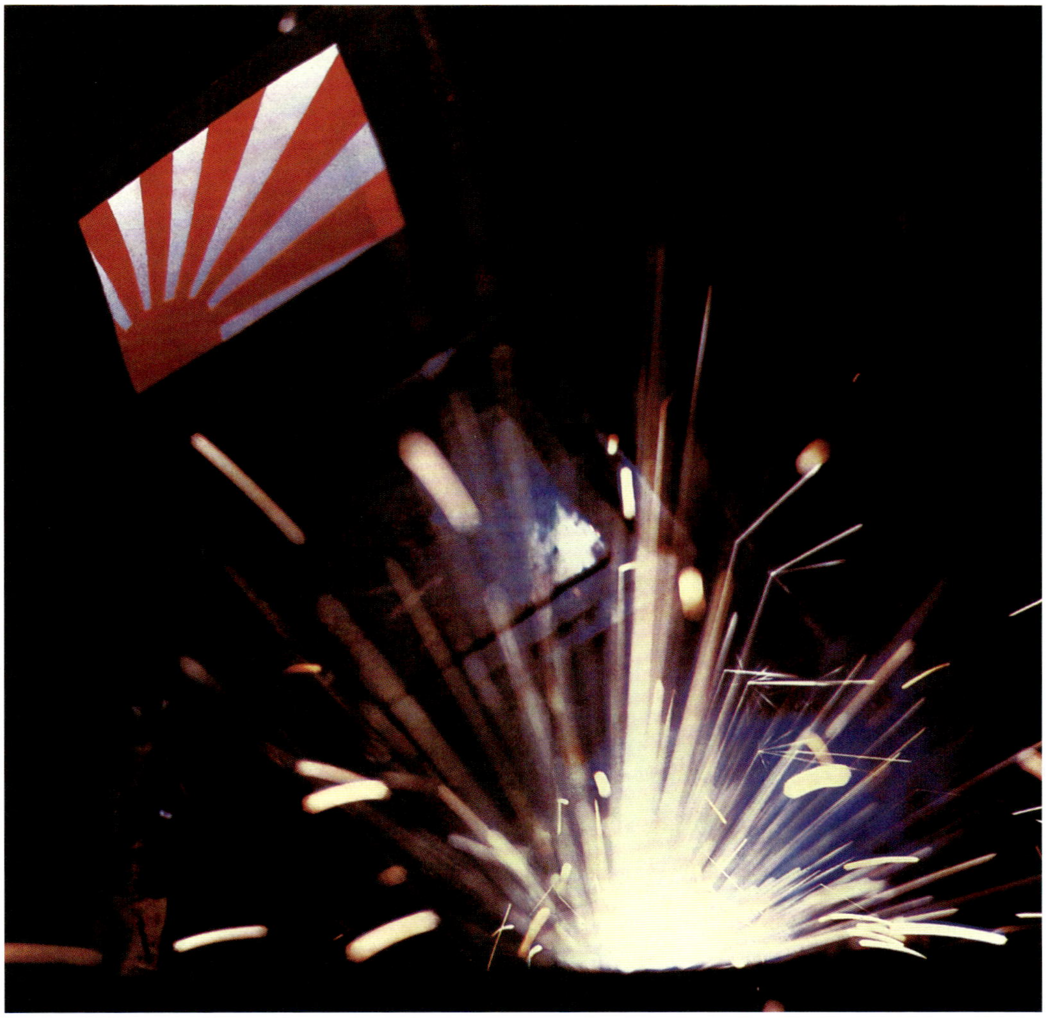

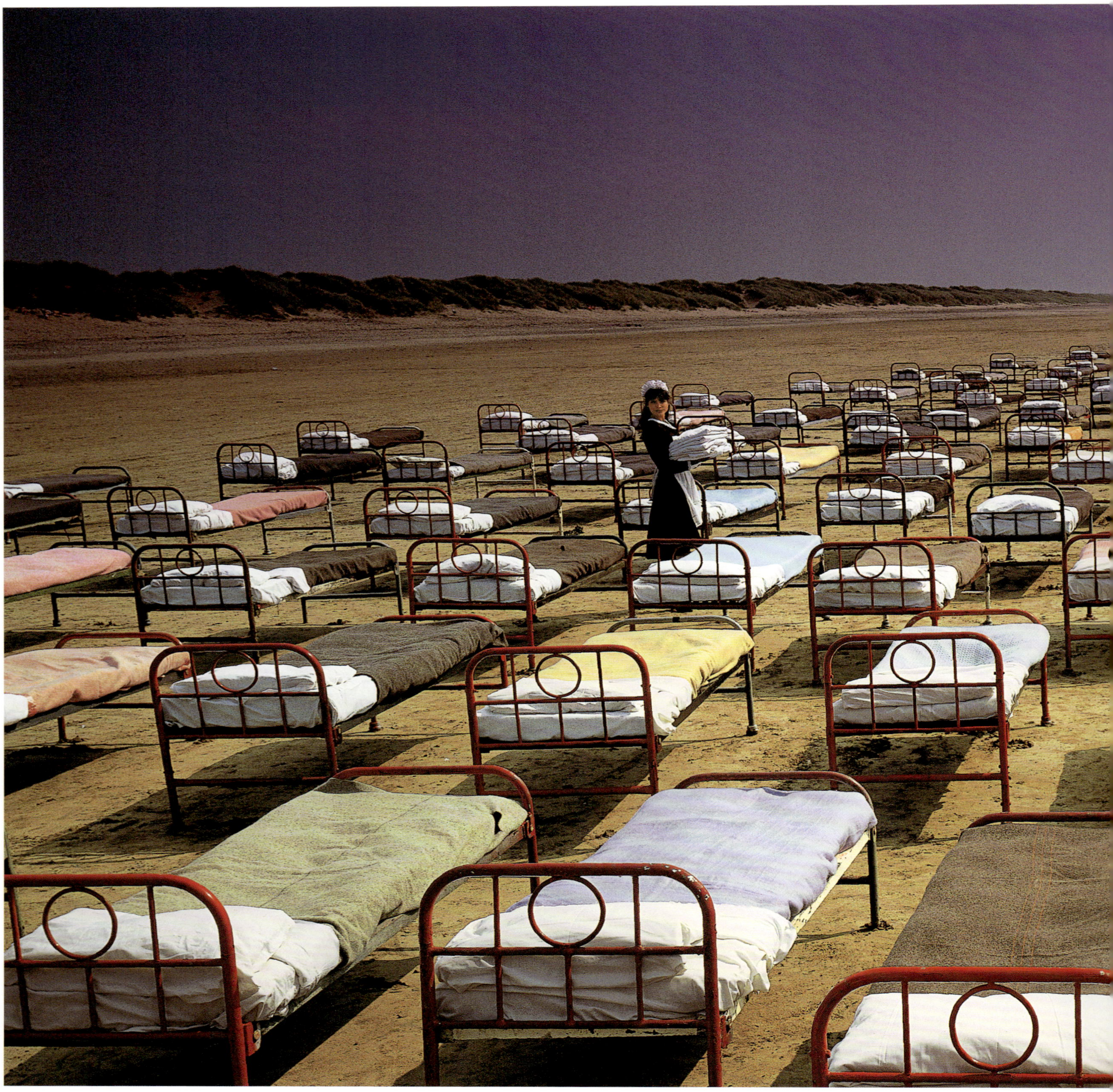

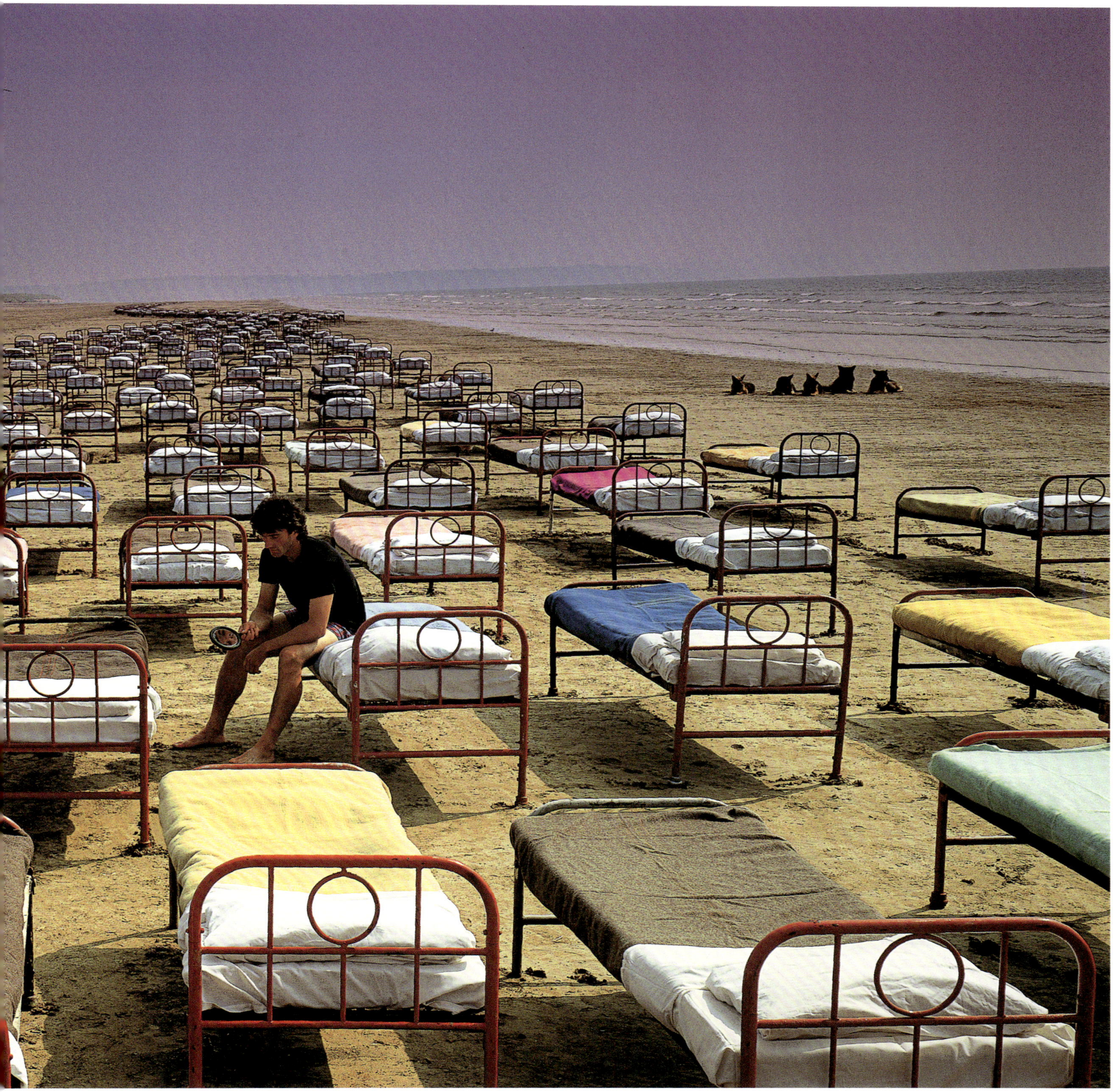

A MOMENTARY LAPSE OF REASON

September 1987 • UK: EMI EMD 1003 / CDP 7480682

220 · PREVIOUS SPREAD · Album artwork, *A Momentary Lapse of Reason*, 1987. Design by Storm Thorgerson and Nexus. Photographs by Robert Dowling.

221 · OPPOSITE · Press reception for the UK tour of *A Momentary Lapse of Reason*, London, 28 January 1988. Photograph by Nils Jorgensen

Like its cover image of 700 hospital beds on a beach, the music on *A Momentary Lapse of Reason* is bold, ambitious and very much a product of the 1980s. The first Pink Floyd album written and recorded without Roger Waters, it was launched in a blaze of publicity and accompanied by a marathon world tour.

But *A Momentary Lapse of Reason* was an album created in trying circumstances. Roger Waters officially left Pink Floyd in autumn 1985. He presumed his departure meant the end of the band, but David Gilmour and Nick Mason thought otherwise. Waters took out a high court application to prevent them using the Pink Floyd name, and so began a war of words and threats of legal action, that continued for the next two years.

Determined to make a new Pink Floyd album, David Gilmour looked for new collaborators. In the coming months, he would spend time with the Liverpudlian poet Roger McGough, Eric Stewart of the band 10cc, and the Canadian singer-songwriter Carole Pope. These brief writing or jamming sessions never led to anything permanent, but talented new musicians were successfully recruited to the project. Bryan Ferry's former keyboard player, Jon Carin, was among the first to be hired, alongside Bob Ezrin, co-producer of *The Wall*. Both would play a prominent role on the finished album. For the first time, Pink Floyd also collaborated with external songwriters, including Phil Manzanera from Roxy Music and the British singer-songwriter Anthony Moore, who co-wrote lyrics with David Gilmour for three of the album's ten songs.

Writing and recording sessions commenced on David Gilmour's houseboat studio, *Astoria*, moored near Hampton Court on the River Thames. While Bob Ezrin and others were often present, huge advances in music technology meant Gilmour could also work alone if necessary.

Unlike previous Pink Floyd albums, there wasn't a concept or a shared theme to this new material. What unified the likes of 'Learning to Fly', 'On the Turning Away' and 'Sorrow' was David Gilmour's voice and expressive guitar playing. Everything on the album, not least the lyrics and occasional sound effects, were tailored to suit the songs and his performance. Gilmour's guitar sound dominated the record. The booming, resonant intro to 'Sorrow' was recorded inside the Los Angeles Memorial Sports Arena for greater ambience. Listeners to *A Momentary Lapse of Reason* rarely had to wait long to hear another impeccably measured guitar solo.

280   The Albums

Although not a concept album, the overall feel of the album suggested new beginnings and a sense of quiet optimism. It was closer to the languorous atmosphere of, say, *Wish You Were Here* than *The Final Cut*'s heavy politicking. This impression was shored up by Richard Wright rejoining the band, albeit not as a full member. His contribution to the album was slight, but the simple presence of his name in the credits lent authenticity to the record.

A Momentary Lapse of Reason was finally completed in Los Angeles with the help of 16 additional session musicians, among them George Harrison's former drummer, Jim Keltner, and Little Feat's keyboard player Bill Payne. Released in September 1987, it immediately went to the Top 5 in the UK and US. Three months later, Pink Floyd, Roger Waters and their respective lawyers reached a settlement, allowing David Gilmour and Nick Mason to continue using the band's name.

Storm Thorgerson, who hadn't worked on an original Pink Floyd studio album since *Animals* 'was brought back to help give *A Momentary Lapse of Reason* a Floyd look and a Floyd feeling,'[3] as he said later. Inspired by the lyric '*a vision of an empty bed*' from 'Yet Another Movie', Thorgerson took delivery of 700 Victorian wrought-iron hospital beds. Each one was arranged on a beach in North Devon 'stretching across the landscape as far as the eye could see', in what was ostensibly a piece of performance art. The late fashion photographer Norman Parkinson would later describe the image as 'an extraordinary picture'.[4] The shoot itself was filmed from helicopter and projected during Pink Floyd's live shows.

A Momentary Lapse of Reason

222 · ABOVE · Steinberger GL3T Headless Guitar played on recording of 'Sorrow', 1986. Built by Ned Steinberger. Pink Floyd Collection

223 · OPPOSITE · Lyrics for 'Learning to Fly', 1986. Anthony Moore and David Gilmour. Courtesy of Anthony Moore Collection

This song was inspired by Dave Gilmour's and Nick Mason's experience of taking pilot lessons, but also speaks to a certain existential angst. Producer Bob Ezrin remembers the completion of this song as a turning point in the challenging process of making the album.

The subsequent Pink Floyd tour was as grand and ambitious as the music and the artwork. The band's first full-scale tour since 1977 featured a vast stage set housed within an 80-foot high steel frame and augmented by flying pigs and aeroplanes, robotic lighting pods and a giant mirror ball.

The tour began in September 1987 and finally ended in June 1990. Between these dates, Pink Floyd played to an estimated 5.5 million people and staged concerts in the former Soviet Union and on the Grand Canal in Venice. A cassette-tape version of the subsequent live album, *Delicate Sound of Thunder*, was taken aboard the Soyuz TM-7 by Soviet cosmonauts and became the first album to be played in space. The popularity of *A Momentary Lapse of Reason* proved that Pink Floyd, both the band and the brand, remained strong.

LEARNING TO FLY

INTO THE DISTANCE, A RIBBON OF BLACK
STRETCHED TO THE POINT OF NO TURNING BACK
A FLIGHT OF FANCY ON A WIND SWEPT FIELD
STANDING ALONE MY SENSES REELED
A FATAL ATTRACTION HOLDING ME FAST, HOW
CAN I ESCAPE THIS IRRESISTABLE GRASP?

CAN'T KEEP MY EYES FROM THE CIRCLING SKY
TONGUE-TIED AND TWISTED JUST AN EARTH-BOUND MISFIT
I

● ICE IS FORMING ON THE TIPS OF MY WINGS
UNHEEDED WARNINGS, I THOUGHT I THOUGHT OF EVERYTHING
NO BEACON TO FIND MY WAY HOME
UNLADENED, EMPTY AND TURNED TO STONE

A SOUL IN TENSION THAT'S LEARNING TO FLY
CONDITION GROUNDED BUT DETERMINED TO TRY
CAN'T KEEP MY EYES FROM THE-CIRCLING-SKIES
TONGUE-TIED AND TWISTED JUST AN EARTH-BOUND MISFIT
I

ABOVE THE PLANET ON A WING AND A PRAYER
THESE LEADEN FEET WILL NEVER KEEP ME STANDING HERE
WEIGHED DOWN BY A PRESENCE OF MIND, I
CAN'T GET AIRBORNE FOR THE WANT OF TRYING,
TO FREE THIS EMOTION THE KICK OF DYNAMITE
COULD BLOW THIS SOUL THROUGH THE ROOF OF THE NIGHT

....
● ....
CAN'T KEEP MY EYES FROM THE CIRCLING SKIES
TONGUE-TIED & TWISTED JUST AN EARTH-BOUND MISFIT, I.

"a sudden suspended emptiness."

(c) A. Moore, D. Gilmour, 1986.

my grubby halo forgotten in the icy air line 2
to wax euphoric and abandon all cares
the air leaves open to anyone who dares
to dream unfettered by the threatening light
to blow this soul right thro' the roof of the night
a soul unburdened a spirit on high
all time suspended as the moments slip by

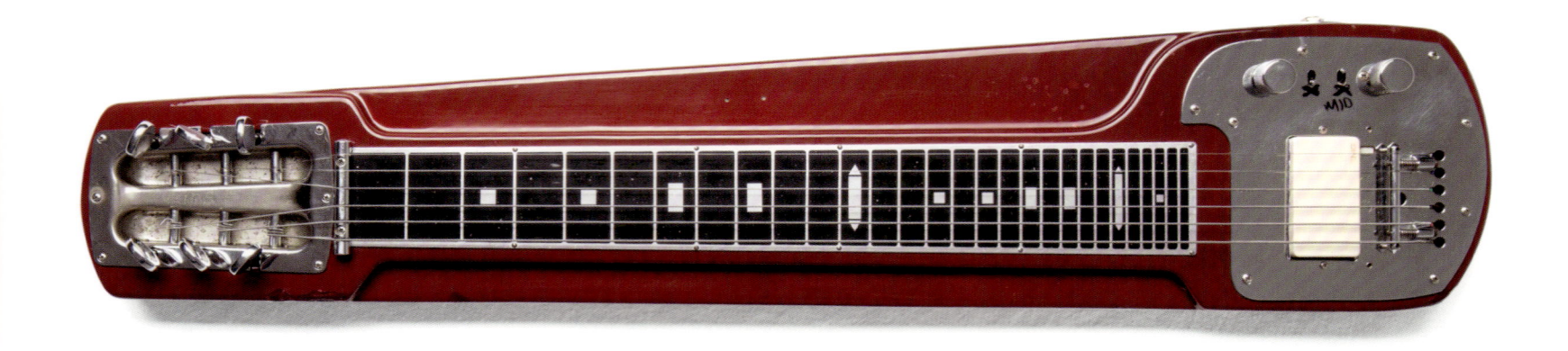

224 · ABOVE · Red Jedson lap steel guitar, about 1974. Pink Floyd Collection

This guitar was played by David Gilmour during live shows from 1974 to 1994. In the 1980s it was further modified and fitted with a white EMG H (humbucker) pickup and used live to play 'One of these Days' from the 1971 album *Meddle*, during Pink Floyd's world tour.

225 · LEFT · David Gilmour playing Jedson lap steel guitar on tour, USA, 1975. Photograph by Storm Thorgerson

226 · OPPOSITE · Candy Apple Red Fender Stratocaster 1957 Vintage reissue guitar, 1983. Pink Floyd Archive

This became David Gilmour's main guitar throughout the marathon two-year world tour of *A Momentary Lapse of Reason* and was also played during recording sessions for *The Division Bell* and many live shows until about 2005.

A Momentary Lapse of Reason

227 · ABOVE · Poster advertising Pink Floyd's concert in Versailles, France, 21–22 June 1988. Pink Floyd Archive

228 · LEFT · Poster advertising Pink Floyd's concert in Luzhniki, Moscow, Russia, 3–7 June 1989. Pink Floyd Archive

Pink Floyd played in the Soviet Union for the first time during the epic world tour of *A Momentary Lapse of Reason*. Other firsts included a spectacular show in the grand setting of the Palace of Versailles, and a free concert broadcast from a gigantic floating barge on Venice's Grand Canal.

229 · OPPOSITE · Fender Telecaster 52V 1952 reissue guitar played live on 'Run Like Hell' during the tour of *A Momentary Lapse of Reason*, 1987. Pink Floyd Collection

286   The Albums

A Momentary Lapse of Reason

230 · RIGHT · Scaled production plans detailing stage, camera and lighting positions for Pink Floyd's 15 July concert in Venice, Italy, dated 4 July 1989. Pink Floyd Archive

Pink Floyd's free concert on the Grand Canal off Piazza San Marco in Venice was broadcast live on television to over 20 countries. The event posed huge design challenges and required a complex system of multiple barges, stabilized with weights and cables, to accommodate the staging, mixing desk, technical equipment and crew areas.

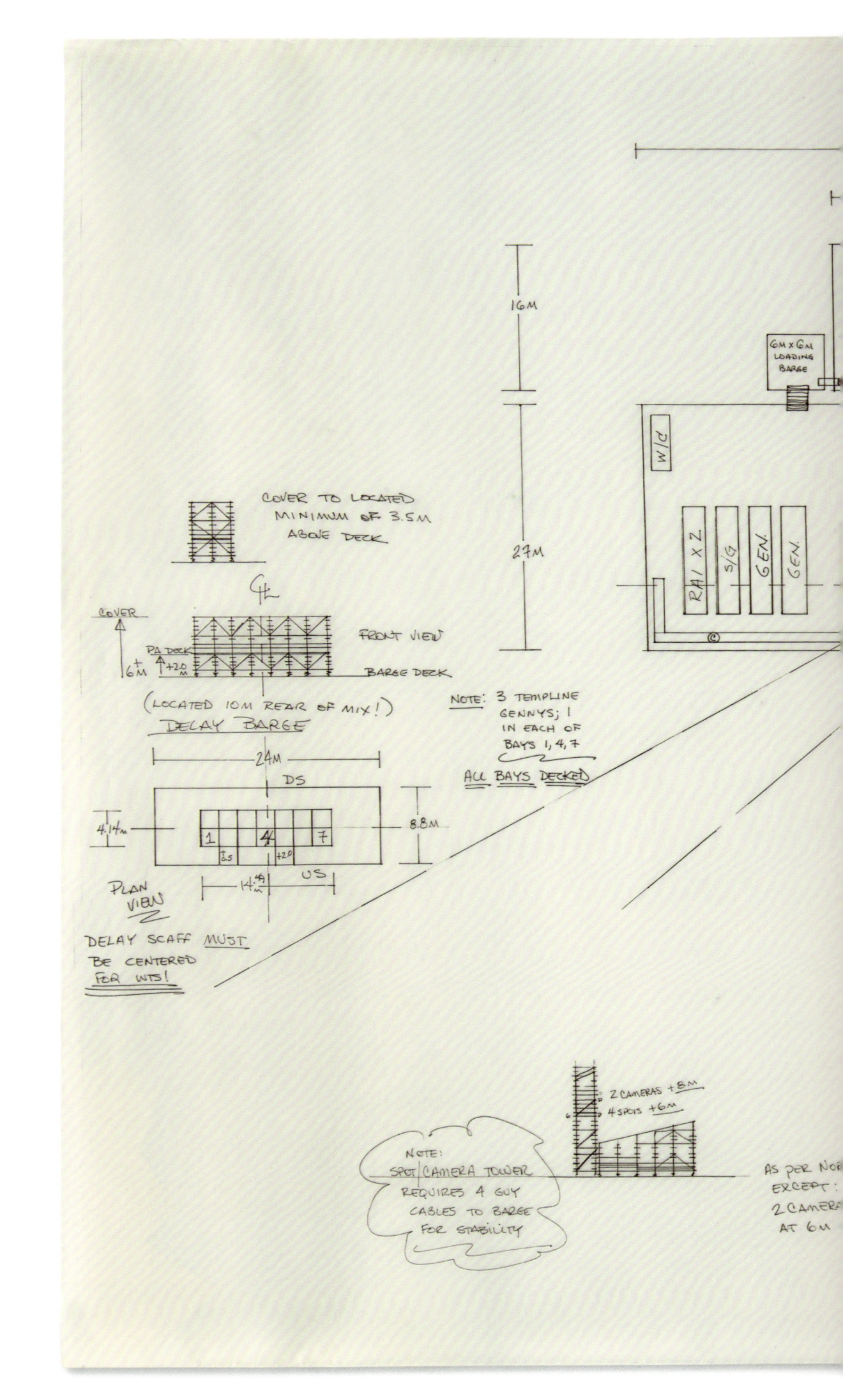

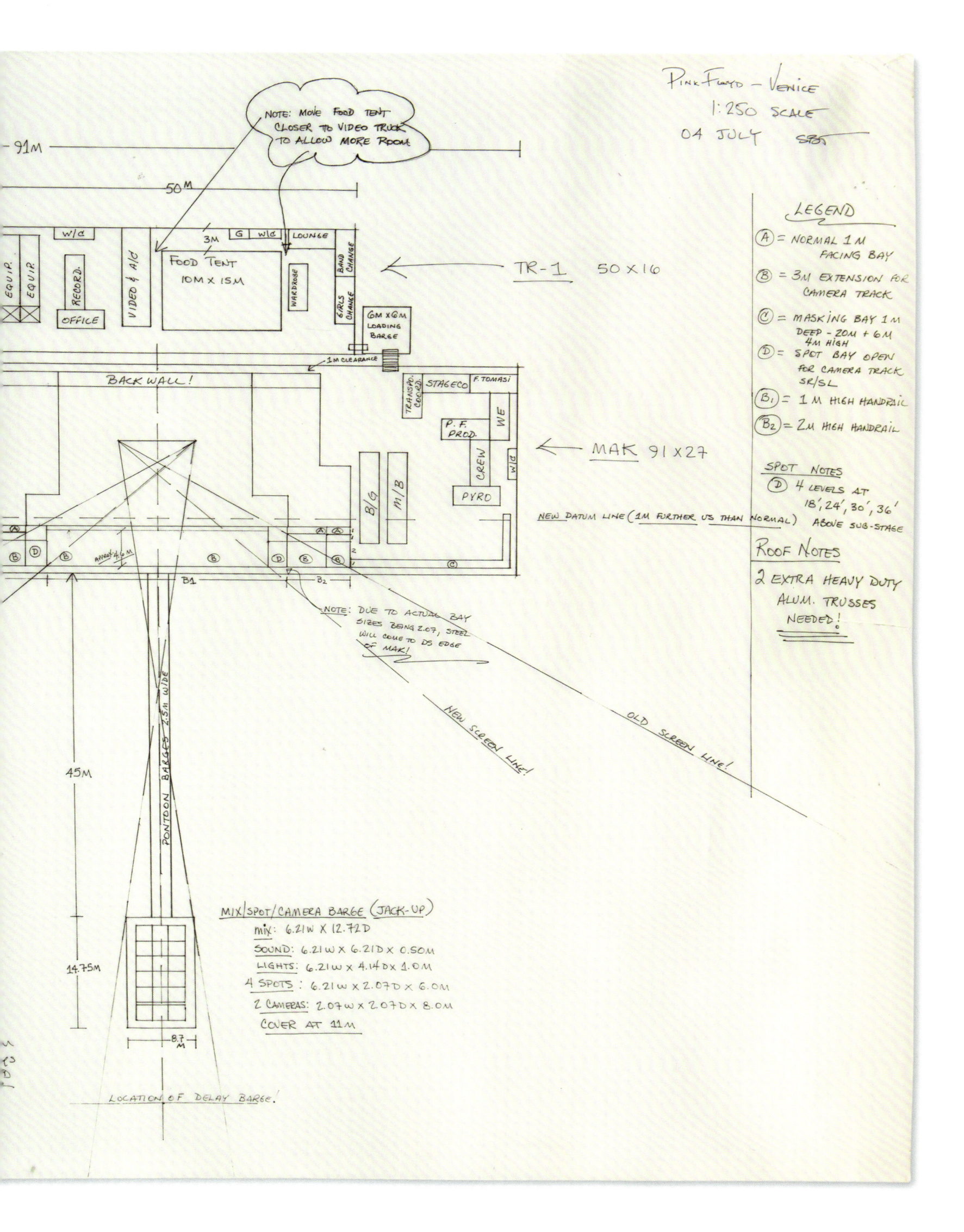

Pink Floyd – Venice
1:250 Scale
04 July SPOT

NOTE: MOVE FOOD TENT CLOSER TO VIDEO TRUCK TO ALLOW MORE ROOM

← TR-1 50 × 16

← MAK 91 × 27

NEW DATUM LINE (1M FURTHER US THAN NORMAL)

NOTE: DUE TO ACTUAL BAY SIZES BEING 2.07, STEEL WILL COME TO DS EDGE OF MAK!

NEW SCREEN LINE!
OLD SCREEN LINE!

- 91M
- 50M
- 45M
- 14.75M
- 8.7M
- APPROX 4.6M
- 1M CLEARANCE

Labels on layout:
EQUIP. / EQUIP. / W/C / RECORD. / OFFICE / VIDEO & A/C / FOOD TENT 10M × 15M / 3M / G / W/C / LOUNGE / WARDROBE / GIRLS CHANGE / BAND CHANGE / 6M × 6M LOADING BARGE / BACKWALL! / TRANSPO. CO./S.D. / STAGECO / F. TOMASI / P.F. PROD. / CREW / WC / WE / B/G / M/B / PYRO / PONTOON BARGES 2.5M WIDE

LEGEND
- Ⓐ = NORMAL 1M FACING BAY
- Ⓑ = 3M EXTENSION FOR CAMERA TRACK
- Ⓒ = MASKING BAY 1M DEEP – 20M + 6M 4M HIGH
- Ⓓ = SPOT BAY OPEN FOR CAMERA TRACK SR/SL
- Ⓑ₁ = 1M HIGH HANDRAIL
- Ⓑ₂ = 2M HIGH HANDRAIL

SPOT NOTES
Ⓓ 4 LEVELS AT 18', 24', 30', 36' ABOVE SUB-STAGE

ROOF NOTES
2 EXTRA HEAVY DUTY ALUM. TRUSSES NEEDED!

MIX/SPOT/CAMERA BARGE (JACK-UP)
- MIX: 6.21W × 12.72D
- SOUND: 6.21W × 6.21D × 0.50M
- LIGHTS: 6.21W × 4.14D × 1.0M
- 4 SPOTS: 6.21W × 2.07D × 6.0M
- 2 CAMERAS: 2.07W × 2.07D × 8.0M
- COVER AT 11M

LOCATION OF DELAY BARGE!

231 · ABOVE · Floating stage for Pink Floyd's concert, Venice, 15 July 1989

232 · OPPOSITE · Audience for Pink Floyd's concert, Venice, 15 July 1989

An estimated 100 million people, including the television audience, heard Pink Floyd's free concert. The crowds in Venice were far larger than the city's infrastructure could handle, and it was claimed that the sound volume damaged local buildings. Yet it was a triumphant feat of staging, a suitably grand performance at the close of an epic world tour, and a gift to Pink Floyd fans across the world.

A Momentary Lapse of Reason

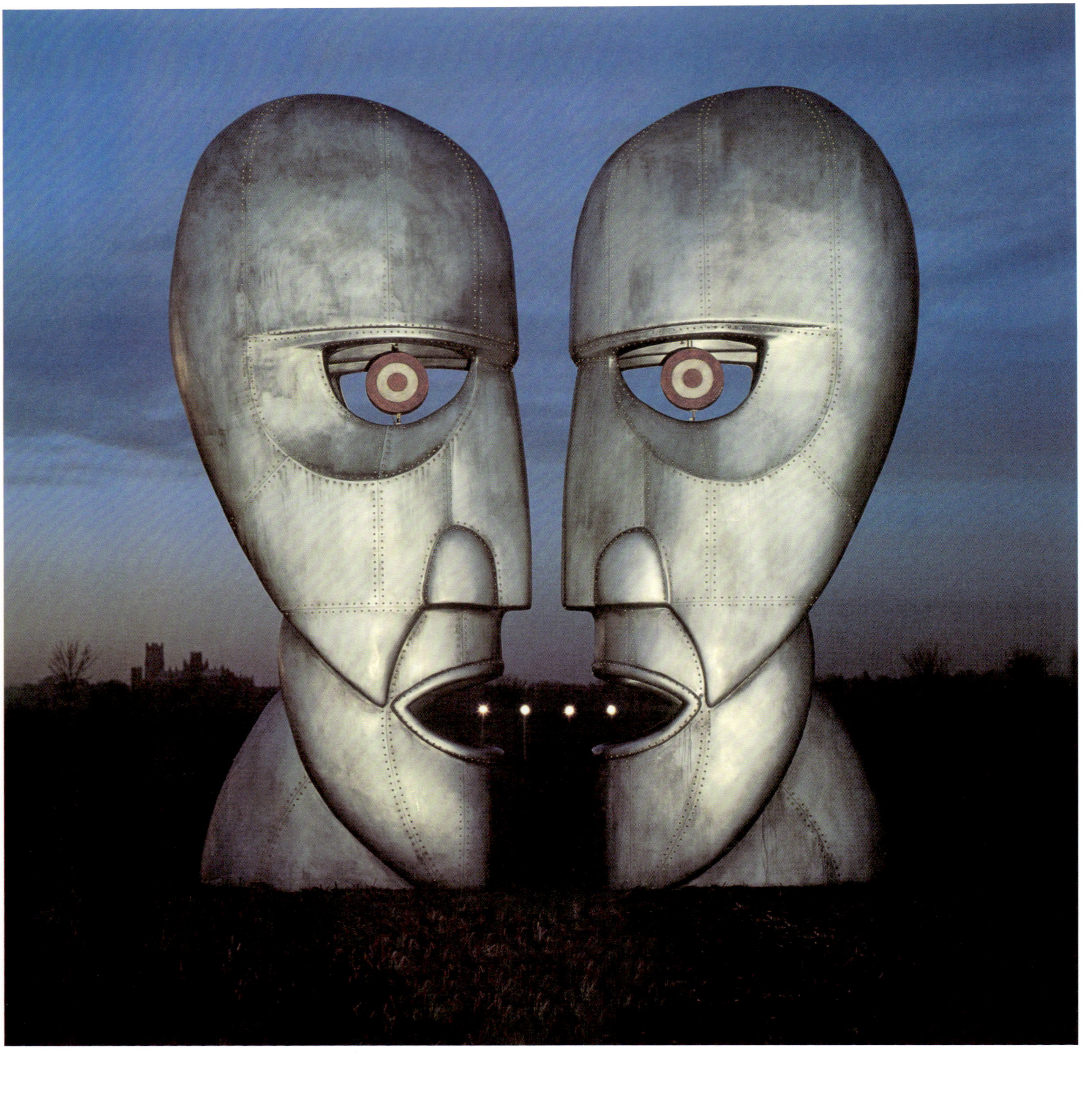

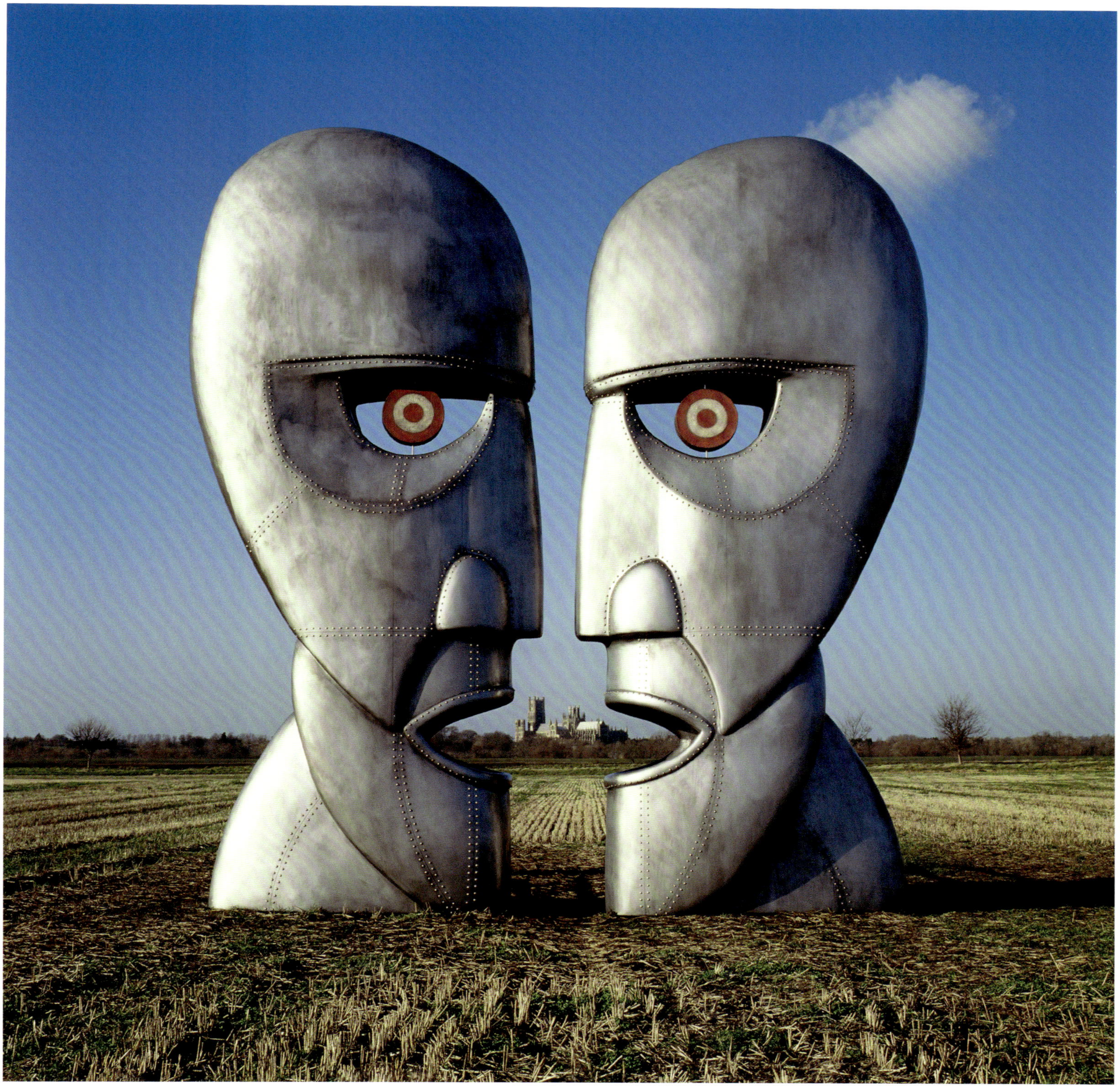

THE DIVISION BELL

March 1994 • UK: EMI EMD 1055 / CD EMD 1055

233–234 · PREVIOUS SPREAD · Album artwork, *The Division Bell*, 1994. Design by Storm Thorgerson at StormStudios. Sculptures by Aden Hynes and John Robertson. Photographs by Tony May / Rupert Truman / Stephen Piotrowski

235 · OPPOSITE · Working drawing of sculpted metal heads, made and photographed for the album cover of *The Division Bell*, 1994. Keith Breeden. Keith Breeden Collection

The Division Bell was an album that looked back at Pink Floyd's past and hinted at a possible future. It saw the return of Richard Wright as a full band member. From the 'talking heads' shown on its front cover to many of the lyrics inside, *The Division Bell* was all about communication. This theme was brought to the fore by the lyrics of Polly Samson, David Gilmour's future wife.

In early 1993, Wright joined David Gilmour and Nick Mason for jamming sessions at Britannia Row Studios and, later, Gilmour's *Astoria* studio. After the lengthy and often disjointed sessions for *A Momentary Lapse of Reason*, this was a return to the way they had made music with Pink Floyd in the late 1960s and early '70s. These improvisations became the starting point for *The Division Bell*.

David Gilmour and sound engineer Andy Jackson ensured that anything worthwhile – a simple guitar riff, chord sequence or melody – was recorded and filed away for further listening. Pink Floyd eventually found themselves with over 50 random pieces, which were then edited down by a very democratic process of elimination. Each band member awarded points to each musical idea. Having whittled the ideas down to 15, they underwent another voting process before the group settled on what became the 11 songs on the final album.

Pink Floyd began recording at London's Olympic Studios in summer 1993. The core trio of Gilmour, Mason and Wright was joined again by co-producer Bob Ezrin and by members of the touring band, including bass guitarist Guy Pratt, keyboard player Jon Carin and old Cambridge friend Dick Parry, who had played saxophone on *The Dark Side of the Moon* and *Wish You Were Here*.

Parry's involvement was yet another link to the past, in an album full of familiar motifs. The instrumental 'Marooned' was a showcase for David Gilmour's dazzling guitar work and felt like a companion piece to 'Echoes' and 'Shine On You Crazy Diamond'. It received a Grammy Award for Best Rock Instrumental Performance the following year. Meanwhile, the gospel backing vocals on 'What Do You Want from Me' echoed those on *The Dark Side of the Moon*, and the sample of a buzzing fly on the album's standout track, the melancholy 'High Hopes', was rumoured to be the same one heard a lifetime ago on *Ummagumma*'s 'Grantchester Meadows'.

However, *The Division Bell* was more than an exercise in nostalgia. Polly Samson wrote lyrics for 7 of the album's 11 songs and was crucial in drawing out the theme of communication and putting her partner's deeply buried feelings into words. 'Poles Apart' was purportedly about Syd Barrett *and* Roger Waters, who had both suffered in the past, in different ways, from the group's collective failure to communicate. 'Keep Talking', featuring the voice of Professor Stephen Hawking, expressed its sentiments in the most direct terms possible: '*My words won't come out right/ What are you thinking?*' In turn, David Gilmour broke his customary silence and composed 'Coming Back to Life' for Polly Samson.

294   The Albums

WORKING DRAWING FOR MODEL NO. 2.

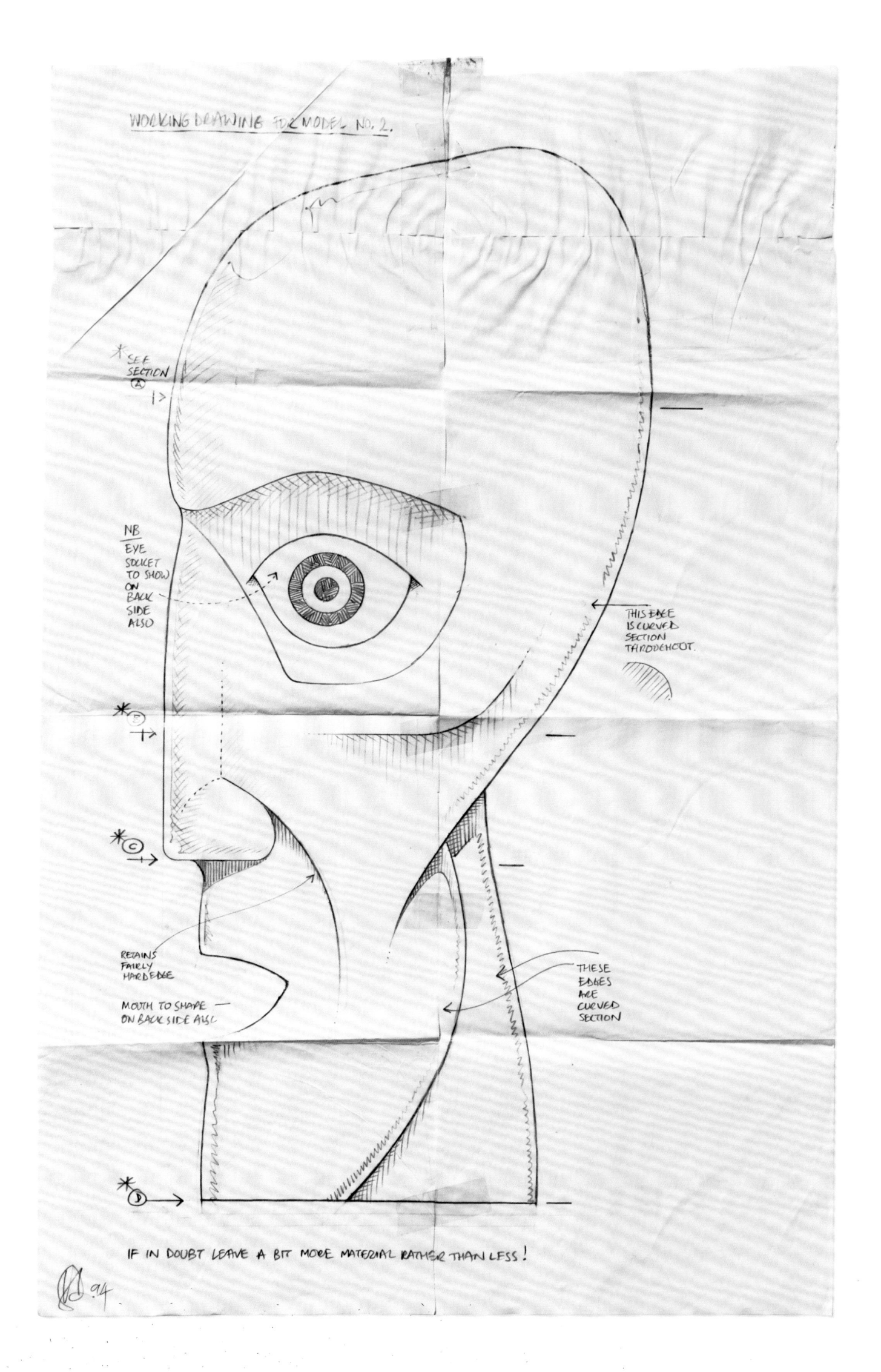

*SEE SECTION Ⓐ →

NB
EYE SOCKET TO SHOW ON BACK SIDE ALSO

*Ⓑ →

*Ⓒ →

THIS EDGE IS CURVED SECTION THROUGHOUT.

RETAINS FAIRLY HARD EDGE

MOUTH TO SHAPE ON BACK SIDE ALSO

THESE EDGES ARE CURVED SECTION

*Ⓓ →

IF IN DOUBT LEAVE A BIT MORE MATERIAL RATHER THAN LESS!

236 · ABOVE · Design illustration of the 'Fish' promotional airship for the UK/European tour of *The Division Bell*, 1994. Storm Thorgerson, Peter Curzon and Stuart Hamsley. Pink Floyd Archive

To promote *The Division Bell* Pink Floyd commissioned their biggest inflatables yet: two airships. The 130-foot long 'Fish' flew over the UK and Europe, while the 'Division Belle' was launched in America. The 'Division Belle', which featured a giant face made up of two fish-like creatures head-to-head, completed a round trip to several cities before suffering damage in a thunderstorm on 27 June. Fans bought the remnants as souvenirs.

Storm Thorgerson's cover image explored the album's theme on a grand scale. Thorgerson commissioned two sculpted metal heads, partly based on the Aku-Aku statues on the Easter Islands, and the height of a double-decker bus. As a further nod to Pink Floyd's earliest days, the metal statues were photographed in a field in Ely, Cambridgeshire, with Ely Cathedral visible between their two heads and with four lights between the mouths denoting speech.

Viewers studying the image would soon notice a 'third' face between the two faces in profile. 'The single eyes of the two faces looking at each other become the two eyes of a single face looking at you, the viewer,' explained Thorgerson, discussing what would be his final original Pink Floyd studio album cover.[5]

Thorgerson, who died in 2013, extended the theme of communication further still: 'It was intended that the viewer should not see both at the same time ... But if one saw both it meant the viewer was interacting, or communicating, with the image directly.'

Released in March 1994, *The Division Bell* and its giant talking heads communicated with audiences worldwide, and reached Number 1 in 12 countries. The corresponding world tour covered the USA, Europe and the UK and was a celebration of both the old and the new.

Pink Floyd re-hired one of their earliest lighting engineers Peter Wynne Willson (who had last worked with them in 1968) to update his liquid light projections and create new effects, alongside the band's regular stage and lighting

296   The Albums

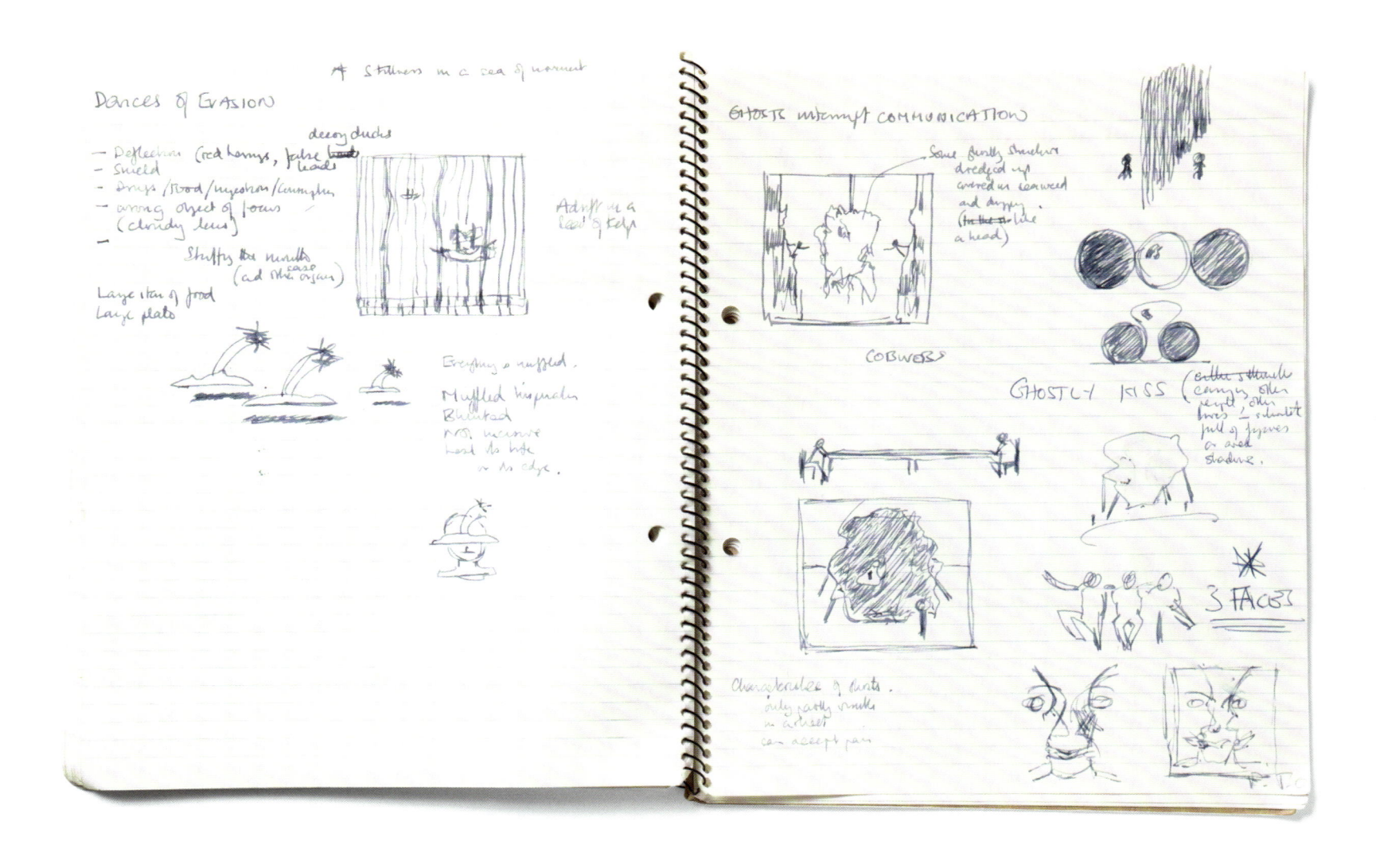

designers, Mark Fisher and Marc Brickman. The set list meanwhile combined most of *The Division Bell* with vintage Pink Floyd tracks, including 'Astronomy Domine' from *The Piper at the Gates of Dawn* and, at some shows, *The Dark Side of the Moon* in its entirety.

The tour broke existing records at the time by grossing over £150 million and was commemorated on the subsequent *Pulse* live album and video. Yet while *The Division Bell* sounded like a new beginning, it turned out to be the end for the next two decades. It would be 20 years before Pink Floyd released another album.

237 · ABOVE · Design notes and (bottom right) an initial sketch for *The Division Bell* album cover, 1993. Storm Thorgerson. Peter Curzon Collection

The Division Bell

238 · LEFT · *Brain Damage* fan magazine, issue 32, April 1994. Matt Johns Collection

239–240 · BELOW · Passes for The Division Bell Tour, March–November 1994. Graphic design by Peter Curzon at StormStudios. Pink Floyd Archive

241 · OPPOSITE · The 'Ten Tour Commandments' for crew on The Division Bell Tour, 1994. Pink Floyd Archive

When you are on the road, you don't do a whole lot. You arrive in a city ... you either have a gig that night ... or you hang around, go out for dinner, get drunk, go to sleep and wake up ... and go to the gig. That is basically how you live and all you do. Very little can get done out there.

—Interview with Marc Brickman and Steve O'Rourke, *Brain Damage* magazine, issue 38, 1994

298 The Albums

THE TEN TOUR COMMANDMENTS

1. **THOU SHALT NOT BE TARDY** - Please observe all call times. Whether it is a baggage call, lobby time, rehearsals, or particularly show time - be punctual. Don't make the many wait for the few.

2. **THOU SHALT NOT BE UN-LAMINATED** - Lamintates should be treasured, never loaned, left behind or lost. They are issued in good faith and for your own protection and convenience. Guests will be issued with stick-on passes. Please ask your guests not to bring cameras or recorders.

3. **THOU SHALT NOT BE OVERWEIGHT** - Members of the band party will be issued with baggage tags and are requested to keep their luggage down to 2 pieces each. Travel lean and light!

4. **THOU SHALT NOT DUCK DUTY** - When departing a hotel please report to the front desk and check-out, taking care of your incidentals. Even if you have no charges - you have to check-out. Always allow sufficient time to do this and still be punctual for our departure.

5. **THOU SHALT NOT FEED THE MASSES** - The catering facility is for touring personnel only. It is not a free restaurant for friends, family or current flights of fancy. Meals will only be served to laminate holders.

6. **THOU SHALT NOT FREE THE WORLD** - There are NO complimentary tickets. All tickets have to be purchased. Please contact Juliette well in advance with your requirements to ensure satisfaction.

7. **THOU SHALT NOT GO WALKABOUT** - If any member of the band party needs to leave the main body of the group at any time, day or night, he or she must ensure that Management knows and is furnished with contact numbers if available.

8. **THOU SHALT NOT COMMIT OVERLOAD** - Do not assume that friends and family can be accommodated on band transport. Ensure that embarrassment and bad vibes are avoided by having your guests make their own travel arrangements.

9. **THOU SHALT NOT COMMIT PUBLIC DEPRESSION** - Try and keep your moans, groans, depression, personal problems and pessimistic observations to yourselves - as nobody wants to hear it.

10. **THOU SHALL BE OBEDIENT** - Do as you are told or you'll get a clump.

view of circular screen looking downwards

242 · ABOVE · Sketch of the stage and circular screen for The Division Bell Tour, 1993. Mark Fisher. Pink Floyd Archive

243 · OPPOSITE TOP · The Division Bell touring stage with psychedelic lighting effects by Peter Wynne Willson, 1994. Stage and lighting design conceived by Marc Brickman and Mark Fisher. Photograph by Mark Fisher. Mark Fisher Collection, courtesy of Cristina Garcia

244 · OPPOSITE BOTTOM · Drawing of the stage design for The Division Bell Tour, 1993. Mark Fisher. Pink Floyd Archive

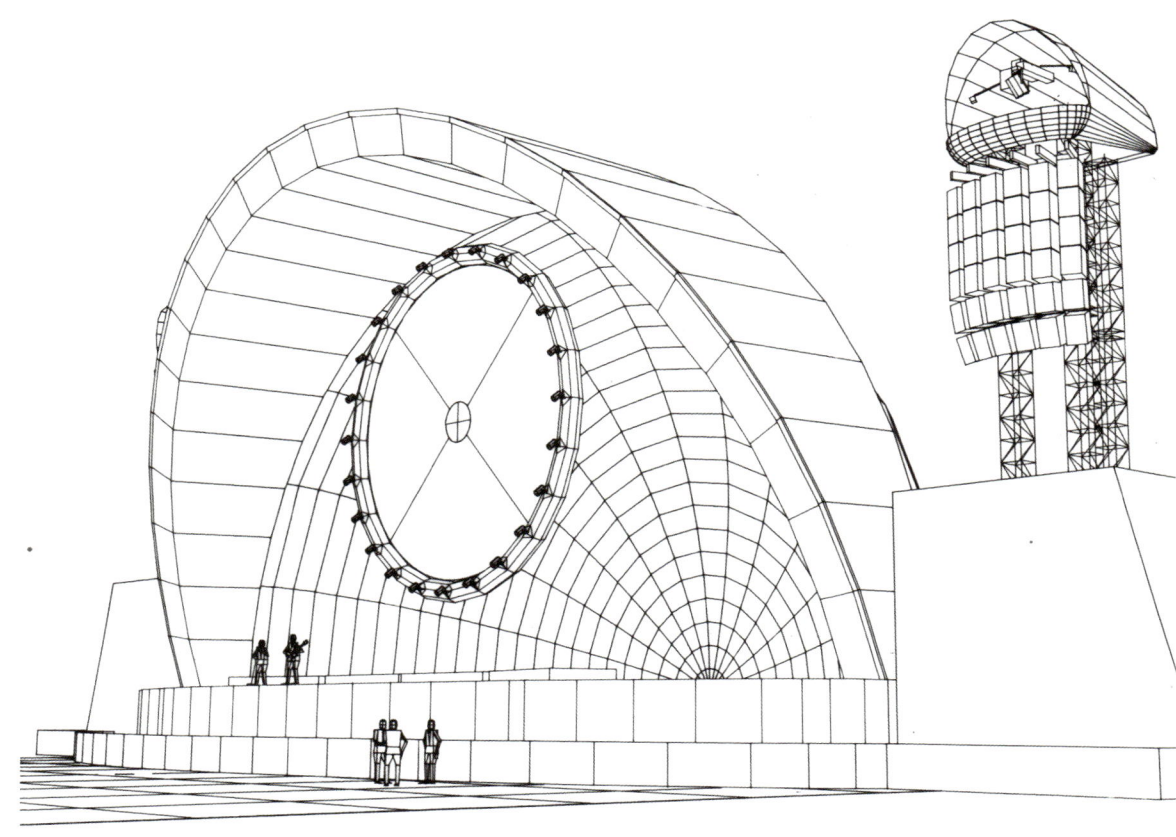

The Division Bell

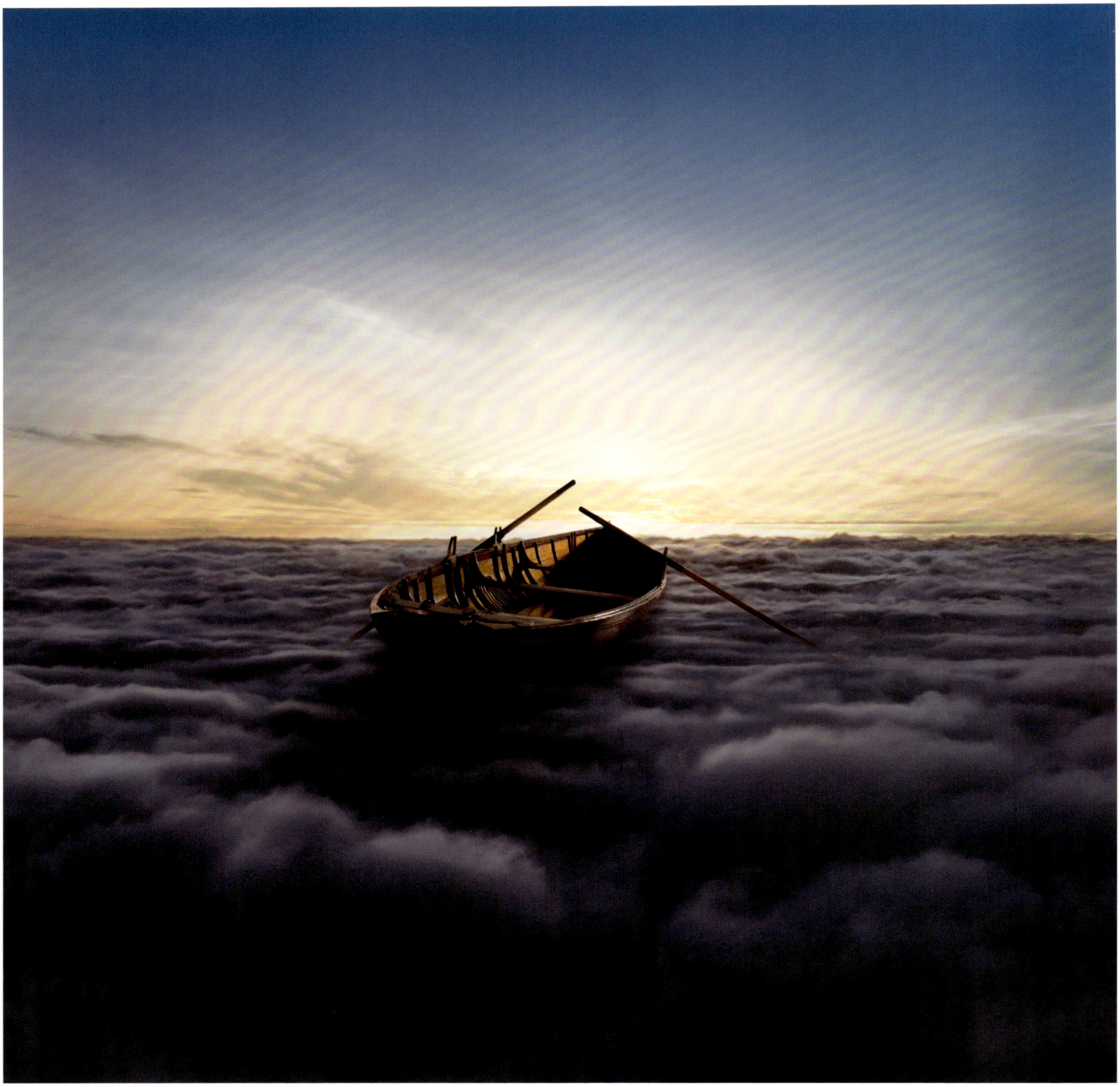

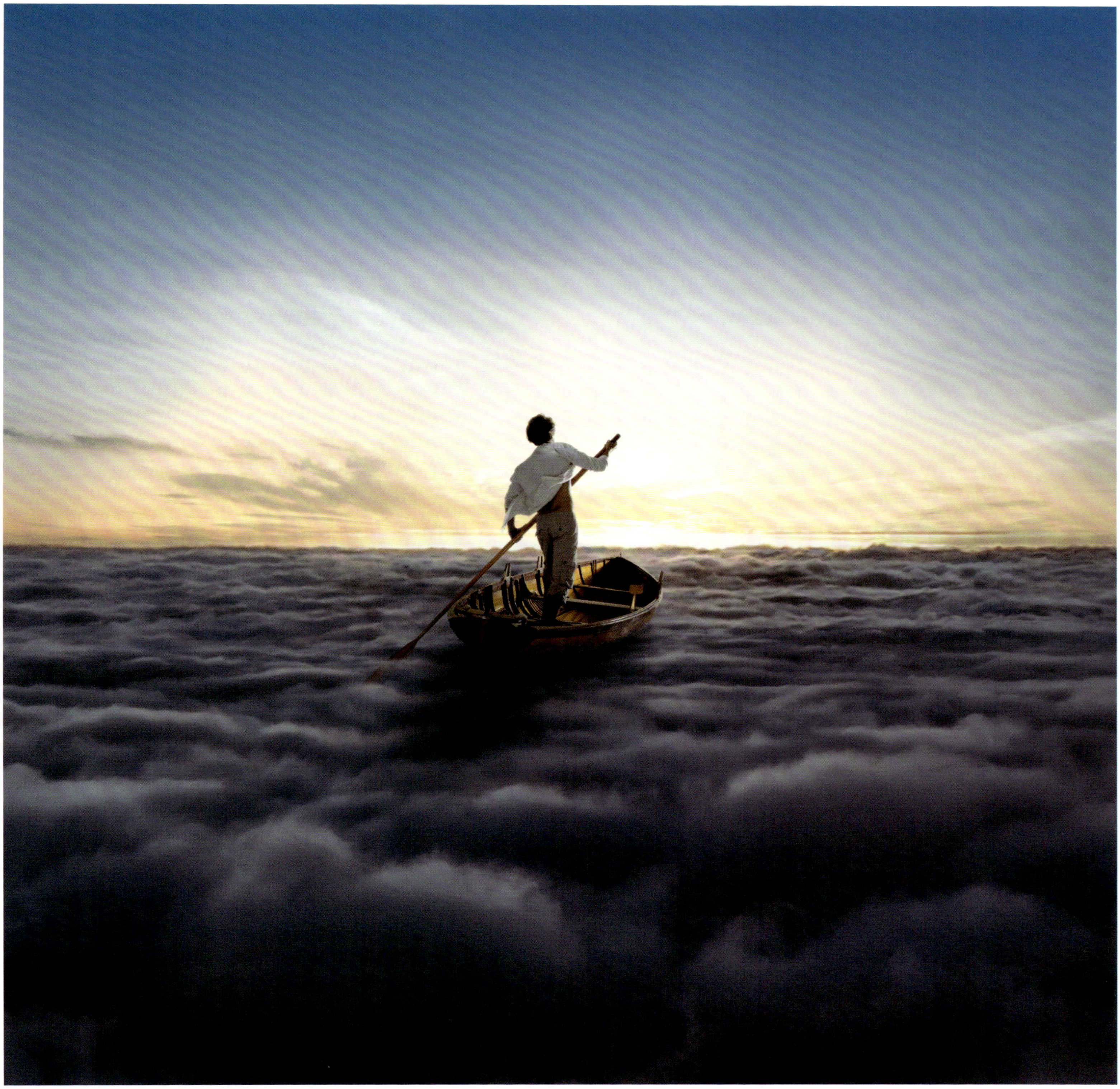

THE ENDLESS RIVER

November 2014 • UK: Parlophone 825646215478 / 825646215423

245–246 • PREVIOUS SPREAD • Album artwork, *The Endless River*, 2014. Creative direction, Aubrey Powell. Cover artwork by Ahmed Emad Eldin. Design and art direction by Stylorouge. Photographs by Simon Fowler, Jill Furmanovsky, Harry Borden, Andy Earl

247 • OPPOSITE • Digital artwork selected as the basis for *The Endless River* album cover design, 2014. Ahmed Emad Eldin

On 15 September 2008, Pink Floyd's co-founder and keyboard player Richard Wright passed away. Wright's contribution to the band had been immense: his songwriting, keyboard playing and vocals were part of the group's DNA. *The Endless River*, released six years after his death, was both a tribute to Wright and a postscript to Pink Floyd's recording career.

The Endless River began where Pink Floyd's last album had ended. *The Division Bell* sessions 20 years earlier had produced more material than the songs on the final record. The band members had spoken before of an album's worth of additional ambient/instrumental music, nicknamed 'The Big Spliff', which had been put together by their sound engineer Andy Jackson.

Starting in 2012, David Gilmour revisited the material. After sifting through over 20 hours of music, he began to take the project further with Roxy Music guitarist and former Pink Floyd collaborator Phil Manzanera. Determined to make 'a 21st-century Pink Floyd album' they, together with Nick Mason and Andy Jackson, slowly culled four 14-minute tracks from the music created largely with Richard Wright in the 1990s, but augmented the material with new ideas where necessary. It was a painstaking process. Additional instruments and overdubs were added with the help of others, including The Orb's producer, Martin 'Youth' Glover.

The Endless River was a fitting tribute to Richard Wright. His voice is heard on the opening track, 'Things Left Unsaid', in an excerpt from a 1972 interview recorded for *Pink Floyd Live at Pompeii*. 'We certainly have an unspoken understanding,' he says, reflecting on the band's way of working, 'but there are a lot of things left unsaid as well.'

Richard Wright's musical fingerprints were all over the rest of the album: in the mournful piano on 'The Lost Art of Conversation' and in 'Autumn '68', which featured a long-forgotten recording of Wright playing the pipe organ in the Royal Albert Hall in 1968. *The Endless River* fully demonstrated how integral, if sometimes overlooked, Richard Wright's contribution had been to Pink Floyd. His voice had subtly complemented David Gilmour's, and his choice of chords had often provided the perfect context for his bandmates to shine. Overall, *The Endless River*'s long, unhurried soundscapes suggested a homage to late-1960s and '70s-era Pink Floyd. As a further nod to the past, one part of the second movement, subtitled 'Skins', was a showcase for Nick Mason's percussion and the closest Pink Floyd had come to a drum solo since Mason's composition 'The Grand Vizier's Garden Party' on *Ummagumma*.

The Endless River was released in November 2014 and preceded by a single, its only vocal track, 'Louder Than Words'. With lyrics written by author Polly Samson, David Gilmour's wife, it addressed head on Pink Floyd's ability to create music – 'this thing that we do' – despite their often tortured personal

The Endless River

248 · OPPOSITE · Richard Wright during rehearsals for Live 8, 2005. Photograph by Tony May

249 · BELOW · Richard Wright playing keyboards during rehearsals for Live 8, 2005. Photograph by Jill Furmanovsky

relationships. Aptly, the song ended with a climactic guitar solo by David Gilmour and a keyboard motif by Richard Wright, which gradually faded from earshot.

The album's otherworldly cover image of a man sailing through clouds into nowhere, appeared on billboards around the world. *The Endless River* debuted at Number 1 in the UK and several other countries in Europe and Number 3 in the US.

Prior to his death in 2013, Storm Thorgerson asked his former design partner Aubrey 'Po' Powell to carry on his work for Pink Floyd. Powell, who had been making films and documentaries, agreed, and was appointed to oversee *The Endless River*.

'We invited half a dozen designers, including Damien Hirst and Peter Saville, to pitch,' he recalls. Hundreds of ideas were submitted, but the band were especially taken with one: 'David and Nick kept coming back to this picture of a man in what looked like a simple wooden boat, punting through the clouds.'

The image had been presented by an ad agency, but Powell discovered it had actually been taken from the internet, and belonged to an 18-year-old Egyptian digital artist, Ahmet Emad Eldin. According to Powell, 'Ahmet spoke a little English, and was astonished to discover Pink Floyd wanted to use one of his pictures on the cover of their album.'

The final cover was put together by designer Rob O'Connor and his graphic design studio, Stylorouge, but there was an element of life coming full circle. Ahmet Emad Eldin later revealed that, just like Hipgnosis, his art was often inspired by Salvador Dalí.

'The image showed a new approach, but it was still in the spirit of the music and of Hipgnosis', says Aubrey Powell. Aptly, there was also an air of finality about the picture; the sense of a curtain coming down. Pink Floyd's journey was finally complete.

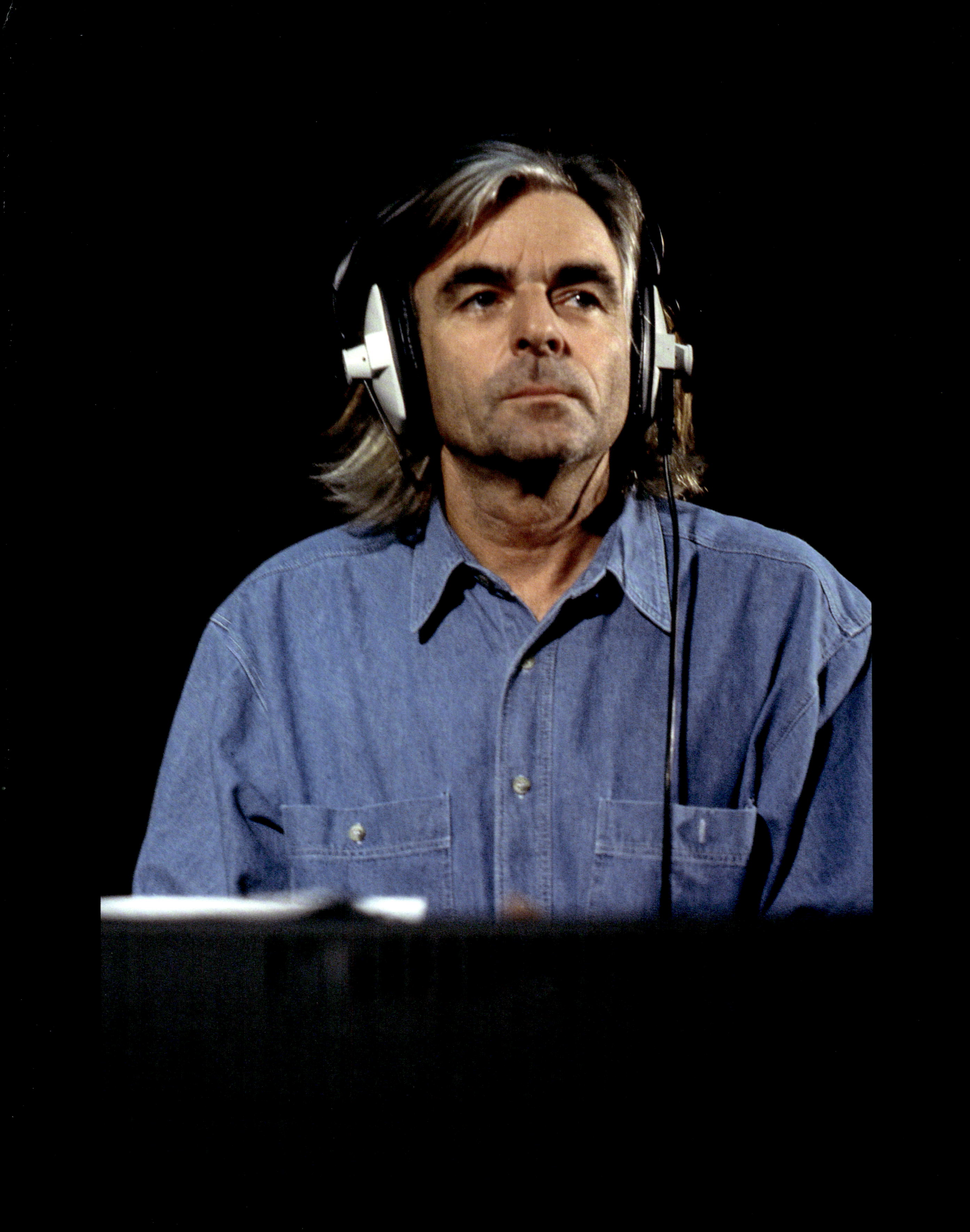

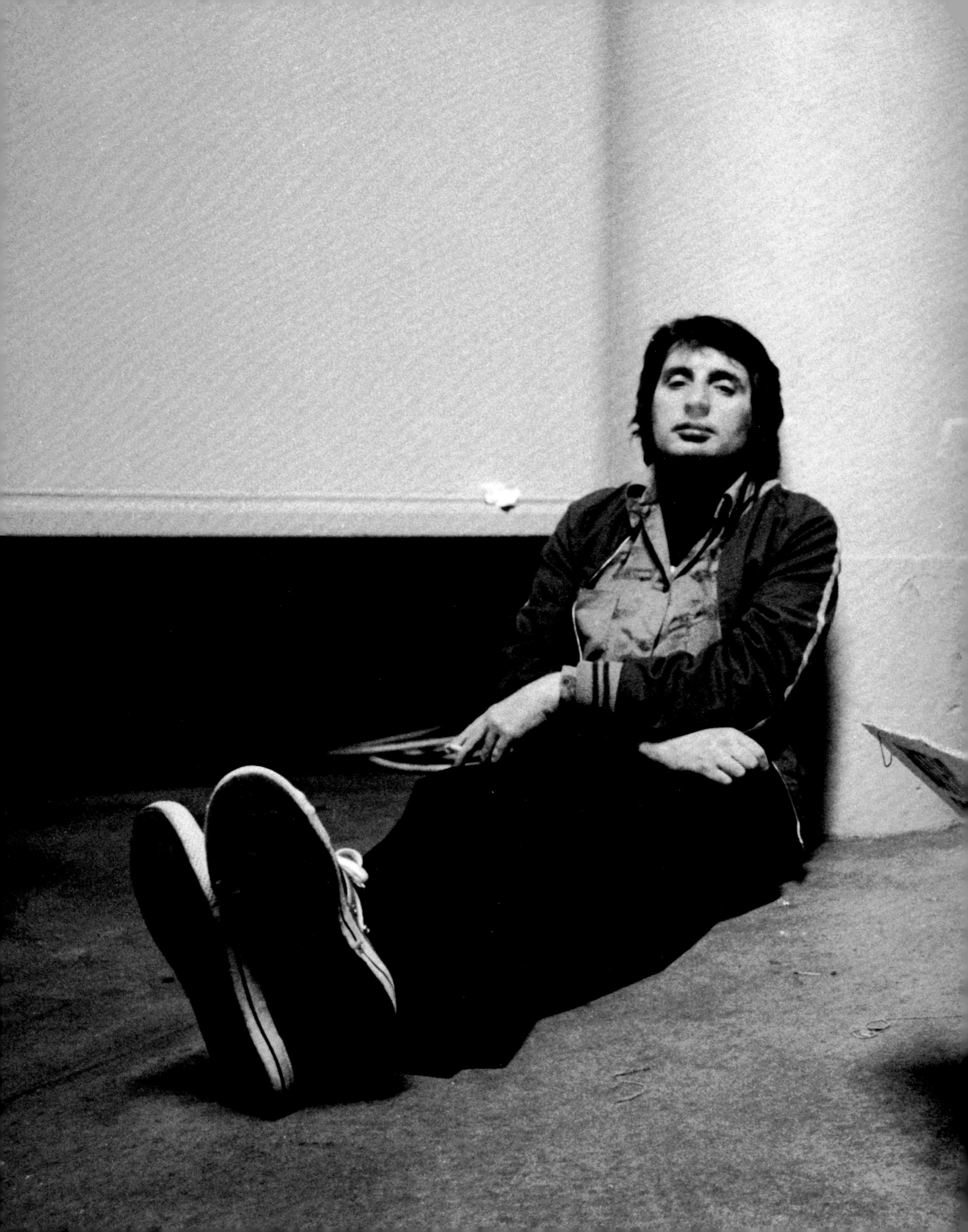

STORM THORGERSON PHOTO DESIGNER

Aubrey Powell

In late 1972, Storm Thorgerson and I arrived at Abbey Road to present Pink Floyd with our cover ideas for *The Dark Side of the Moon*. The band were friends of ours, but it was still an apprehensive moment, walking into their recording session and hoping we'd cracked the brief.

We presented a dozen designs, including a sketch of the now-famous prism, so rough it could have been drawn on the back of a napkin. The band cast their eyes over the designs, and one by one pointed at the prism and said, 'That's the one'. An aggrieved Storm tried to pitch them our other ideas, but Pink Floyd were unanimous. 'No,' they insisted. 'That's the one.'

I walked out of the studio feeling exhilarated, but Storm was nonplussed. It didn't matter that Pink Floyd had chosen one of our ideas, Storm was upset that they hadn't considered the others. He was downcast. But that was Storm. Brilliant but contrary, he was never able to fully embrace his own success. Little did he know that *The Dark Side of the Moon*'s prism would become an iconic album cover.

To the outside world Storm could appear difficult and disorganized. He was always probing and often seemed more interested in someone's psychological well-being and personal life than in getting the job done – and he was always late. At the same time, though, he was extremely funny and very kind. Artists had to be quite strong to deal with him, but if they persevered they were rewarded with a grand design. Some clients made the grade; others didn't and walked away.

I first met Storm Thorgerson on the rugby field. We were in rival school teams and Storm was as bullish and no-holds-barred on the pitch as he was off it. He was a pupil at the same school as Syd Barrett and Roger Waters, and we both knew David Gilmour from the Cambridge scene.

One Saturday afternoon Storm invited me to his house. When I arrived, I found Storm and some of his bohemian set lounging around his bedroom, its walls covered with graffiti and montages of surreal art, deep in conversation and listening to the blues. It was all going well and I was making new acquaintances until the police arrived in the hope of an easy drug bust. They went away empty-handed, but from that day on Storm and I became the best of friends.

Storm emerged into a world at war on 28 February 1944, and from the start he marched to a different beat. Both his parents were dedicated Communists. Until the age of nine Storm attended Summerhill, a radical boarding school in Suffolk that allowed pupils to choose which lessons to attend. You could say that the seeds of Storm's alternative approach to life were sown there. Storm was unafraid to challenge anyone in authority. One old friend still recalls the teenage Storm driving his tank-like 1940s American Studebaker down Cambridge's main shopping street, pausing only to crack an egg on the roof of a stationary police car. He then went back and did it again. And again ...

In 1965, Storm moved to London to study film at the Royal College of Art and became a photo designer by accident when a book publisher hired him to come up with some modern-looking covers for their latest titles. Storm asked me to help. He was like a mentor to me and suggested I try photography too. He lent me a Pentax camera and showed me how to compose pictures, process film and develop prints.

Soon after, Pink Floyd asked an artist friend of ours to design a sleeve for their second album, *A Saucerful of Secrets*. He turned them down, so Storm volunteered our services, which Pink Floyd accepted. Storm once candidly described this early artwork as 'the result of messing about without being weighed down by knowledge or preconception'. Neither of us had a clue what we were doing, but we learned on the job.

Before long, Storm and I were being asked to design sleeves for other groups, beginning with The Pretty Things, Marc Bolan and Free. We borrowed £500 each and rented two floors at 6 Denmark Street in the middle of London's Tin Pan Alley. The studio became Hipgnosis' home for the next 15 years.

Storm always claimed he wasn't a photographer and said he couldn't 'draw for toffee'. Ideas came to him in dreams. 'Plundering the goldmine', he used to say, meaning his busy mind. It was Storm's concept to put a cow on the cover of Pink Floyd's fifth studio album *Atom Heart Mother*, with no band name or album title; this upset EMI's senior management but delighted the band. Storm realized that in his role as a renegade designer he could be a man without boundaries. And Pink Floyd made music without boundaries. They trusted us, and gave Hipgnosis the freedom to design whatever we wanted.

Storm would listen to Pink Floyd's music, read the lyrics, and cast himself as a translator. He saw his job as turning an audio event into a visual event. He thrived on ambiguity and contradiction, on strange juxtapositions and visual puns, making the real unreal: 'Exploring the impossible and suspending disbelief,' as he once put it. And it was Storm's fascinations that drove the extraordinary covers for, among others, *Ummagumma*, *The Dark Side of the Moon*, *Wish You Were Here* and, later, *A Momentary Lapse of Reason*, *Delicate Sound of Thunder* and *The Division Bell*. It was his idea to wrap the cover of *Wish You Were Here* in sealed black shrink-wrap, a homage to the artist Christo who famously wrapped the coast of Little Bay in Sydney, Australia, in fabric in 1969. You had to buy the album and tear off the wrapping to see the cover.

Storm and I spent 14 years designing album covers between 1968 and 1982, for much of that time with Hipgnosis' third partner Peter Christopherson. If Storm had the ideas, then I was the practical one, directing and photographing the shoots, making sure Hipgnosis ran smoothly and ensuring we all got paid. The work was relentless and the relationship between Storm and our clients wasn't always easy.

Storm was uncompromising, often far too clever for his own good, and he expected the same from others. His mantra was always 'a good idea is a good idea'. If Storm believed in an idea and one group turned it down, he'd offer it to another. And he'd repeat that mantra to Led Zeppelin, Paul McCartney or any artist who discovered they weren't the first to be pitched a particular concept for their new long-playing vinyl.

While Storm would often dazzle people with his brilliance, he could also upset them with his bluntness and unwillingness to accommodate their own ideas. I often found myself playing referee, and our own relationship was not without problems. We argued furiously, and I once threw a very expensive Hasselblad camera across the studio at him. But we always made up. We both believed passionately in what we were doing, and the work always came first.

Storm stopped working with Pink Floyd for some years, after a misunderstanding over the cover design of *Animals*. In some ways, it was also the beginning of the end of Hipgnosis. In 1982, Storm suggested we cease creating photo designs. I was resistant to the idea, but with his usual foresight Storm had seen the future. Hipgnosis' expensive gatefold sleeves had become redundant in the DIY post-punk era; the 12-inch LP would soon be replaced by the compact disc, and MTV had just arrived, meaning groups were spending money on big-budget videos rather than cover shoots. It was time to move on.

Storm and I formed a new company, Greenback Films, and made videos for many of the artists we'd once designed sleeves for. But we fell out and parted ways in 1985. It was ten years before we spoke to each other again. Storm continued to direct videos and make TV commercials, a medium which, in typical Storm style, he later denounced as 'emotionally, and intellectually bankrupt'. But he returned to designing album covers and created the incredibly ambitious artwork for Pink Floyd's 1987 comeback album, *A Momentary Lapse of Reason*.

David Gilmour, discussing *A Momentary Lapse of Reason*, recalls handing Storm a drawing of an empty single bed for inspiration. Storm's response was 'Great! But let's have 500 empty beds'. And that is exactly what he ended up with: ignoring common sense, the budget and the inclement elements to photograph the beds on a beach in Devon.

Storm suggested using a suit of lights, an idea taken from the embellishments of matador's bull-fighting costume, for the sleeve of Pink Floyd's live album, *Delicate Sound of Thunder*. Putting two businessmen wearing dark suits covered in glowing bulbs in locations around the world was bound to catch the attention of any record buyer. It was a unique and inspired idea.

Storm brought the same visual drama to Pink Floyd's next album, *The Division Bell*. To acknowledge its theme of communication he commissioned two huge, Easter Island-style heads, which he photographed, facing each other as if in conversation, in a field in Ely, Cambridgeshire. Others might have 'faked it' and created the images on a computer. Not Storm. It had to be real. 'I prefer the computer in my head to the one on my desk,' he said.

The computer in Storm's head – 'the goldmine' – continued to serve him well. He made films for Pink Floyd's live shows and designed the artwork for compilations and box sets, including the Immersion editions of *The Dark Side of the Moon* and *Wish You Were Here*. Storm's taste for conundrums and visual puns was still evident. Pink Floyd fans puzzled over the significance of the marbles included in these box sets. But it was just one of Storm's jokes: you've all lost your marbles, and he was giving them back.

Sadly, in 2003 Storm's health deteriorated, yet he never stopped working. Storm died aged 69 on 18 April 2013. The next day, the *Guardian*'s Martin Rowson used the prism from *The Dark Side of the Moon* in a political cartoon. No explanation was needed. Storm's big ideas had become an instantly recognizable part of modern popular culture. He would have been delighted.

250 • PAGE 308 • Storm Thorgerson backstage on tour with Pink Floyd, USA, 1975

THE NOTES

'Lift Off': Syd Barrett, Pink Floyd and the London Underground
—JOE BOYD
1. Cited in Eric R. Danton, 'Exclusive First Listen: Robyn Hitchcock covers Nick Drake', *Wall Street Journal*, 7 March 2013.

What Have We Done to England? Pink Floyd and the Lure of the Pastoral
—ROB YOUNG
1. https://www.theguardian.com/uk/2003/jun/30/arts.greenpolitics
2. Rob Chapman, *A Very Irregular Head: The Life of Syd Barrett*, (London, 2010), p. 152.
3. Barry Miles, *Pink Floyd: The Early Years* (London, 2006), p. 82.

A Long-Term Prospect
—JON SAVAGE
1. Peter Jenner interview by Jon Savage, December 2014.
2. Bob Farmer, 'Meet the Pinky Kinkies', *Disc and Music Echo*, 25 March 1967.
3. 'There's such freedom artistically...', *Disc and Music Echo*, 8 April 1967.
4. Maureen O'Grady, 'Light Entertainment from the Pink Floyd', *Rave*, June 1967.
5. David Hughes, 'Pink Floyd: Freak out comes to town', *Disc and Music Echo*, 22 July 1967.
6. John Peel, 'The Perfumed Garden', *International Times*, no. 34, 28 June–11 July 1968.
7. Peter Jenner interview by Jon Savage, December 2014.
8. Ibid.
9. Maureen O'Grady, 'Light Entertainment from the Pink Floyd', *Rave*, June 1967.
10. 'Notes Towards the Illumination of the Floyd', *Zigzag*, no. 32, June 1973.
11. Ibid.
12. Peter Jones, 'Ladies' Clothes, Free Form Music, Anarchy and the Pink Floyd', *Record Mirror*, 8 April 1967.
13. Peter Jones, 'Your Guide to this Week's New Singles', *Record Mirror*, 17 June 1967.
14. Penny Valentine, 'Britain's Top Singles Reviewer Spins This Week's New Discs', *Disc and Music Echo*, 17 June 1967.
15. 'Notes Towards the Illumination of the Floyd', *Zigzag*, no. 32, June 1973.
16. Mike Godwin, eye witness account, http://www.ukrockfestivals.com/International-Love-In.html
17. 'Pink Floyd Hit 8: Album All Set', *Disc and Music Echo*, 22 July 1967.
18. Quote from http://www.pinkfloydonline.com/discography/thepiperatthegatesofdawn
19. Peter Jenner interview by Jon Savage, December 2014.
20. Ibid.
21. 'Notes Towards the Illumination of the Floyd', *Zigzag*, no. 32, June 1973.
22. Roger Waters quoted in Mark Blake, *Pigs Might Fly: The Inside Story of Pink Floyd* (London, 2007) p.114.
23. 'Notes Towards the Illumination of the Floyd', *Zigzag*, no. 32, June 1973.
24. John Peel, 'The Perfumed Garden', *International Times*, no. 34, 28 June–11 July 1968.

Great Gigs in the Sky: Pink Floyd and the Architecture of Rock
—VICTORIA BROACKES AND ANNA LANDRETH STRONG
1. Pink Floyd's collaboration with Hipgnosis began in the 1960s and continues today with the band's work with Aubrey Powell and with StormStudios.
2. The authors thank the following individuals for contributing their words and insights to this chapter:
MARC BRICKMAN, lighting artist and production designer: *Recognized as a cutting-edge innovator in the industry, Marc Brickman has painted some of the world's most iconic landmarks with light including the Venice Grand Canal, the National Gallery of Art in Washington DC, and the Empire State Building in New York. He has collaborated with Pink Floyd and David Gilmour since 1987.*
BRIAN CROFT, pioneer of stage and rock performance lighting: *Brian Croft began his career in theatre and stage management and was a founder member of the National Youth Theatre, London. He entered the music industry in 1970, working on The Rolling Stones' tour of Europe. He went on to found and direct lighting companies supplying lights and staging to the music industry, culminating in the chairmanship of Vari-Lite Production Services (now PRG). Working with Mark Fisher and others, Croft oversaw and implemented huge changes in the entertainment touring industry.*
SEAN EVANS, Creative Director: *Sean Evans is the Creative Director behind Roger Waters' 'The Wall: Live', which toured the world from 2010 to 2013, and director of the 2014 film* Roger Waters: The Wall. *He is the Founder and Director of Deadskinboy Productions.*
CRISTINA GARCIA, architect and wife of Mark Fisher: *Cristina Garcia has spent 20 years designing award-winning and environmentally sustainable buildings across Europe and Asia with architectural practice KPF. Having studied architecture at the ETSAB in Barcelona, Garcia built her career in London from 1990 onwards. Her relationship with Mark Fisher began after she worked with Fisher Park on the Seville Expo '92; the couple later married in 2009.*
JONATHAN PARK, engineer and founder of Fisher Park and Studio Park: *After studying engineering at Cambridge University and working as a Senior Engineer at Arup Associates, Jonathan Park became a lecturer at London's Architectural Association (AA). There, he met Mark Fisher, and the two began working together as Fisher Park. In 1995, Park formed Studio Park and continues to work on high profile shows and projects. His work includes the exhibit* The Wall *in the Rock & Roll Hall of Fame Museum, Cleveland.*
RAY WINKLER, CEO of Stufish Entertainment Architects: *Founded by the late Mark Fisher, Stufish's work has redefined the live entertainment experience from design to set build, from show creation to production. Ray Winkler joined Stufish in 1995 and now leads the studio in their sector-leading work in music, theatre and live event architecture. Stufish's music portfolio includes concert tours for Pink Floyd, The Rolling Stones, U2, Madonna, Lady Gaga, Michael Bublé and One Direction.*
3. Interview with Nick Mason, 'Architecture Hits The Wall', *AArchitecture 20* (London, 2013), p.12.
4. Nick Mason, *Inside Out: A Personal History of Pink Floyd*, ed. Philip Dodds (London, 2011), p.50.
5. Danish TV interviews with Pink Floyd in 1992. Quoted in Glenn Povey, *Echoes: The Complete History of Pink Floyd* (London, 2007), p.34.
6. *Queen*, review of a Pink Floyd performance on 5 January 1967. Quoted in Povey, 2007, p.51. (*Queen* magazine subsequently merged with, and was then subsumed by, *Harper's Bazaar*).
7. *Melody Maker*, 22 October 1966.
8. Mason, 2011, p.82.
9. *Melody Maker*, 9 December 1967.
10. *Croydon Advertiser*. Quoted in Povey, 2007, p.142.
11. For more information, see http://archigram.westminster.ac.uk
12. Simon Sadler, *Archigram: Architecture without Architecture* (Cambridge MA, 2005), p.143.
13. Reyner Banham, 'Centre Pompidou', *Architectural Review*, no.161, May 1977, pp.270–94, cited in Stanley Matthews, 'The Fun Palace: Cedric Price's experiment in architecture and technology', *Technoetic Arts: A Journal of Speculative Research*, vol.3, no.2, 2005, p.87.
14. Transcript of Mark Fisher, 'There is no Theory only Practice: A Slide Show about Rock and Roll', Lecture to the Architectural Association School of Architecture, London, 27 February 1996 www.aaschool.ac.uk/public/audiovisual/videoarchive
15. See Eric Holding, *Mark Fisher: Staged Architecture* (Chichester, 1999), p.24.
16. For details of the Automat and Dynamat projects, see Holding, 1999, pp.20–23.
17. Mason, 2011, p.225.
18. Transcript of Mark Fisher, 'RDI Address 2012: Armies of Pleasure', RSA, London, November 2012 www.rsa.org.uk
19. Transcript of Mark Fisher, 'Tribe Style', Lecture to the Architectural Association School of Architecture, London, 23 May 2000. www.aaschool.ac.uk/public/audiovisual/videoarchive
20. Ibid.
21. Ibid.
22. Quoted from an interview with Marc Brickman for *The Pink Floyd Exhibition: Their Mortal Remains*, 2017.
23. Holding, 1999, p.35.
24. Transcript of Mark Fisher, 'RDI Address 2012: Armies of Pleasure', 2012.
25. Transcript of Mark Fisher, 'There is no Theory only Practice: A Slide Show about Rock and Roll', 1996.

The Albums
—MARK BLAKE
Quotes from Aubrey 'Po' Powell in these texts are taken from conversations with the author in 2016.
Quotes from Vic Singh, Willie Christie and Barbet Schroeder are taken from interviews conducted for: Mark Blake, *Pigs Might Fly: The Inside Story of Pink Floyd* (London, 2007).
1. Storm Thorgerson and Peter Curzon, *Mind over Matter 4: The Images of Pink Floyd* (London, 2007), p.22.
2. Quotes from Gerard Scarfe are taken from an interview with the author, October 2016.
3. Thorgerson and Curzon, 2007, p.100.
4. Norman Parkinson quoted by *A Momentary Lapse of Reason* cover photographer Robert Dowling, Q Magazine, Pink Floyd Special Edition, October 2004.
5. Thorgerson and Curzon, 2007, p.130.

THE PICTURE CREDITS

© Archigram Architects 1974: 84
© Syd Barrett Family Ltd / Collection of Libby Gausden Chisman: 12
© Syd Barrett Family Ltd / Collection of Jenny Spires: 19
©Paul Berriff: 95, 97
© Peter Blake. All rights reserved, DACS 2017 / Image © Victoria and Albert Museum, London: 31
©1994 *Brain Damage Magazine*: 238
© Bill Brandt: 176
Courtesy of Warren Dosanjh / Photograph by Rupert Truman © Pink Floyd Music Ltd: 21, 36
© Ian Emes / Photograph by Rupert Truman © Pink Floyd Music Ltd: 143, 144, 145, 159, 160
© Michael English / Image © Victoria and Albert Museum, London: 5, 6, 7, 8, 32
© Jill Furmanovsky: 2, 55, 57, 59, 60, 61, 192, 249
© Wendy Gair, 1966. Courtesy of Lindy Mason / Photograph by Rupert Truman © Pink Floyd Music Ltd: 71
© Ron Geesin: 128, 129
© Ron Geesin / Richard Stanley: 51, 52
© Bill Graham / Lautrec Litho / Photograph by Rupert Truman © Pink Floyd Music Ltd: 86
© Nick Hale / Hulton Archive/ Getty Images: 72, 73
© Hipgnosis 1970 Photograph by Aubrey Powell: 23
© Peter Jenner / Sincere: 44
© Nils Jorgensen / REX / Shutterstock: 221
© Kip Lornell / The University of Mississippi: 17, 18
© Tony May: 248
© Clive Metcalfe: 10
© MGM / UA / REX / Shutterstock: 25
© Moviestore / REX / Shutterstock: 119
© Pink Floyd Music Ltd: 1, 28, 43, 48, 49, 50, 53, 56, 58, 62, 76, 77, 93, 94, 99, 107, 108, 115, 117, 118, 120, 121, 122, 124, 125, 126, 136, 139, 142, 146, 147, 148, 150, 153, 154, 157, 158, 170, 171, 178, 180, 182, 183, 185, 186, 187, 214, 215, 217, 218, 219, 225, 250
© Pink Floyd Music Ltd / Image © Victoria and Albert Museum, London: 74, 75
Photograph by Rupert Truman © Pink Floyd Music Ltd: 16, 40, 46, 68, 70, 80, 81, 83, 89, 101, 102, 103, 131, 134, 135, 137, 138, 149, 151, 152, 155, 156, 162, 163, 164, 165, 166, 167, 168, 169, 181, 179, 184, 188, 189, 191, 193, 194, 195, 196, 200, 201, 202, 203, 204, 205, 206, 207, 208, 212, 216, 222, 224, 226, 229, 230, 237

Pink Floyd Music Ltd © 1979, Pink Floyd Music Pubs. Ltd © 1979: 190, 213
© Pink Floyd Music (1987) Ltd: 24, 220, 223, 227, 228, 232, 233, 234, 239, 240, 245, 246, 247
Artistic trustee of the estate of John Nash / Image © Victoria and Albert Museum, London: 27
Image courtesy of *The Wire Magazine* / Eddie Prevost © Frazer Pearce: 13
© Philips Records Ltd / Image © Victoria and Albert Museum, London: 15
© Colin Prime. Courtesy of Sheila Prime / Image © Victoria and Albert Museum, London: 37
© PRISMA / REX / Shutterstock: 231
© Michael Putland / Hulton Archive / Getty Images: 22, 130
© Denis O'Regan / Premium Archive / Getty Images: 34
© Adam Ritchie: 64, 67, 105
© Adam Ritchie / Redferns / Getty Images: 66, 104
© Gerald Scarfe: 210
© Marc Sharratt / REX / Shutterstock: 35
© Ray Stevenson: 33
© Ray Stevenson / REX / Shutterstock: 111, 112, 113, 114
© Peter Still / Redferns / Getty Images: 26
© Rob Verhorst / Redferns / Getty Images: 88
Image © Victoria and Albert Museum, London: 29, 106
© Nigel Waymouth and Michael English / Image © Victoria and Albert Museum, London: 4, 42
© Andrew Whittuck / Redferns / Getty Images: 3

THE ΔCKNOWLEDGEMENTS

AUBREY POWELL, VICTORIA BROACKES AND ANNA LANDRETH STRONG

Pink Floyd have stood astride the British rock scene over six decades and on the global stage since the launch of *The Dark Side of the Moon* in 1973. Fifty years since their first breakthrough single 'Arnold Layne', *The Pink Floyd Exhibition: Their Mortal Remains* is an opportunity to look back over these years, with the help of many individuals who have been part of the band's story, who have shared their thoughts with us, and in so doing, have enriched the exhibition and accompanying book. We are enormously grateful to the executive curator, Nick Mason, along with David Gilmour and Roger Waters, for their belief in and commitment to the exhibition and for generously sharing both their knowledge and wonderful collections. Similarly, our heartfelt thanks go to Gala and Jamie Wright on behalf of Richard Wright. Thanks also go to Polly Samson, principal lyricist for *The Division Bell* and *The Endless River*. We are grateful for the support of Syd Barrett Music Ltd.

Michael Cohl, Glenn Orsher and colleagues at Iconic Entertainment Studios, along with co-producer Paul Loasby and his team at One Fifteen, deserve huge thanks for making the show happen and keeping it on the road. We have benefited from the expertise of the band managers alongside Paul – Mark Fenwick, Tony Smith and Garth Tweedale. Profound thanks go to the Pink Floyd curatorial team led by Aubrey 'Po' Powell: Paula Webb Stainton, co-curator; Tracey Kraft, archivist, and Catriona MacDonald, curatorial assistant.

Production director Nick Levitt of Live Gallery Media Events, together with Ian Greenway, Jo MacKay and Molly Iredale of LarMac Live, have collaborated to bring the vision of this outstanding exhibition to life. At the V&A, we thank: Geoffrey Marsh, Director of Theatre and Performance, and Alex Stitt, Director of Commercial and Digital Development, who helped to bring the exhibition to the V&A and have supported the project throughout; Dina Ibrahim and Olivia Oldroyd, exhibition managers, and their colleagues in the V&A Exhibitions department; Kathryn Johnson, content editor, and Corinne Jones, research assistant, whose contributions have been extensive and crucial. To ensure the essence of Pink Floyd flows through the exhibition from beginning to end it was vital to integrate the look and feel of long-term collaborators: Ray Winkler, Rachel Duncan, Jasna Jevremovic, David Morgan, Dan Dodds and Jenny Melville at Stufish; Roger Waters' Artistic Director, Sean Evans; designer Peter Curzon and photographer Richard Evans of StormStudios; and Laserium designer Richard Turner, video content director Richard Kenyon, content producer Beki Gaskin, and Ellie Clement at Lucky Frog.

Acknowledging the historical importance of, and the ground-breaking designs created by Peter Wynne Willson, Arthur Max, Marc Brickman and Gerald Scarfe, we would like to thank the following for making the designs and concepts a reality: Patrick Woodroffe, lighting director, with Terry Cook and Rob Casey at Woodroffe Bassett; Scott Willsallen, Head of Audio, and Bobby Aitken, audio consultant; Lana Topham, Pink Floyd film archivist; Ian Emes; Fiz Oliver, exhibition film producer; Laurence 'Benny' Trickett, editor; Barry Trulat, archivist; Alistair McCaw and David Germond at Real Studios for their valued advice and direction; Phil Taylor, equipment archivist; Roger Waters' archivist Paul Warren and text editors Glenn Povey and Simon Wells.

The partnership with Sennheiser was paramount to the creation of a quintessentially Pink Floyd visitor experience. For this we thank Andreas and Daniel Sennheiser, Guy Holmes, Uwe Cremering, Norbert Hilbich, Robert Genereux, Edelgard Marquardt, Gregor Zielinsky, Mareike Oer, Victoria Chernih, Stephanie Schmidt, Uwe Greunke, Michelle Downey and Alexander Haeberlein from Sennheiser. For the audio content on behalf of Pink Floyd we would like to acknowledge long-time Pink Floyd co-producer and mastering engineer James Guthrie and audio mixing and mastering engineer Andy Jackson, along with Damon Iddins, Simon Franglen, Simon Rhodes and Joel Plante, for their commitment to achieving the phenomenal audio experience that Pink Floyd are renowned for.

For editing, designing and creating this wonderful book, we would like to thank: the expert contributors, authors Mark Blake, Joe Boyd, Howard Goodall, Jon Savage and Rob Young; designer Jonathan Abbott at Barnbrook; photographer Rupert Truman of StormStudios; copy-editor, Kate Bell; One Fifteen's Andy Murray and Elena Bello; and the team at V&A Publishing, Kathryn Johnson, Tom Windross and Emma Woodiwiss. Thanks to them and to our expert contributors, this publication is valuable not only as a window on to the exhibition and the extraordinary objects on show, but also as a lasting record of Pink Floyd's legacy. Our gratitude also goes to the photographers, artists and designers of all creative disciplines who have allowed us to show their work in both the book and exhibition, and to the countless external people who have contributed thoughts and advice, including: Brian Croft, Alan Edwards, Cristina Garcia and Jonathan Park.

We are grateful for the assistance, advice and passion of the following people who have helped keep the exhibition and its myriad of moving parts flowing: Bernard Doherty, Doug Wright and David Cox from LD Communications; colleagues at AKA Marketing for Public Relations; John Harper, COO at Iconic; production co-ordinators Liam Cohl, Jonathan Uda and Katherine Boener; associate to Mark Fenwick, Kate Watkins; associate to Tony Smith, Jo Greenwood; PA to Nick Mason, Victoria Gilbert and Cat Peoples, EA to Michael Cohl.

The support pillars to any project of this scale are: the accountants Cameron Farzad of LarMac; Stephen Rath of CPI; Anupam Palit and Andrei Poledaev of Iconic; Justin Morris, CFO of Pink Floyd Companies; Pink Floyd accountant, Davie Meunier; Legal Advice courtesy of James Harman from Simkins Partnership; James Earle from Fladgate LLP; Marc Stollman at Iconic; object handing by Frances Halahan and Sophie Budden; object mounting by Richard Rogers; and props by Nigel Talamo.

Thanks also go to: Norman Perry of Perryscope and Steve Hatton of Nylon for bringing together fantastic merchandise concepts to capture this milestone exhibition; Peter Robson from Jabeye; Rob O'Connor and Jamie Gibson from Stylorouge and Matt Johns for all things website and digital; colleagues from Onsight; ABC Inflatables; Lisa Ryan from EFM Management; Graphitecture; Media Powerhouse; Power Logistics; White Light; Set Square; Matilda Dunne, Chiara Felice, Ben Levy and Valeria Strachevskaia.

Many others have also contributed hugely to the project, and while space does not permit us to mention every name, we would particularly like to thank at the V&A: Tim Reeve; Bill Sherman; David Bickle; Linda Lloyd Jones and Rebecca Lim; Sophie Brendel; Olivia Rickman; Zoe Franklin; Jane Rosier; Kathryn Havelock; Veronika Tarasidis; Kati Price; Holly Hyams; Keith Hale; Camilla Graham; Bethan Garland; Cara Williams and the V&A Learning team; Clair Battisson; Jane Rutherston; Sarah Sevier; Philip Contos; Liz Edmunds; Fred Caws; Daniel Feeney and the Security and Visitor Experience teams; Technical Services and Health and Safety staff; Sophy Thomas and our colleagues in the V&A Department of Theatre and Performance, and also those who have since moved on to pastures new but played a vitally important role during their time on the project: particularly Martin Roth, former Director of the V&A.

Everybody we meet speaks of their personal connection with band; a first record, an unforgettable concert or another inspiration in their life from Pink Floyd. We would therefore like to thank these many old and new contacts and friends, parts of the wider Pink Floyd family, and the team both within and outside the V&A who have been incredibly generous with their time.

Finally, we should like to pay tribute to those who have, through various means, influenced the story of Pink Floyd: Peter Jenner and Andrew King; Bryan Morrison (1942–2008); Steve O'Rourke (1940–2003) and Storm Thorgerson (1944–2013).

THE ΔCKNOWLEDGEMENTS

In addition to the many lenders included opposite, we are also grateful to the following people and organizations who have also made loans to the exhibition:

Barbie Antonis
Peter Barnes
BBC
Symon Bland St Pauls Gallery, Birmingham
Theo Botschuijver (The Evenstructure Research Group)
Keith Breeden
John Davies
Peter Dockley
Warren Dosanjh
Richard Evans
Duggie Fields
Bob Follen
Libby Gausden Chisman
Andrea Gaeler
Ron Geesin
Marc Gerstein (Lead and Light)
Bryan Grant (Britannia Row Productions)
Ian Harvey (Hills Road Sixth Form College)
Tim Hunkin
Matt Johns
AlexandLiane Large
Adrian Maben
Lindy Mason
Dave Mills
Christopher Milner
Anthony Moore
Hector Proud (Proud Gallery)
Andrew Sanders
Julio Santo Domingo (Collection Courtesy of Rock 'n' Roll Hall of Fame and Museum, Cleveland, Ohio, USA)
Gerald Scarfe
Wilf Scott
Piers Sellars
Jeffrey Shaw (The Evenstructure Research Group)
Jenny Spires
Paul Staples
Nigel Talamo
Bruce Tippen
Your Music Memory Collection, Toronto
Zoe Zurstrassen
Battersea Power Station Collection
StormStudios Collection

Finally, our thanks also go to:
John Barton
Jacques Boumendil
Clive Brooks
Fiona Dauppe
Lucy Davenport
Katy Hepburn
Tony Howard
Mick Kluczynski
Colin Lyon
Alexandra Popoff
Vanessa Rinaldi
Jane Sen
Shuki Sen
Neil Warnock
Robbie Williams
Caroline Wookey

The End

THE COLLABORATORS

Photographers / Designers
Dan Abbott; David Appleby; Lee Baker; Paul Berriff; Thierry Boccon-Girod; Willie Christie; Peter Christopherson; Eloise Collins; Tony Collins; Finlay Cowan; Jon Crossland; Julie Davies; Roger Dean; Hans Jurgen Dibbert; Bob Dowling; Andy Earl; Ahmed Emad Eldin; Richard Evans; Sean Evans Jill Furmanovsky; Nick Hale; George Hardie; Robin Harries; Dezo Hoffman; Bush Holyhead; Aden Hynes; Bob Jenkins; Sebastian Jenkins; Peter Jenner; Nils Jorgensen; Kip Lornell; Jean-Denis Mahn; Richard Manning; Tony May; Mike McInnerney; Brian D McLaughlin; Clive Metcalfe; Sally Norris; Rob O'Connor/Stylorouge; Denis O'Regan; Stephen Piotrowski; Cedric Price; Colin Prime; Michael Putland; Adam Ritchie; John Robertson; Mick Rock; Marc Sharratt; Vic Singh; Richard Stanley; Martin Starnes; Ray Stevenson; Storm Thorgerson; Rupert Truman; Rob Verhorst; Carinthia West; John Whitely; Andrew Whittuck; Irene Winsby; Ian Wright

Producers
Joe Boyd; Norman Smith

Co-Producers
Bob Ezrin; James Guthrie; Michael Kamen; Phil Manzanera; Youth; Andy Jackson

Engineers
(in chronological order)
John Wood; Malcolm Addey; Jerry Boyes; Geoff Emerick; Graham Kirkby; Michael Sheady; Michael Stone; John Barrett; Richard Langham; Ken Scott; Jeff Jarratt; Peter Mew; Brian Humphries; Peter Bown; Alan Parsons; John Leckie; Rob Black; Roger Quested; Dominique Blanc-Francard; Andy Scott; Peter James; Chris Thomas; Nick Griffiths; Patrice Quef; Brian Christian; Rick Hart; John McClure; Michael McCarthy; Robert Hrycyna; Andy Canelle; Mike Nocito; Jules Bowen; Marc Desisto; Stan Katayama; Jeff Demorris; Keith Grant; Hugo Zuccarelli; Damon Iddins; Eddie Banda; Michael Rendall

Mastering Engineers
Harry Moss; Doug Sax; Bernie Grundman; Joel Plante

Musicians
(in alphabetical order)

Album abbreviations in the following list:
PGD: The Piper at the Gates of Dawn
SS: A Saucerful of Secrets
SM: Soundtrack from the film More
UM: Ummagumma
AHM: Atom Heart Mother
MD: Meddle
DSM: The Dark Side of the Moon
WYH: Wish You Were Here
ANM: Animals
W: The Wall
FC: The Final Cut
MLR: A Momentary Lapse of Reason
DB: The Division Bell
ER: The Endless River

Chris Adamson (Spoken word, DSM); Carmine Appice (Drums, 'Dogs of War', MLR) ; Gilad Atzmon (Sax and Clarinet, ER); Billie Barnum (Backing vocals, 1973 European tours); Andy Bown (Bass, W tour 1980–81, FC); Sam Brown (Backing vocals, Knebworth 1990, DB album and tour); Sarah Brown (Backing vocals, ER); Vicki Brown (Backing vocals, 1973 UK dates and Knebworth 1990); Jon Carin (MLR, DB album and tour, Live 8, ER); Doreen Chanter (Backing vocals, FC); Irene Chanter (Backing vocals, FC); Joe Chemay (Backing vocals, W album and tour 1980–81); Ray Cooper (Percussion, FC); Nawasa Crowder (Backing vocals, 1973 North American tours); Joe DiBlasi (Guitar, 'Is There Anybody Out There', W); Chris Dennis (early years Pink Floyd); Candy Dulfer (Sax, Knebworth 1990); Lesley Duncan (Backing vocals, DSM); Bob Ezrin (W, MLR, DB and ER); Stan Farber (Backing vocals, W album and tour 1980–81); Venetta Fields (Backing vocals, 1973–75 tours and WYH); Claudia Fontaine (Backing vocals, DB tour); Steve Forman (Percussion, MLR); Cynthia Fox (MC, W shows 1980); Roberta Freeman (Backing vocals, MLR); Rachel Fury (Backing vocals, MLR tour); Juliette Gale (early years and pre-Pink Floyd); Ron Geesin (Orchestration, AHM); Bob Geldof (Vox, 'In The Flesh', W film); Donnie Gerrard (Backing vocals, MLR); Stéphane Grappelli (Violin, 'Wish You Were Here', WYH); James Guthrie (W > ER); Jim Haas (Backing vocals, W album and tour 1980–81); Bobbye Hall (Congas, W); Roy Harper (Vocal, 'Have A Cigar', Knebworth 1975 and WYH); Stephen Hawking (Electronic voice sample, DB, ER); John Helliwell (Saxophones, MLR); Damon Iddins (Keys, ER); Andy Jackson (Bass, ER); Peter Jenner (Vocal intro, 'Astronomy Domine', PGD); Bruce Johnston (BVs, W); Jon Joyce (BVs, W album and tour 1980–81); Michael Kamen (Orchestration, W, FC, DB, keys Knebworth 1990); Jim Keltner (Drums, MLR); Carol Kenyon (Backing vocals, DB, Live 8); Clydie King (Backing vocals, 1973 European tours); Radovan 'Bob' Klose (early years and pre-Pink Floyd); Darlene Koldenhoven (Backing vocals, MLR); Jim Ladd (MC, W shows 1980); Nick Laird-Clowes (Lyrics, DB); Michael Landau (Guitar, 'One Slip' MLR); Rebecca Leigh-White (Backing vocals, DB); Mike Leonard (keys, pre-Pink Floyd); Patrick Leonard (Synths, MLR); Tony Levin (Bass and Chapman Stick, MLR); Mary-Ann Lindsey (Backing vocals, 1973 North American tours); Phyllis Lindsey (Backing vocals, 1973 North American tours); Durga McBroom (Backing vocals, MLR tour, DB album and tour, ER); Lorelei McBroom (Backing vocals, MLR tour); Henry McCullough (Spoken word, DSM); Fred Mandel (Keyboards, W); Roger 'The Hat' Manifold (Spoken word, DSM); Frank Marocco (Concertina, W); Louise Marshall (Backing vocals, ER); Lindy Mason (Penny Whistle, UM, SM); Members of EMI Studios session musicians (AHM); Members of Escala (Strings, ER); Members of the John Alldis Choir (AHM album and 'Atom Heart Mother' live shows 1970–71); Members of the National Philharmonic Orchestra (FC); Members of the New York City Opera ('Bring The Boys Back Home', W); Members of the New York Philharmonic Orchestra (W); Members of the New York Symphony Orchestra (W); Members of the Philip Jones Brass Ensemble (Brass, 'Atom Heart Mother' live 1970); Members of the Salvation Army International Staff Band (Brass, 'Jugband Blues', SS); Members of the Stanley Myers Orchestra (Brass, 'Corporal Clegg', SS); Clive Metcalfe (bass, pre-Pink Floyd); Geoffrey Mitchell (Conductor, 'Atom Heart Mother' live 1971); Anthony Moore (Keys, ER, Lyrics MLR, DB); Andy Newmark (Drums, 'Two Suns In The Sunset', FC); Keith Noble (Vocals, pre-Pink Floyd); Sheilagh Noble (Vocals, pre-Pink Floyd); Jerry O'Driscoll (Spoken word, DSM); Nobs the dog 'Mlle Nobs' (Live At Pompeii); Blue Ocean (Snare, 'Bring The Boys Back Home', W); Scott Page (Sax, MLR album and tour); Dick Parry (Sax, DSM, WYH and 1973–75 tours, DB album and tour, Live 8); Bill Payne (Hammond, MLR); Jeff Porcaro (Drums, 'Mother', W); Joe Porcaro (Snare, 'Bring The Boys Back Home', W); Guy Pratt (Bass, MLR and DB albums and tours, ER); Pupils of Islington Green Primary School ('Another Brick in the Wall', W); Raphael Ravenscroft (Sax, FC); Tim Renwick (Guitar, W film soundtrack, MLR and DB albums and tours, Live 8); Lee Ritenour (Guitars, W); Andy Roberts (Guitar, W tour 1981); Polly Samson (lyrics, ER, DB); Tom Scott (Sax, MLR); Seamus the dog ('Seamus', MD); Edward Shearmur (Orchestration, DB); Jackie Sheridan (Backing vocals, DB); Norman Smith (Drums, 'Remember A Day', SS, and 'Sysyphus', UM); Phyllis St. James (Backing vocals, MLR); Barry St. John (Backing vocals, DSM); Tom Stoppard (playwright, Darkside); Liza Strike (Backing vocals, DSM, 1973); Alan Styles (Voice, 'Alan's Psychedelic Breakfast', AHM); Margret Taylor (Backing vocals, MLR tours); Toni Tennille (Backing vocals, W); Willi Thomczyk (MC, W shows 1981); Vernon Thompson (Guitar, pre-Pink Floyd); Clare Torry (Vocal, 'Great Gig', DSM, backing vocals, UK dates 1973, Knebworth 1990); Doris Troy (Backing vocals, DSM); Carmen Twillie (Backing vocals, MLR); Trevor Veitch (Mandolin, W); Gary Wallis (Percussion, MLR and DB tours); Harry Waters (Voice, 'Goodbye Blue Sky', W); Patricia Watts (Spoken word, DSM); Snowy White (Guitar, ANM album and tour, W tour 1980); Carlena Williams (Backing vocals, 1974–75, WYH); Larry Williams (Clarinet, W); John 'Willie' Wilson (Drums, W tour 1980–81); Peter Wood (Keyboards, W tour 1980–81); Ace Young (MC, W shows 1980); Trudy Young (Groupie voice, W); Gary Yudman (MC, W shows 1980); Hugo Zuccarelli (Holophonic FX, FC).

316   The End

THE INDEX

Page numbers in *italics* refer to illustrations and their captions

Abbey Road Studios
   1960s 65, 71, 82, 150, *151*, *152*, 153, *154*, *156*, 178
   1970s 82, 88–9, *91*, 92, *105*, *106*, *109*, 184, 194, 216, 230
'Absolutely Curtains' (*Obscured by Clouds*) 96, 206
'Alan's Psychedelic Breakfast' (*Atom Heart Mother*) 188
album tours
   1974 'Dark Side of the Moon' world tour *10–11*, 94, *100*, 125, *125*, *196*, *218*, *222*, 230, *234*
   1975 'Wish You Were Here' tour *222*, *236*
   1977 'Animals/In the Flesh' UK and North American tours 9, *112*, 114, 128, *130–1*, 132, *136*, 139, *242*, 250
   1980–81 'The Wall' stage show tour 9, *38*, *39*, 107, 114, 137–9, *139*, *141*, *144*, *234*, 252, *255–7*, *259*, *260*, *262–3*, *268–9*
   1987–90 'A Momentary Lapse of Reason' world tour 9, 108, 125, 139, 282, *285*, *286*, *288–91*
   1990 'The Wall' stage show world tour (Roger Waters) *141*, 252
   1994 'The Division Bell' world tour 9, 44, *55*, 114, 120, 125, 139, *140*, 141, 142, *143*, *296–7*, *298*, *299*, *300–1*
   2000 'The Wall' stage show tour (Roger Waters) 252
   2010–13 'The Wall' stage show world tour *39*, *141*, *255*
Animals 43, 52, 106, 238–47
   album cover and artwork 126, *238–9*, 240–2, *243–5*, 311
'Another Brick in the Wall' (*The Wall*) 52, 107, 251, *258*, *264*
'Any Colour You Like' (*The Dark Side of the Moon*) 100, *222*
'Apples and Oranges' single (1967) 72, *73*, 164
'Arnold Layne' single (1967) 15, 28, 30, *31*, 58, 59, 60, 63, 65, 82, 150, *156*
   invitation to the press launch *59*
'Astronomy Domine' (*The Piper at the Gates of Dawn* and *Ummagumma*) 66, 84, 153, 178, 297
Atom Heart Mother (1970) *36*, 40, 86, *88–9*, 90–3, 124, 182–91, 194
   album cover and artwork 40, *182–3*, 188, 310
   vocal and instrumental arrangements *186–7*
'Atom Heart Mother' suite (*Atom Heart Mother*) 90, 91–3, 194, 234
'Autumn '68' (*The Endless River*) 108, 304
Azimuth Co-ordinator quadrophonic sound controller 122, *122*, *123*, 178, *222*

Barrett, Syd 14, 25, 35, *156*
   alienation 63, 71–2, 76, 153, 164, 250, 294
   career after leaving the band 32–4
   cigarette lighter experiments 62, *158*
   death 32
   drawings and paintings 23, 27, *63*
   guitar and guitar playing 24, 25, 62, 150, *156*, *157*, *158*
   'leader' of the band 15, 45, 60, 83
   leaves the band (1968) 8, 28, 32, 33, 51, 72, 76, 85, 105–6, 122, 164, 174
   life before the band 8, 21, 23, 62, 115, 153, *266*, 310
   and LSD 8, 23, 27, 31, 153, 164
   mental illness 33, 48, 62, 72, 85, 97, 105, 164, 219
   the reluctant pop star 16, 28, 63, 153
   songwriting 20, 27, 28, 31, 34, 47–8, 54, 71–2, 85, 150, 153, 154
   star qualities 28, *29*, 59, 62, 63, 65, 66

'Bike' (*The Piper at the Gates of Dawn*) 34, 48, 68, 85, 153, 164
Binson Echorec 25, 27, 62, 65, 74, 153, *158*, *159*, 195
The Body (1970, film soundtrack, Waters and Geesin) 90–1, 184, 216
Boyd, Joe 15, 28, 32, 120, 121, 150
'Breathe' (*The Dark Side of the Moon*) 98, 100, 101, 104, *196*, 216, 217
Brickman, Marc 114, 116, 120, 139, 141, 297

'Candy and a Currant Bun' single (1967) *31*, 65, 68, *156*
'Careful with that Axe, Eugene' (single and *Ummagumma*) 76, 90, 126, 178
'Chapter 24' (*The Piper at the Gates of Dawn*) 18, 48, 153
'Childhood's End' (*Obscured by Clouds*) 52, 206, *210*
'Cirrus Minor' (*More*) 86, 174
'Comfortably Numb' (*The Wall*) 107, 252
The Committee (1968, film soundtrack) 87, 90, 174
concert venues
   1972 Japan *95*
   1966 Hornsey College of Art *119*
   1966 Marquee Club *119*
   1966 AA School of Architecture *114*
   1967 Commonwealth Institute *118*
   1967 Alexandra Palace *31*, *33*, 66, *121*
   1967 Queen Elizabeth Hall *46*, *47*, 60, *120*, *121*, 121–2
   1967 Saville Theatre *70*
   1968 Rome *167*
   1968 Hyde Park *168–9*
   1968 Sound Factory, Sacramento *166*
   1968 Avalon Ballroom, San Francisco *171*
   1969 Royal Albert Hall *87*, 178, 304
   1969 Royal Festival Hall 122, *123*, 124, 178, 184
   1970 Hyde Park *185*, 188, *188*
   1970 Bath Festival of Progressive Rock 184, 188
   1971 Crystal Palace Bowl 124–5, 194
   1972 Brighton Dome 216
   1972 Portsmouth Guildhall 216
   1972 Rainbow Theatre 216
   1972 Japan *95*, 96
   1972 Pompeii, Italy *145*, 206, 304
   1974 Sophia Gardens Pavilion, Cardiff *124*
   1975 Seattle Center Coliseum *102–3*, *110–11*
   1975 Knebworth 132
   1977 Oakland Coliseum *136*
   1977 Olympic Stadium, Montreal 250
   1979 Madison Square Garden *144*
   1979 Nassau Coliseum *268*
   1988 Versailles *286*
   1989 Luzhniki *286*
   1989 Venice *288–91*
   see also named concerts
'Corporal Clegg' (*A Saucerful of Secrets*) 74, 86, 167, 274

The Dark Side of the Moon (1973) 9, 40, 52, 82, 85, 90, 94, 96–8, 104–5, 125, 174, 206, 209, 214–27, 230, 252, 294, 297
   album cover and artwork 8, *214–15*, 219, *225*, *226–7*, 240, 309, 310, 311
   live performances planning chart *224*
   press reception, London Planetarium (1973) 9
Delicate Sound of Thunder
   live album (1988) 282
   album cover and artwork 310, 311
   publicity launch *281*
The Division Bell (1994) 9, 54, 106, 108, 125, 192–301, *285*, 304
   album cover and artwork 54, *292–3*, *295*, 296, *296*, *297*, 310, 311
   launch promotion *296*
Dockley, Peter 122, 124, 180, 194
'Dogs' (*Animals*) 230, 240, *247*

'Echoes' (*Meddle*) 93–4, 100, 126, 194, 195, *196*, 216, 234, 294
Emes, Ian 114, 125, *200–3*, *218*, 219
The Endless River (2014) 54, 108, *236*, *302–7*
   album cover and artwork *302–3*, *305*, 306
Ezrin, Bob 108, 250, 251, 280, *283*, 294

Farfisa electric organ 86, 98, *159*
'Fat Old Sun' (*Atom Heart Mother*) 40, 188
'Fearless' (*Meddle*) 194–5

The Final Cut (1983) 52, 92, 107–8, 272–7
   album cover and artwork *272–3*, 276, *277*
Fisher, Mark 114, *114*, 126–8, *129*, 132, *132–3*, 137, *138*, 139–41, 142–3, *143*, *144*, 267, 297
'Flaming' (*The Piper at the Gates of Dawn*) 68
'The 14-Hour Technicolour Dream' concert (1967) 31, 121
'Free Four' (*Obscured by Clouds*) 96, 206

'Games for May' concert (1967) *46*, *47*, 60, 66, *120*, *121*, 121–2
Geesin, Ron 90–2, *91*, 184, *186–7*, 188
Gilmour, David *10–11*, 22, *196*, *207*, *236*
   the albums
     Animals 240, *247*
     Atom Heart Mother 90, 188
     The Dark Side of the Moon 98, 101, *196*, 217
     The Division Bell 9, 106, 108, 109, 284, 294, 296
     The Endless River 304, 306
     The Final Cut 276
     Meddle 94, 194–5, *196*, 284
     A Momentary Lapse of Reason 9, 108, 280, 283, 311
     Ummagumma 178
     The Wall 107, 251, 252, *258*
     Wish You Were Here 101, 230, 232, *236*
   Astoria houseboat recording studio 54, 280, 294
   guitars and guitar playing 8, 74, 86, 93, 101, 108, 167, *189*, *196*, 217, *236*, *259*, *284*, *285*, 294, 306
   life before the band 22, 72, 109
   replaces Syd Barrett (1968) 8, 32, 74, 76, 85, 115, 164
   songwriting 40, 54, 78, 106, 107, 109, 178, 188, 194–5, 230, 240, 280, *283*, 296
'The Grand Vizier's Garden Party' (*Ummagumma*) 86, 178, 180, 304
'Grantchester Meadows' (*Ummagumma*) 39, 40, 86, 178, 180, 294
'The Great Gig in the Sky' (*The Dark Side of the Moon*) 98, 100, 108, *196*, 219

Hammond electric organs 86, 92, 94, 98, *213*, *222*, *251*
'Have a Cigar' (*Wish You Were Here*) 230, 232, *236*
'High Hopes' (*The Division Bell*) 54, 109, 294
Hipgnosis (Thorgerson and Powell) 8, 9, 174–5, 180, 209, 219, *233*, 281, 310
   Pink Floyd album covers and artwork 8–9, 76, 167, 174, 180, 188, 195, 209, 219, 221, *226–7*, *231*, 232, *233*, 242, 310–11
Hopkins, John 'Hoppy' 16, 28, 31, 32, 120, 121

The End   317

THE INDEX

'If' (*Atom Heart Mother*) 93, 188, 194
inflatable pig ('Algie') 126, 128, 240, 241, *241*, 242, 244–5 *see also under* staging concepts
International Times 17, 19, 28, 117
'Interstellar Overdrive' (*The Piper at the Gates of Dawn*) 84–5, 150, 153
'It Would Be So Nice' single (1968) 76

Jenner, Peter 58, 60, 63, 72, 76, 120, 153, *156*, *160*, 220
'The Journey' musical suite 122, 178, 180
'Jugband Blues' (*A Saucerful of Secrets*) 51, 62, 71–2, 74, 164

'Keep Talking' (*The Division Bell*) 108, 294

'Learning to Fly' (*A Momentary Lapse of Reason*) 280, *283*
'Let There Be More Light' (*A Saucerful of Secrets*) 51, 74, 167
'The Lost Art of Conversation' (*The Endless River*) 304
'Lost for Words' (*The Division Bell*) 108
'Louder Than Words' (*The Endless River*) 304, 306
'Love-in Festival' concert (1967) 33, 66

'The Man' musical suite 122, 178, 180
'Marooned' (*The Division Bell*) 294
Mason, Nick 22, *25*, 30, *115*, *152*
 the albums
  Atom Heart Mother 90
  The Dark Side of the Moon 97, 216, 224
  The Division Bell 9, 294
  The Endless River 304
  Meddle 195
  A Momentary Lapse of Reason 9, 108, *283*
  Obscured by Clouds 206
  Ummagumma 178
 drums and percussion 85, 86, *190*, *197*, 206, 242, 304
 life before the band 21, 22, *115*, *115*
 personality 59, 66
 on the singles 60, 76
 songwriting 86, 178, 304
 on the tours *67*, 122, 128, *224*
'The Massed Gadgets of Auximines' concert (1969) 122, *123*, 124, 184
'Matilda Mother' (*The Piper at the Gates of Dawn*) 48, 153
Max, Arthur 114, 125, 141, *219*
Meddle (1971) 81, 93–4, 96, 192–203, 206, 216, 219, 230, *284*
 album cover and artwork 192–3
A Momentary Lapse of Reason (1987) 9, 54, 108, 125, 139, 278–91, 294
 album cover and artwork 278–9, 310, 311
'Money' (*The Dark Side of the Moon*) 98, 125, 217, 219
'Music in Colour' concert (1967) 118

'The Narrow Way' (*Ummagumma*) 86, 178, 180

A Nice Pair (1973) *165*

Obscured by Clouds (1972) 52, 92, 94, 96, 204–13, 216, 252
 album cover and artwork 204–5
'On Noodle Street' (*The Endless River*) 108
'On the Run' (*The Dark Side of the Moon*) 217, 219
'One of these Days' (*Meddle*) 125, 195, *196*, 200–3, 219, *284*

Park, Jonathan 114, 128, 137, 143
Parry, Dick 98, *99*, 219, 294
Phase Linear 400 PA amplifier *195*
'Pigs (Three Different Ones)' (*Animals*) 240
'Pigs on the Wing 1 & 2' (*Animals*) 240
'A Pillow of Winds' (*Meddle*) 94, 194–5
Pink Floyd 234
 albums *see* named albums
 changes in line-up 44, 54, 82
  Richard Wright leaves and later rejoins 251, 281, 294
  Roger Waters leaves (1985) 9, 139, 276, 280
  Syd Barrett leaves (1968) 8, 28, 32, 33, 51, 72, 76, 85, 105–6, 122
 concerts *see* concert venues; named concerts
 dislike of publicity 8, 9, 18, 54, 105
 film soundtracks 52, 60, 86, 87, 90, 104, 172–5 *see also Obscured by Clouds; Pink Floyd – The Wall; Soundtrack from the film More*
 gigs 8, 15, 25, 27, 28, 30, 31, 62, 67, 83, *116*, 120, 121, 150, *160*
 recording studios
  Astoria houseboat 54, 280, 294
  Britannia Row 240
  Strawberry Studios, Château d'Hérouville 83, 92, 96, 206, *207*, *209*, 211, 216
  see also Abbey Road
 singles 31, 42, 44, 65, 68, 71, 72, 73, 74, 76, 126, *156*, 164, 174, 274 *see also* 'Arnold Layne'
 staging of shows *see* staging concepts
 tours 30, 44, 65, 66, 67, 71, 72, 76, 166, *171*, 180, *196*, 232, *236 see also* album tours
 photos
  1966–67 20, 56, 61, 64, 69, 73, 114, 151, 154, 155, 170
  1968–69 42, 75, 78–9, 87, 168–9, 177, 181
  1970s 6–7, 77, 80, 84, 92, 95, 102–3, 105, 127, 188, 198–9, 209, 211
Pink Floyd Ballet (Roland Petit) 126, *127*, 141

Pink Floyd Live at Pompeii concert movie (1972) 206, 304
Pink Floyd – The Wall (1982, film, Alan Parker) 38, 38–9, 43, 44, 107, *138*, 234, 252, *255*, 274
The Piper at the Gates of Dawn (1967) 9, 39, 47, 48, 51, 60, 68, 83, 84–5, 121, 148–51, *161*, *165*, 274, 297
 album cover and artwork 148–9, 153, *155*
'Point Me at the Sky' single (1968) 42, 44, 74, 76, 174
'Poles Apart' (*The Division Bell*) 294
'The Post-War Dream' (*The Final Cut*) 274, *275*
Powell, Aubrey 'Po' 10–11, 114, 310, 311
 Pink Floyd album covers and artwork *165*, *167*, 174–5, 180, 188, 195, 209, 219, 221, 232, 240–1, 242, 306, 309–11
 see also Hipgnosis
Pulse live album (1995) 297

'Reaction in G' (unreleased, 1967) 71
'Remember a Day' (*A Saucerful of Secrets*) 51, 71, 74

Samson, Polly 54, 108, 109, 294, 296, 304
A Saucerful of Secrets (1968) 8, 51, 74, 76, 85, 162–71, *165*
 album cover and artwork 8, 76, 162–3, *167*, 310
'The Scarecrow' (*The Piper at the Gates of Dawn*) 48, 68, 85, 153
Scarfe, Gerald 39, 44, 114, *234*, 250, 252, *268*, 270–1
'Scream Thy Last Scream' single, (1967) 71, 72
'Seamus' (*Meddle*) 195
'See Emily Play' (single and *The Piper at the Gates of Dawn*) 54, 60, 63, *63*, 66, 68, *69*, 82, 83, 153, 232
'See-Saw' (*A Saucerful of Secrets*) 167
'Set the Controls for the Heart of the Sun' (*A Saucerful of Secrets* and *Ummagumma*) 27, 51, 71, 85–6, 167
'Several Species of Small Furry Animals . . .' (*Ummagumma*) 86, 178
'Sheep' (*Animals*) 52, 230, 240
'Shine On You Crazy Diamond' (*Wish You Were Here*) 100, 101, 104, 105, 194, *196*, 230, 232, 234, 294
'Skins' (*The Endless River*) 304
'Sorrow' (*A Momentary Lapse of Reason*) 280, *282*
Soundtrack from the film More (1969, film soundtrack) 86, 87, 172–5, 180, 206, 252
 album cover and artwork 172–3
Speak (1967, film soundtrack) 174
staging concepts 9, 114, 115, 120, 122, 219, 224, 226–7, *268*, 288–9, 290–1, 300, 301
 animation 39, *39*, 125, 218, 219, 252

inflatables 9, *112*, 114, 124–5, 128, *130*–1, 194, 267, 282, 296
light shows 8, 18, 25, 60, 62, 115, 116, *117*, 120, 122, 141, 150
lighting 9, 114, 115, 125, 126, 139, 296–7, *301*
projections 25, *39*, 55, 120, 121, *121*, 141, 219, 252
puppets 137, *138*, *139*, 252
roof structures 132, 137, 140, 141, *268*
'Stay' (*Obscured by Clouds*) 96, 206
synthesizers 48, 86, 98, 206, 212, 217, 220, 221, 222, 223, 232, 251, 254
'Sysyphus' (*Ummagumma*) 86, 178

The Tea Set (later Pink Floyd) 24–5, *25*, 26
'The Teacher' (*The Wall*) 39, *138*, *139*
'Things Left Unsaid' (*The Endless River*) 304
Thorgerson, Storm 8, 9, 141, 180, 266, 281, 306, *308*, 310, 311
 Pink Floyd album covers and artwork 9, 40, 54, 164, *231*, 281, 296, 306, 309–11
 see also Hipgnosis
'Time' (*The Dark Side of the Moon*) 40, 125, 217, *218*, 219
Tonite Let's All Make Love in London film (Peter Whitehead, 1967) 62, 121, 150
Torry, Clare 98, 100, 108, 219

UFO club, London *18*, 19, 20, 28, 30–1, 60, 62, 121, 150, 154, *160*
 Pink Floyd gigs 8, 15, 27, 28, 31, 62, 83, *116*, 121, 150
Ummagumma (1969) 40, 86, *171*, 176–81, 188, 194, 294, 304
 album cover and artwork 176–7, *179*, *181*, 310
'Us and Them' (*The Dark Side of the Moon*) 90, 98, 104–5, 125, 216

La Vallée (1972, dir. Barbet Schroeder) 52, 96, 206, *208*, 209
 see also Obscured by Clouds
'Vegetable Man' (unreleased, 1967) 71, 72

The Wall (1979) 9, 52, 81, 86, 92, 106, 107, 108, 232, *236*, 248–71, 274
 album cover and artwork 248–9, 250–1, 270–1
 movie *see Pink Floyd – The Wall*
 stage show 39, 250, *253 see also under* album tours
Waters, Eric Fletcher (father of Roger Waters) 52, 86, 96, 206, 274
Waters, Roger 10–11, 22, *25*, *115*, *156*, *168*
 the albums
  Animals 240–1
  Atom Heart Mother 93, 188
  The Dark Side of the Moon 97, 98, 101, 105, 216, 217, 219
  The Final Cut 52, 274, 276
  Meddle 194–5

318   The End

THE INDEX

Obscured by Clouds 96
The Piper at the Gates of Dawn 153
A Saucerful of Secrets 71, 85, 86, 164, 167
Ummagumma 40, 86, 178
The Wall 38, 39, 106, 107, 114, 250, 251, 252, 264, 265, 266
Wish You Were Here 230, 232, 236
on 'Arnold Layne' 58, 60
The Body soundtrack (with Geesin) 90–1, 184, 216
career after the band 86
disconnect with audience 65, 107, 137, 250
leaves the band (1985) 9, 139, 276, 280
life before the band 8, 21, 22, 30, 38, 52, 115, *115*, 266, 310
songwriting
   1960s 40, 68, 71, 74, 85, 86, 153, 164, 167, 178
   1970s 93, 96, 98, 105, 188, 194–5, 206, 217, 219, 230, 232, *236*, 240, 252, 264
   1980s 52, 274
on tours 65–6
Watts, Peter *181, 191, 195*
'Welcome to the Machine' (*Wish You Were Here*) 230, 232
'What Do You Want from Me' (*The Division Bell*) 294
'When the Tigers Broke Free' (single, 1982) 274
'When You're In' (*Obscured by Clouds*) 206
Wish You Were Here (1975) 9, 52, 85, 100, 101, 104, *105*, 105–6, *106*, *109*, 194, *196*, 222, 228–37, 281
album cover and artwork 228–9, *231, 232, 233, 235*, 310, 311
'Wish You Were Here' (*Wish You Were Here*) 230, 232
'Wot's ... Uh the Deal?' (*Obscured by Clouds*) 96, 206
Wright, Richard 25, *207, 306, 307*
the albums
   Animals 240
   Atom Heart Mother 90, 188
   The Dark Side of the Moon 219, 222
   The Division Bell 9, 106, 108, 294, *307*
   The Endless River 304, 306
   Meddle 194
   A Momentary Lapse of Reason 9, 110, 281
   A Saucerful of Secrets 71, 85, 164, 167
   Ummagumma 86, 178
   The Wall 251, *251*, 252
   Wish You Were Here 232
death 108, 304
leaves and later rejoins the band 251, 281, 294
life before the band 21, 115
organs and organ playing 30, 62, 85, 86, 98, 104, *159*, 213, 304
other keyboards and synthesizers 86, 178, 219, 222, *251*, 304, 306
songwriting 71, 86, 96, 164, 167, 178, 188, 206
Wynne Willson, Peter 114, 120, *165*, 296–7, *301*

'Yet Another Movie' (*A Momentary Lapse of Reason*) 281

Zabriskie Point (1970, film soundtrack) 87, 90, 104, 184, 216

First published by V&A Publishing, 2017
Victoria and Albert Museum
South Kensington
London SW7 2RL
www.vandapublishing.com

Distributed in North America by Harry N. Abrams Inc., New York
© Victoria and Albert Museum, London

The moral right of the authors has been asserted.

Hardback edition
ISBN 978-1-85177-916-1

Paperback edition
ISBN 978-1-85177-932-1

Library of Congress Control Number 2016960604

10 9 8 7 6 5 4 3 2 1
2021 2020 2019 2018 2017

A catalogue record for this book is available from the British Library. All rights reserved. No part of this publication may be reproduced, stored in a retrieval system, or transmitted in any form or by any means, electronic, mechanical, photocopying, recording or otherwise, without the written permission of the publishers.

Every effort has been made to seek permission to reproduce those images whose copyright does not reside with the V&A, and we are grateful to the individuals and institutions who have assisted in this task. Any omissions are entirely unintentional, and the details should be addressed to V&A Publishing.

Front jacket/cover illustration: Barnbrook
Art Direction: Jonathan Abbott and Anıl Aykan Barnbrook at Barnbrook
Design: Jonathan Abbott
Copy-editor: Kate Bell
Index: Sue Farr
Repro: DL Imaging Ltd, London

New photography by Rupert Truman, StormStudios
V&A Photography by V&A Photographic Studio

Printed in Italy

FSC MIX Paper from responsible sources FSC® C013123

V&A Publishing
Supporting the world's leading museum of art and design, the Victoria and Albert Museum, London

SENNHEISER

The audio experience in *The Pink Floyd Exhibition: Their Mortal Remains* is created by sound experts Sennheiser. Their AMBEO 3D technology enables captivating audio, including a new mix of Pink Floyd's 'Comfortably Numb' from the band's last performance together at Live 8. Sennheiser systems are used throughout the exhibition for all audio elements, including the highest-quality delivery of arrangements taken from Pink Floyd's archived audio documents: a perfect fit, as the band have used Sennheiser and Neumann audio equipment throughout their career.

On Sennheiser's involvement, Nick Mason has commented: 'We have been using Sennheiser equipment ever since Pink Floyd started out as a live band and used the MD 409 microphones for our performances, so it is only fitting that they provide the audio experience at our exhibition. Sennheiser has been at the cutting edge of audio technology for a very long time, and we have no doubt that they help make "Their Mortal Remains" something special.'